# The

John Bentley

http://www.theroyalsecret.info

# The Author

John Bentley is a first-time novelist. After winning Harrow School's coveted Coward History Prize, he emigrated at age 18 to Australia. Two years later in 1960 he returned to England overland via India and Iran, and regions now known as the Islamic Republic of Pashtunistan and Kurdistan, on a route little changed since the days of Alexander the Great. By thirty he controlled a global media empire, which included the UK's largest movie company and film studios producing the cult movie *The Wicker Man* among others. At thirty-two, described by the international press as a corporate buccaneer, he sold up to retire, forgoing a promising political career. Living between New York, Paris, St Tropez, Ibiza, and the highlands of Scotland, he studied philosophy, metaphysics and transcendentalism.

Returning to the UK in 1980, he started a video retail business that became the largest in Europe. By the mid 80's he sold out of his video venture and disappeared from the headlines to sail half way round the world. From 1990 he immersed himself in the new digital world, seeing its possibilities for social revolution. By 1995 he had created and brought to market the world's first Internet TV as a social media product which he launched in the USA in 1995. (www.johnbentley.biz)

In 2006 he retired to Portugal's Algarve coast. With *The Royal Secret* he has now fulfilled an ambition to be a writer. His novel combines his love of history, mystery and philosophy with his view that to save itself from destruction mankind today needs to rapidly establish a new paradigm of joint social and scientific evolution. Always controversial, he has written an audacious, thought-provoking epic thriller with a solid foundation in reality. Fans of Dan Brown to those of Bernard Cornwell, CJ Sansom and Umberto Eco, and of the Holy Grail, the Tudors and the Templars will enjoy this scintillating blend of 16th century intrigue and modern day conspiracy.

# Acknowledgements

To my wife Janet for her love and patience in giving me space while I wrote this book; yet providing both hope and the driving force to achieve its completion. Also to our various dogs who tried hard to refrain from interrupting my work.

To sundry early readers and skeptics for their forthright advice. The others who have followed its progress with encouragement will know who they are.

To my long-gone father who instilled in me a love of reading, and my mother a love of words. To chance and whatever deity rules my life for the gift of duration to find time to write as I have long wanted and waited to do.

I should not forget Elizabeth Gallup, Alfred Dodd and Margaret Barsi-Greene and their books. Their endeavors in times past well surpassed mine in providing information which gave much of the historical detail to the book's principal character. I have enjoyed with them an affinity and desire to restore the damaged reputation of one of England's greatest men.

# Reader Interaction

*The Royal Secret* was devised to offer readers instant access to online information related to people, places and background in the pages of the book, consisting of photos, articles and news which can be accessed online on *The Royal Secret* Pinterest and Pearltrees social media sites and *The Royal Secret* web site as listed below. In place of a bibliography those books to which the author has referred, and alluded in **The** *Royal Secret*, can also be found in the online sites below:-

Web: http://www.theroyalsecret.info

Pinterest: www.pinterest.com/theroyalsecret

Pearltrees: www.pearltrees.com/the_royal_secret

# Introduction

Following the death of an American bio-billionaire a thrilling exposé of mystery and intrigue links the conspiracy politics of today directly to the seamy spy rings of Queen Elizabeth I. Through the eyes of a woman seeking to uncover the truth about the death of the man she loves, *The Royal Secret* reveals the story of one of the world's best known men: a great writer, philosopher and prince, whose real identity and rightful claim to the thrones of England and America has been concealed until this day.

From Washington to London, Paris and the castles of the Templars, Mrs. G has only weeks in which to decrypt clues from the distant past of the Kabbalah and the bloodline of Christ himself. As she delves into a world of mysticism she exposes modern day science to criticism in its suppression of an occult intelligence sought by those who have ruled the world over past centuries, as they still do today.

# PROLOGUE

## The Royal Secret

*"Ancient code of order stand*

*Beneath the souls of lesser grand*

*Secret hold that bound their world*

*To guard their chance of second hurl.*

*Dormant want to those that deem,*

*That reap the chance to end their beam.*

*Silent men, women and child,*

*Forever lost in centuries wild."*

**Secret Code of Order. Chevaliers de Sangral.**

*"A great part of Europe, to say nothing of other countries, is covered with a network of secret societies. The world is governed by very different people from what is imagined by those not behind the scenes."*

**Benjamin Disraeli. 19th Century British Prime Minister.**

*"And nothing, not God, is greater to one than ones self is,"*

**Walt Whitman. 19th Century American Humanist, Transcendentalist and Poet.**

*"We are such stuff as dreams are made on."*

**William Shakespeare. The Tempest**

It's not what we know, but what we don't know that divides the majority of us from those few who do. Not just of access to knowledge by which we might succeed, but also of the misdeeds and malefactions by which others prosper.

From the beginning of time the peoples of the world have sought to govern their own destinies. A multitude of cults and creeds have risen and fallen, destroyed by the corruption and greed of those in power. The circle of bondage, to faith and courage and from liberty to complacency, to dependence, to dictatorship continues without end. Dynasties and dictators have come and gone, all consigned to the dustbin of history.

Great names down the ages have contrived to bring every art and science to question mankind's place and purpose in the world, and to achieve peaceful co-existence. Among them philosophers and prophets, scientists and spiritualists, artists and artificers, mathematicians and monks; and those of the anti-Christ; the shamans magicians and witchdoctors.

Some wrestle with equations of the Universe, of protons and neutrons, and others with the spiritual positives and negatives of good and evil, as to what and who we are, and where we go. It is only too easy to forget what we have already learned, and so to repeat the same mistakes. Incurable plagues, starvation and wars that have ravaged the world throughout its history can return to threaten our existence at any moment.

Without knowledge of the past we cannot truly understand the present or even guess at the future. Yet one long-forgotten genius provides the vital missing link to the saga of humanity from its beginning to the present, and perhaps to its end. Rediscovered today, above all, this story is his.

President Thomas Jefferson called him one of the three greatest men in the world. A founder of America and the origin of its Constitution; a man who rose to the heights of his day as Regent of England. Prolific writer, scientist, chemist, politician, pacifist, poet, philosopher and mystic. A half-bastard descendant of the most famous of English Royal lines. Nietzsche, the German philosopher, condemned to perdition all those who would not recognize his genius. Yet, apart from a few occult societies, he is virtually unknown today. His reputation destroyed by his enemies and his name dragged in the dirt and dust of decades, condemned by his critics as corrupt, disloyal, and as a homosexual. To all intents and purposes he died bankrupt and disgraced taking his secrets with him to an unmarked grave.

It took a brilliant American woman in the 19th century and a determined English lawyer in the early 20th century, the best part of their lifetimes to investigate the real identity of this seemingly supernatural Elizabethan. By decrypting codes devised four hundred years ago, they uncovered a veil of silence long drawn over conspiracies of the past. Of murder and mayhem, of disguised identities, of incest and ignominy, to be finally exposed only now by a woman of the 21st century.

In *The Royal Secret* Mrs G is a fictional character in her role as a botanist, but her modern day story revolves around present day events and those from a hidden past. From Jesus and Mary Magdalene, to the turbulent reign of the Tudors, to big business of today. From the torture of the Dark Ages to the licentiousness of the Renaissance. Of phantom writers, of revolutionaries, and of covert societies conspiring to regain prestige, in a world where the passions of men and women to scramble tooth and nail to the zenith of power never ceases.

On her husband's death Mrs G sets out on her quest to discover the truth of her own existence, her personal Holy Grail. In this she finds herself on the same path as an Elizabethan living four hundred years before her. As his true persona is unmasked, he becomes her hero and guide, and she finds herself unwittingly in the shadowy sphere of a cabal whose members intrigue to shape and control the modern world, as their forbears had done in the past. She finds herself torn between the powers of good and evil and discovers that, as with her Elizabethan counterpart, those she trusts are not all they may seem.

Her trail leads her through a labyrinth of history from the pyramids of Egypt to the Temple of Solomon, to the Washington Monument to London's Temple Inns, to Paris and further south in France in the chapels and castles of the Templars, and finally in the Carpathian mountains of a past Transylvania. In her adventure she takes strength from the heroines of womanhood's past.

It is the tale of humankind itself, illuminating the essential missing truths that unite the ancient and the modern worlds. Can the clever, but unworldly Mrs G find her answer in her own race against time running parallel to her hero, their enemies threatening their existence at every turn? On her travels Mrs G finds herself accompanied by a shadowy figure in whom she puts her trust, as she seeks to unravel clues to finally join the man she loves, and so that the two teenage children of whom she is the guardian and stepmother may be sure of their heritage and exist in a better future.

# Cast of Principal Characters

*(In alphabetical order)*

Abe, geneticist and cryptographer

Ahriman, a devil

Bacon, Francis writer, philosopher and politician

Bacon, Anthony adoptive brother of Francis Bacon and spy

Boleyn, Anne: 2nd wife of Henry VIII and mother of Elizabeth I queen of England

Buckingham, née George Villiers courtier to King James: later Duke of Buckingham

Buonarroti, Phillip CEO of Washington Order and descendant of Michelangelo

Cecil, Robert later 1st earl of Salisbury, courtier and state official

Coke, Sir Edward lawyer, parliamentarian and husband of Elizabeth Hatton

Compton, (Lady Mary) mother of Buckingham

Crick, Francis scientist, Nobel Prize winner and co-discoverer of DNA.

Crowley, Aleister adventurer, occultist and mystic

Dee, John magician, occultist, writer, philosopher, entrepreneur and spy

Dudley, Robert later Earl of Leicester, epicurean supporter of arts and theater

Mrs G. cryptographer and second wife of Abe (née Jane Fenn Gallup)

Edward, 6th son of Henry VIII and briefly king of England before death at fourteen

Elizabeth, Queen of England daughter of King Henry VIII and Queen Anne Boleyn

Essex, Robert Devereux 2nd Earl of Essex, adopted son of 1st Earl & Lettice Knollys

Ethan, a priest

Esther, housekeeper to Abe

Gerry, grandson of Abe and Marilyn, and brother of Marianne

Hatton, Lady Elizabeth wife of Edward Coke and mother of Frances Coke

James I, King of England and Scotland

Jonson, Ben playwright and friend of Francis Bacon

Marianne, grand-daughter of Abe and Marilyn, and sister of Gerry

Marguerite, Queen of Navarre and later of France. Wife of King Henry of Navarre and France

Marilyn, Merovingian descendant and first wife of Abe

Mary Magdalene, companion of Jesus Christ

Matthew, Toby lawyer, priest and epicurean

Merovech, first Merovingian king

Pallas Athene mythical Greek goddess of knowledge

Popper, Karl philosopher and professor of economics

Raleigh, Sir Walter, adventurer, entrepreneur and advisor to Queen Elizabeth I

Robsart, Amy first wife of Robert Dudley

Shakespeare, William Actor and mask. Later known as the Bard of Avon

St Germain, Compte occultist and Ráckóczi heir

Tudor, Mary Queen of England and daughter of Henry VIII and Catherine of Aragon

Wriothesely, Henry Earl of Southampton

# Chapter 1

## London, England. 1554

The grey roughhewn stone walls of the Tower were barely reflected in the swirling waters of the Thames hastening by, as if the river had no desire to take heed of the day's events inside the grim guardian on its northern bank. For the Tower of London had history. Not just of defending the entrance to London by river from the sea for the previous five hundred years as a fortress that had never succumbed to attack, but one of a terrible past. Of the two boy Princes gruesomely murdered in it only half a century before to deny them their rights to the throne of England. Of the thousands tortured and imprisoned within its prison cells for life, never to leave, and of the beheadings and executions by the axe and sword of the mighty that had fallen, as well as the flighty.

Among the latter were two of the wives of Henry VIII, or Henry the Great as he was known in his day. One, Anne Boleyn, his young second wife, had been accused by a jealous Henry of flirtations with Harry Percy, the youthful and handsome heir to the great Northumberland family castle at Alnwyck, whose fortunes stemmed from their defense of the English border against bloody Scottish raids for over half a millennium.

But on this day in 1554 it was not one of Henry's adulterous wives who faced the black wooden block of execution that stood in the fifty-foot-high walled yard of the Tower Green. It was Elizabeth, Henry's own daughter by Anne Boleyn, accused by her half-sister Mary Tudor, now Queen, of treachery to the crown and of being a Protestant heretic. Mary was a Catholic, married to King Philip of Spain, and her pursuit and execution by sword and fire of those who did not support her Catholic regime had earned her the label of "Bloody Mary".

The then Princess Elizabeth had been brought to the Tower by boat, entering under protest through the massive portcullis bars of the dreaded Traitors Gate from which there was said to be no return. Aged twenty-one, Elizabeth now looked through a tiny slit of a window high up in the Bell Tower out onto a patch of grass where the execution block stood. The flag of the English red cross of St George hung drably in a slight breeze and drizzling rain. Several carpenters were finishing the wooden scaffolding to seat visitors, since executions of those of rank were required to be witnessed for the record by selected officials of status. There were near to one hundred prisoners in the Tower and which one of them was to have their life ended that day was known only to the Queen and a chosen few court officials.

In amongst the scaffolding two jet black ravens fought, bilious yellow in beak and claw, tearing apart the entrails of a rodent, screeching raucously as flesh and fur flew. The ravens were considered as much part of the Tower as were its famed Beefeaters, the Yeomen of the Guard. The latter, present in number this day some fifty strong and armed with their halberds, pikes equipped with razor-sharp axes, had long held their position as the Tower's guardians in their impressive uniforms of red and gold. Should the ravens leave, it was fabled, the Tower would fall and with it the British monarchy and its peoples.

As Elizabeth looked on the scene below from her cell-like room, a ray of sunshine broke through the low grey clouds. It fell across the lawn onto the block on which the Queen intended the young princess to have her head severed from her body that very day. Elizabeth's own mother, as Queen, had knelt there only eighteen years before to be beheaded by the sword. Anne had not given her husband the son he so desperately wanted as an heir, and had accused the King of a flirtation with the sour-faced girl Jane Seymour whom he married just days after Anne's execution.

Elizabeth's heart was beating fast and she made the sign of the cross on her small freckled bosom, praying that the good Lord might somehow realize she was not guilty of anything in this world; apart, that was, from being a threat to her half-sister as a replacement Queen. Under English law Henry's daughter Mary by his first wife, the Spanish Catharine of Aragon, ranked ahead of Elizabeth in the succession. Their half-brother Edward VI, born of Jane Seymour, having died, aged fifteen, in 1553.

"I am innocent," Elizabeth kept repeating to herself over and over, "guilty only of birth," as she felt tears of anger and despair welling in her blue-grey eyes. Thoughts tumbled furiously through her mind. My life finished before even started, and yet with every advantage of a noble birth. "Damn Mary Tudor, and her Catholic mother. May she perish of the plague in a slow death worse than mine," Elizabeth swore to herself.

What possible request could save her now? Many supplications had been made to her cold-hearted sister, and not one had been considered as far as was known. If deliverance was at hand, it had to be now or never. The heavy wooden door to her cell opened on its iron hinges. She turned to face three men. One the Lord Warden of the Tower, and the others two armed halberdier guards, who approached her grim-faced. They were there to do their job for queen and country, and Elizabeth was not the Queen. The Lord Warden was attired in a long red velvet tunic over dark brown breeches with black patent knee-high boots and a tall crown hat, one brim fixed by a blood red garnet jewel, as befitted the occasion and his standing. His facial expression was impassive as he unrolled a small scroll of parchment. Elizabeth bit her lower lip. Small beads of perspiration ran down her neck into her cleavage. She clenched her fists, so much so her nails cut into the palms of her hands, as if to hang on to the world and life as though it were a precipice down which she was unstoppably sliding to her doom.

"I am here," pronounced the Warden in stern tones, "to decree your fate, Madam. By a High Order I am commanded there is to be a stay of execution." With a slight bow of his head he turned to go, added "I beg your leave, Ma'am," and departed with the two guards. Elizabeth gasped.

Could this be true, was she to be spared, and if so who had intervened on her behalf? "By the Devil or by a guardian angel? – what salvation!" she exclaimed. By whose order, she wondered. Higher than the Queen? If so, who? What had happened she did not know, but she felt as if she were flying. Released from death as if an angel on wings. She felt sure that after such a reprieve God was on her side and now England's throne would be hers. It was her birthright. Her father Henry would have turned in his grave to see the

Catholics returned to power in his kingdom. She would extract her revenge on her bitch of a sister.

"Come quick, Beth," said a voice, as through the door came a body in a long dark cloak out of which a hand took hers. "Let's celebrate our good fortune. We are to be freed soon, but must stay in the Tower until our release. I have it on good authority! Hush!" He held his finger to her lips. "Don't speak; there is no need for words now. We have time enough. Your end is not yet to be."

Elizabeth knew the voice and as the cloak fell from his face a pair of laughing eyes caught hers. Those of Robert, her second lover. Her first, when she was but fourteen, had been executed for impregnating her. He had been an older man, some twenty years her senior, who had taken advantage of her youth to seduce her. Robert was her own age, young, virile and handsome, and Elizabeth was in love with him. Deeply and passionately so. Cupid's dart had struck at her heart at the first sight of his fierce good looks in the dark recesses of the Tower.

Elizabeth took Robert's hand as he quickly led her through a narrow winding passage to the adjoining Beauchamp Tower where he too had been imprisoned. In it was a small anteroom, a chamber with leather-bound chairs and a low couch covered in drapes over which he laid her body. Shutting the door behind them, he quickly lifted her long gown waist high to her short linen bodice, and as quickly he undid his own doublet and his breeches to hold his firm flesh against hers. She was ready for him and put up no resistance nor felt shame, since it was not for the first time in these last few weeks of waiting their bodies had come together in hot embrace. What else had been their prospect but to take pleasure while they could with only death awaiting them?

But now that was behind her. The double excitement of her imminent release and the sight of Robert, who only minutes before she had thought she would never see again, aroused all her senses and the blood coursed through her heart and veins. They fell onto the couch as one, heaving and panting in a mad flurry of kisses and embraces until the union of their young bodies could be satisfied no more. In her dreams she was Queen, and Robert Dudley was to be hers. He would be the father of her offspring. That her resolve would reward her with joy she felt sure, but the grief it was later to cause her was to remain concealed from the public gaze until the 21st Century, over four hundred years later, and it would change the course of history forever.

# Chapter 2

It was early fall in Boston and the low rays of a late afternoon sun slanted through the amber and scarlet foliage of the maple trees gently rustling in the light breeze. On a wide avenue in the Brookline district a large New England house of early 20th century design stood set back in its garden, protected by a ten-foot-high brick wall and electric, double wrought iron gates. Specimen trees of various types, shapes and sizes shaded a large, even and manicured green lawn, well-watered by a sprinkler system in a garden of immaculate order. Great care had been taken of the many species of vegetation brought there from the world over by its owner. A range of glass hothouses stood against a far wall, filled with rare plants and herbs. Not just of decorative intent, but ones that had purpose. The owner of the house had been a man who had built a great fortune from a lifetime of botanical study.

French doors opened wide from the house onto the lawn, and it was through them that two teenagers in shorts and T-shirts ran laughing through spurting water sprinklers and into the house. A boy of seventeen and a girl of fifteen; brother and sister. "Hi, Mrs G," they both called out to an attractive woman of small to medium build seemingly in her mid-50s seated at a large 18th Century oak desk. Sharing the highly polished desktop with two multi-colored glass Tiffany lamps and a pair of simple early American silver candlesticks, stood a large smart-internet TV at whose screen Mrs G had been staring intently.

As the two came in she sat back in a deep red leather Chesterfield chair and clapped her hands. "Come and see my new toy," she said. "It's mind-blowing to me that I can sit at home and find information which would have taken me a lifetime not long ago. Wonderful! You kids take it for granted, but it's an extension of intelligence you can't now do without, just a click away on Google. Einstein believed once you had found an answer you needed to write it down to keep your mind clear for new thoughts. Now everything we know of the

Universe is sitting there on the Cloud. Einstein would have loved it Technology's answer to telepathy." "Exo-Brain!" came the reply from the boy, grinning. "T.M.I. Too much information though"

Mrs G smiled. "Well we had to search books in my school days, so you are lucky to have it all at your fingertips. Soon it will probably be in a chip placed in your head. Your Grandpa was an inventor but if he hadn't learned from history, he would have wasted his time proving what was already known. It's why studying is important." Mrs G saw herself as the unofficial guardian of Gerry and his sister Marianne since their granddad had died.

"Your Grandpa utilized the Fibonacci Code for his theories to grow plants for medicinal purposes. Without its discovery nine hundred years ago, he would have had to invent it. It's a mixture of science and divination. Science is a progression of human thought, while true art is an irresistible creative urge, as Einstein explained it. It seems to me that art today is little more than fashion for the sake of fashion. It has no spirit. As for science, what is believed true one day is not the next. Nothing is absolute except death."
"And I'm not entirely sure about that either," she voiced to herself.

This was a good opportunity for Mrs G to catch the children together and she wanted to make the most of it. She was leaving for Europe in two days and did not know exactly when she might be back.

"Your Grandpa's inventiveness revolutionized the decoding of plant genetics and made him the fortune that you'll inherit one day, and, I hope, use for good purpose. The way things have turned out life has decreed I am to help you now he is dead, and your poor parents too. Fate has many twists and turns. But you must put the bad behind you. You have your lives ahead of you and it's time you gave some thought to your future. You'll soon need to make your own decisions. I can only help you so much."

Gerry grimaced. The memories of his Grandpa's death, not so long after that of his parents and Grandma in a car crash, still greatly pained him. The events had hurt him deeply and made him introspective. He was not at all sure yet what to make of life, but he listened to what Mrs G was telling him. Both he and Marianne had respect for her, and for the time being she was the closest person they had in the world, apart from each other.

"Grandpa was a code-buster?" Gerry asked.

"He was," said Mrs G, "and I was too for many years in my work as his assistant while he was married to your Grandma. Codes have been used from the beginning of time to exchange concealed information. The internet today has two sides. The one most people see, and the Dark Web which most people don't realize exists; where coded messages are used by terrorists and criminals to avoid discovery. Everything that exists in this world can be used for good or bad. Positive or negative in equal effect. We have a choice. Let me show you what I mean, as this one is nearer home."

Mrs G quickly Googled and pointed on the TV screen to a plant with dark red berries.

"See this, it's Belladonna; it can be used to cure pain, or it can kill you. Some call it Deadly Nightshade, or the Devil's Weed. There's one in the garden hothouse right now. Juice from its berries was once applied by girls to make their eyes dilate and look more beautiful, but it could kill them if they overused it. The same with most drugs which is why you need take care with them.

"Belladonna is used medicinally now for Parkinson's disease and as a painkiller. It has a strange, dark beauty and it was a favorite of your Grandpa's first wife, Marilyn. She had a good knowledge of herbal medicines and poisons, as all old families did, handed down from times past before the days of pills. The word medicine is associated with the Medici family in Italy who made their fortune using herbs and plants. Not just to cure people, but also by poisoning their enemies with secret potions. Many of the species in your Grandpa's greenhouses here can be deadly. You should never touch them until you know which is which; so stay clear of them until you do. Their leaves can be toxic and cause sickness, even death.

"There is a book known as *The Poisoners Bible*, or in its proper name as *Dreisbach's Handbook of Poisoning*. It can be found on your Grandpa's library shelves and makes interesting reading. There are many books there, including some on your mother's family history. Try to use the time while I'm away to study them. It's your history too. As you know, your mother's Mom, Grandma Marilyn, was French - and descended from an ancient bloodline -The Merovingians, who claim they go back to King Merovech of Gaul, or France as it has now become and five hundred years before Merovech to Mary Magdalene. Both your names have ancient origins. Gerry's Christian name is Germain, which comes from Germanus, an ancient saint, and Marianne from Mary Magdalene who was known as Maryam. Your grandmother insisted on you having them. St. Germain is a popular area of Paris, once famous for its artists and bohemian lifestyle which I will be visiting this trip to research my new book. Next time I'll take you for a tour of Europe to understand the great European Renaissance of art and literature and the beginnings of science. It will give you a much better understanding of human progress than you can learn at school. Only after the European Renaissance does America's own history even start!"

While Mrs G was talking, a rotund lady of Afro-American origin had come into the room with a jug of coffee and biscuits. Esther was five-foot-three tall and almost as round. She had a yellow and green bandana on her head and two large amber-flecked brown eyes which stood out like an owl's from their whites. A flowing and colorful dress to near her ankles swayed as she walked.
"Hi, Mrs G," she said with a big grin on her face. "How about some sust'nance?" and placed the tray by the side of the TV.
"What'll the chill'n have? Or will they wait for mealtime?"
"It's okay, Esther," said Mrs G. "It's your day off. We can get some supper together easily if you'll defrost some pizzas for us."

She turned to the children. "While I'm away, Esther will cook for you. Ask her for anything you want, but be nice to her. She served your Grandpa well for many years at his laboratory in Georgia and knows a lot about plants, so she might just slip some Belladonna into your soup if you don't behave."
"No problem, Mrs G," they'll be just fine with me," Esther happily assured her in her broad Southern accent.

"When are you off, Mrs G?" asked Gerry.
"Soon now, Mrs G replied. "I'm leaving for England to search for ancient codes to know more about the subject of the book I'm working on.
"Will you see the Queen?" joked Marianne.
"Not on this trip. I expect she's a mite too busy, but as it happens, the first Queen Elizabeth was a code-buster for real. She started England's first spy network, the British Secret Service."
"Oh cool," Marianne laughed.
"Sub-zero!" Gerry retorted.

"But first I'm stopping off in Washington to see a publisher whom I hope may help with my book. He's an old friend of your Grandpa." Mrs G spoke her words sadly.

"He was interested in your Grandma's heritage, which your Grandpa felt was best left alone. Grandpa was devastated when your parents both died with Grandma in that awful car crash. He wanted to show many things to you as you got older, but with his own death soon after, it was not to be. When your Mom died your Grandpa asked me to help you both as best I could, so I do what I think he would have done. Your family has an interesting history on your mother's side which your parents would have told you if they had lived. Its time you knew about it and I'll do my best to tell you the story. It starts many years ago in a past that I helped re-discover with your Grandpa and which my book will be about.

"Brill!" exclaimed Marianne. "When can we start?" She jumped up and pointed at the TV. "What are those drawings? They're weird!" Mrs G laughed. "They're images of old codes. If you're finished in the garden for the day, I'll tell you what I'm investigating for my book and then we'll get some pizza and ice cream together for supper. I hope when I come back from Europe I'll have more clues sorted and I can tell you better where it's all going. It's an adventure into the past and maybe the future too."

"Yo!" exclaimed Gerry "we're up for it. We'll be back - give us twenty minutes to shower and chill out." Gerry chased his sister upstairs laughing. It was good to know more about their 'fam'.

# Chapter 3

Mrs G settled herself in her high-backed chair and thought how best to begin her story. She would use video material she had assembled for her book. Images were a good way to show kids things, just as were the Egyptian hieroglyphics of the past. A picture really could be worth a thousand words. She would talk at the same time as clicking through the screen shots and answering any questions the kids had.

She hadn't too much time as she needed to pack and be at Boston's Logan Airport in thirty-eight hours on her way to Washington. Then on to London on the red-eye overnight flight to be there the following morning. But there is a time for everything and this was as good as any to tell the kids more about the world of their past and how it might affect their future. They had the whole evening ahead of them.

The kids were bright enough intellectually and were quick at absorbing knowledge that was of interest to them. They had grown up fast this last year and had begun to think about life and death too, since the untimely ends of their parents and grandparents. A gentle cough which had tickled the back of Mrs G's throat for the last few months irritated her and reminded her that she needed to take care of her own health. There were many things she had to do in the next few weeks before she could find time for the examination her doctor had recommended she have. She would sort it out when she returned.

She caught a glance of herself in the Lalique Art-Deco mirror on the wall. Still looking good for sixty-two. A trim slight figure with a good complexion. Could easily pass for a few years less. Her brown hair had highlights to disguise her newly emerging gray roots. It was shoulder length but well cut and neat and easy to keep. She was not good at chit chat with her hairdresser and preferred to avoid time spent there. Nor was she keen on too much artifice. Just some lipstick and a light foundation cream were as much as she could be bothered with, and some natural colored nail varnish. A touch of eye pencil to enhance her brown eyes completed the picture.

She looked at her hands. No liver spots yet, and still some tan from the spring break in Bermuda and a few days of sailing this summer on Nantucket Sound on the Ta Chiao 50 foot sailing ketch of Abe's friends, a vacation she had shared with him before he had died. Abe did not care for the glitzy, gin palace, motor yacht cruising of the Florida Keys and the blue rinse brigade of Palm Beach.

She had dressed today in a knee length, plain, gray pleated skirt with a close-fit, duck-egg blue, cotton half-sleeved T-shirt, bare brown legs and sneakers. She had played a couple of boisterous sets of American tennis with the kids earlier in the day and was pleased not to have been too puffed.

The kids needed more friends to come round, but it was the trouble with being super-rich. After their mother and father had died, Grandpa Abe had put a protective ring around them. He had set aside a large amount of money into a foundation whose purpose was to benefit them one day along with charities and projects in which Abe was involved. Aware of his advancing age, Abe had asked Mrs G to be a trustee of the foundation in the children's interests, which she had accepted so as to please him. Although sociable within her small circle of friends, she was not a naturally social person of the type found in Boston's classy society. That task she had left to Abe's former wife Marilyn. It was from the foundation that Mrs G was supplied with any funds she required for herself and the children since Abe's death in her role of unofficial guardian. She had only to call Abe's lawyer in Boston and funds would arrive.

In a way it was her fault, she thought, that the children did not get out and about more; but she was too old now to mix with the mothers of other kids of the same age. A stand-in mother who wasn't really cut out for the job, but as much as she could, she made it her job nevertheless. Abe would have wanted it that way. Why else would he have married her if not to give his grandchildren the protection they needed with their parents both dead? He had always trusted her as she trusted him.

Yes, they were good friends and had spent much time together, interested in the same intriguing subjects and how to find the answers. Two sleuths together, but ultimately she had been his assistant and was in awe of his knowledge. As a student at the old Boston University School of Medicine, she had seen his rise in importance and had known he would one day become famous in his chosen profession.

She had joined his pharmaceutical research company as a junior botanist soon after leaving college and had become an assistant to him at twenty-seven. Abe had liked her quiet and responsible manner and her enthusiasm for working at all hours. That was well over thirty years ago now. She had always respected his close family life and his clever, but eccentric, aristocratic wife Marilyn. Abe had enough on his hands with his work, and with the excesses of his wife and daughter, both of whom enjoyed travel and mixing in a world of high society to which they belonged by birthright. They were fortunate that Abe was able to support their lifestyles.

Mrs G enjoyed her professional work with Abe and had become almost one of the family by gradual adoption, known by them always as Mrs G. Marilyn was smart enough to know that Mrs G was important to Abe's work and the trust it required. After Marilyn's death, Abe had married Mrs G and they had slept together for shared comfort, but without carnal knowledge of each other. She loved him for his brilliant mind and had felt it transcended all else. Sex at her age, she told herself, was of no importance to her, but good companionship was.

Mrs G's full name was Jane Fenn Gallup. Her background was that of a hard-working professional family. Her great-grandmother Elizabeth was a highly intelligent woman who had worked for the US government deciphering codes at the time of World War One. Elizabeth Gallup had been previously employed as a researcher for an Illinois textile millionaire whose interest was to discover more about the life of William Shakespeare. In her time she had become famous in American literary and scientific circles, having written a four hundred page paper entitled *The Shakespearean Ciphers.* She had used her cryptology skills to examine hidden codes in the works of Shakespeare and her paper was the result of thirty years of painstaking investigation.

Mrs G's parents had given birth to her in February 1953, under the star sign of Aquarius, and like her mother she had chosen to continue a tradition of the females in her family by carrying on the distinguished name of Gallup. Her own parents had both died from the gas fumes from a faulty motel water heater when she was eighteen, so she was more than sympathetic with Gerry and Marianne. Their parents had died in a car crash, together with Abe's wife, Marilyn, on an icy road in Vermont not a year before Abe's own death. None of those in the car had survived. There had been some local publicity at the time, but with no witnesses the coroner had returned a verdict of accidental death.

It was the first time the family as a whole had been exposed to the press who considered their wealth to be newsworthy, and Abe had asked Mrs G to tell the children the news before they heard it elsewhere. In the years in which Mrs G had become Abe's close confidant, the children's mother had travelled extensively in her occupation as a horse breeder. As a result, the children had frequently stayed in Abe's Brookline house where Mrs G had got to know them well.

Abe had been head down in his efforts at home to complete a major experiment. The older he became the more withdrawn he had grown, his mind on his work and what he might best bequeath to the world from his billion-dollar fortune and his pharmacological discoveries, and what to his grandchildren.

It was not long after the car crash that Abe had proposed marriage to Mrs G and they had wed in a quiet, private ceremony at the local Boston synagogue, Abe being Jewish. He was by then in his mid-seventies and had little left in the way of family. After the marriage, at Abe's request, Mrs G had studied the Jewish religion, and its origins in the Kabbalah four thousand or more years ago whose teachings were handed down in complex numerical codes of the type Mrs G enjoyed interpreting.

Mrs G and her sister had attended Wellesley College near Boston for a short period before moving on to medical school. Her sister, who was equally studious, had been employed by NASA for a time, before working for CERN in Geneva on the large Hadron Collider in the particle physics laboratory. She had become so absorbed in her work of splitting atoms to ever more minute proportions that she had found no time for marriage or a family. She had died of myeloid leukemia in middle age as a hazard of her occupation before the discovery of the Higgs Boson "God Particle" at CERN in 2014 which was now changing scientific perspectives. Mrs G's own tendency was towards healing, both of the mind and body, believing in natural solutions from her understanding of plants. It was a territory in which she had assisted Abe in his lifelong dream to find a cure-all concoction to solve humanity's ills.

# Chapter 4

## Brookline, Boston

Mrs G had got her presentation together just as the kids came back in and stretched themselves out on a giant-sized, floral, chintz-covered couch, the design of which was echoed in the voluminous curtains that hung on rings from mahogany rods across the tall windows. The chintz was to dress the room for the summer only and was due to be changed for warmer colors as the days of autumn drew to an end. The room's polished parquet floor showed off the several luxurious antique oriental carpets of Persian and Indian origin that Abe had collected over the years.

Paintings by Norman Rockwell of an earlier America adorned the oak paneled walls along with a few European Impressionists, Gauguin and Chagall among them. Mrs G had chosen a Pop Art picture by Ed Ruscha of various amphetamine capsules floating in space on a red background as if planets encircling the globe; which it had amused her to buy for Abe long before Ruscha's prices went sky high. Abe had kept it out of sight from visitors in his library room. His personal experiments with drugs were a secret he preferred to keep to himself.

Mrs G pointed at the large TV screen. "Now pay attention. These are mystic Egyptian signs - hieroglyphics of symbolism and allegory." She clicked on her mouse. More signs appeared.
"See these. Numerical codes instead of words. The Jewish Kabbalah is based on one. Your Grandpa understood them. Although seemingly mysteriously magical to some, they are actually fixed rules of cause and effect determined from one single creative source. They reveal the amazing energy forces in and around us. Magic is not about playing tricks. It's for real. You will learn more in time and l hope; inherit your Grandpa's intellect. Incidentally, the subject of my book invented his own bilateral code at your age, similar to the binary code used by your computer today."

"What is allegory exactly?" asked Marianne.

"Something that isn't what it seems. An illusion or a disguised message. Something that can be interpreted to reveal a hidden meaning," Mrs G replied.

"My book will tell of a writer and inventor four hundred years ago. President Jefferson called him one of the three most intelligent men of all time. The other two were Isaac Newton, the physicist, and John Locke, the social philosopher. They all influenced the Founding Fathers' vision of America and its Constitution.

Dusk fell outside in the garden and Gerry got up to close the French doors. The large LED screen now shone brightly in the darkening room. As Mrs G moved her mouse, a scene of Knights on horseback appeared, their chain armor covered with a red crosses emblazoned on white tunics.

"I know these guys," exclaimed Gerry. "They're the Knights Templar. Crusaders; the Holy Grail; the Ark of the Covenant and all that holy shit! King Arthur and Lancelot and his round table knights were once my heroes, but people say they're just a myth."

"No, wrong Gerry." That the Templars existed is well known, and that there was an Ark of the Covenant in some form is certain. As for King Arthur, most modern historians now concur that he existed. I am sure you've read the poem of the Excalibur sword, and of Parsifal, the German knight, and his story of the Holy Grail. They are based on real events even though they may have been seen later as myth."

Mrs G started to cough and quickly took a couple of throat lozenges. "The tombstones of the Templars can be seen all over Europe. So listen up good! It's where my story starts, and it's for real. Hear me through and try to avoid interrupting. If you have questions please keep them until later. It's for your benefit I'll tell you this tale."

"The Templars were founded over a thousand years after Jesus' death. At first they were poor monks helping Christian visitors to the Temple of Solomon in Jerusalem. But after a few years in 1128 they discovered the Ark of the Covenant and King Solomon's treasure. It had been buried under the Temple to hide it from the Babylonians who destroyed an earlier Temple there six hundred years before the birth of Jesus. Documents from that time called the Dead Sea Scrolls were not found until quite recently in 1947 and told of an enormous treasure of gold and jewels.

"What was in the Ark?" asked Gerry.

"It's believed it may have held the tablets of Moses' Ten Commandments together with secrets of an ancient faith placed there by David and Solomon, both kings of Israel. Jesus was said to be descended from the kings' royal Jewish bloodline. Mary Magdalene was also royal. Her grandmother was Princess Selene, the daughter of Queen Cleopatra, and Mary's grandfather was Juba, the pagan King of Nubia."

"But," said Marianne, "I thought Mary was a Christian."

"Well, yes, after she fell in love with Jesus, she became a Jewish Christian," replied Mrs G. "You will see what I mean by that later."

"Jesus was good looking by all accounts. There is an image of his face on the Veronica Veil at Manotelo in Italy. He was said to have auburn colored hair and blue eyes. Many people fell under the spell of his charisma. He was a rebel at heart, but not the militant leader the Jews hoped might save them from the Romans. He was a student of John the Baptist who recognized that Jesus had a sensory gift, a karma that inspired people.

"When Jesus laid his hands on the sick they had faith in his touch. It was an intimate transfer of energy by which people healed themselves. To Mary it was the power of both faith and love. A magical chemistry of touch. In the Gospel of Philip it is said that Mary and Jesus would often openly kiss one another. Jesus exuded a magnetism which can easily be confused with magic as it cannot be proved. Yet it is innate in us all. But today people have lost their understanding of it, preferring to be cured by pills than faith.

"The wealthy Jews saw Jesus as an anarchist, a political trouble maker who thought to represent himself as a new Messiah, which to them was heresy. But Jesus had not pretended that he was any more than a man of the people, offering simple messages of faith which conflicted with the pomposity of the Jewish High Priests. While he kept his preaching to small villages, the priests ignored him, but when he threw the money changers out the Temple in Jerusalem, they reacted. The High Priest Caiaphas appealed to Pontius Pilate, the Roman Governor, to get rid of Jesus.

"Pilate was married to a woman of the Jewish Essenes sect, with similar passive beliefs to the Nazarene tribe of Jesus, and he saw no reason for Jesus to be punished by death. But Caiaphas demanded Jesus' crucifixion, and you know the rest of the story as does the whole world."

Mrs G drew breath and continued.

"The Roman Empire in Jesus' time consisted of most of Europe and North Africa, and as Christianity spread it split into different versions. One preached by Jesus' brother James, and one by Mary Magdalene. Another was proclaimed by Paul, which had an appeal to the gentile Greeks and Romans. Paul had never met Jesus. He rejected the old Jewish Hebrew beliefs and asserted Jesus was the Son of God.

"James was stoned to death on the orders of Caiaphas, and Mary escaped to the Languedoc, a country in what is today part of southern France. Helped by Joseph of Arimathea, a wealthy friend of Jesus, Mary converted the pagan Languedoc people to Jesus' Nazarene beliefs reflecting ancient Egyptian ideals, and Mary was revered as a Priestess of the Egyptian goddess Isis."

"Mary taught a belief in a god of two parts. One of a creator god and the other his bad adversary. The concept was an old one called 'Dualism'. It soon spread to a pagan England and took root in Glastonbury which was later the home of the English King Arthur. Before that, the English Druid priests believed in androgynous gods combining male and female characteristics equally. They were little different from the Hindu gods of India thousands of years before Christ. It goes to show how beliefs spread across the world many thousands of years ago.

"The Nazarene version of Christianity preached by Mary Magdalene did not claim Jesus was divine, whereas the Catholic Church of Paul did. Four hundred years after the time of Christ a band of warrior kings from the Languedoc known as the Merovingians ruled most of France and Germany in an area then known as Gaul. They took their name from King Merovech who claimed his descent from Mary Magdalene whose faith the Merovingians adopted.

"The dispute as to Jesus' divinity split the people of Europe in half for a period of nearly a thousand years. The Romans had rejected their old pagan gods and adopted Paul's version of Christianity. Over hundreds of years the religious power in Europe shifted from the Roman emperors to successive Italian popes in the name of the Roman Catholic Church. The Merovinigians continued their belief in the Nazarene creed but over time as Catholicism spread westwards in Europe the popes gained the upper hand. Their use of fear and torture suppressed other beliefs in a time known as the Dark Ages which set back the advance of scientific knowledge by nearly a millennium.

"The Catholic Church made images of the devil they claimed the Nazarenes worshipped, with horns and cloven hooves and a forked tail, and gave the devil names. Satan and Lucifer, who had once been angels but were corrupted by riches as the Catholics claimed the Jewish Kings David and Solomon had been. Ahriman was another, the god of greed and envy. Others were Beelzebub; The Lord of the Flies; Astraeth the female god of lust; Bile, the Celtic god of Hell, and so on. The androgynous Baphomet was another, depicted as the goat-headed god of illicit sex.

"Each time the Nazarene creed re-appeared the Catholics would try to silence it. Eleven hundred years after Jesus, the Pope declared war on the last stronghold of the Nazarene Jewish Christians in the Languedoc who were known as the Cathars. They held beliefs from the Gnostic Gospels which stemmed from ancient Jewish concepts and before them from the Egyptians and of a sect known as the Zoroastrians. It was a belief based on the cosmos and in God and the Devil, in which God represented a pure life to be found only in heaven, while the Devil was the tempter of man on Earth to wage war and to possess wealth which destroyed the true soul."

"The Cathars believed, as their Merovingian ancestors did, that Mary Magdalene had given birth to a child by Jesus whose descendants were the true Christians. They believed in equality between men and women and swore vows of honesty. They believed in reincarnation and saw no purpose in formal marriage. They saw sex as an enjoyment for all persuasions, not just for the procreation of children as the Catholics maintained. The pope claimed the Cathars were devil worshippers and homosexuals and urged the French King to destroy them and their Albigensian royal family. In a war which went on for many years with appalling atrocities over half a million people were slaughtered. Many were burned to death in huge bonfires of over five hundred bodies. The French Crusader knights, some of whom were Templar mercenaries, finally won by storming the Cathar's fortress of Carcassonne. In one day they killed seven thousand men, women and children. But not long after the French King turned against the Templars with encouragement from the Pope.

Mrs G cleared her throat, speeding through pages of downloaded information on the screen in front of her, stopping at a picture of a rose emblazoned on a cross.

"Mary adopted the single red rose as a symbol of the blood of Christ. It had once been the emblem of love to the Egyptians as it was to be with the Cathars and later that of King Arthur Pendragon and his Knights of the Round Table. The Pendragons claimed ancestry from the Merovingian's and adopted their Nazarene beliefs.

"In 1455, a thousand years after King Arthur, descendants of the Celtic Pendragons in Wales called Tudor joined the nearby Lancastrians at the battle of St Albans against the Yorks of Saxon origin in the War of the Roses. When the Tudors eventually won they laid claim to rule over England, overlaying their larger red rose with the smaller white rose of the Yorks in unity, which became the symbol of the England of Henry VIII and Elizabeth I . In the days before most people could read, symbols were important, and the rose was seen as an icon of purity to ward off the evil of Satan."

"Satan?" Gerry suddenly exclaimed. "So did they think he was for real?"

"They certainly did, and so should you. Temptation by another name. The Devil has many names. The early Christians believed you had an angel sitting on your left shoulder and a devil on the right. Life is full of choices. You can take your pick!" Mrs G said with emphasis.

# Chapter 5

Mrs G wiped a tear from her face. The import of Abe's death had flashed in front of her. Had he perhaps taken his own life in error? It was unlike him to make mistakes with dangerous drugs after a lifetime's experience. Was there another reason? But if so what? He had been rich but he had not set out to be and his wealth had bothered him. It was why he had set up his foundation to give his money to cure disease in the world. He was a good man, she reminded herself.

"Just want to stretch my legs," she said, opening the doors into the garden and going out to the edge of the lawn to hide her tears. It was dark now and as she looked up at the starlit night sky, she hoped that Abe was there in heaven, and nowhere else!

She shivered a little in the night air as she looked towards the range of hothouses near where she had found Abe those few months ago one early evening in May. She recalled their damp fetid smell. Even now as she looked into the dark she felt she could see him lying there near an open door under the trees. She had called out to him, but with no response, her heart had begun beating faster. She had started to run, calling his name. When she got to him at first she had noticed a slight discoloring of his skin and a thin line of blood running from the corner of his mouth, but nothing more. The paramedics she called had come within fifteen minutes to take him to Massachusetts General Hospital in Boston, but he had been dead on arrival.

Abe had put on weight and had kept to a diet to control a diabetes problem. The trouble was he did not take enough exercise. He had too many meetings he needed to attend and scientific functions where he was in demand as a speaker and benefactor to many Boston charities. Abe had been aware of his health and had made it his mission in the last year or so to get his affairs in order. Firstly, to put his great knowledge of bio-engineering on record for posterity for the benefit of the scientific community. Secondly, to settle his estate and the money he wanted to leave to continue his research on plant genetics, and thirdly for the children's inheritance. This had been the main purpose of the foundation he had created. He had called it the Magdala Foundation at his first wife's request. The word Magdala meant "The Tower" and had been the name of the birthplace of Mary

Magdalene. In recent weeks Mrs G had sensed Abe had been uneasy about something. It was unlike him, but she knew better than to ask. He was a man who liked to solve his own problems.

Mrs G had never given a thought to what Abe might leave her on his death. In her eyes he was immortal. He had not spoiled her, nor did she expect him to. She knew his proposal of marriage was more for the children's sake to have someone he trusted to look after them if he died. Nevertheless she had loved him deeply for his kindness and wisdom and his belief in mankind. In this she felt at one with him.

Abe had been a loner in many ways. His thoughts constantly pre-occupied him and he would spend days alone scribbling his ideas and calculations down on pieces of paper which Mrs G would collect, type out and scan to file away on her laptop. He had little time for a social life or the usual leisure time activities of the typical corporation executive. Playing golf at Boston's smart private golf clubs or drinking at the 19th hole all evening he saw as a waste of time. People had thought him introverted, but then they didn't know him and the things that excited his passion for genetic engineering and what it could reveal for the good of humanity. Often in the evenings Abe and Mrs G would sit unraveling codes of all descriptions to amuse themselves, as others might do crosswords puzzles.

There was a certain snobbery in Boston about its past that Abe had not liked, and Mrs G was reminded of an old verse Abe quoted on occasions about Boston society.

*And this is good old Boston,*
*The home of the bean and the cod.*
*Where the Lowells talk only to Cabots,*
*And the Cabots talk only to God.*

John Cabot was an Englishman who claimed in 1497 to be first to discover what is now Canadian territory, having sought a northern route from England to China. As it later turned out, the route to Canada from Scotland had been known to the Templar Knights a hundred years before and to the Vikings before them. Nevertheless, Cabot claimed the whole of North America as British territory, and his family had settled in Boston. Abe's family had had no such luck.

Abe had come from a background of Orthodox Jews, of which he was the only boy. His mother had been the creative one in the family. She was a dressmaker, but had found her pleasures in the small back yard of their terraced house in New Jersey growing medicinal plants. Her own mother, who had come to America as one of the huddled masses at the end of the 19th century, had imparted to her a knowledge of herbal remedies handed down to her by Livornese Jews from Tuscany. Medicines in her day were rare and expensive, as were doctors. The poor needed to look after themselves and they often knew better than the medics of whom many were quacks and charlatans. Natural solutions then formed the basis of most medicines in which herbs and roots were ground and mixed into paste with a pestle and mortar.

Abe's mother gave him an interest in natural medicine and what little else she had best to give. Her determination was strong to make life better for her family through her inherited knowledge. She had little time for books and reading and would sing Jewish folklore songs handed down from generations before her. What's bred in the marrow comes out in the bone, as she liked to say.

Abe had liked his music, particularly Mozart and Brahms and had an ear for harmonic tones and how they could affect the mind and emotions. How some strains of Wagner's opera *Tristan und Isolde* could make the hair rise on the back of the neck. He would look for geometric patterns in music and their iteration. The same applied to plants, but although repetition occurred almost exactly, it was never quite identical. He felt it tallied with his friend Karl Popper's theories of chaos out of order, and order out of chaos.

Popper was a professor at the London School of Economics with whom Abe often corresponded, and was respected as one of the 20th century's new breed of philosophers. He believed with Abe that too much tolerance in society led to the disappearance of tolerance. Although concurring with Darwin's theory of the origin of the species and Mendel's concept of genetics, Popper saw them as unscientific until proven. Popper believed that the more complex the answer to a solution, the more questionable it became.

Abe was not an atheist, as Popper was, nor as rigidly Jewish orthodox as his parents had been. Popper had felt the existence of a god could neither be proved nor disproved, but out of tradition Abe gave respect to the ancient teachings of the Kabbalah and a Creator while trying to rationalize them to his experience of science. It was said that religion was the redemption of man's solitude, but Abe saw no cause for solitude in a world in which man and nature were one.

Towards his end Abe felt he had resolved the much-disputed problem of Creationism. He knew as a scientist that the Universe had a design. That order existed within it meant to him that it must have been devised by a divine authority of exceptional intellect, since it was a creation of great complexity, however undetermined it might seem. Abe had been excited when Mrs G's sister had told him that findings from the atomic Hadron Collider at CERN in Switzerland into bio-carbons linked directly to the Fibonacci code, as it also did into theories of sacred geometry from the Kabbalah and man's distant past.

It was logical to conclude that nothing existed except from the mind and will of an extraordinary power and that power was God, whatever form that God might take, or however it might be described. There was no reason to believe its Creator would beget the Universe other than for its good, but it required balance to achieve this. Abe saw science as part of a greater whole, but to him it came first in his quest for answers. In this Mrs G would often disagree as she felt faith itself could provide solutions without need for scientific deduction.

John Keats, the 19th century poet of the Romantic Movement, had proposed that people could think and find solutions without restraint of previous knowledge. Keats believed science followed the imagination of man and of those poets and artists who rated inspiration over knowledge. The novelist, DH Lawrence, once wrote to the mathematician Bertrand Russell: *"When everything else is gone ...there is always the sense of God, of the Absolute. Our sense of the Absolute is the only sense left to us."* It did not require a religion to feel this.

Abe's father made little money but he had managed to get Abe into a good Jewish school in the Bronx. It was there Abe had learned about the balance of harmonic tones and about the Fibonacci theory of sequence and its pertinence to the genetic codes of all life on Earth. Its use in computing and artificial intelligence had been discovered in 1940 by Alan Turing, the English inventor of modern computing. Later Abe had understood how morphogenesis, the study of the growing shapes of animals and plants, could be similarly applied across a whole number of disciplines.

Abe's experiments required first-hand knowledge and he was interested in those before him who had explored the use of plants which could alter states of consciousness. He saw it as no coincidence that Lewis Carroll, the writer of the fantasy tale of *Alice in Wonderland*, had once lived in the same English town as Turing, and both were brilliant mathematicians. Turing's ideas for deciphering the German codes in World War Two were largely responsible for Britain's eventual victory, but had at first been seen as bordering on lunacy. After the war he was given treatment to cure his homosexuality which was at the time seen as a form of derangement.

Carroll was known to take a potion made from the laburnum tree which induced hallucinations and gave birth to the strange dream worlds of Alice. Perhaps the minds of Carroll and Turing had not been delusional at all, but by using drugs they had altered their states of consciousness to levels of imagination that could not otherwise be achieved. The English academic and philosopher Aldous Huxley had said as much of his own experience in his book *The Doors of Perception* having ingested mescaline, the psychedelic drug which had started the flower power generation of the 1960s in California in Abe's youth. The mysteries of the mind and of mathematics intrigued Abe, and the Fibonacci Series became for him a revelation of life and the answers it could provide, not just for plants but for humanity and their interconnection. If it was necessary to use them to open the mind Abe had decided he would do so, but with caution.

Abe had been fascinated by the work of Francis Crick, an English Nobel Prize winner who, as the world's most famous contemporary scientist, had admitted shortly before his death in 2004 that he had come to his discovery of the double helix of DNA as a result of taking lysergic acid diethylamide to expand his intelligence. LSD, as it was known, was a manufactured hallucinatory drug with a cosmogenic power. Crick claimed it had opened his mind to a fourth dimension, similar to the use of a drug known to the shamans of Brazil and Peru by the name of Ayahuasca, containing the chemical Tryptamine, as did LSD. The shamans had believed they could ascend to a real world on beams of light where truth would be revealed, rather than the unreal world in which man lived on earth.

Crick had believed that the intelligence of modern man had not evolved as Darwin had proposed, but that it had been received at a single moment of time by our anthropomorphized ancestors around 25,000 years ago, give or take 5,000. He saw as likely it had been brought to earth by an alien race.

Crick evidenced that the woven strands of human DNA, similar to ancient symbols of interlaced vines or entwined serpents, carried not only our genes which took up no more than three per cent of man's DNA, but were present in every living thing in the universe. Crick had further realized that what was seen as the greater part of unused DNA, or "Junk DNA" as it became known had its own hidden code but that without the use of psychedelics its secrets could not be explored. The full intelligence capability of DNA in man was said to be one hundred trillion times greater than the most sophisticated information storage devices currently in use. Not only might it connect man telepathically to every living thing in the Universe but it might also reveal the secret to life.

Crick's view on aliens was extraordinary for a man of science. Abe himself had considered that it was not until the equation of blending psychotropic plants had been discovered that the intelligence "minded" in DNA had given rise to the wisdom of the cultures who had built the pyramids. How primitive people thousands of years earlier had discovered the solution was a mystery unless they were more intelligent than mankind was now. That there might be parallel universes of the mind fitted with the relatively new theories of quantum physics, and of experiments in the gene splitting of plants needing millions of combinations to discover radical solutions.

Often Abe would experiment with concoctions of consciousness-altering potions on himself and Mrs G would need to help him recover while his mind came back to Earth, sometimes days later. She felt it was quite likely that one of his personal experiments would kill him one day given the risks he took with himself and which he would not allow others to take, including Mrs G.

One particular area that had intrigued Abe was the sulphonamides, which although poisonous were the basis of antibiotics, the miracle cure-all drugs of the 20th century first discovered by the British scientist Alexander Fleming in 1928. Recently the power of antibiotics to heal was fading fast by reason of their over-prescription for almost every complaint. Given to animals and crops, they had entered the food chain in a process which could not now be reversed. Abe had long ago predicted that germs would develop their own reactive super strains and that humanity would again fall foul of the plagues that had once wiped out half of the world's populations.

Abe specialized in genetic engineering of plant life and its advances in splicing which he believed might allow the discovery of a combined vaccine to defeat common viruses as well as mycobacterium. He had come to realize that the genetic coding of plants was extraordinarily similar to that of humans. A solution to cure all ills was the stuff of his dreams, but it was a huge task that required many millions of speculative combinations.

His experiments of the past few years had brought some success to the cure of tularemia, a virulent bacterium endemic in the USA and Europe. He had kept the results of his most recent experiments to himself particularly that of a universal antibiotic combined with psychosomatic drugs based on the tryptamine compound DMT, a substance which improved observation, rather than being hallucinogenic. With the right balance it could produce a race of disease-free super-intelligent people who could utilize their hidden store of unused DNA.

As Mrs G reflected, she saw Abe clearly in her mind exactly as she had found him. He was lying on his back, his head to one side, and as she bent towards him she had touched the small line of blood on his face and recoiled as his dead glazed eyes had looked into her own. She was not religious in any orthodox way, but somehow she felt this could not be the end. Somehow there had to be more, and if she did nothing else in her life she would try to find out what.

# Chapter 6

Mrs G came back into the room still shaking a little from the memory of that dreadful day. Gerry and Marianne were on the couch talking together. She composed herself and sat down.

"I hope I'm not talking too much," she began once more.

"That's quite a brief, but battleship-sized piece of history for you to absorb, but I expect you may know a lot of it from school, and from your grandmother. If you do, then let me know and we can skip it and move on.

"In the thousand years following King Arthur and his Knights, the Catholic Church slowly became the religion of the English whose kings adopted it in fear of the popes and their alliances with powerful European rulers. Several English kings mixed their bloodlines by marriage to foreign wives to keep the peace with the stronger Catholic countries of France and Spain. Catholicism was a theological ideal with rules known formally as the Nicene Creed which went hand in hand with state laws. Its insistence that people should commune with God only through its priests gave it control of people and their confessions. It was not anywhere near the esoteric Nazarene faith of Jesus and Mary Magdalene which encouraged a direct personal communion with God, whose followers had been driven underground.

"In the 20th century some ancient writings were found in a cave near the Dead Sea where the Essene sect had once lived. They were written in Hebrew soon after Jesus' death and are known as the Dead Sea Scrolls. Similar Hermetic texts were found soon after at Nag Hamada in Egypt. They showed clearly that in Jesus' time he was not seen as the son of God. It was not a view the Catholic Church had wanted known, nor did they want people to know of the importance to Jesus of Mary Magdalene.

"In the 9th century the seven hundred year old Gospel of Mary Magdalene was unearthed. In it her status at the time of Christ was shown to be above that of all Jesus' disciples, which the Catholic Church refused to acknowledge. The Church had named the Vatican cathedral in Rome as St Peter's and commissioned artistic works of Jesus' mother Mary to substitute her image in place of Mary Magdalene."

As she spoke Mrs G found an image on her TV screen.

"See this. It's the wonderful statue of "La Pieta", known the world over as Jesus dying in his mother's arms. But the face of the mother is that of a beautiful young woman whom the sculptor Michelangelo had dared to make in the image of Mary Magdalene. His family name was Buonarroti and he and his descendants were known in later years to be secret Nazarenes and Freemasons.

"In 1606 the Italian painter Caravaggio painted Mary Magdalene, said by the Catholics to show her reclining in ecstasy, when it is clearly apparent she is pregnant. However much the Catholics tried to destroy Mary Magdalene, her name lived on, as did the Nazarene creed, resurfacing in the religious rebellions of the Protestants Luther and Calvin in Germany. In France the Protestant Huguenots were massacred in their thousands by Catholics, and they fled to Germany and to England and then on to America. It's how your mother's family came here with their Nazarene faith, and their claim to the bloodline of Mary Magdalene known as the Rose Line."

Marianne had been waiting to speak and nervously asked Mrs G a question.

"If it's true that Grandma and the Merovingians were descendants of Mary Magdalene then she must have had a child. So was Mary married?"

Mrs G smiled. "She was said to have taken a daughter named Sarah to Egypt when she first fled Israel, and from there to the Languedoc where it's claimed she was carrying Jesus' son on her arrival. Certainly the Merovingian monarchs who claimed their descent from her believed so. It is what I believe and want to investigate on my trip to Europe for your sake. It is known that some of Jesus' disciples were jealous of Mary, particularly John who had been intimately close to Jesus. Why would they be if she was not Jesus' wife or partner?"

It was dark now outside and Gerry yawned loudly and stretched himself out on the couch. "Is there much more of this, Mrs G? I need to get me a Coke; and what about our pizzas?"

Gerry said it impatiently. He was getting bored. His interest was in the Templars and Mrs G was going a long way round about it.

"The Templars are next up," smiled Mrs G, "and then that's it. So hear me to the end if you want to make sense of it all."

# Chapter 7

Mrs G was more concerned about Gerry than she was about Marianne. Gerry was seventeen. Not yet man, nor still boy. As for Marianne, she had been pleased to be treated with empathy by Mrs G, but Gerry was now without any man as his mentor. His mother had been distant from him, preferring her love of horse breeding which she shared with her husband, Gerry's father, an Englishman who had devoted himself to his wife and the lifestyle and fortune she brought with her rather than to their children.

At the age of thirteen Gerry had been sent to a boarding school in England to broaden his education before returning to college in America. Along with science as his preferred subject, he had learned Latin and French. Math came easily to him. He enjoyed being at his grandfather's Brookline home in Boston, where with his sister they had moved after the death of their parents, and the space it afforded him. His studio room at the top of the house was equipped with every form of entertainment and digital information device modern technology could offer. A set of drums lay idle now, as did the punch bag hung from a ceiling beam. More serious things were on his mind.

Physically he was of medium height with a wiry, but athletic build toned from swimming and the workouts he did dutifully at home every day. His eyes were blue-grey with a mop-head of chestnut-colored hair. Gerry had one or two close friends at college, but was neither gregarious, nor a team player, preferring stand-alone sports. He played squash, had a Fifth Kyu Karate blue belt, and was a good rifle shot. He and his sister sailed a small laser dinghy in South Boston harbor.

Since the death of his parents, and now of his Granddad, Gerry was becoming aware that he would soon need to take on responsibilities which had not previously concerned him. He had not mentioned his distant heritage to his friends who had little interest in ancestry or how past history might have importance. Americans in general were happy to go along with Henry Ford's famous maxim that "history is more or less bunk". To Americans that might be so, but not to Europeans as Gerry had learned. To them the separate cultures and history of Europe's nearly fifty nations were essential to their self-belief and old feuds of war and religion died hard.

Fewer than a quarter of Americans had ever traveled outside the North American continent. That it had largely been English settlers who had fought to gain independence from the English monarchy, or that the American Founding Fathers were mostly English Masons, was now of little consequence.

Gerry had got on well with Abe who had not tried to shape his political views. Rather Abe had been keen to discuss the world of scientific discovery as the realm which offered adventure in space travel. Abe had directed Gerry towards the sci-fi books of Isaac Asimov, a Russian biochemist at Boston University whom Abe had known well. The recent movie *Interstellar* had captured Gerry's imagination, as had the private space tourism venture of Virgin Galactic, and it was in science and space that his interests lay.

There were other interests Gerry had not talked about with Abe. Those relating to the occult. Gerry had read some of the works of Aleister Crowley, an English explorer of the Edwardian era, who had traveled the world studying religious cults, including devil worship. India's Buddha and Hinduism, Egypt's ancient god Horus, Arabic and other ancient languages all attracted Crowley's attention as he investigated a world that had passed. He had ventured to the Sahara and South America and had attempted a climb of Kanchenjunga in Nepal to seek whatever god he might find on its summit. Crowley's stories had excited Gerry's imagination and he wanted to know more. What underlay religions? Hindus said we are ignorant of who we really are, while Buddhists said we are ignorant of who we are not. It was the niceties that were important, and Gerry was a perfectionist, as had been Abe.

Like so many prophets in the past Crowley used opium and hashish to open his mind to a metaphysical world. Crowley had advocated scientific naturalism and created a religion of "True Will." There had been and would continue to be many like him throughout the ages with varying philosophical and religious standpoints from the cults of the Theosophists of the Victorian age to the Indian gurus of the 1960s. Most were self-convinced idealists. Some were frauds. The words of John Lennon's album *Imagine* for a new Aquarian age were vastly influential at the time, but today amongst the self-acclaimed musical revolutionaries and rap stars the chaff needed separating from the wheat.

Gerry had smoked grass with his schoolmates and was aware that he had a rebel side to his nature. He believed it came from his eccentric grandmother. He had considered visiting a shrink to discuss this part of his personality, but Abe had deterred him saying psychologists were mostly pseudo-scientists along with Freud and his like. "The insane lecturing the sane", as he had put it. Better to press on confidently seeing rebelliousness as an asset. For Gerry adventure beckoned on all fronts. He knew knowledge was power Abe had told him so and it was the key to his future as someone who was to have great influence.

# Chapter 8

Gerry returned to the room with two Cokes and some water for Mrs G.

"This is the last leg," croaked Mrs G, taking a long draught to relieve her vocal chords. "You can get your pizzas after this."

"By the 12th century the Muslim religion of Islam had spread rapidly and battles for control of the holy site of Jerusalem raged between Muslims and the Catholic Christians. The Temple of Solomon was protected by the Templar monks, but their ranks were soon joined by crusading nobles from all over Europe who came to fight for the Holy Land in the name of Christ.

"At first the Templars were sworn to poverty, but after discovering King Solomon's treasure they became rich and fought alongside the Crusader knights to whom they acted as bankers. In 1187 the Crusaders lost control of Jerusalem to the Muslim Saracen army of Saladin after a series of fierce battles. The Templars retreated to Europe, building themselves castles and fortresses and continuing their role as bankers.

"Having first professed Christian Catholic beliefs, the Templars now turned to practice Dualism as had the Merovingians and Cathars before them. It is believed they were influenced by writings they found in the Ark of the Covenant. This together with their wealth soon put them at odds with the Catholic Church who sought to destroy the Templar's power. First by reputation, claiming they were sodomites who took magic potions and were in league with the Devil, as they had once accused the Cathars of being; and then by military force.

"On Friday 13th October 1307 the French King Philip, hand-in-glove with the Pope, ordered the murder of the Templar leaders in Paris where he had invited them as guests. The date has been seen as unlucky ever since. Those Templars left alive fled, some to the remote Swiss and Hungarian mountains, and some by boat to Scotland, taking their treasure hoard with them, aided by the Scottish King Robert the Bruce who claimed Merovingian descent. A part of the treasure was buried at Roslyn Chapel near Edinburgh. The

English King Edward learned of the treasure and attacked the Scots at Bannockburn, but retreated when his army was taken by surprise by the well-armed and ferocious Templar knights. Knowing the English would be back, the Templars planned to take the remaining treasure, including the Ark of the Covenant, to a safer place.

"From an encryption at the Roslyn Chapel we know that its owner, Prince Sinclair knew of the old Viking sea route to Nova Scotia in Canada. The Templars sailed there, hiding the treasure on Oak Island, just off the Canadian coast, in a labyrinth of tunnels under the sea set with traps to flood and drown any strangers attempting access. Many efforts to find it since have failed. To hide their identity the Templar descendants in Canada changed their name to Arcadians, after the Ark of the Covenant, and over time many of them joined French settlers in the French city of New Orleans in Louisiana. Since then Louisiana has become part of the United States and the Arcadians are known today as Cajuns, still speaking with their own, Old French dialect."

# Chapter 9

Gerry and Marianne, hungry by now, went to cook their pizzas. The large old cooking range in the kitchen heated the water all year round, so the baking ovens below were always hot and ready for use. Their dogs, a black Labrador and two Jack Russell terriers, lay on the dark red tiled floor near the ovens for warmth. In ten minutes Gerry and Marianne were back with their pizzas to hear how Mrs G's tale would end. It was getting late and the night seemed very silent in their enclosed domain. It was good to disappear into the past world of her story.

"You need to know about the Roslyn Chapel in Scotland. It's named after the Rose bloodline of Mary Magdalene from which you are said to be descended. Your mother went to visit the Chapel there with your grandma not long before they both died. In a second I'll show you photos she took."

Mrs G clicked away at the PC and recent pictures of Roslyn appeared on the screen, standing alone in a field. Instead of being a ruin it was a large robust building in Gothic style, now over five hundred years old, looking much like a church without a spire, with medieval architecture of flying buttresses, and the hideous faces of gargoyles to ward off evil spirits. More shots appeared, this time of the interior carvings. "They are symbols that tell the story of life itself," Mrs G explained. "From the beginning of intelligent mankind, twenty thousand or more years ago."

Mrs G scrolled down through pictures, closing in on an eclectic mix of Egyptian, Hebrew, Christian and pagan symbols covering the walls and floors. In the roof a starry firmament of pentagram-shaped stars looked down as it had done in the Great Pyramid of Unas, depicting Osiris the god of afterlife. The vine of life and fertility emerged from the mouth of a green man which Osiris was said to be. Roses adorned the arches over the entrance signifying the Rose Line, on whose geographical meridian Roslyn sat, in a direct line from cathedrals in Spain and France to Scotland. It was the route of pilgrims for hundreds of years to this day. On the floor was an immense symbol of the Star of David, the symbol of male and female sexual union. At the far end were the two Pillars of Wisdom of

Solomon's Temple.

Mrs G continued scrolling down the screen images of Roslyn and its interior, showing its mystic origins. How ignorant we are of the meanings of the past and yet everything is here for all to know, she mused. She pointed at the screen. "See this. The pentagram with its five points has meaning to many faiths including Christians, Muslims and Jews. The Masonic Dome of the Rock is depicted here as in other ancient Templar chapels, and there," she pointed, "you can see Christ on the cross. In the roof you can see a pendant keystone, the last stone to be inserted in its building as with the pyramids. And there are the steps that lead to an underground crypt as large as the Chapel above, where it is said the treasure was kept for a while. Some say Roslyn was laid out in the manner of Solomon's Temple in Jerusalem where many thousands of sacrifices of animals were made on its huge altar of blood-stained golden horns as payment to the High Priest for his forgiveness of sins. But there is no altar at Roslyn that compares in any way, nor any talk of sacrifices. Your mother had wanted to meet with the Chapel's owner, but instead she saw a deputy. Despite being polite he did not add much more than was well known. 'There are many legends about Roslyn,' he had told her. 'It was built by the Sinclair ancestors on ruins of a previous chapel.'

"It seems the Sinclair name means "clear light" in Occitan which was the language of Langue d'Oc in France where the Sinclair family originated as Merovingians. The Sinclairs are custodians of Roslyn's premises and its secrets. Many people travel there to try to decipher the meaning of the codes."

It was strange, thought Mrs G, that the secrets to life from thousands of years stood in a field owned privately and unguarded, as if it was of little importance. Was humankind never to learn from history, but just to push on relentlessly in its search for knowledge evidenced only by facts, rather than having faith in the knowledge of the past?

"The Sinclair family history is recorded in a book called *Rosslyn* written by a family member. They have long been connected to the Scottish Rite of Masonry. Strange as it would seem, a female Sinclair descendant of the present time is married to a Lord Rothschild, a supporter of a prestigious sect of the Jewish faith connected to the Kabbalah. The Rothschild family raised the funds to build the Israeli parliament building, the Knesset, and the nearby Supreme Court on which is the image of a pyramid with the all-seeing eye of the

Egyptian god Horus."

As I see it, the marriage is hardly a coincidence. It may have been a closing of the circle in which the original Hebrew faith stemming from mystic beliefs of the Egyptians came together once more with that of the Nazarene Christianity of Jesus. It is said that around 780 A.D. a Rabbi Makhir had reinstated the Kabbalah's teachings from the lost text of the Sepher haBahir, said to be the same as that which the Templars found in Solomon's Temple. The Rabbi, who claimed he was descended from King David resided on sacred ground in Narbonne only thirty miles from Carcassonne in the place where Mary Magdalene had once found refuge on her arrival there and where the Cathars also lived. Yet one more coincidence!" Mrs G concluded.

Are you going to Roslyn Mrs G?" questioned Marianne, looking slightly perplexed from a thought she had just had. "My music teacher taught me last week that the five notes on my piano's black keys are pentatonic and are magic, as you can play any tune on them without needing to use the white keys."

Mrs G smiled. "The pentagram is seen as a magical symbol. As for Roslyn I don't think I will discover any more there than your mother found out. I am more interested in the hero of my story, as I hope him to be. He knew all I have told you and a good deal more. He was a scientist, cryptographer and philosopher. He believed in an afterlife as did the Egyptians who built the pyramids so that the spirits of their kings could ascend from their tombs on beams of light to the stars above. The geometrical skills to build the pyramids have been unsolved ever since, even with the massive computer power of today. The pyramids once stood in deep moats, which could be flooded from the river Nile. Their architects devised that at given planetary moments, a powerful electro-magnetic current would transport the souls of the dead to the stars from whence they had once come. The cones on top of the pyramids were made of solid gold as powerful energy conductors. The sides of the pyramids were not steps as we see them today, but were flat surfaces of white stone which could be seen from space and absorbed solar energy to power the electronic forces required.

"The pyramids at Giza and elsewhere were built to imitate the dog leg pattern of the heavenly Orion constellation. The stars Orion and

Sirius represented Isis and Osiris, the principal god and goddess of the Egyptians. The Egyptians believed their ancestors had once come from the star Sirius and there are carved stone tablets today still hidden in under-ground caves in the Sahara desert that tell the same tale. If they are right, then the people from Sirius were most likely the start of Homo sapiens, who brought intelligent life to Earth. Sadly, Islamic terrorists have recently found and destroyed many of the tablets, as they conflict with the views of their Prophet Mohammed."

"Far out!" exclaimed Gerry. "Grandpa Abe used to say if men are descended from apes, then why are there still apes. But what are the Egyptians to do with my Merovingian ancestors?"

"That's what I intend to find out for my book," Mrs G replied. She was tired now, running her fingers through her hair, as if in exasperation at Gerry's impatience. "I want to know if they shared the same secrets as the Egyptians. I must have more time to find the clues I need. I have to go to see a publisher first to see if he thinks it will be of enough interest to publish. When I do you two can have the first copy."

Mrs G clicked back to the picture of the interior roof of Roslyn on the TV screen depicting starry signs of the heavens.

"You two in your adult lives will be witness to a new age in the history of the Universe, which astrologers call the Harmonic Convergence of the Planets, the Age of Aquarius, which started only in 2010," she explained.

"Your Grandpa was a scientist who dealt in facts. He knew that plant-life was controlled by the rhythms of the planets, but it took a leap of faith for him to see that if all life forms are at one with the Universe they might be able to be transposed anywhere in it. He saw belief in an afterlife as paranormal and difficult to believe without evidence. But I think an after world may very well exist in reality, as there is much science does not know, least of all of the brain, and of the spirit, nothing at all. Sadly the world is short on faith. Love cannot be proved as fact, yet we know it exists. Because we have lost trust in our natural selves we seek scientific evidence to give ourselves assurance, but much of what we believe as fact constantly changes as new 'facts' emerge. The new 'Rainbow' theory of gravity in which there is no beginning and no end in a world of parallel universes has now debunked the old 'Big Bang' idea of how the world began.

"The subject of my story I believe to be the missing link between the past, present and the future. He was born with every possible advantage and achieved great fame which turned to disaster, but from it I believe he found the truth of our existence. He saw that faith and science might be as one in a parallel universe. That everything we see in the physical universe only comes into existence when the mind gives it form. The quantum physics of the human soul."

Coughing, Mrs G reached for her glass of water and drank it down. Her throat was parched now and her eyes stung from looking at the screen. "No more history now," she just managed to whisper. "That's enough. My real story has yet to begin, and when I am back from Europe I hope I can tell you it all."

With that she switched off the TV to turn in for the night, heading upstairs to the bed she had not long ago shared with Abe. Nothing ever stayed the same. Gerry and Marianne followed to their rooms shortly after.

# Chapter 10

## York Place, White Hall, London. August, 1560

Elizabeth, now Queen after her sister Mary Tudor's death from flu in November 1558, is visibly pregnant belying her normally slim and wiry young body. She had inherited her youthful gaiety from her father Henry and his love of music, both being accomplished players of instruments. Despite her slight build, with her light red hair and penetrating blue-gray eyes, she had a commanding presence and had inherited her father's steely resolve in making decisions.

She turns to a man across a paneled room, hung with tapestry scenes of deer pursued by huntsmen on galloping steeds. Elizabeth was herself a good huntswoman, riding side-saddle with ease. She had learnt to ride at a young age following in the footsteps of her father, himself a renowned sportsman, before his death from overweight and syphilis. Henry had been a serious athlete, playing tennis and rounders and a feared champion at jousting with his fellow knights. In one joust he had been taken for dead. Elizabeth lacked none of his courage or forthrightness.

"I am four months with child, Robert," she exclaimed. "We will need to wed before it is born.
"My darling, Beth," he replied "you have given me your love, a home, and now our child. Everything I could wish for, but to marry you now? What of my wife? My betrothal to her was witnessed!"
"Do you forget the secret vows we took with Father Cornelius in the Tower? They annulled what may have gone before them. I am your wife now, and Queen besides. That of your past is yours to resolve," spat out Elizabeth. I am with child - she is not. 'Tis time to make a virtue of necessity. We need to be wed formally so that our child should not be born a bastard, and you will vow to keep our pact a secret forever. That is my will."

Without a shrug of hesitation Robert nodded in agreement. "We are as one," he replied. "That I vow."
Elizabeth waved her hand imperiously. "My wish is to rule as Queen

alone. You will not share my throne, Robert, nor ever be acknowledged as my husband to my people. For your own good as you will see one day."

"Your wish be my command, Ma'am," Robert acquiesced. He knew where his best course lay.

"Well then, draw near me and show me you love your Queen", Elizabeth smiled winningly, and held out her hand expectantly.

# Chapter 11

**Cumnor Hall, near Oxford, England. 1560**

Amy Robsart had married Robert Dudley in Richmond in 1550 when they were both eighteen. The wedding was of social importance and the thirteen year old King Edward VI, heir to his father Henry VIII, had attended it. Robert and Amy had taken up residence in Norfolk where they were to start married life. They had had no children when, in 1553, after the death from illness of the young King Edward, Robert had been arrested with his father, the Duke of Northumberland, for plotting to overthrow the new Catholic Queen Mary - by replacing her with their protégé Lady Jane Grey.

Robert was imprisoned by Mary in the Tower of London where he met and seduced the Princess Elizabeth with whom he was later released, but with his possessions confiscated. For a while he had fled to France leaving Amy to fend for herself. She had moved to Cumnor Hall in 1558 near her former home with Robert.

In 1557 Elizabeth, then twenty-five, following the death from flu of her half-sister Mary Tudor, had been crowned Queen of England and Ireland. Soon after she had given Robert the title of Master of the Horse so that he was to be near her at court almost daily. Two years later she granted him the high title of Knight of the Garter. If she gave any thought to Robert's former backing of her once rival to the throne, Lady Jane Grey, she paid it no attention. Being opportunist herself in resisting objections to her claim to the throne, she recognized the same character in Leicester with whom she had shared her escape from execution.

Little doubt word of their romance had filtered back to Amy in the countryside, but Amy was still in love with Robert. He was dashingly good looking and they had married as young lovers in the brief five year Catholic reign of Mary before Elizabeth became queen. Amy hoped in time her husband would return to her when he had reestablished his fortunes. Elizabeth was rumored to be fickle in her fancies and to quickly discard those with whom she became bored. For her to be married it would most likely be with a foreign king or prince for political reasons to cement England's relationship with France or Spain, so to avoid the threat of future wars.

Amy and Robert had seen little of each other after he had sought refuge in France and so they had delayed starting a family. Rumor had it that Amy had developed cancer of the breast while pining for her husband whom she was last known to have seen when he visited her in 1558 in the house at Cumnor, near Oxford, which he had rented for her.

But Amy had not known, nor had anyone else, of Robert's and Elizabeth's bigamous vows of marriage taken in the Tower four years before in 1554, nor of Elizabeth's pregnancy by Robert six years later, shortly after which Amy had been found dead. Some said she had taken her own life but the coroner's verdict was that she had died from a fall through the balustrade railings of a staircase at Cumnor in which she had hit the back of her head on the floor below. The date of her death was established as September 8th 1560.

A more unpleasant rumor was that she had been thrown over the railings or that they had been cut to weaken them. On later investigation it was found that there were few if any witnesses called by the coroner, since the staff at Cumnor had been given the day off, and the coroner's court papers had somehow since been lost. As for Robert he did not manage to find the time to attend Amy's funeral due to his attendance on the Queen at court.

# Chapter 12

A few days after Amy Robsart's death, Elizabeth in her private chapel in the palace at York Place, regally attired, but visibly pregnant, appeared nervous. Her own private priest was in attendance together with her staunch friends Lady Anne Bacon and Lord Puckering. Lady Anne was herself pregnant, expecting the child's arrival in four months, as was Elizabeth her own. Elizabeth thanked them for coming and spoke of the consequences of what they were about to witness. Lady Anne's husband Sir Nicholas Bacon was a lawyer who held the title of Lord Keeper and was a close confidant of the Queen, as he had been previously to her father, Henry.

Elizabeth spoke to those present with firm authority.
"This ceremony is to be witnessed by you as required in law. But it is to remain a secret until the day I decree otherwise. Neither you, nor any other, will ever speak of this, lest you face sentence of death. I have put my trust in you and you shall be well rewarded."

At this warning she beckoned to the priest to commence her marriage to Robert. They stood with heads bowed as they took their marriage vows in Latin. When the short ritual was completed the priest left the Chapel and Elizabeth spoke again to the dignified Lady Anne. She indicated her pronounced stomach, noticing the co-incidence of Lady Anne's own rounded belly.
"When this child of mine is born, God willing, I will give it into your care to raise as your own. It will henceforth take your family name and you are never to disclose from whence it came.
"The child is adulterine, half-bastard, conceived before wedlock. I cannot now risk my throne or endanger the child's life through any future claim to my throne. Better now it should go with you. I know you both as of good repute and good education and that you have your own children. You shall have use of York House here next door to me, but I ask too that the child should be-times live at Gorhambury House in Hertfordshire, which was my father's grant to you and shall

remain so in my reign. I may on occasion ask to see the child, but your lips must forever remain sealed that it is born of the Queen."

Elizabeth rose to bid them leave. "I shall always be in your debt," were her parting words to them as they bowed and left her with her now husband, Robert Dudley, soon to be made Earl of Leicester. She turned to take his hand as a tear ran down her cheeks, and buried her face on his chest. No peace for the wicked, she thought, although she had no desire to deserve the opprobrium of that term. She soon regained her composure.

Four months later on 22nd January 1561 at Windsor Castle the Queen gave birth to a blue-eyed boy, whom she named Francis, born under the sign of Aquarius, the New Age sign said to give intuition, insight and a oneness with nature. That he shared his Taurean moon sign with his mother, was to prove him an equal to her in strong mindedness, but at odds in their future battles of will. As for Lady Anne, her own child died stillborn, providing a useful cover for the newborn child whom the Queen handed over to her on his entrance into the world. Later it was found that the papers to record his birth by the Queen had been destroyed.

# Chapter 13

## Washington DC. USA. Fall, 2014

Mrs G was led by Phillip Buonarroti's secretary into a sumptuous office suite on the sixth floor of his offices. From large floor-to-ceiling windows the offices overlooked the famous five hundred and fifty foot high Washington Monument, named after America's first President, the founding father of the nation. As Mrs G entered, Phillip cut short a phone call and walked over to greet her.

He was around fifty-five, she guessed, with dark hair now showing silver streaks and impeccably styled. Sleek, but good looking in a perma-tanned way, now a little too chubby, although well concealed in an expensive, well-tailored, light grey check suit. The Rossetti brogue shoes with their tassels just a little too new and shiny. He looked every part a smart Italian American.

"Welcome to Washington," he said in a voice with manly charm, stretching out his hand.
"I'm Phillip; Phil to my friends. Great to meet you. Abe told me how much he had relied on you and about your shared interests. What brings you here? I hope I can be of assistance."

He looked hard at Mrs G, trying to sum her up through his tightly-lidded eyes. She seemed much as he had imagined she might. Neatly dressed in a slightly old fashioned secretarial sort of way. No expensive jewelry apart from a small Patek Philippe watch with a lapis lazuli face and black leather strap which Abe had bought her the previous Christmas. A fitted blue bolero jacket, as part of a suit with matching skirt in a classic Chanel style, and smart, black patent shoes with low heels. A colored silk Gucci scarf topped it off. She stood around five-foot-five in her stockinged feet. She was, he reckoned, probably pretty straightforward to deal with, but a little shy and possibly naive outside the protected Boston environment afforded to her by Abe. Phil considered himself good at making snap judgments on people when he first met them. First impressions were the best, he believed.

Mrs G took his handshake firmly as he indicated a black leather chair opposite his expansive glass and steel desk. As she settled into the seat she coughed and asked for a glass of water. A little nervous, thought Phil, I wonder what's on her mind. He spoke to give her reassurance.

"Abe and I were good buddies for many years. I expect he told you." He looked at her enquiringly as if her answer would decide how he might treat her. She didn't answer and so he continued:

"I got your email, thanks. So what is this book of yours? Sounds interesting. All about the life and secrets of Francis Bacon. Isn't he the British artist with those contorted soul-suffering paintings which cost a king's ransom? I saw one in the last Sotheby's sale here which went for over fifty million bucks! Looks to me as if it's all done on dope or with distorting mirrors. Easy if you know how, I guess, but not to my taste." With that he sat down opposite her in a large leather-backed steel swivel chair and faced Mrs G. "I am a publisher, but I am not so sure this is in my domain. Not art. I do political stuff mainly."

"Uh uh", mouthed Mrs G, shaking her head. "You've got the wrong one. The artist Bacon died only twenty years or so ago. Mine lived four hundred years back. By comparison his genius blew away the contemporary one." Phil was surprised at the vehemence in Mrs G's expression. He had teased her about the artist. He had an idea why she had come to him.

"So tell me more," he said. "Four hundred years is a long time." Mrs G sensed a lack of interest, but she was not going to be diverted. She told him about the curiosity that she and Abe had in relation to the Francis Bacon of Elizabethan times and how he was a vital link to the Masonic origins of American history. She pointed at the grand spire of the Masonic Temple which could be seen in the panoramic view of the Washington Monument from where she sat, so as to emphasize her point.

"I believe my findings can reveal ancient knowledge of mankind's origins in the Universe which Bacon took to his death. They relate to Bacon's Masonic connections and to the past lineage of Abe's grandchildren from their grandmother. I am sure you know that the whole of Washington is laid out on a design of sacred geometry on astrological principles from Egyptian times. The Capitol building was built to resemble the original Temple of Solomon in Jerusalem.

On the Washington obelisk there are hieroglyphics linking the spiritual past to the future and a prediction of the end of the world as we know it. George Washington and the Founding Fathers knew their meaning and few today are aware of it."

"Um" said Buonarroti, slowly picking his teeth, knowing perfectly well what she was saying.

"I am not so sure Abe would have approved. You know he liked to deal only in facts and wanted to protect Marilyn and her family from their antecedents. Did he know of your intentions? Without real evidence it is often best to leave speculation alone."

"It's not speculation. I've uncovered evidence which I hope to prove in my book when I've completed my research. It's why I'm off to Europe tomorrow. I'm sure Abe would have approved of my goal. His death will not defeat my purpose. He was a wonderful human being and he dedicated his life to medicine and to his family. There was no reason for him to die. His autopsy was unsatisfactory." Tears came to her eyes as she spoke about him. "I can't believe he would have taken his own life."

"Yes," said Phillip, "a terrible shock for his family, and for us all. He always seemed full of life, on a mission to save the planet from all ills. You may not know he was a friend of our charitable Order here in Washington of which I am a member. We don't broadcast our good work." He looked at her quizzically. "What was the problem with the autopsy? He worked hard, but I can't believe he was depressed in any way."

Mrs G was surprised. Abe had not mentioned his connection with the Order but she knew he regarded Phillip as a good friend and had appointed him a trustee of Abe's Magdala Foundation. She felt Phillip was unsympathetic to her cause. It was possible that Abe may have made an error by somehow ingesting the sulphonamide potion on which he had been experimenting, but it would have been unlike his usual caution. She knew he had developed a particularly strong strain, which would form the basis of a new breed of antibiotics that were urgently required. She decided to ignore Phil's inference and instead changed tack to ask him a favor with a big smile on her face.

"Please can you help me with my book?" she implored, "It's important to me. It's my Holy Grail." She moved in her chair slightly as if about to leave. She had a plane from Washington's Dulles Airport to London she needed to catch the next day.

Buonarroti looked at her and felt slightly sorry for her. He checked his watch, a large, gold Rolex, and saw he had another meeting due. Best to appease her, he thought. What harm could come from it? What could Mrs G really reveal from the past, which would now be of any great interest? The American public was not that interested in history. But what else might she disclose? Then he suddenly realized she might have more importance than he had considered after Abe's death. He turned away for a minute to think of the best tack to take with her.

"Okay. If you stick to facts I will help you publish once it's finished. But," he added, "on one condition." Once more he studied her suspiciously. Was she as naive as she seemed or was there more under the surface than just her idealism? Why had she come to see him? He moved away from the window in which he had been studying her reflection and said:
"So long as I approve the final draft. Is that a deal? If you find that Grail of yours, that would be really something," and he smiled at her benevolently.
"I'll let you know when I have, but it may surprise you," said Mrs G, rising from her seat. She smiled, and Phillip smiled back as graciously as he could manage.

As she went out of the door he picked up the phone and dialed the number of the caller he was speaking to before her arrival.
"Hi," he said. "I thought I'd let you know I don't think there's a problem, but we should keep an eye on her. She's recently taken up Abe's old position as head trustee of his Magdala Foundation and so is able to veto how the funds are applied. I'm a co-trustee and can run rings round her if necessary, but what's more of a problem is to find out if she knows about Abe's antibiotic formula, or whether he took it to the grave. She's leaving for London tomorrow, but she'll be back in a few weeks. Better stay on standby." He put the phone down, slicked back his hair with his left hand, and grunted.

# Chapter 14

Phillip Buonarroti sat down to think. He cast his mind back a year or so ago, soon after Yom Kippur and before Thanksgiving. Abe had come to see him in this very office with his news. He was excited and had immediately produced a small green phial which he had placed on Phillip's desk. He looked tired, but elated at the same time. "This is to be my epitaph," he had said pointing at the sealed bottle. "In there is the most powerful antibiotic strain ever developed. In the right dosage it can save the lives of billions from recurrence of disease and the plagues that have ravaged mankind in the past and will soon reappear. The world ignores them at its peril, over-prescribing drugs without a thought to the harm that will be done to this generation, let alone the next."

Then Phillip had put an arm round Abe's shoulder and congratulated him with words of praise. He knew that this was likely to be the culmination of Abe's research and hard work these last few years. But in the same office only a few months later, it was a different proposition. Abe had not been happy. He was getting old. His face had looked drawn and tired. He must be pushing eighty, Buonarroti thought. "How can I help you, Abe?" he had asked with his usual charm. But it was clear Abe was here for a purpose and in no mood for small talk.

"If you don't already know, you will now," Abe had said. "I want out. I've helped you people enough, and I will not have you take advantage of me!" Abe glared at Phillip. "I am not here to cause a scene, but from the beginning of next year, don't expect the Order to get any more funding from me or my foundation, and don't contact me again!"
"Take it easy, Abe," Phillip had said. "What has changed? You know how much the Order value your contributions. I thought the Foundation's arrangements with the Order had been made permanent with the trustees so they can't be altered" Abe grimaced.
"That may be, but while I'm alive I can change them if I wish, and I intend to, as soon as I can get to it."
"Hold on, Abe, just what do you think you'll achieve? Who's to get your fortune? It must be well past a billion dollars by now. Do you want to leave it all to your kids and spoil them for life? Or give it all

to the taxman? The Order will protect your children if anything were to happen to you. The continuation of their heritage through their mother and grandmother is vital in its link to the past. Your grandchildren are the last of the bloodline. You can be sure they will always have us onside."

"Dammit," Abe replied searingly. "It's nothing to do with that. I don't give a cuss for the whole Merovingian thing any longer. The kids are better off without it in this day and age. My entire involvement with your Order has bedeviled me. Just a chain of bad events. My wife dead and my daughter too. So much for your protection!"

Buonarroti came from a long line of Italians who as revolutionaries in 18th century Italy in the name of Masonry had fought for freedom against Europe's Catholic monarchs. His family had been a tough breed and he was proud of it. As with Abe's, they had also been settlers in the early days of America's independence and its own Masonic revolution of a fraternity for all religions. In the two centuries since, many of its precepts had become forgotten, and it was clear to Phillip new attempts were being made by enemies of America to subtly undermine its democracy, both from within and without.

The terrible event of 9/11 was only a foretaste of what was to come. It was now clear that the planes which had hit the Twin Towers could not have brought them down alone. That the buildings had crumbled to pure dust in just minutes indicated the use of an unknown science of a high order. If it was a known technology it had never been declared publicly. If it was not known by the Americans then whose expertise was it?

The use of explosives placed inside the building was not a hypothesis that made sense. Many theories had been put forward as to the assassins. That they were Islamic fanatics was generally believed but there were other assertions. The evidence required for proof was lacking in a way that smelt strongly of a cover-up. There were many unresolved issues. One theory was that the attack may have been organized as a false flag event by Jewish Zionists to conjure up hatred for Muslims in the never ending battle of their religious ideals. Both groups had a foothold in America, but the Jews were predominant. Phillip knew many of the latter and he was sure they would not support such an outrage which in any event had killed many of them in the buildings at the time, along with several hundred Brits. At least this time the Russians had not been indicted having given moral support to America along with the gift of the striking memorial monument known as "The Teardrop" which now stood in New Jersey.

Since China had not been suspected the only other possible contenders were religious fanatics. For two centuries the once revolutionary Masonic cause worldwide had remained passive, refusing any militant involvement. To Phillip's mind it was time to reassert its old ideals of a proactive non-sectarian Masonic meritocracy. Abe's invention was just what Phillip needed for his plan if he could only control it. The time had come for action before the incessant argument between Jewish and Islamist zealots blew the whole world up with them.

Phillip was not going to have Abe stand in his way. He faced Abe and spoke firmly to him.

"Hold on, Abe, take a step back for a moment. Who helped you in the early days if it wasn't the Order? Who introduced you to your wife and the prestige you got from her background, and the grandchildren you now have? Perhaps you forget?"

"No I don't," Abe said. "I have repaid my dues many times. I have the right to disagree. We fought to get individual liberty in America, not controls by the state or anyone else, including you! I want no more of your secret cabal. What I have heard disgusts me. I agreed to share my findings with you to prolong life with my new discovery and now you intend to keep its use only for those you consider worthwhile. I share your views on democracy, but we need to convince others of them, not to refuse medical aid for political reasons or to control population growth. It's a total abuse of power!" Abe's face was grey with rage.

"Well," said Buonarroti, losing his own cool now, and wagging his finger at Abe.

"Perhaps you forget a bit too conveniently. What of those who died from that earlier drug experiment of yours? Who was it that suppressed the media in relation to a story which could have ruined your career for good? You forget who you are dealing with. Do you want it to leak out to the press at your time of life? The Order has powerful friends. You well know our aim is to make a better world with the knowledge we have from the past. It is us, we, who control this knowledge, who are the highest order of man. Long may it remain as it is ordained. Look what you have achieved through us. Great fortune and fame in your profession. Are you now to betray the faith of those who have helped you?" Phillip spoke grandiosely, as he could do when it suited him.

Abe was shocked at what Buonarroti had said. Was he being threatened now with exposure years after the event? Nothing had been more upsetting to him than those few who had died from his experiment years before. But they had been near death in any event and elected to try a new drug that might prolong their lives, if only for a few months. He had personally helped their families in their grief and few had complained. Yes, it had all been hushed up, but it was to the benefit of everyone. Was his greatest ever achievement now to be abused by way of recompense?

He stood to go. "I won't suffer blackmail from you. I have done all I can and more for your cause, but I will not be party to what I see to be the Order's betrayal of the ideals I believe in. I will have no truck with eugenics. I am a man of science and of the people. It's all very well to talk of faith. Nobody has done more than I have to bring science and faith together as one. You have no right to act as God. You accuse me of causing the death of a handful of people when you would deprive life to millions to pursue your goal of making the world the way you want it. There is no more to discuss. It is you who forget!" He crossed the room to leave.

Phillip looked flushed. He had not expected Abe to be so resolute. After all the Order was known to be a patron of good works both in Washington, where it had its headquarters, and through its contacts around the world. It would be their word against anything Abe might say. They certainly didn't want to lose the benefit of future funding from Abe's foundation, but they had other rich subscribers who could be relied on. The Illuminati, as the press liked to portray them, had always been a moving feast of new applicants seeking a position at the high tables of influence and power, and Phillip was a broker and arbiter of that power.

What concerned him more would be the loss to the Order of Abe's discovery which could solve many of the resource issues the world now faced. As present antibiotics failed and incurable diseases and plagues spread, they would endanger vast numbers of people as they once had. Those who could not afford good medication would die in any event. Phillip considered he was better equipped to handle the distribution of such an essential commodity, which would take a good deal of administrative capability and time to put into production and market. Far better to manage it discriminately and save those who stood for the same principles as America. If Abe was not to play ball, his plan would come to nothing. As Phillip thought, the furrows on his brow suddenly unfurled with relief. He called to Abe as he approached the door to leave. "Just one thing Abe," he said, "that you forget. I have the formula. You left it with me when you were last here."

Abe turned on his heel. "Wrong again, Phil," he replied: "You have a phial but no formula. What is in the bottle if duplicated and released will kill not half the world, but pretty much all of it. Solanaceae spores are airborne and in their strongest form could kill most of the population of America in weeks. You talk of having superior knowledge, but yet you don't realize a simple fact of science that many medicines can be deadly poisonous when in concentrated form, and need exactly the right mix to administer if lives are to be saved."

Abe was enjoying lecturing Buonarroti now. Who did these money men think they were?

"It is not only the index of the ingredients that you don't have, but more importantly the quotient of the mix. Without it if you break the seal on that bottle you will die within hours. But I do have it and you will not get it from me. Your simple mind may think it's an easy matter of dilution but I can assure you it is not!"

With that Abe left, exhausted, but satisfied with the painful meeting he had needed to accomplish. Equally he was bitterly disappointed with the realization that the Order, in which he had long put his trust to do good in the world, had thought to abuse what was to be his greatest contribution to mankind. Was this to be the end of his dream? The formula for its use as a life saver was a complex one, but simple enough to administer once it was known, so to whom could he now entrust it? What was the point in continuing? Perhaps best now he should take its secret to the end of his days and confound the Order forever.

"Damn their souls," he snorted indignantly to himself. He would get his revenge. Only he knew what was in the phial he had left with Buonarroti and the details of its potency and specifications. He was glad he hadn't mentioned the addition of a psychosomatic ingredient to produce a super-intelligent species of disease-resistant humans. Given to someone like Buonarroti it could mean he could control the world. Whatever his alleged intentions for the good of intelligent man, that sort of power could lead to corruption in anybody's hands.

Buonarroti was reeling from Abe's words. How stupid he had been not to realize those few months ago what Abe had just said. Soon after Abe left he took out his handkerchief to take the phial from a filing cabinet and carefully wrapped the bottle in it, taking it to a small concealed wall safe in his office, hidden behind a picture of a pyramid. At the top of the pyramid was drawn an eye. Swinging open the picture on its hinges, he clicked the combination lock numbers to open the door of the safe behind it and put the phial gently inside. "There it will stay," he said aloud. The problem now was had Abe been bluffing? Or was his own death warrant sitting in his safe waiting to be opened, he brooded as he loosened his shirt collar. "Shit!" he exclaimed.

# Chapter 15

## London, England. October 2014

Mrs G's flight to London had passed without incident. She had booked herself a seat in business class and fortunately found no-one beside her on the flight and had skipped the unappetizing dish offered so not to be disturbed. On arrival the London autumn weather was damper than in Boston and she was pleased to have brought a warm coat and walking shoes for the rainy streets. She had booked in at the Savoy Hotel, as its location in the Strand was a short distance from the site she had wanted to investigate first. The Temple Chapter House in London's Inner Temple was just off Fleet Street, famously home to the English press, and once to a notorious prison for those in debt.

The Inner Temple itself was one of four Inns of Court which had been the training ground and home of English barristers-at-law for centuries past. Its buildings were contained in a three-acre plot which ran down to the banks of the Thames in Shakespeare's time, but now the Embankment road had intervened. Eight hundred years before the Knights Templar had given their name to it in building a Temple House there.

Mrs G set off the following day, walking through the soft drizzle past the grey Gothic towers of the English Law Courts. She was soon to turn right into a narrow-gated entrance leading to a maze of cobbled alleyways until she found the Temple Chapel she had come to see. As she entered its dark, cold interior from the daylight outside, her eyes blinked to look at the tombs of past Templar Crusaders. Their swords and spears carved in stone by their side where they lay in their armor, as if to rise from the dead to fight at the first clarion call of battle.

For some reason many of the knights had their feet crossed. She shone the light beam from her i-Phone onto their inscriptions and wished she had brought a bigger flashlight. As she backed away from a tomb she looked up to see high on the wall above her a carved two-winged Pegasus, and stumbled on the uneven floor, nearly into the arms of a person behind her. She turned to apologize and saw a man, just under six foot tall and in his mid-forties, or so she guessed, wearing the white dog collar of a priest with a light grey vest, cream jacket and matching cream Panama hat. He was of a slim, but fit-looking build with a tanned face, and his warm brown eyes smiled at her. He looked out of place on a rainy day.

"Oh, so sorry, I didn't see you," she exclaimed.
"No matter," said the man. "No problem." He looked quickly at the Pegasus above them and said "As above, so below." Mrs G looked puzzled. The man smiled. "An ancient saying'. 'Deus inversus," he said by way of explanation and gave the sign of the cross. The phrase had a dual meaning he did not mention, but why bother, she had the innocent face of a type he liked.
"I saw you looking at the knight's feet," he continued, changing the subject. If their legs are crossed, it means they had been in battle. They are not tombs but effigies," he told her obligingly.
"So is this holy ground?" asked Mrs G.
"Not really. The Knights' beliefs were esoteric and spiritual, but not theological. The true Templars respected all religions. They believed in faith, hope and charity. The words from Corinthians in the St James' Bible in which the greatest of all was charity. In those days charity meant kindness," the man said by way of explanation.

"Sorry, I should have introduced myself. Ethan." He offered her his hand to shake, which she did.
"Do you work here?" she asked.
"No, but while I was in London I wanted to come here. It's of interest to my work. Are you on vacation?" He had noticed her New England accent.
"Researching for a book," Mrs G said. "It's of interest to me too."
Ethan nodded. "Yes, you and many others. The Templars may once have followed the Christian cross, but in the name of Mary Magdalene and the Nazarene faith, rather than as Catholics. They were not necessarily Crusaders as many believe. The Crusaders were a mixed bunch of militants, even fighting on the side of the Pope at times as mercenaries, as they did in their massacre of the Cathars at Carcassonne on charges of devil worship. Faith has many roads."
His grin showed his white teeth.

"You seem to read my thoughts," Mrs G said. "I'm off to Paris in the next few days, and then to Carcassonne. Now I need to go do some shopping in the Strand and I'm off to The Tower of London tomorrow. She held out her hand to say goodbye. She did not give her name. With that she walked out of the Temple and into the sunlit garden of Elm Court with its colorful, late-flowering dahlias of hallucinatory hues and trees of falling, golden autumn leaves, and shook herself a little. It had been cold in there.

# Chapter 16

## Leicester House, London. 1573

In the years of Elizabeth's reign the palaces and houses of those in a position of power stood on the northern riverbank of the Thames. The roads being only of dirt, the river was the main thoroughfare for travel from the Queen's palace at Greenwich near the Thames estuary to the east, and to her palaces of Richmond and Hampton Court in the west. In between was the palace of York Place where the Queen lived, near the White Hall complex where the business of state was conducted; later to be of larger size than the French palace of Versailles.

The population of London was some two hundred thousand and the river was a constant scene of activity. Sailboats carrying goods and produce imported from Holland, Germany and France returned having delivered English exports of woolen goods on which England's economy was principally based. No bridges over the Thames existed other than London Bridge on which many houses and shops were built similar to the Rialto Bridge in Venice. Many small boats operated as water taxis which would row their hirers between the muddy north and south banks of the river for a half-penny. At times a salmon could be seen in the grey waters among the carp fish and mullet which fed many Londoners.

Those in positions of importance had their own grand boats, the Queen having a launch of galleon-like proportions. Its superstructure was painted in colors of red and gold, manned by twenty or more oarsmen who would speed her up and down between her palaces for meetings or sporting out of town, hunting deer in Richmond Great Park or at Hampton Court, or to her stud of racehorses at Greenwich.

Elizabeth had not seen the young Francis for some time and had now to decide on his future role. She had summoned Lady Bacon to have Francis brought to her at the more private Leicester House for a reason. She had bought it for Francis' father Robert and it was where he now lived, and she wished to introduce Francis to him, without revealing his parentage. Francis was twelve years old and his education was under the Queen's personal control. As Francis entered he gave her a full bow, as he was accustomed to do in her presence. She bade him sit by her side, and gave him a quick glance.

"This house we are in, Francis," she declared, "is one built on an ancient site once occupied by the Knights Templar and contains secrets of England's heritage of which I wish you to learn."
Francis spoke: "Of the Holy Grail?"
Elizabeth smiled. "I see Lady Bacon has been teaching you well. My Tudor ancestors have been living by the ideals of the Templars for centuries. I hear you are a bright pupil and it is why you are of interest to me as I need to train those of intelligence in the service of my realm. You are to advance your learning at Trinity College in Cambridge to study there from now on, together with your brother Anthony. Arrangements have been made for you both to leave this week and you are to go with Sir Amyas Paulet who is to be your tutor."

A few days later Francis bade farewell to Lady Anne and travelled to Cambridge with Anthony in a coach and four from the Queen's own stables. The roads were little more than rutted mud tracks, but outside the period of the winter rains the going was fairly easy, and starting out at daybreak they made the sixty miles there by late afternoon. Francis and Anthony had been brought up from childhood as if they were true brothers and, although Anthony was three years older, they were good friends. Apart from football, and playing chess and chequers, they shared a common interest in cryptology, which the Queen had especially requested they should study.

The high spires of Cambridge's churches and the university places of residence came looming through the dusk and the two youths jumped out to be allotted their rooms. Their tutor, a man of somber disposition, but with intelligent perceptive eyes, had said nothing on the journey, but had sat listening to their chatter. He now spoke to tell them where they should meet him the following morning.

In the classroom the next day before the tutorial which they were to share with only a handful of other boys, Sir Amyas had singled out Francis.
"It will be my pleasure to broaden your knowledge here in Cambridge to assist in whatever task Her Majesty might bestow on

you. I will call you Francis and you may call me Paulet. Firstly, I wish to enquire as to your religious viewpoint."

Francis spoke without hesitation. "I recognize truth as love in which woman is the awakener."

Sir Amyas raised one eyebrow at the strange response of his twelve-year-old pupil.

"And pray whose conception is that?"

"It is that of Dante, my favorite poet. My aim is to establish a creed only of good and self-enlightenment," responded Francis.

Sir Amyas nodded wisely. "Tut! Forsooth you have learnt fast it seems, but you are in a fool's paradise to think you can abolish evil, as our good King Henry discovered in seeking to abolish Catholics. They hide, but they are still among us."


But as he spoke he quickly understood that the level of learning which Francis had already acquired was likely to make him an outstanding scholar, as the Queen had believed. He looked down at some figures on a piece of paper on the desk on which Francis had been writing.

"You have an understanding of cryptology? Impressive in one so young. This appears to be of a complex nature."

Francis smiled a broad grin at Paulet and knew he was going to enjoy his education.

# Chapter 17

Mrs G returned to the Savoy, turning into its entrance off the Strand with the large 1920s stainless steel name sign emblazoned on its exterior, over which stood the statue of the Templar Baron Peter of Savoy whose palace had once stood on the same site in Elizabethan times. Mrs G had just returned from Harley Street, London's home of specialist medical practitioners, where she had been to get a second opinion on her irritating cough.

She had made some interesting discoveries at the Tower the day before to include in her research. Before she had left Boston she had discovered on Google a London bookseller who had some rare, fine print copies of early editions of Shakespeare said to be written in their original form. She had tracked him down to a small bookshop tucked away in the Burlington Arcade where he had the books ready to collect. They had not been cheap, but money was no obstacle, and so she had gladly parted with the ten thousand pounds the bookseller had asked. It would be cheap at double the price, she thought, if they contained what she needed to find. She had billed her purchase to the debit card she had received from the Magdala Foundation.

She sat for some hours at the desk in her room with the books at her side, busy typing notes into her Apple laptop. She made clicking noises of satisfaction with her tongue as she progressed and stopped to rub her eyes from reading the small print of the books in their antiquated format.

At last she got up to stretch, and going over to her window directly overlooking the Thames on whose opposite banks a replica of Shakespeare's famous Globe Theatre stood, she let her thoughts roam. The books had been disappointingly small to decipher all that was written, but had given her sufficient clues to what she hoped for. No need to go to Roslyn now, she thought to herself. It seems the signs were here all the time. I need more time to study them. I wish I could have seen these long ago. This double writing disguised it. No wonder he concealed his identity! If only I could get hold of a genuine first edition to make sure.

### An antechamber, Palace of White Hall, London. 1576

Elizabeth had been on the throne of England for the past twenty years maintaining a felicitous, but strict rule over her subjects from whom she had kept England's enemies at bay. She had been a popular monarch. She contrived that her popularity should be her best form of defense against the often turbulent nobility, half of them still concealed Catholics who had lost power and position after the new Anglican Protestantism had been made England's official religion by Henry VIII.

Elizabeth claimed her right to the throne was inviolable since her half-sister Mary was the product of an illegal marriage between her father Henry and Catharine of Aragon. Catharine had previously been married to Henry's older brother Arthur who had died and some versions of the Bible forbade a woman to marry her former husband's brother. As a result, Elizabeth felt self-righteous in her own claim. Love of self overcame most of her other emotions, and although she might be susceptible to a change of opinion, rarely would she apologize, and much enjoyed the silver-tongued flattery of her sycophantic courtiers.

As Good Queen Bess, as her public called her, she had been a benefactor of the theater, and the arts of dance and music, encouraged in this by her husband Robert Dudley, now the Earl of Leicester. He had played his part and had kept silent about his marriage to her and the existence of their two joint children. The youngest named after him, Robert, his favorite, whom he was to bring up in his own image as a military man. Often Elizabeth would tease her husband by her flirtations with foreign wooers who sought her hand, in their attempts to bring England back into the Catholic fold by marriage. Elizabeth's open dalliance with her suitors at court often upset and offended him. She had received marriage proposals from Charles Archduke of Austria and later from the two French princes of Anjou, Henry and Francis. Despite the attention she had confided extraordinarily to a friend:

*"If I am to follow the inclination of my nature it is this: beggar-woman and single, far rather than be Queen and married!"*

Even so, she played a skillful game to appease her government ministers, informing them, without any intention of marriage, that she was seriously looking for a suitor and would not rule any out. This too helped her relationship with the English Catholics to refrain from attacking her in the belief they could eventually manipulate the monarchy back to their religion.

Elizabeth would never reveal her secret marriage to Leicester and her only concern was that neither he, nor her offspring by him, should divulge it either before or after her death. Few knew of it and those who did kept quiet in fear of retribution. As for Francis, now almost sixteen, he was nearing the end of his time at Cambridge, and had been told by Lady Anne that he would need to attend the Queen's court regularly to learn its practices.

Soon after Francis' arrival at court a young lady-in-waiting to the Queen, no more than sixteen years of age, is being entertained by a youth of similar age, Robert Cecil, a courtier, in a brown velvet tunic and matching brown breeches with a small, black, flat cap. He whispers to the young girl and nods his head towards a figure standing nearby. The girl in turn re-joins the other young ladies of court who gather round and giggle as she repeats what she has been told. Cajoled by them, she leaves the group and goes over to a figure standing alone and only recently seen at court. The young woman approaches him, a saucy smile on her face.

"Sir, may I enquire? You are most pleasing to us. We hear you are a virgin – of our own Virgin Queen. A miracle to behold!" she says tongue in cheek.
Francis looks shyly at her, and flushes with embarrassment, while there are peals of laughter from the other girls. Robert Cecil, short of stature, smirks at Francis' discomfort.

Suddenly the laughter stops as they notice the Queen standing by the open door. She crosses the room in a fury and seizes the teasing girl, slapping her face and beating her, tearing and ripping at her flimsy clothes until she lies stripped, bruised and naked, cowering and whimpering on the floor. Seething with anger, Elizabeth banishes her from court, and turns to the other, now trembling Ladies-in-Waiting, her voice a crescendo.

"Whatever you have heard this day you will forget and ne'er repeat, as if one word of it shall reach my ears again you shall face death. That I promise. Now out of my sight. All of you. Thou dost infect mine eyes. As for you, sly Cecil, I will speak to your father to find you other employment. He will deal with you as you deserve. Meanwhile, you are banished from my Court.

Robert Cecil's father, Lord Burleigh, was a trusted adviser to the Queen for whom she held respect, but she need warn him to tell his son to keep his lips closed in court, whatever he may have heard from his father. Cecil had a deformity since birth of a splayed foot and hunchback and Elizabeth could see why he might have cause to resent Francis and his natural comely attributes, and of his true parentage if known to him.

Elizabeth turned to Francis, who was now standing as if frozen to the spot, her brows still knitted in fury.
"Well didn't you hear me? Be gone!"
Francis, white in pallor, and near tongue-tied, stutters out: "Is it true? Are you my mother?"
"Stay thy voice. Do as I say. Be gone! I am your Queen. Go forthwith!" As Francis turns away, she calls out after him, more in sorrow than in anger. "You have done well at Cambridge, but there is no place here for you now. You will go with Paulet to France to continue your education."

Francis tried again to speak. "You have not answered my question," he says.
"Leave!" commanded Elizabeth. "And hold your tongue! By Jove, you test me! I am your monarch and answerable to no man. See what happens to those who disobey me." She pointed to the window facing The Strand where the grisly severed heads of those who had countered her wishes still rotted on a line of spikes. "Now go!"

As the room emptied and Francis walked to the door to leave, Elizabeth called out after him and as he turned to face her she exclaimed:
"It is true, you are my born son, but you, though Royal, shall ne'er rule England."
She strode toward him, her face white, and wagged her finger in his

face to conclude her tirade.

"I will have you leave my realm posthaste to pursue your education in France and no more is to be spoken of this by you. Is this clear? You have done well at Cambridge, now it is time to move on. Without ado you will go this next morn with your tutor to France. 'Tis for the best, as you will see."

Francis crossed the courtyard to his parents' home at York House in shock and with his blood running high. He had often played in the yard in his youth whilst unknown to him Elizabeth had watched him from the windows of her own rooms in York Place. He entered his parents' chambers to confront them. Lady Anne Bacon was alone, and as Francis explained what had just passed he sat down and sobbed, now unsure from her silence who or what he was. Looking her directly eye-to-eye he asks her quietly: "So it is true?"

"One day you will understand more," Lady Anne replied. "I have oft feared this day might come. The Queen gave you to me to as an infant to raise on oath I should never reveal her secret. You know you have seen her here and at Gorhambury on her visits and she has your best interests at heart.

You were a handsome child at birth as you are now, with the same blue grey eyes of your mother. You need swear now for me and for yourself to keep this secret. Take no notice of court gossip. Only you and I and the Queen know the truth for sure. Ignore those who taunt you. They can only surmise. Nor go against the Queen. Since you were ten she has called you "Her little Lord Keeper" as you know. She has always been impressed by your wit and cleverness. You are dear to her heart. She has her reasons and they are to protect you and your future. Swear to me now you will do as I ask," Lady Anne requested, her hand trembling as she held that of Francis, more out of fear for him than for herself.

Francis went to kiss her cheek. "I do not have to," he replied. "I will honor what you ask for the love you have given me, and of mine for you, until the day the Queen should change her mind of which I feel sure. She has said that I am to be sent to France."

Francis realized that his entire life had now changed and that he was to enter a new world for which much of his education had prepared him, but there would be far more yet to learn. He had not liked the sneering face of Robert Cecil, which he realized now was one of jealousy. Francis would have to learn the ways and manners of the

Court and the deception practised there. There was one last question he had not dared ask Lady Anne. If the Queen was his mother, then who was his father? It was a question not to be answered for some time, and when it was he would discover he had a new brother born of the Queen, some five years younger than he was.

Within two days he was on a naval frigate with Paulet bound for Calais in France. The ensign of the Royal Navy flying bravely on its aft mast in the cold, strong winds of late winter. He stood watching the power of the spume-topped grey sloping waves heave the boat up and down in their rises and troughs. His stomach churned as he realized now his life was no longer to be the plain sailing of the past, and he considered the uncertainties of his future. He was pleased to have left Cambridge. Its teaching was too theological, taught by professors set in the ways of Aristotle, in which new thought was discouraged. It had been time to go. Now he needed to become a man and think for himself. To create his own world.

# Chapter 18

## The Louvre Palace, Paris. March 1576

Accompanied by Paulet, who had travelled to Paris with him, Francis entered the crowded state rooms of the French Court. He was now just sixteen years old. Sir Amyas Paulet had been expediently appointed by Elizabeth as Ambassador Extraordinaire to take up residence in the British Embassy in Paris and to assist Francis in his further knowledge of Europe and its history. After some days passed Paulet considered it time to introduce Francis to the French king, as Elizabeth had commanded him.

Francis knew of the battles of Crecy, Poitiers, and Agincourt in which the English had defeated greater numbers of French forces. The superior weaponry of the English archers with their long bows and their iron-tipped arrows could pierce the heavy armor of the French knights. But he knew too of the more recent Hundred Years' War, in which the English had lost a large slice of Burgundy which they had controlled. The battles between France and England were the stuff of ages. At times foes and at others allies.

English and French knights had fought side by side against Muslim armies to defend Jerusalem, and Christendom itself, but had been finally beaten by the superior force of the Saracen Saladin. Not so long ago his Muslim warriors had ousted the Crusaders and conquered Spain, Italy and North Africa, and half of France itself up to the walls of Lyon. Since then the English had developed a formidable navy of small swift fighting ships armed with the new invention of iron cannon, less costly and more reliable than bronze. Together with their use of ships of hardened oak stronger than iron, it had given the English control of much of the north Atlantic and Mediterranean seas and so induced a peace of sorts between France and England. At the Field of the Cloth of Gold, Francis' grandfather King Henry VIII had met his French counterpart King Francis I in a show of rival magnificence at Calais in 1520, where they had struck a truce which was still hanging by a thread to this day.

Francis had learned at his mother's court of the Renaissance reformation sweeping the capitals of Europe, reawakening wisdoms and cultures from the Greeks and Romans. A rebirth of art and literature in place of the dark ages that Europe had endured for the previous seven hundred years under Catholicism since the collapse of the Roman Empire. However, all the nations of the European continent were still in thrall to Rome. From there, powerful popes wielded power over Europe's monarchies with their threat of excommunication from God whom they claimed to represent. All, that was, except for England, where Henry had banished the Catholic religion, substituting in its place the Anglican Church of which Henry had appointed himself as head. His daughter Elizabeth had carefully chosen her title deliberately as the Church of England's Supreme Governor, so as not to symbolize herself as God's agent on earth.

As Francis was led through the rooms of the French court among groups of chattering people, they slowly parted to regard him, and as his name was called out, the sound of their voices lessened as he and Paulet were presented to King Henry of France. The King was notorious for his dalliances with his "mignons," the young good-looking boys and pages to his Court in their tender years. Who was this new young Englishman who was to be presented? Would he find favor with their effete King? Rumors and gossip hummed round the room with all eyes on Francis, but even as Francis bowed low to the seated monarch, his eyes were on the young woman sitting near him. He was struck by the sight of the most beautiful woman he had ever seen. That others shared his thought he was to later discover.

Marguerite de Valois, Queen of Navarre, was twenty-four years old, and had been married at her mother's wish to the young stalwart, but boorish, Henry King of Navarre. He was not in attendance on the French court that day, nor had he been for some time, since neither of the two King Henrys enjoyed each other's company. Nor had Marguerite managed to hold the attention of her husband, despite being the belle of the French court. As once flatteringly described by Alexandre Dumas, Marguerite was:

"… *the object of all the poet's eulogies … a beauty without rival in that Court in which Catherine de Medici had assembled the loveliest women of the age and country."*

Marguerite looked directly at Francis and their eyes met for a fleeting moment. His eyes of blue-grey and Marguerite's of a deep, dark brown. Her long raven hair, parted in the middle, fell from under a small diamond and ruby tiara onto her bare, white shoulders and low cut black gown. As described at the time, 'a voluptuous eye veiled by long lids, coral and delicate lips, a graceful neck, a full enchanting figure.' Concealed in satin slippers were tiny feet, little bigger than those of a child. She beckoned to a courtier and whispered a short message to him. She wanted to know more about this young Englishman.

### Paris, France. October 2014

Mrs G had booked herself into the five-star Hotel de Crillon facing the Place de la Concorde. From her balcony she could see the Louvre Museum, the former palace of France's monarchs. The hotel was generally unknown to tourists as it catered for a small clientele of the discreet rich rather than to the more showy Middle East and African guests at the Plaza Athené and the Paris Ritz. She had crossed the arched bridge of the Pont de la Concorde to visit St Germain-des-Prés earlier in the day. There she took coffee at the famed Les Deux Magots café to watch the world go by and to do a spot of thinking. There was a connection between St Germain and the Templars she needed to reconcile in her mind. Her mobile sounded as she sipped her black café taken with a dash of cognac and a pain au chocolat. When in Rome, enjoy yourself like a Roman, she thought. Except this was Paris. Answering she heard the voice of her prospective publisher. She had not expected his call.

"Hi there, Mrs G," the voice crackled. "It's Phil Buonarroti. So where are you today? Tried to get you at the Savoy but tracked you here. Your maid in Boston gave me your cell phone number. I told her it was urgent as she would not have told me otherwise. Sorry about that. I just wanted to know how it's all going. Have you found your Philosopher's Stone yet?"

"What was that?" queried Mrs G.

"You know," Phillip replied. "Your Holy Grail quest. Thought you were going to Scotland. What takes you to Paris? A good place to find the elixir of life for many, and the prince of your dreams. Have you found any good-looking frogs to kiss yet?" He quipped in poor taste.

"I have a lot yet to do," said Mrs G, wishing that Esther had not given away her mobile number.

"Okay, when you need any help just let me know. Stay in touch." He paused and then added:

"Oh, and one last thing, did you happen to work with Abe on the antibiotic solution that may have killed him? Abe's friends are concerned that it shouldn't fall into the hands of anyone else it may harm."

Mrs G had not realized that Abe had discussed his project with Buonarroti, nor could she see why this should be any business of his, but she explained that Abe had worked alone on his last project, without her. She knew he had high hopes for it, but nothing more, she said. She felt it was a strange question to have asked. It was true that Abe had been more secretive about his work than at any time before, perhaps because of its dangers.

# Chapter 19

After his presentation at court as Le Seigneur Bacon, Francis had been pleasantly surprised at his reception. He already had a full understanding of French which was commonly spoken in Elizabeth's English court, and he had been quickly surrounded by people inviting him here and there. They were convinced he was of some importance to have been brought to meet the King, and as with the gossip at all courts, someone new and foreign needed to be discovered and dissected.

A week or two following Francis' introduction to the King he had been invited to stay on the premises of the Louvre Palace, and Paulet had decided there was no harm he would be likely to receive if he transferred from his room at the British Embassy. Marguerite had given word she would like to assist him during his stay in Paris and they had met on several occasions with Paulet present. She had promised she would introduce him to her friends and others who would be useful to him to know more about Paris, and on the further travels that had been planned for Francis in the capitals of Europe.

Francis had been greatly attracted to Marguerite, as much for her wit and gaiety as for her beauty, and they had quickly become friends. Shortly after he had taken up residence at the Louvre, Francis had received a sealed invitation delivered to him by Marguerite's own pageboy. He had opened it to see she had requested his attendance on her that very evening to share a light repast in her private apartments at the Palace. The page had returned at the appointed hour of nine o'clock to escort him. He had washed and completed his toilette, perfumed himself and put on his best blue brocade jacket and white lace cravat for the occasion. His young legs were still slender in his white stockings and blue velvet evening shoes with their silver buckles. He had not far to go along several corridors, lit by flickering candles reflected in gilded mirrors. On entering he was surprised to find Marguerite alone, having expected other guests to be there.

Marguerite informed Francis she preferred to see him in private without Paulet's presence so she might get to know him better. She told him she had married Henry of Navarre some four years before, but that he lived in his own small mountainous kingdom in his castle on the border with Spain in a corner of south west France. She had no children by him, and he needed to attend to his duties there. She herself preferred the ways of the sophisticated French court as opposed to the trite simplicity of Navarre.

She beckoned Francis to sit with her together on an ornate gilt chaise longue, while from a small crystal decanter she poured red wine from the Burgundy vineyards into his glass, and proffered some foie gras, together with sweetmeats, quails eggs and truffles from a silver tray.

She related to him her own history. That her family had descended from the royal Albigenses who had been all but destroyed as heretics four hundred years before as Cathars for their beliefs in the Nazarene Creed. Those of her family who had escaped had found for themselves new roles in Europe, so long as they were seen to practice Catholicism. She told Francis how much she admired the English Queen as a strong woman ruling alone, managing to steer England as head of its new Church of England against powerful Catholic enemies.

Marguerite waited a while for the wine to take effect and took Francis' hand to hold on the low-cut bodice of her dress against her breasts and looked into his eyes. She had quickly realized she was dealing with an innocent. Francis' head was spinning now from the wine he was unaccustomed to. Marguerite told him how she had met the English Queen on a visit to England and how his blue-grey eyes were similar. Maybe she is aware of my birthright, Francis thought.

He felt exhilarated that he would be the next King of England one day succeeding his mother's reign, whatever she had said to the contrary. It was his right, so how could she stop it? No wonder he was here now with Marguerite. She must know, he felt sure. But who else did? The Queen had said he had no place at the English Court. But that was now. What of the future?

His mind whirled with these thoughts and the wine. He could not have known that Marguerite had added an aphrodisiac potion of her own concoction she had learned from her Medici family. He looked at her unsure what next to say or do, his consciousness drifting slowly into the scenario that was soon to take place as if in a dream world of neither time nor place.

*Now was she just before him as he sat,*
*And like a lowly lover down she kneels;*
*With one fair hand she heaveth up his hat,*
*Her other tender hand his fair cheek feels.*

After Francis' initial hesitation, and sensing his receptiveness to her touch, Marguerite took her advantage, slowly leading him to her bed where she disrobed him gently, but decisively, as a child is undressed to his full nakedness. She was not to be done out of her planned evening's entertainment. That he was slightly built, but strong, she could see as she stripped him of his clothes. He was of medium-to-tall height, but still nubile in the way of a young woman. He had offered no resistance and followed her every wish, almost as if hypnotized by her. She had drawn the cream damask curtains of the four-poster bed around them to give him a sense of privacy and entered into the pleasurable task of mischief she had given herself of being first to seduce this virgin youth - the future King of England, as she knew him to be. She unveiled herself in front of him from a barely transparent gown of gossamer silk to watch his reaction and had quickly realized she would have to guide him to fulfill her desires. In the theater of her mind he was to be her Adonis and she his Venus.

*"Fondling", she saith, "Since I have hemmed thee here*
*Within the circuit of this ivory pale,*
*I'll be a park, and thou shalt be my deer:*
*Feed where thou wilt, on mountain, or in dale;*
*Graze on my lips, and if those hills be dry,*
*Stray lower, where the pleasant fountains lie.*

His head hazy, as if entranced, Francis did as he was bid, slowly rising to the task as his own passions stirred. Soon satiated by his attentions, Marguerite was on top of him now, her small but strong thighs astride his as if riding a pony, having encouraged his manhood to full strength with deft hands and mouth caresses learned as part of her Latin upbringing in the arts of seduction. Her body rode him gently, but with slowly increasing, undulating strokes, as she listened to his breathing coming faster and faster, so that she could reach her point of climax at the same time as his. Faster now, and she gripped his arms, pinning his shoulders to the bed as he struggled, his body writhing under her as her nails cut into his flesh.

He could feel himself reaching far into her as her inner muscles clasped him into position. She was not to let him go easily until she was well satisfied. Her long black hair fell across his face as he smelt the scent and heat of her body as his own sweat ran from his brow. He opened his eyes to see her small porcelain white breasts with their long dark nipples hard and erect. Her devilish black orbs were alight with passion as she cried out in a long drawn-out banshee wail. With an explosion that seemed to rip him apart, he felt as if his body was turned inside out, and that his soul had left him to enter into her body somewhere in time and space; he knew not where. He felt himself truly possessed, as she had intended.

As she rolled her body away from his, he felt their juices warm on his flesh and hers, and started to feel embarrassment. He tried to speak but, still light-headed from the potion he had drunk, could only whimper. He had lost track of time and Marguerite had measured her pace to prolong her enjoyment. She placed her hand over his mouth and laughed out loud, a long and happy laugh. Her new pony had proved an enduring stallion. She would keep him on a short leash for her exclusive pleasure. "Hush! *Mon bébe; dit rien,*" she said. "It is time to rest and wonder at what God has given us that the Catholics would deny us. Now you know the power of women for which men give up their kingdoms and their souls, and which empowers them to fight for their desires. This is the way to truth, as Dante knew, and Christ before him. The divinity of union and the seed that giveth life."

"Now tell me the truth," she said, as they lay face to face on a silken pillow soft with goose-down. She put her finger to his lips and asked; "Why did your mother send you here? Do you think I don't know who you are? It was not just for the study of books," she joked. "My brother, the Duke of Anjou has courted your Queen. From what I know of her she is well versed in the pleasures of the flesh, as too with those of wine and music. I feel sure she has sent you here to learn, and so I will be your teacher."

She was testing him to see what he might reply, but he had said nothing in response, his mind still trying to return from his trance to reality. "So now you have made my association in my carnal knowledge," she quipped, "I will tell you more of my history and of my spiritual nature. I am the daughter of Catherine de Medici, of Italian descent, and a Catholic. My mother is the Queen of France. Our Medici family became rich from their use of opiates from plants for pleasure and relief from pain, and too from the lending of money. Two days after I was wed my mother ordered a massacre of Protestant Huguenots in Paris in which thousands met their death. It was on the day of St. Bartholomew. There had been a revival of Mary Magdalene's teachings practiced by the cults of Gnosticism and Theosophy. My husband is next in line to the French throne and it was a warning to him since his Albigensian ancestors were Cathars. So are my own, but my mother taught me that in life it is wise for women to take the side of those with power. My husband had to leave the French court because of his association with the Huguenots. He has no need of me since he has a mistress in Navarre with whom he lives.

Francis at last found his voice. "So, what do you believe in?" he asked her.

"That Christ's message was one of purity," she said softly. "He did not use fear or force to persuade. The language of love and faith required neither rule nor reason. To him it was a personal joy in which we need look for peace within ourselves. Not in theory, but in practice, without need for wealth or power. It is the creed of the Cathars as taught to them by Mary Magdalene.

"It was an ideal from the past, which the Egyptians, Persians and the Indian Sufis had practiced long before in their belief in the Atman, or belief in one's own soul. I feel sure Jesus experienced all the natural senses as we have just done. His love affair with Mary Magdalene was no secret. You may ask me what I believe. I am not sure any more, or even whether I care. I am accustomed to a style of living. St Paul told us that the flesh lusteth against the spirit and the spirit against the flesh. But to leave the delights of the flesh would necessitate sacrifices which I would loathe to make. They are to enjoy as God intended us. My Cathar ancestors recognized two gods in one, a good one and a bad one. They said one was the reflection of the other and if we didn't recognize evil, we could never redeem ourselves. They took their beliefs from the ancient Kabbalah as did Mary Magdalene. Perhaps the choice it gave us offered the best of both worlds." She laughed. "I prefer the natural pleasures the Catholics say are sinful so to enjoy my sins all the more! What do I care for their virtue? I have no shame. It is love of joy I seek in both

body and mind."
She closed her eyes and was talking now as if in a soliloquy.

*"Or for love lacking vestals and self loving nuns,*
*That on the earth would breed a scarcity,*
*With barren dearth of daughters and of sons?*
*Love comforteth, like sunshine after rain,*
*But Lust's effect is tempest after sun;*
*Love's gentle spring doth always fresh remain,*
*Lust's winter comes ere summer half be done.*
*Love surfeits not, Lust like a glutton dies;*
*Love is all truth, Lust forged full of lies."*

Francis was perplexed now. Lady Anne had been careful to guide him strictly in the ways of the English Protestant Church, and away from sin. Grasping for his senses in his still hazy mind he tried to change the subject. "Wasn't it the Cathars who protected the Holy Grail?"

Marguerite smiled. "Yes, in a way. Mary Magdalene, as the story is told, brought to Carcassonne the chalice into which blood had spilled from the spear wound on Jesus' side. The *Sang Réal*. But whatever it may have been it was a symbol of a far greater treasure – of the soul – and of Jesus' love and purity. This is what I would prefer to believe if it was as simple as that, but I am born to riches and power which are not easy to disown. As much as I have ever loved, I love you now."

She spoke softly to him, kissing his bare chest. "You have a beautiful and innocent soul."
Francis looked at her with adoring eyes. "So, that is what you have shown me. The path to heaven through love, to share our bodies and minds forever. You have told me of the new Reformation of the Renaissance. Now together we can give rebirth to the whole world with our knowledge!"

Marguerite smiled. "You are yet a novice in many ways, but you are ambitious *mon jeune coz*, for one so young. There's beggary in the love that can be reckoned, so take it for what it is you feel in your body, and not try to make it into something else in your mind. If it's reformation you are after you can start with me. I will continue my lessons in lust; after which if pure love may follow we shall be blessed indeed. You should not confuse the two, since some consider love a madness. They say your mother the Queen was once zany for your father's love and would openly kiss and hug him in her court among many people, as I feel sure Mary Magdalene did with Jesus. You should not be embarrassed by your emotions. They are natural and, so, God-given."

She rolled over Francis' moist body once more, her naked flesh pressed on his in their now-cold sweat. "Less talk is what you need best appreciate. Those do not love who do not show their love." She pushed his mouth away from her erect nipple and kissed him full and long on his tender lips. As she lifted her head she bit his lower lip with her small sharp white teeth. "There now, don't dare fall in love with me!" She exclaimed." You are a boy whom I will make man, but until then I will protect you. My husband has not seen me for two years, but he has his spies, and he will not happily know of our liaison." She laughed once more. "The devil offers many temptations. You may share them with me both in pleasure and in pain, so you might choose between good and bad as you desire."

Francis tries to rise from her bed, somewhat dazed and trifled in expression. "But, he stutters, I thought you believed in the purity of Christ's teachings."
"I do," said Marguerite, pushing Francis' young, angelic, white body back down on the bed.
"What can possibly be impure in what our bodies and souls have just shared? You have much to learn, but original sin is a good start. When you are done with me you will have improved your swordsmanship in more than one way," she joked as she once more pulled him to her and guided him for her pleasure.

*Hot, faint, and weary, with her hard embracing,*
*Like a wild bird being tam'd with too much handling,*
*Or as the fleet-foot roe, that's tir'd with chasing,*
*Or like the infant, still'd with dandling,*
*He now obeys, and now no more resisteth,*
*While she takes all she can, not all she listeth.*

*Once more the ruby colour'd portal opened,*
*Which to his speech did honey passage yield,*
*Like a red morn that ever yet betokened*
*Wrack to the seaman, tempest to the field.*

They were the words to be later echoed in the erotic love poem of Shakespeare's *Venus and Adonis*.

In the delirium that followed Marguerite almost swooned in delight with the sedulous attention of her new-found lover. The words she uttered came whispered from her lips:

*Oh where am I ... in earth or Heaven,*
*Or in the ocean drenched or in the fire?*
*What hour is this or morn or weary even?*
*Do I delight to die or life desire?*
*But now I lived and life was death's annoy,*
*But now I died, and death was lively joy.*

More time passed......

*And having felt the sweetness of the spoil,*
*With blindfold fury she begins to forage;*
*... her blood doth boil,*
*And careless lust stirs up a desperate courage*
*Planting oblivion, beating reason back,*
*Forgetting shame's pure blush and honour's wrack*

*Once more the engine of her thoughts began:*
*O fairest mover on this mortal round!*
*Would thou wert, as I am, and I a man.*

Hours passed in which they took their pleasure of each other and finally, their bodies both exhausted beyond all measure, Marguerite bid Francis cease his exertions and stroked his hot brow.
"There, what better way to expiate sin? What does your body tell you?"

She became serious. "You need to meet with good people and to beware the devil at your door. Hell is empty and all the devils are here. Trust me, you will need all the knowledge you can get. Not just from books, but from life itself and your own conscience. Let it be your guiding light. *"No se preoccupe,"* she said in Spanish, the language of the Navarre court. "Don't worry." There is time yet; I am told you are to remain in France one year or more yet for us to enjoy our time together. When the time comes that we must part I will write recommendations to my friends in Madrid, and Venezia and Roma, where you are to visit to complete your education in their ways and in their languages. To learn wit and wisdom and to become a man of letters and better still, of the world."

Francis felt the taste of blood on his lip from her bite and looked at her strangely. "Have I ever known you before?" He felt somehow that he had always belonged to her, and no-one else, yet it also scared him and he wanted to leave her room and escape the power she now had over him.

"Who knows what has gone before?" came her answer, "from whence we came or where we go? Our love has reached the doors of heaven. My senses tell me you are blessed with a tender and beauteous soul Francis, and there will be new worlds for us to meet, in this or next. I am psychic and I sense the same in you. We are rare and special people. You must go back to your chambers and rest and sleep your dreams, but for now you must stop your questions, for parting is such sweet sorrow that I shall say goodnight 'til it be morrow."

She put a finger to his lips, and watched him go. He had the face of an angel. When love and lust came together, she thought as she felt the pang of her heart, this was the moment when heaven and earth united, held somewhere in an unknown abyss of time and space.

*For pity now she can no more detain him*
*The poor fool prays her that he may depart,*
*She is resolved no longer to restrain him*
*Bids him farewell, and looks well to her heart,*
*The which by Cupid's bow she doth protest,*
*He carries thence encaged in his breast.*

The next day a messenger delivered her a note from Francis. In it the short message proclaimed in his handwriting:

"*Where both deliberate, the love is slight. Whoever loved, that loved not a first sight?*" Francis B.

That moment she knew he loved her more than she did him, and he could not let her go, but love him she would do as she knew his soul cried out for it. His affections starved for years. That her love would pass as did all the others she had wooed and loved, she knew, and the tear she wiped from her eye she could barely believe since she had not cried for some years now. As for Francis his father had warned him that 'no man can at once be wise and love,' but it was too late now, although he did not know it. The magic spell was woven, and it would take an age to break.

Like Romeo and Juliet the sensibilities of Francis for Marguerite, and those which she returned, were to be: *as a rose of pleasure drinking the sweet dew of early delight, and every hour was to be that of honeyed love, with tender notes bearing fragrance of those untold joys only immortals know.*

For years to come the love that Marguerite had taught Francis would both fire and quench the angry passions that were to rise in him against his own mother and her denial of his birthright. The countless poems and sonnets he was to write to his love revealed his young and innocent soul.

*"Unless I look on Marguerite in the day, there is no day for me to look upon. I will love her everlastingly, for I am as constant as the Northern star."*

# Chapter 20

Mrs G's search in Paris for clues of the Knights Templar had amounted to little. It was as if all traces of their existence had been wiped off the face of French history. The Catholic Church had slow-roasted Jacques de Molay, the old Templar leader, to death in 1314 after he had recanted his confessions of devil worship and sodomy made under torture on the rack, tearing his limbs and senses apart in agony. It had taken the Roman Catholic Church over a thousand years, but it had now finally eradicated all open practice of Christ's original Nazarene teachings and its followers. Mrs G pondered that perhaps she should have better gone to Germany, or Portugal where the Templars had once ruled. Switzerland too held many traces of their symbolism and their tradition as bankers.

At least that was to all appearances, but underneath the surface many of Christ's Nazarene believers had in time quietly regrouped under new names. Many of the Templars became the Knights Hospitaliers, who devoted themselves to the poor and good causes at their own expense. Similarly the Rosicrucians in Germany, whose symbol was the rose and cross. They practiced their beliefs in concealed lodges with rituals of membership which would condemn with expulsion or death those members who revealed their secrets, since to do so would risk exposure to the Catholics. All worship of Mary Magdalene, known by the Templars as the "Black Madonna", was seen by Catholics as heresy.

Many had become self-help organizations for those who rejected Catholicism and abhorred how it had confused the image and purpose of Christ for its own ends. All the while the Catholic Church taxed the rich with threat of excommunication; and that of hell and damnation to the poor whom they forced to pay Church dues.

Michelangelo and Leonardo da Vinci, among many others of huge talent, had been required to produce works of a religious nature by the Catholic Church. Many of these artists were considered and paid only as would-be builders or house painters for work the Church saw no more than being decorative. Their genius was often not fully recognized until decades later. Popes were no more than sharp politicians and money lenders, often poisoning their enemies to keep the papacy within their grasp. The Jesuit priests, trained at the Vatican, were an intelligence service employed as spies and clever proponents of arguments to convince doubters of the Catholic message.

Nevertheless, art under the Catholics flourished. Often with concealed messages unknown to their patrons. Paintings would contain secret messages tucked away in the fold of a cloak, or in a reflection of a mirror, recognizable only to those in the know. As printed books became more available so they too would reveal coded messages. After Henry VIII's purge of papal control of the English Church it became the turn of the English Catholics to hide, often in the priest's holes built into the walls or floors of their homes. A priest would hide there, because if found conducting a Mass or christening or marriage ceremony he risked his life along with the lives of the family who hid him, and confiscation of their assets.

Both Henry VIII and his daughter Elizabeth had filled their own coffers and those of the state from such seizures. The Queen's navy under Drake and Raleigh roamed the oceans seizing Spanish galleons full of gold pillaged in the name of Christendom from the native Mayan and Aztec tribes of South America. Why bother to land troops on South American shores to find gold when your Spanish enemies did the work for you? The huge wealth gained had helped the start of England's own Renaissance and many European craftsmen and artists had come to London to seek their fortune.

Mrs G considered her stay in Paris needed to be limited. She had studied the story of St Germain with great interest, since he had in the distant past been connected in some way to the Knights Templar, and his name had also strangely come up in connection with America and its Constitution. There had been a Germanus in England in the 4th century who had gone to France as the Bishop of Auxerre and had later been made a saint.

Mrs G knew Gerry would be interested back in Boston. She had taken note of where she might pick up clues in her travels and passed them on to him by email. But now she needed to hasten to

Carcassonne. There nearby in the foothills of the Pyrenees was the small 12th century Chapel in Montsaunés whose walls were said to be inscribed with coded signs and symbols of the Templars. There was much that needed to be done, and time pressed on her.

She ordered a taxi from the Crillon to Orly Airport for a midafternoon flight to Toulouse, passing down the broad avenue of the Champs Elysees and by the eternal flame of the tomb of the unknown French soldier under the Arc de Triomphe. She realized now that much of what she needed to discover in her search had been deliberately concealed over the centuries by secret societies of those in power, many of whom still remained. Nothing changes she thought, "Plus cá change plus c'est la même chose" as the French would say. Abe's friendly Washington Order too, it occurred to her, might be one of them. Perhaps Phillip Buonarroti knew more than he had let on about his Order and his relationship with Abe. But then would Abe have been associated with him? Being trusting by nature, Mrs G rejected the thought.

## Paris. The British Embassy. 1578

Francis Tudor, blood heir to the English throne, sits with his childhood companion Anthony Bacon, several years his elder. Francis is in a serious mood and speaks earnestly: "Anthony, it is my wish to wed Marguerite. I have given my heart and soul to her and we are of the same mind and spirit; for this I feel sure she will see sense in our union."
Anthony had followed Francis to Paris soon after his arrival there. The Queen had a mission for him in her intelligence services he was to pursue for many more years. He shook his head. He did not know yet that Francis was of royal blood.
"Brother, love is blind and lovers cannot see. I fear you are deceived by passion alone and are besotted by your need for her which you mistake for true love. Take heed that those who marry in haste oft need repent at leisure. She has told you herself that you need to travel to seek knowledge and wisdom. You are too young to wed and have not the status to do so. Besides Marguerite is married to another; but if you must write to her; do so in verse to express your deepest

feelings. Put poetry to motion. Time is a healer and you are young."

Francis had retorted, his head and heart full of emotion.
"Love is not love which alters when it alteration finds. She is
beautiful, and therefore to be woo'd, she is a woman and therefore to
be won."
He felt his sense of manhood rising inside him. What Francis did not
know was that Ambassador Paulet had soon become aware of
Francis' liaison with Marguerite. It had continued for a year or more
and become a major cause of gossip at the French court, as had been
previous affairs of Marguerite. Paulet had no choice but to inform the
Queen of England as he had been tasked by her to report on Francis'
actions. He had become fond of Francis and protective of him. In an
attempt at helping the lovers he had proposed to the Queen that
Marguerite should divorce her husband and marry Francis whom he
presumed would one day be the future king of England. He had
written to the Queen: *At first sight they have changed eyes and are
both in either's powers.*
Despite the fact that Elizabeth and Marguerite were both related
through Catherine de Valois, once reputedly the most intelligent and
sophisticated woman in Europe, Elizabeth had not approved of
Francis' choice of dalliance, since Marguerite was seen as a Catholic,
and married. The Queen had told Sir Amyas it was time for Francis
to leave for new travels in Europe, but she was not displeased at his
initiation by a woman of good birth and standing during his sexual
coming of age. Elizabeth knew of Marguerite's reputation, and her
intimate initiation of Francis had come as no great surprise to her,
nor perturbed her, since Marguerite was a woman of her own kind
and ancestry.

Sir Amyas, knowing of Francis' disappointment, had sought to
redirect his thoughts and ambitions to the business of life. "Be not
afraid of greatness," he had told Francis. "Your time will come.
Some are born great; some achieve greatness, and some have
greatness thrust upon them."

# Chapter 21

Mrs G joined other disembarking passengers from Paris and found herself a waiting taxi.

"Carcassonne. *Tout droit,*" she said, practicing her small knowledge of French. The bearded driver replied gruffly in the local Occitan accent, a tongue from centuries past, which Mrs G could barely distinguish. It was to take an hour in the gathering dusk before the vast and menacing battlement walls of Carcassonne and its town within could be seen towering in the dusky hills above. Lights glimmered high over them as the taxi crossed the bridge over the black waters of the River Aude and up a steep winding road.

The entrance to the fortress was over a narrow bridge across a deep but now waterless moat. Then through massive iron-studded wooden gates with a rusting portcullis overhead. Mrs G thought of the Crusader knights who had once crossed the bridge and stormed its portals on behalf of the Pope, and of the many thousands of Cathar men, women, and children put to death within its walls.

She had booked a room through an agency in Paris in a private guesthouse in the old part of the town overlooking views of the southern countryside, as there was no hotel of note within the inner castle precincts. Its tiny, narrow, winding cobbled streets, unchanged over a thousand years, were unsuitable for traffic and access was now largely restricted to pedestrians. She paid her driver and walked the last two hundred meters to the small guesthouse where she went straight to her room to rest. The rush to get out of Paris and her trip down had tired her. It was there she woke early the next morning with a view across red tiled roofs and stone parapets on a cold, but sunny October day. As she took *petit déjeuner* of a large cup of milky coffee and a croissant she looked out on the tall spire of a church in the fields below standing out clearly against a pale blue sky.

## A French Bastide Summer House on the Estate of the King of Navarre near Carcassonne. Le Jardin, June 1578

Marguerite of Navarre, lightly dressed in finery of batiste and white lace, is seated in her herb garden under a parasol held by her lady-in-waiting, fanning her face with a sandalwood-scented fan to keep the summer flies away. The tall spire of a local church is in the background. The musical notes of a madrigal being played on a mandolin fill the air, while the aroma of lavender and honeysuckle pervades the warm breeze. The borders of Le Jardin are alive with the colors of the pink, red and white oleander bushes. Other members of Marguerite's retinue disport themselves idly, walking or sitting on the grass lawns surrounding a small ornamental pool in whose center stands a statue of a cloven hoofed satyr playing his flute. It was Pan, the erotic half-beast, half-god of nature and animals beloved by children.

A bewigged footman appears with a silver tray on which is a folded letter tied with a red ribbon sealed with red wax. Marguerite glances at the imprinted symbol on the seal, to be sure of the sender, and breaking it open, reads the words with an enigmatic smile on her face.

"Qu'est que c'est Madame?" enquires her lady companion.

"C'est une carte, de Francis, c'est un poème d'amour. Tu veut l'apprendre?"

She read the opening lines of the poem out aloud.

*"Shall I compare thee to a Summer's day?*
*Thou art more lovely and more temperate.*
*Rough winds do shake the darling buds of May,*
*And Summer's lease hath all too short a date."*

*"Le Doux"* Sweet boy, Marguerite thought. She had given Francis the nickname at the French court and it had stuck. What a darling lad he had been. Perhaps her liaison with Francis had gone too far, she mused. She had hoped he would soon forget his adoration of her after his departure from the French court, but it seemed the memory of their nights of passion had not left his head nor his heart. She had played with his affections too long, but he had been a very special boy, and in her own way she had loved him even though she knew in her heart she could not keep him.

She would not forget his sweet lips and sensuous body, and his seriousness when they had talked for long hours to put the world to rights; and they had laughed too. Laughed at the world from inside the gilded cage of her apartments decorated with silken tapestries of birds and animals of the field looking out over the Seine. There, often naked, they had romped and frolicked alone day and night, playing games of make believe, conscious of neither time nor place. Reciting poems they exchanged in secret codes in which each had to un-fathom their hidden meanings and unspoken desires. An unrepeatable dream forever gone and swallowed up by the inevitability of the politics and events that comprised their lives. Still, it had been an enjoyable year or two. Quite delightful!

It seemed that she must still be his only lover. How flattering that she should have been his first. It was best she should not respond to his poetry; it would soon douse the vapors of his infatuation. *Le pauvre!"* She mused, twirling her lace parasol like a carousel. "Some rise by sin and some by virtue fall," the words escaped her lips aloud.
What would become of Francis? She had wanted to show him life, and now he needed to make the best of the experience she had gifted to him. She clapped her hands for the minstrel to stop his music.
It was time for lunch of *terrine de caille*, spiced *jambon*, and the local *pain de compagne* made of oatmeal and barley, washed down with the aromatic *Ugni vin blanc* from her own vineyard; and then to her boudoir for an afternoon siesta with her new, older lover. Today she would be the slave to his passions, variety being the spice of life.

### Carcassonne. October 2014. Lunch Time

Mrs G had wandered through the old citadel that morning, its ancient buildings holding each other up, faltering over its narrow alleyways and lanes. Fortunately there were not many tourists at this time of year, and she looked for any place where she might find authentic clues about the Templars. Many of the tourist shops had small, replica plastic knights on horseback and postcards of them in armor. Their white tunics carried the red Christian cross of St George, the emblem on the English national flag to this day.

Mrs G had found a small bistro out of the cold breeze and in the sun where she had taken a table outside and was waiting to be served lunch. Among the books she had purchased in London was a miniature, leather-bound volume of the complete works of Shakespeare. The print was too meager to read without her strongest glasses and some good sunlight, both of which she had where she sat, and she had turned to the sonnets on its back pages. She had read several before she came to one that commenced with the question: *"Shall I compare thee to a summer's day?"*

She remembered her mother reading it to her long ago and the beguilingly romantic lines that followed. None of the sonnets had published the name of an author although they had been attributed to Shakespeare. Mrs G had not read them for a while and shook her head at the thought that Shakespeare and Francis Bacon had lived at the same time. It may well have been that Francis had taken Shakespeare's verse to send to Marguerite.

As she looked up she saw a man looking at her as he approached. He seemed to have come from nowhere, as the cobbled square she was in was otherwise almost deserted. She recognized him now as he came nearer.

"Hello, I thought it was you. Remember me? From the Temple in London? Ethan," he said.

Slightly taken aback, Mrs G replied. "Yes, of course, what are you doing here?"

"Sorry, it must seem strange to you, but I had intended to visit Carcassonne before you told me in London you might also come here. So not so much of a coincidence really, considering our similar interests. I had hoped I might see you again. Do you mind if I join you?"

He asked pleasantly enough and Mrs G indicated a chair next to hers, knowing she had little choice but to offer it out of politeness. It was not that she didn't like him, but she was on a mission and did not welcome interruptions. Ethan looked in the reflection of the window across the street to read the day's menu written in chalk on a board outside the restaurant where they were sitting.

"What are you having?" he asked her. "The lamb I think," said Mrs G.

"Good choice," said Ethan. "I'll have the *pot au feu*, and if you like wine I suggest a Bandol rosé. It's a local wine which suits your quest here. The rose symbol of the Grail. How's it all going? By the way lunch is on me, please."

Mrs G nodded her acceptance. She felt he was a little pushy but it was good to have a companion in a foreign land, and they had something in common to talk about. She hadn't particularly noticed his urbane good looks, but she liked his charm and quiet intelligence. During lunch she had told him her reason for being in Carcassonne. "I'm here to chase down the Grail story," she explained. "There are one or two places nearby where I want to check out symbols. One is at Rennes de le Chateau, said to be haunted by the Devil. It's a bit of a tourist trap connected to an allegedly fraudulent story some years ago of the Priory of Sion. The other is a small chapel at Montsaunés which is much less known to tourists and so likely to be more interesting, with many mysterious signs and symbols from a thousand years ago whose meaning no-one has yet interpreted. The two are not more than a hundred kilometers from each other."

"History can be at its most interesting in its darker moments," Ethan commented cryptically as they finished their meal. "Can I help you in any way?"

"Thanks, said Mrs G, getting up to leave the table, "but I prefer to do things my own way. I hope you understand. When I know more I might contact you if you don't mind. Perhaps when I'm back in London if you're there. Can you give me a mobile number to make contact?" she smiled at him.

"Happy to. Call me when you're ready. It'll be a pleasure," Ethan replied.

It was difficult to place his silky accent. Italian perhaps, or what? She couldn't quite define it. He wrote down his number and held out his hand to shake hers.

"I aim to take a stroll. Some places of interest here. The Rue des Barbés has been recommended to me as a place for the redemption of sinners," he joked gently, aware she did not know the town. "May good fortune be with you," he had said paternally in the manner of a priest. It comforted her that someone took an interest in her endeavors. She felt less alone.


Mrs G had planned to leave early the next day to go to Montsaunés, a small village less than a two-hour taxi drive away as she estimated. As she lay in bed later that night a huge clap of thunder startled her from her sleep. She went to the window to see streaks of forked lightning flash several times through low, blackened clouds over Carcassonne's grim ramparts, and after a few minutes went back to bed, shaking a little.

The room had become cold. The sound of thunder rolled around the hills re-echoing. Was it an omen? she asked herself, as she slowly regained her sleep. If so, of what? She dreamed she was transported into a church with a high stone altar on which bare slab bodies lay naked with their flesh slashed from a bloody massacre; and then suddenly she was in Buonarroti's office in Washington in which knights cloaked in full regalia of weird images and icons sat at a round table performing a ceremony of initiation while she watched. Abe was on his knees kissing an insignia emblazoned on an apron worn by a man in front of him. Was it a just a dream or a revelation of the past, or even of the future? Perhaps it was the medicine her doctor in London had given her playing tricks on her mind. The reverie passed and she fell sound asleep.

The news Mrs G had heard from the specialist she had seen in London for a second opinion on her cough had not been helpful as he could not define its cause and she was feeling progressively more tired. The specialist had felt her Boston doctor might have given her the wrong antibiotic and had prescribed a new one in place of it. She was concerned, but had no time to worry over it. The urgency now was to complete her mission in the short time she had remaining in Europe and then have a full medical examination on her return to Boston. She needed to find the secret of the Grail. Perhaps faith could heal as well as science. Did one cancel out the other or was it that they might somehow come together as one and the same? This was uppermost in her mind. Her concern now for her health was that it could prevent the completion of her undertaking.

# Chapter 22

**Gorhambury House, St Albans, County of Hertfordshire, England. 1581**

Francis had woken up to a storm raging outside. He had dreamed the house was covered in a thick black tar. The rain lashed at his window and beat on its leaded glass panes. He rose sleepily and stared into the dark scene outside. The moon appeared momentarily from behind a threatening sky of scudding, grey clouds, and in its fleeting gleam he saw in the grounds a large monument in the shape of a pyramid. Its peak glowed gold illuminated by a beam of light and in it a single all-seeing eye looked directly at him. Around it sat a group of men in a circle. They were in the armor and tunics of the Templar Knights, and they rose as one to face him and salute him, as if he were their leader. He stared further into the sheets of rain and gloom, but suddenly the ghostly light he had seen them by had gone, and he could see the scene no more. In the morning he remembered the vision and considered that despite the vividness, he must have dreamed it all.

His return to Gorhambury from the European continent was a sad occasion. During his absence of several years he had received news of the death of his foster father, Sir Nicholas Bacon, aged seventy. Paulet had told Francis the Queen had determined he should remain on his grand tour of Europe and so he had had no option but to write to Lady Anne to express his condolences to her. Anthony had returned earlier to comfort his mother while Francis continued his journeys. On his arrival Lady Anne had asked to see Francis privately the following morning.

During his time abroad Francis had traveled widely, accompanied at all times by Paulet, spending time in all the great capitals of Europe to learn their languages, to study their art and history, and to learn the new fashions and styles of the great European Renaissance. It was over two years since they had departed from Paris. They went first to Lisboa, then to Madrid and Cordoba, and on to Verona, Venezia, Firenze and Roma. In Paris he met and held talks with Pierre de

Ronsard, then fifty-five, the philosopher poet of the French Renaissance. While on his travels he visited Greece and Egypt and several countries of the ancients and learned of their mystical Orders. He studied the teachings of Arabian lore and Egyptian mysticism, and of the Kabbalah and their ability to write and transcribe codes in a printed page with messages which were invisible to the uninitiated.

In Europe he studied the medieval Guilds and the German Steinmetzin stemming from the Knights Templar. He visited the new theaters that were becoming part of European everyday culture. Roman and Greek dramas and comedies of the past were being staged which had been banned for centuries by the Catholics as sinful. He heard the music, not just hymns played on the organs of the many great cathedrals he visited, but also the light airs played on the new instruments of the harpsichord and mandolin.

Paulet had made sure that by the time Francis returned to England he was a man of culture and knowledge, not just of the past, but also of the latest developments in technology and creative arts of the day. Of new artists who captured the exact image using a camera obscura, which revealed to Francis both the magic of art and its artifices. He became familiar with the recent works of the Dutch artist Hieronymus Bosch and his symbolism of life and death, good and evil, and of heaven and hell. His paintings were said to imitate the heretical beliefs of the Cathars and their dreams, inspired by magical potions, according to the Catholics' accusations.

The land at Gorhambury had formerly been the site of an abandoned ruin inhabited by the Knights Templar, and later by the monks of a Benedictine Abbey seized and destroyed by Henry VIII. In years long before, it had been the site where St Alban, an English martyr, had been beheaded by the Romans in the 4th century for following the Nazarene creed of Jesus and Mary Magdalene.

Both Henry VIII and Queen Elizabeth had bestowed use of the site to Sir Nicholas Bacon. On it he had built a fine house and adjoining temple with the Pillars of Wisdom of Solomon's Temple as a main feature. The design also signified the liberal arts and sciences, later used as a Masonic symbol. Altogether the house had become known locally as The Temple, and the Queen had visited it on occasions during its construction to give it her stamp of approval, as well as to visit Francis to see how his education was coming on. Despite

Elizabeth's confidence in the Bacons' own knowledge, and the strong Protestant leanings of Sir Nicholas and Lady Anne, the Queen had herself appointed a personal tutor for Francis from the age of two.

In the morning Francis had gone down to breakfast with Lady Anne, but thought it best not to tell her of his experience that night. They had drunk some wine with their meal of cold meats, cheese and dried fruits when Lady Anne sat back in her chair to speak.

"I need inform you of news of which you need be made aware," she said quietly.

"On the occasion of Sir Nicholas's passing no right or benefit under his Will and Testament was given to you. My two sons Nicholas and Anthony are to inherit all of Sir Nicholas' worldly goods, and full title to Gorhambury, where in my lifetime I am to reside."

Francis rose to kiss the hand she proffered him. She had been good to him, but strict in behavior as had Sir Nicholas. If he had ever seen them as his parents, it somehow now seemed in abstract form, but he had a great affection for them, as they did for him. His relationship with his real mother, the Queen, he felt was only now beginning. Her visits to him as a child had usually been brief and questioning.

Lady Anne had said no more than she needed to say. She had done her duty as the Queen had requested, but from her words Francis knew not to discuss the subject of his real mother, or even of his real father of whom he still had no knowledge. Further, that since his foster father had made no provision for him it was a sure sign of his real parenthood. He felt that his future was now surely to be in the hands of the Queen. This caused him some trepidation about the new existence that was opening up before him.

He wondered just who did know about his birth and the secret of it that his foster parents had been sworn to. Who else knew other than his real father? Francis himself had not yet confided his true birth to Anthony. They were good friends as students and enjoyed each other's company as if blood brothers. Anthony was now twenty-four and had a command of languages well suited to his leanings for a life involved with the Queen's diplomatic service, as she had planned for him. He and Francis spent days talking of their adventures, as Anthony too had travelled widely and had many tales to tell of European politics and the schemes of the French and Spanish to invade England to reinstate the Catholic religion once more.

As for Francis his adventures in Europe had taught him many things about the senses. He had not forsaken his passion for Marguerite. He had written her many sonnets to express his love for her, but had received no reply. She had been in his thoughts nearly every day and despite attempts by Paulet to introduce Francis to as many young princesses of European blue blood as possible, he had done little more than dance and joke with them, ignoring their sometimes obvious advances. But with his good sense of humor and gentle wit he had charmed his way into the hearts of many who were to remember his name in future.

Francis had written an ode to Marguerite and, having not heard from her, had not sent it, so as not to show her how much her denial of him injured his feelings. He had heard rumor of her affairs, both of those past and new, and for the first time the green-eyed monster of jealousy had disturbed and dismayed him. His poem had lain for many moons in a drawer of his bureau unsent since he had first written it and Francis would read it from time to time hoping one day he could bring himself to destroy it, having dispensed with the feelings for Marguerite that tugged daily at his heart. Perhaps one day he might publish it anonymously and that she might discover it, leaving her conscience to guess at its origin.

*"My love is as a fever, longing still for that which longer nurseth the disease;*
*Feeding on that which doth preserve the ill, the uncertain sickly appetite to please.*
*My reason, the physician to my love, angry that his prescriptions are not kept,*
*Hath left me, and I desperate now approve, desire is death, which physic did except.*
*Past cure I am, now reason is past care, and frantic-mad with evermore unrest;*

*My thoughts and my discourse as madmen's are, at random from the truth vainly express'd.*
*For I have sworn thee fair, and thought thee bright, who art as black as hell, as dark as night."*

Among men generally, he had been friendly enough, but preferred those with good humor to the more earnest, or the womanizers, or those destined for military roles, or for the Church. He had no calling for either Church or Army, seeing both as a requirement to follow orders in a life that was mapped out for those who had little mind of their own. He felt confident in himself and in his knowledge and imagination. That apart, he was the son and heir of the Queen, with the right one day to be King. Not just King of England, but also of its dominions in the new world.

What his mother had in store for him he did not know and, other than Marguerite, this was the only question with which he was uneasy. He had not reckoned on the Queen's motives, nor could he, since he hardly knew her mind from the brief occasions on which they had met. She had shown him some care and clearly had taken an interest in his education and ability. That was all. She was an enigma known to none but herself, as Francis was to discover.

# Chapter 23

**The British Museum Library, Archive Rooms, London. October, 2014**

Mrs G was sitting peering over a page of a large book, covered in a thin plastic film underneath which was a parchment of faint print on a yellowing background. She looked up to say hi to Ethan who had just arrived and was now standing beside her. She had sent his mobile a text the day before to ask him to meet her there and as he had not replied she was pleasantly surprised he had made it.

"Thanks for coming," she said as she looked up at him.

"Did you have any problem finding me? I left directions for you at the desk. This building is a warren of rooms and corridors."

"No problem," replied Ethan, "how did you get on in France? Any luck?"

"Montsaunés was full of clues, but I need time to decipher them. Rennes le Chateau gave little up. No devil that I could find. A wild goose chase and a tourist trap. The only thing they haven't claimed to have found there yet is the Loch Ness monster." She laughed. "But more interesting is what I'm finding here." She pointed to the cover page of a Shakespeare play in front of her.

"This is a copy of the frontispiece that appeared on a number of the early publications of Shakespeare plays."

Ethan looked down at a lithographed figure. "Isn't she Pallas Athene, the Greek goddess of knowledge and enlightenment? Her spear was a symbol of her fight against ignorance. The two columns she's standing between are the Pillars of Wisdom from the Temple of Solomon in Jerusalem."

Mrs G nodded. "Yes, of course, I know that; every reader of Shakespeare knows her meaning, but it is these pages which are of interest to me." She turned to a following page. "You see these marks," she pointed at tiny marks down the side of the page and among the written lines.

"They are concealed codes intended to be found by those future generations clever enough to understand them. My parents told me about their discovery by my great-grandmother, but these are too unclear through this plastic to decipher with assurance. I need to see an original work in best possible condition. The markings are said to run through most, if not all, of Shakespeare's plays, so it is quite a task, but the people here won't allow me the time without special permission, and time is not what I have right now. I need to find access to first editions somewhere else. They are very rare."

Looking at her watch she picked up her notes and went to leave. "My time is up for this morning." She frowned in annoyance.

"Cheer up," Ethan smiled. "How about lunch at the Balthazar? It's a hot spot right now and not far away in Covent Garden near the Opera House. Do you like devilled kidneys?"

"Okay, you win, it'll take my mind off it all," Mrs G replied. "Do you like the theater? I was going to get tickets for *The Comedy of Errors* at the Globe Theatre tonight. It's one of Shakespeare's plays about a mix-up with two pairs of identical twins and it's really funny. The expression 'too much of a good thing' comes from it. Have you seen it? My hotel can get an extra ticket if you'd like to come."

Ethan nodded. "Okay, if you twist my arm. My preference has always been for the romantic tragedies, *Romeo and Juliet* and *Othello*. Love turned to disaster. I like a bit of real drama." He chuckled.

They hailed a taxi outside the Museum after walking through long entry lines of students from the world over. Even in these days of Google, Mrs G thought, there was no substitute for the real thing. The codes she had recognized this morning had confirmed it. She had not wanted to tell Ethan of their true significance.

# Chapter 24

**Twickenham Hall, Richmond, London, 1582. Afternoon.**

A small, lone boat crosses the Thames from its north bank to its south. A man in a black greatcoat stands at the arm of the tiller while two others at the oars pull hard upstream against the newly ebbing tide. Sitting huddled at the prow is another smaller cloaked and hooded figure. As the vessel draws up at a low, wooden jetty, rising from the reeds on the muddy bank opposite, the figure steps out lightly and walks rapidly up the lawns of a superb Tudor mansion facing the river.

The door of the house is opened by a servant who takes the cloak of the wearer as its occupant flings it off and moves into a large hall with a dark oak staircase leading to an overlooking gallery. Down its stairs comes a lightly-bearded young man in elegant attire, lace ruffles at his neck and cuffs, in tight red breeches and white stockings, with a small jeweled dagger in the belt by his side. This was a moment he had long waited for, and now it had arrived. This week he had seen his twenty-first birthday come and he had received a message he was to meet the Queen at this very place, and to ensure that he was there before her arrival. His earlier arrival and curiosity had taken him to explore several of the rooms.

The woman from the boat comes towards him. Her arms outstretched to embrace him as they near. "So, what do you say?" she exclaims, "to my gift of Twit'nam Hall on your coming of age."

Noticing his dagger she takes it from his sheath and places it on a side table out of harm's way. Francis looked at her and the splendor of the hall in which they stood as she took his hand.
"Come," said his mother. "I will show you what is to be yours." She led him to a magnificently furnished drawing room overlooking the river. "See," she pointed, "across the river is my palace at Richmond. We shall be neighbors, you and I. This is to be your place of residence, one fit for your future. I have engaged servants to tend to your new home and your needs."

"Your Majesty is too kind," Francis responded, bowing low before her. "Please be assured I will do all in my power to reward the generosity you bestow on me."

"Have no fear," said Elizabeth, "your time to show your gratitude will come, but for now I want to hear all about your travels. What you have learned these last years? What news from Europe? Who have you met and what role do you intend to pursue in your life?"

Francis' puzzled expression gave him away and Elizabeth knew it was the moment to tell him. She had never been one to avoid speaking directly.

"As I have told you, you are not to succeed me, Francis, as sovereign. I wish you to renounce any claim to the throne. The circumstances of your birth were such that I could not have declared you as my legal heir without complications which might have endangered my claim to the throne, and so your own. You will know the Salic law forbidding women the right to reign. In some eyes you would be seen as the bastard son of a bastard queen, since under Catholic law my father was already married to another when he married my mother; and soon rid himself of her too." She said with emphasis.

"Now that the years have passed and I am forty-six years of age it is too late to publicly claim you as my son.

"I swear that it will be the best for you." She sighed for a moment before she spoke again.

"Uneasy lies the head that wears the Crown."

"What I have done for you I have done also for your father. He will never rule as King. You know him as the Earl of Leicester and until recently he has been my companion since the time of your birth. He will wish to discuss with you your future plans. From what I hear you have inherited his love of the arts and theater in which he encourages us all in our brilliant new English Renaissance. I am sure you will have much to share with him.

"I propose you come to my court in these next few days where from now on you will be welcomed as Francis Bacon, Esquire. You will find some there who suspect your true birth and name, but you may never breathe a word of it or you will endanger your life and mine," she said somberly.

Then in a lighter tone:

"You must come soon to tell us all at court of your travels and the gossip and practices of the foreign courts you have visited that we may learn of new music and dance and of their latest plays, and of their *'liaisons dangereuses.'* I hear you have been well taught!" she smiled amusedly.

"To give you the status you will require I will appoint you my Ambassador Extraordinaire. How does that suit you?" She laughed and clapped her hands with glee to witness the surprised pleasure on his face. Francis had grown to a good height and stature with a pleasing countenance of which she approved. His dark hair, pointed beard and demeanor gave him an air of manly sophistication. Elizabeth looked him directly in the eye, her look changing to one of warning.

"If you displease me, I will take this away from you," she gestured at the house. "It is for your use now and one day it will be in your ownership when you have proved worthy of my trust in you. I have in mind that you need to study the law. It will forever be of use to you and if required could make you a living. For now I have made you a generous monthly allowance from my personal funds to further your life, which I hope will be one of equal study and leisure. My advice for a contented life is neither a borrower nor a lender be. I hear you don't gamble since you neither sport nor joust, although practiced with your rapier from your exploits in France I am given to understand." She raised a smiling, but knowledgeable eyebrow, not wanting to touch further on her son's sexual adventure. "So, pray tell me, what have you in mind to do?"

Francis had been warned by Paulet to say nothing to the Queen of his dalliance with Marguerite or of any plans to try and see her again. He had thought hard about his future desires, but until now had not known what duties might be required of him. He could not be more delighted to hear that his mother and father enjoyed theater and the arts and literature. It was known that Elizabeth herself was an accomplished musician, playing the lute, and that she loved to dance every day, often practising the steps of new dances as an exercise when she rose in the morning, under the instructions of her personal dancing master.

"I would like for my leisure to write and to use the theater to convey my knowledge and to entertain," Francis earnestly explained. "I wish to tell our English people in their own language of the great history of the Tudors and their desire for peace and freedom. I intend too that they may know of the best of dramas from stories of the Greeks and Romans that I have learned in my travels, and of the great romances and tragedies of past times from the world over, and of comedies too. Without jest and laughter life would be dull indeed."

Elizabeth smiled at his enthusiasm.

"I would not bid to discourage you from your father's love of theater, but it is best you should not involve your name. Write by all means, but my wish is that you should be learned of the laws of England. I have asked Lord Burleigh, who is my Lord Treasurer and Keeper of the Royal Purse, to arrange for you to have chambers at one of the Inns of Temple to study. I want that you be a source of wellbeing for my nation. To stand for good order, liberty and the pursuit of happiness, that my people deserve. But to prove your own intent why not write me a play? A comedy. Let it be your first to please me. I command it. We shall see your literary merit thereby!"

She laughed with delight. This would test his youthful fervor.

Elizabeth saw the serious look on his face and decided to stage her own play to try out his other skills.

"Come now," she exclaimed with a grin showing on her face. "Let me show the steps to the Turkeloney. 'Tis a new quick dance all the rage at court, where you must prove yourself with the other young bloods."

She took his hands and lightly danced him round the room so he could follow her steps, which she was pleased he quickly copied.

"'Tis best accompanied by the words of a song our young men sing:

*"If I ever marry I'll marry a maid. To marry a widow I'm sore afraid."* She chuckled as she sang.

She saw his surprise and then the twinkle in his eye that he had seen in hers. At last she had got from him the smile she wanted. His nervousness dispelled. She had disarmed his ingenuousness with her ingenuity, as she had so many others in her life. She was happy at last to see her son and converse with him as an adult after his years away. She felt they could talk freely now he had understood he was not to inherit her throne. He had shown no outward disappointment at what she had told him. Francis was the scholar of her family, of immense intelligence and profound in thought, as his tutors had reported to her. He had shown signs of genius from an early age in matters of mathematics and philosophy and was proficient in Latin, Italian and Greek, apart from the French he had spoken from birth as did all the nobility at the English Court. Francis was unlike his younger brother to whom Elizabeth had given birth, also from her husband Leicester. Her second son looked more like his handsome father, taller than Francis and with a fiery demeanor at a young age. She had named him Robert to please his father, and already at fifteen years of age she knew he would give her more problems than Francis. He was a hothead, but he would be the warrior she might one day need to defend England's shores. She had left much of his education to his father and he had opted for a military career. Elizabeth and Francis talked and laughed for several hours and as she took her leave they stood by the open door while the twilight closed fast round them and the evening star of Sirius appeared alone in the sky above them. Elizabeth summoned a servant for her cloak and asked Francis to accompany her to her waiting boatmen.

"You may visit me in my Richmond Palace by boat when my court is there. It is but a short distance away. No need to stand on ceremony," she declared, as they walked down the lawns where she stopped at the water's edge to hand him a small velvet bag. As he took it from her she held his face gently in her hands and kissed him lightly on his cheek. It was the only kiss she was ever to give him. "In the bag you will find two gifts," she told him. "One a ring to wear at all times. To be returned to me only as a sign of your direst need. The other is a symbol of your destiny."
With that she boarded the waiting watercraft, and Francis watched her quickly disappear from sight in the gathering dusk as her oarsmen rowed downstream across the river in the calm water before the tide turned.

As Francis re-entered the doors of his new home ideas flooded his mind one after the other. He knew now the path that lay before him. His tutors gone, his way forward was to please and obey his Queen and country as a loyal servant. He would do so by making England far greater than it was now through education of its people and knowledge of the mind and spirit, and from new inventions. His eyes sparkled at his thoughts until they crowded his head and overcame him, and a wave of exhilaration swept through his whole being at the future that lay ahead of him. He had not felt so excited since his introduction to the French Court in Paris and the first days he had spent with Marguerite. She was gone now. He appreciated what she had taught him, yet still he could not forgive her. It had been a moment in time only. This he realized. No turning back. His new future was before him.

# Chapter 25

**Globe Theatre, Thames South Bank, London. October, 2014**

Mrs G and Ethan left the Globe Theater together and walked into the cool night air. The play, *The Comedy of Errors*, had been a highly amusing performance set in a contemporary London scene with one of England's most famous black comedians in the lead role. Yet a more important reason that Mrs G had wanted to visit The Globe was that it was an exact replica of the original theatre of Shakespeare's time. She had learned of the relatively recent discovery of codes hidden in the wall of a building which had once belonged to a young member of the Royal Society, the world's first ever scientific institution founded in 1660. Francis Bacon and his friend John Dee had been members of its forerunner, Gresham College, some sixty years before. She had heard that Bacon had given instructions for his manuscripts to be placed in secret hiding places for the benefit of posterity, should his writings otherwise be destroyed.

The codes discovered had taken some years to unravel but among their findings had shown that the Globe was built to a specific structure using the central number 72, which according to the scientist Isaac Newton, one of the Royal Society's first members corresponded with the structure of the Universe. It gave the Globe extraordinary qualities of sound in an experience of interaction of audience and players which had been considered mystical.

Strangely the Globe had been built in 1599 or some forty years before Newton's declaration of the discovery of the structure of the Universe. Also odd was that Newton had tried to prevent this information being made public on the grounds that its knowledge could endanger the entire world in future. Perhaps it had been known before him. After all, the laws of mathematics were thousands of years old, although many of them had been lost and obscured over time.

The night was fine, but cold and Mrs G and Ethan strolled together over Waterloo Bridge before hailing a taxi. Inside the cab Mrs G opened her Mulberry handbag and took out her i-Phone to Google up the information she was looking for. Having found it she looked puzzled.

"It's strange, but I had the same feeling in Carcassonne. The Shakespeare sonnet number 18. 'Shall I compare thee to a Summers Day' was first published in 1609 in a volume of other sonnets and verse, yet thirty years beforehand Francis Bacon had sent it to his lover Marguerite, whose love letters were found after her death. It was well before any work was attributed to Shakespeare who would have been only thirteen at the time. How could he possibly have expressed the depth of passion shown in it?

"Something else I discovered recently was that the Earl of Leicester had been known as 'The Shield of Pallas' even before Shakespeare's birth. Its title had been conferred on him as a protector of knowledge. Illustrations of Pallas Athene also appeared on covers of Shakespeare's plays before the Shakespeare name was attributed to them. Leicester was known for his support of the theater at a time when actors were considered as undesirables, and they had been outlawed until Henry VIII had allowed play-acting at his Court. Leicester organized the licensing of actors so that acting might be seen as a profession. He was a charismatic man and held the Queen's attention in mind and body for the first twenty years of their relationship. After that, of the amorous dalliances they had both engaged in, his became greater than hers, which she resented."

"Leicester?" queried Ethan.

"Yes, the husband of Elizabeth and father of her two sons: Francis Bacon, and Robert Devereux. Robert Essex, as he became known. Ethan lifted an eyebrow. "So, how come they both had different family names?"

Mrs G smiled knowingly. "Because Elizabeth farmed them both out at birth to people she knew well and could trust as foster parents. She had never said she was married, although she was, and so got herself into a lie she could not get out of. It also suited her as she hated interference in her wily ways, and so she gave her husband and sons jobs they could do for her without crossing her path."

Mrs G flicked through some photo shots on her i-Phone which she had filed from their web sites. "Look," she pointed to one. "That's Alnwyck Castle, where they film the Harry Potter movies. It's in Northumberland near the English Scottish border, and has some scary history. One of its heirs was the lover of Anne Boleyn, the mother of Elizabeth I, and both Anne and her lover had their heads cut off by Elizabeth's father for their troubles.

"Wow!" exclaimed Ethan, "They didn't mess around in those days. Why do you have its picture?"

"Because I have a hunch it could be the place to confirm my theory," she said excitedly.

"What of? The Grail?" Ethan enquired.

"No, forget that, this is something else. I can get the US Embassy to call up the present incumbent, the Duke of Northumberland, to say I would like to do some research. With luck I may get to meet him. Apparently the Duke's a nice guy who likes meeting people who might help contribute funds to some of his pet projects, or those of his wife. I am told she has made a fantastic garden there with one of the world's great formal waterfalls, and another full of herbs and plants. I know a lot about plants and we should have plenty to talk about. I expect I shall be gone for a day or two as I need get there by train."

With that the taxi pulled up at the Savoy entrance and Mrs G left, leaving Ethan to go on. She had not thought to ask him where.

# Chapter 26

## Richmond, London. 1584

Francis sat at his desk at Twickenham Hall. He had come in from an early morning walk in its park-like grounds of magnificent cedar trees seeded from the Lebanon, and old English oaks many hundreds of years of age. Silver birches glinted in the morning sun as white swans courted ritually on the riverbank of the Thames. He looked at the ring his mother had given him, which he now wore on the index finger of his right hand. On it was a motif of a five-pointed rose set in a crown. It was the old symbol of the Tudors, but also one that later became recognized as that of a Prince of Masonry. Francis well knew this from his studies of his heritage and its lineage from Mary Magdalene to the Tudors. The rose in the image of a woman's vulva was seen as the eternal symbol of love and female generative power from the times of the Greeks and Egyptians.

He reached to pick up the other gift his mother had given him. A small but heavy wedge-shaped piece of stone he held carefully in both his hands. It looked as if it had been reduced in size and was worn smooth with one side engraved with the same Celtic rose as the ring. He knew it was a symbol of the keystones that formed the last stone put in place in the ancient Egyptian pyramids and in the temples of the Templar knights. He replaced it on his desk. It made a good paper weight for the many manuscripts that lay on the desk. A mixture of plays and ideas for books and poems, as well as law cases. He did not notice the barely visible graphic etched on its underside.

The Queen had been as good as her word and the Lord Burleigh, her trusted confidant, had found Francis rooms at a law chambers in Gray's Inn where he would stay in London to carry out the Queen's wishes for him to become a lawyer, which final exams he was to have successfully completed at twenty three. Having finished his studies he felt relieved that he could now spend more time where his heart lay; in his grand home at Twickenham and the space it afforded him and the group he had collected there to share the creative work he planned.

He got up from his desk to enter a large adjoining room, where he was met by a chorus of cheerful greetings from the team he had assembled. Each one of them had congratulated him on his law degree as they came up to shake his hand. Ben Jonson, a red-faced bear of a man, had given him a huge hug. Francis was pleased with his new found acolytes whom he had handpicked to create a new world of English literature. One task the Queen had in mind was for him to reflect the new Protestant interpretation of the gospels in English. She had recommended him to Robert Fludd, a man with whom Francis was to work to produce the New English Bible from unfinished translations by William Tyndale of earlier Latin versions. The Queen had considered it would be a good test of her son's language skills learned at Cambridge and abroad.

Since Chaucer's times nearly two hundred years before, the English language had progressed rapidly, taking on many new French words. French, Latin and English were spoken at the Court of the Queen, but the Law Courts still largely used Latin, so that a commoner on trial would have difficulty understanding the proceedings against him. Francis was determined to put this to rights.

All those in his new team were men. Not just skilled writers learned in the classics, but those interested in the new theories of philosophy and science. He wanted men with experience of life too with knowledge of life in the taverns and the whorehouses to assimilate the language of the streets into one he would create to last forever. His aim was to give them a single purpose for a complete reformation of English life. Not that they could not think for themselves. Francis wanted that of them, but that they should experiment with new words and thoughts for the purpose of educating and entertaining all the English public rather than the few. They were to do so, not just by words in books and poems in a greatly expanded English language, but by enacting stories and dramas in plays for the public to see. He had decided to call them his "Good Pens".

In the room he now entered they sat talking one to another or in groups, while some wrote notes with quill pens. The room started to buzz with conversation after his arrival and there was a hum of activity. Most were his own age, in their twenties. Many were smoking tobacco newly brought from the Americas. On several desks stood wine glasses and pewter jugs.

Apart from Ben Jonson, closest to Francis in friendship were Fletcher, Beaumont, Chapman, Dekker, Massinger, Marston, Ford, Heywood, Hobbes, Bushell, Nashe, Bright, Burton, Peacham, Betterton, and Rawley. In all about twenty who would come and go rotating with newcomers in the years ahead. Digges, an astronomer, was one. Another, Richard Field from Stratford who from 1589 was to print many of the works stemming from the Good Pens. Some were friends from Francis' days at university, and others were literary adventurers and new age reformists who were to change the English language forever in England's own Renaissance. Francis clapped his hands to get attention.

"Gentleman. A toast to Pallas Athene and her spear of knowledge," he exclaimed. It was Leicester, Francis' birth father, who had suggested they use her name as their group symbol. Not only did the ancient Greek goddess Pallas represent knowledge, but her helmet was by lore said to have given her the invisibility that the Good Pens were to seek for many of their works to come. They stood as one to the toast as Francis continued.

"Here's to good wine to freshen the mind and the good weed to dream on! Let our goal be to start a New England in our own English tongue. I promised Her Majesty a play and it will be our first endeavor to please her. Since we are all novices who find much amusement in our errors, I propose it shall be a comedy, and it shall be named *The Comedy of Errors.* Pray raise your glasses once more gentlemen. To the Queen, our benefactress."

They stood to echo his words. "The Queen."

At this instance Francis's butler announced a newcomer's arrival. "Walter Raleigh, Esquire".

A military-looking man in his late twenties, in a flowing cloak, with a sword at his side, strode into the room. He doffed his feathered cap as Francis went to greet him.

"I understand you have been informed by Her Majesty of my business here and of my intentions." Raleigh spoke, frowning slightly at the scene of merriment in front of him. "I trust, Sir that my visit is not too intrusive."

"Why, Sir, no indeed, you are most welcome. Her Majesty has told me of your plans to settle our new dominions in America, which are to be named Virginia after our queen, and that you seek our advice. It will be my pleasure. You are among friends, Sir, please speak your mind. May I introduce my partner in wit and writ, Mr Ben Jonson?"

"With respect, I would seek your knowledge alone," stated Raleigh determinedly, and Francis led him to his private study. "Pray, how may I assist you?" inquired Francis.

"My learned friend," replied Raleigh, "I understand you have been devising new laws for living in our lands in the New World. I am told that you have plans for the development of the land and property for exploitation by settlers of all class and denomination. You are a bold man indeed to advance such a view. You appreciate I am not a man of letters, but rather one of action, and so seek your advice on how I may best proceed for my next visit to our dominions."

"Indeed, Sir," said Francis respectfully, since Raleigh's name was famed for the foreign discoveries he had brought back to England. Tobacco was one and the potato another, which Raleigh was growing on his estate in Ireland. Raleigh was in good stead with the Queen to whom he was immensely loyal, a virtue she considered uppermost among all others, and for which she was shortly to grant him a knighthood.

Francis continued enthusiastically.

"I believe those Englishmen who have good knowledge of care of the land need be encouraged to make their fortunes there. We need ensure good leaders are found from those among our landed families whose loyalty can be trusted. Growth of population need be encouraged to explore this undiscovered continent since it has the resources of water and soil to maintain many of Her Majesty's future subjects. I intend to start work on a thesis to be called *The New Atlantis* which is to set out the principles of our newly found lands so that all men there shall live a life of liberty in the pursuit of happiness. It shall be their guide. Now Sir, will you not join with us in our repast and walk with me in our magnificent gardens."

"I must decline as I need to return to London this day," replied Raleigh. "But these are brave words. A Utopian world is more easily conceived than performed. Please take heed, we shall need to fortify settlements with men and arms with which to keep our acquisitions from falling into Spanish hands. I shall inform Her Majesty of our meeting, but now I must take my leave. You are much spoken of lately and I find pleasure in your acquaintance. I bid you farewell and a return to your books and friends."

Raleigh bowed his head curtly and departed. Although young himself he had already seen much of the known world and his experience had given him a practical nature. He was no dreamer. He knew men needed laws and that laws needed protecting.

Alone in his study, Francis felt satisfied that his mother had trusted him well enough to advise one of her most favored stalwarts. Each day now was to bring Francis new laurels to reward his past studies. His dearest wish was to please his Queen. He knew that her wish, now that England had freed itself from Catholic influence, was to pursue the tenets of her Tudor forbears and of King Arthur's Knights of the Round Table. It was for this he had named the principal members of his team of Good Pens more formally as the Knights of the White Helmet, of which he was to be their first Grand Master.

# Chapter 27

Alnwyck Castle, built in 1096 after the Norman conquest of England, had been home to the presently incumbent Percy family for the past seven hundred years. It stood among the dark green slopes and steep granite spurs of the Northumberland hills. It was a gaunt and foreboding building at any time of year, but in November with snow on the nearby craggy peaks and the slate grey clouds speeding over its bulwarks, it appeared as if from some distant fantasy of a battle scarred realm, dwarfing the tiny homes of its retainers in the shadow of its walls. It was here that Robert Dudley, the lover and secret husband of Queen Elizabeth I had been born and raised nearly five hundred years before, as one of thirteen children of his parents.

Mrs G had been greeted by the Duke's butler and taken to the vast galleried library of the Prudhoe Tower. There she was confronted by one of the greatest collections of written English history comprising over fourteen thousand volumes. It struck her that in the days of manuscripts written by hand, only families of noble birth had access to knowledge, which they had kept exclusively for their own benefit. From 1476 on, the impact of Caxton's inventive printing press and its low cost mass production of books had enabled literacy among Londoners to be over sixty percent by Shakespeare's time. But today Mrs G had come to find out finally exactly who Shakespeare had been, and whether it was who she suspected, that had actually created the great number of works that had spring from his mind.

As Mrs G stood gazing at the library's paneling of oak inlaid with sycamore, and its ornate Italianate ceiling, the Duke himself appeared, dressed casually in a tweed jacket and corduroys. He mentioned the US Embassy had spoken to him about her botanical interests and introduced himself as Ralph Percy. He had enquired why she was interested in the particular manuscript she now asked to see, since it was a rare item of which few other than historians were aware, but as he led her to it, he sensed the curiosity in her.

"It is known as the Northumberland Manuscript and is in the original." He said: "I will leave you to examine it at your leisure. Please let me know when you have finished and I will introduce you to my wife Jane to take you on a tour of our gardens. Fortunately today is one they are not open to the public. I expect our Poison Garden will be the one of most interest to you."

The Duke had drawn up an old high stool for her in front of an airtight glass cabinet in which the manuscript was laid out at the page she wanted to see. There she saw what she had long hoped to be true. She coughed nervously as she peered at the scribbled notes and doodled drawings, and checked and rechecked the words and writing. There was the mirror of Pallas Athene with her spear in hand, and below it the helmets of Pallas and Pluto, symbols of invisibility and concealment. There too she saw in black ink the names written: Francis Bacon – William Shakespeare, and the words Richard II and Richard III clearly identified. She had stared at them for so long that she had hardly noticed the Duke's return. He was standing behind her, and she turned to thank him.

"I am told this is the only written evidence of Francis Bacon's involvement in Shakespeare's plays, she said hesitantly.
"That is correct," the Duke replied. "Bacon was many things to many men, but known only to a few. What is your interest in him, may I enquire?"
"My late husband and I spent many years deciphering the genetic codes of plants using the Fibonacci sequence. I had learned from a paper written by my great grandmother of secret ciphers hidden in the original plays of Shakespeare, and this whetted my appetite to continue her investigations. As she did, and as I also believe, either William Shakespeare himself was highly talented in the language of codes, of which there is no evidence, or that some other person of great cryptological skills must have taken the name of Shakespeare as a pseudonym. There is, of course, the possibility that both of them wrote plays at the same time."
"That may be so," the Duke replied. "You are by no means alone in thinking it was Bacon. One of my Northumberland ancestors, known as the Wizard, was the patron of various friends of Bacon here at Alnwyck who were advisers to Elizabeth I. They practiced their alchemical arts here. One of them was the Queen's personal astrologer, John Dee. My ancestors were nothing if not political and they got themselves into all sorts of trouble. One was accused by King Henry VIII of being the real father of Elizabeth!"

The Duke looked at Mrs G enquiringly, wondering if the sexual shenanigans of English royalty might be best left alone from the scrutiny of foreign inquiry.

"There is a Francis Bacon Society in existence which has some noted members and may advise you helpfully. One of whom I am told is the Marquis of Northampton who knows a good deal about the authorship of the Shakespeare's plays which he may wish to share with you. If you like, I'll try to contact him for you. He lives some way from here at Compton Wynates, the greatest Elizabethan house in England and said to be the most haunted! Queen Elizabeth visited it quite often. If you meet him, you should ask him about his tower building in London's Islington where I believe the Queen often met with Francis Bacon. It is almost as unknown to the public today, I am told, as it was then."

Mrs G, coughing furiously, asked for a glass of water which was brought to her, and soon after she was introduced to the Lady of the house, Jane Percy, who too shared a love of botany. She had inaugurated her Poison Garden at Alnwyck after a visit to Padua in Italy where she had visited the Poison Garden of the Medici family founded hundreds of years before. The Medicis were renowned for their knowledge and use of plants. Not just to cure, but also as poisons and aphrodisiacs, and in their psychosomatic use to achieve altered states of consciousness.

Mrs G and Jane Percy spent some hours discussing new discoveries of plant uses for medical purposes and their narrow line between bringing life and death. Time flew by and she had hardly any left to see the famed grand waterfall Jane had created, or more of the grand Gothic interiors where much of the Harry Potter film footage had been shot, and where Francis Bacon's father had once been raised. She promised she would return, and as she left she could not quite bring herself to her senses in knowing which world she was in. The past or the present? More than ever now she realized they were eternally interconnected and that time in the cosmos had no meaning.

# Chapter 28

**York Place. Queen Elizabeth's Residence. 1596**

The Queen clapped her hands with delight. The play *The Comedy of Errors* was being performed tonight by the Queen's Company of actors licensed by her royal command, and had been written for her by her son Francis some fourteen years before. She had seen it performed several times and had never failed to be amused at the ingenious farcical fun of its mistaken identical twins. She was pleased she had a son who shared her own sense of amusement and theater. Francis was with Elizabeth tonight, as too was his true brother Robert now aged thirty and some five years younger than Francis. How time had flown by, Elizabeth mused.

The Queen remembered too another play Francis had written in his early twenties. It was a play on words in which the Danish King had been killed and which Elizabeth had suspected Francis had intended to allude to her. She would not have known if Leicester had not pointed out the inference. He had visited the young Francis without notice to find him directing a rehearsal of actors in the play and had caught him by surprise. Francis then had called it *Ur Hamlet; "Ur"* meaning prodigal in Danish, a reference to a returned wanderer or prodigal son, as Francis had seen himself on his return to England after his travels. On finding out he was not to be the future king he had written the play in recrimination.
When Elizabeth first knew of it she had scolded Francis with her whiplash tongue, and Francis had thought better of admitting the play had any reference to her, and withdrew its performance. It was not for many years, until after the Queen's death, that a new version by the name of *Hamlet* was staged in public.

Today Francis and Robert were both seated behind their mother amongst her other courtiers, as she wished neither of them to be known as her offspring, particularly given the inquisitive eyes and ears of visitors. It had been the Queen's personal amusement to keep the foreign Ambassadors at her court guessing as to which country she might one day make a marriage alliance with, but now at her age of sixty- three they had given up any hope. It appeared as far as most could see that it would be the end of the great, but short Tudor royal lineage; but then they did not know about Elizabeth's two sons.

In former days the Queen had a reputation for her liking of younger men. She had seduced Francis's childhood companion Anthony when he was sixteen despite his preference for his own sex, for which he had later stood trial in France for an act of sodomy with his pageboy. It had been rumored that the poem of *Venus and Adonis* was a warning by Francis to his friend, the young Earl of Southampton, of Elizabeth's desire to bed the handsome earl, and what it might entail if she were to lay her hands on him

There had long been gossip in the Court about Elizabeth's relationship with Robert Essex, and it secretly amused her that he was thought to be her lover, when unknown to the gossips he was her son. She and Leicester, Robert' s father, had parted thirteen years ago in 1583 after he had bigamously married Lettice Knollys, Elizabeth's cousin and close friend, some ten years younger than Elizabeth. Lettice had raised the young Robert Essex as her son but Elizabeth was to banish her and Leicester forever from her Court when she heard of their marriage and of the concealed liaison they had carried on for many years beforehand. Some eight years had passed since Leicester had died from drinking a glass of poisoned sherry.

Elizabeth and her son were fond of each other's company. She and Robert both loved dance and music, and were often seen together at plays of Court and masked balls where their identities were supposedly hidden. It flattered Elizabeth that people should mistakenly think she had a lover at her age, and Robert had at times played up to her game. He had been back and forth for many years fighting the Spanish at sea and had recently returned after a naval coup. In command of the English navy he and Francis Drake had surprised the Spanish war fleet at anchor off Cadiz and routed it.

Robert and Francis had not met for some time before this evening. "So what say you, Robert, on return from your adventures? Do you not find pleasure to laugh at our Francis' *Comedy of Errors*?" Elizabeth enquired mischievously, knowing of her sons' contest for her affections. Robert and Francis not only had an age gap between them, but had led very different existences, and although having been friends in their teenage years were entirely unalike in character. Robert knew that Francis had been content to give up his claim to the throne of England, but Robert with his fierier disposition had not. As brothers they bonded in their interests against their joint enemies at Court but nevertheless their rivalry came to a head at times.

"Since Francis chooses to flatter Her Majesty with his pen, so shall I flatter her with my sword, and we shall see which is the mightier," Robert proclaimed.
"Let me tell you of my exploits in Cadiz with Sir Francis Drake. How we singed the King of Spain's beard, burning and sinking his fleet and putting many to the sword! How on our return we seized the great library of the infidel Moors from the Bishop of Faro bearing their ancient teachings and the science of *Algebra*, which I have donated to Sir Thomas Bodley to form a new library at Oxford." He ended sarcastically: "Of which our dear Francis may avail himself in the pursuit of all knowledge, but to what end best known only to himself. To my mind brevity is the soul of wit. The first thing we should do is to kill all the lawyers!"

Elizabeth's smile vanished, but she quickly recovered. She knew Robert well and that he was seeking her praise and due reward. She considered his jibe at Francis was to diminish his scholarly leadership qualities and any claim to the throne. Robert knew from his father, whose favorite he was, that having been conceived after his parent's secret marriage, he had a better claim than Francis who had been conceived before marriage, and so was adulterine. He also knew Francis was the cleverer of the two of them and was never quite convinced of Francis' vow to refuse the throne. He would poke fun at Francis' learnedness while in turn Francis nicknamed him 'Rash Robert'.

Elizabeth did not think that Robert would ever try to depose her while she was Queen, but she had developed eyes in the back of her head to protect against her enemies at home and abroad who might try to conjoin him in their plans. She knew it was best to keep Robert occupied, and if possible out of England where he was inclined to stir up internal politics and Court gossip.

As the play ended and the audience of courtiers slowly left the room, she turned to Robert.
"You shall take the fire in your belly to command my army in Ireland

and resolve our problems with their Catholic rebels. As for Francis, you forget he serves me well in word and in deed. I will have no bad blood between you!"

She gathered her gown and departed for her bedchamber; Robert and Francis bowed low to her with her other courtiers. The signs of tiredness showed now in her face. She no longer liked the look of herself in her mirror. Her teeth were blackening and beneath her heavy makeup the smallpox scars and worry lines the years had brought her showed through. She had had enough of the eternal strife of European politics, and was not pleased to suffer the petty jealousies of her Court.

Those who angered her or spoiled her waning pleasures soon found themselves out of favor and banned from Court, or their assets seized, or worse their heads cut off and placed on pikes lining the streets outside her palaces with the more common offenders against her laws. The thought of her absolute power gave her renewed strength as her ladies-in-waiting undressed her before she retired for the night. She set the tiny alarm clock timepiece she wore on her finger from which a small prong would extend to prick her hand to wake her up. It was an age of new gadgets and inventions in which she took a close interest.

As she lay between the four ornately carved and turned wooden posters of her bed, its curtains drawn and her lady of the bedchamber sleeping nearby, her mind turned to her life and how it had sped by so quickly despite the extraordinary number of events she had encountered. She mused happily that despite its problems she had managed to enjoy much of it. Not for nothing was she known as "Good Queen Bess" from early on in her reign. It was a description of her admirers which she relished and later had added to it "In memory green" to reflect her long held interest in the turf. Not only had she hunted regularly, often twice a week in Richmond Park, or on her frequent tours of England with her Court retinue, but she had kept a string of racehorses at her stables in Greenwich providing her many winners at her royal racecourses at Richmond and Ascot.

She enjoyed a good gamble especially when she was onto a winner, but was more cautious than some of her noble friends. Many gentlemen of means had galloped out of their fortunes, leaving their heirs bankrupt. Elizabeth had followed in her father's sporting footsteps, as did Robert. Gambling and sport were synonymous in their day. Betting took place on everything possible. Cockfighting, bear-baiting, archery, jousting, cards and dice. In all of which Elizabeth had once found respite from the world of politics and intrigue. Her favorites at Court were all sporting men of good physique, practiced at dueling, or in hunting, and as energetic dancers who would whirl their partners round the dance floor.

As her eyes closed her lips pursed with a smile as she thought of Francis. He was not one of such men. The Bacons had been a good choice to raise him, but they were quiet people of a temperament opposite to her own volatile nature. Francis was intelligent and had a love of theater and poetry, which Elizabeth too liked, while Essex was her good-looking fighting son as his father Leicester was. She would often refer to him as 'her wild horse'. Her sons were well matched in many ways, but true opposites. One could not be all things to all men without pretense it was said, but that had been her forte. She had been given no choice in life. Few knew her well, and he who once did best had now deserted her. She was a victim of circumstance and destiny and had made the best of it she could. Life was a battle, she surmised, but it was the very purpose of existence to survive.

# Chapter 29

London. November, 2014

Mrs G was standing on a busy north London street in Islington in front of a Starbucks coffee store, polystyrene cup of coffee in hand, looking up at an old, but impressive, structure the other side of the road. As the red double-decker buses rolled by in procession with a black London taxicab or two scattered among them, she could hardly believe what she was seeing. Here among the dust and fumes and noise of London's traffic was the headquarters of Elizabeth I's secret service, still standing to this day.

She had managed to contact the Marquis of Northampton with some difficulty. Had it not been for a good word from the Duke of Northumberland at Alnwyck she was unlikely ever to have been where she was standing now. But two days ago she had received an invitation from the Marquis to stay at his home of Compton Wynates for a night, and so had made haste not to lose the opportunity. She had arrived up the splendid drive to the house at dusk to be shown quickly to her room by a waiting servant who was expecting her arrival. Her chamber was furnished in the heavy drapes of the Elizabethan period, with a large, dark oak four-poster bed with capacious curtains.

She had been informed she was to attend drinks before dinner at eight thirty that evening and was free to wander the grounds beforehand if she wished. She had taken time to have a bath in a massive cast iron bathtub poised on feet carved as talons, so high she could hardly get in or out of it. The water trickled from the taps slowly in the manner only those who lived in old English homes thought adequate, as if water were in short supply.

When she came out of her room the light was dim in the long corridor leading to the top of the massive staircase between the upstairs gallery and the cavernous hall below. She had changed into her best evening outfit of a full length blue-grey form-fitting silk dress cut low over her still pert breasts and slim stomach. She thought herself unfortunate not to have found time to have had children of her own, but her figure was her reward. She looked a good deal younger than her years.

She wore a necklace Abe had bought for his first wife at a Christies auction sale of antique jewelry in 2007. It consisted of a gold chain heavily set with diamonds, rubies and pearls, and it had cost Abe half a million US dollars. Abe's wife Marilyn had not worn it as it had belonged to Marie Antoinette, the former Queen of France, beheaded by the guillotine, and she had thought it unlucky. Abe had mistakenly believed it had a connection to the Merovingians and on Marilyn's death insisted Mrs G should wear it, since he reasoned its legend would not bother her more practical mind. She had not since had many occasions to wear it, but tonight, not to be outdone in smart English society, she was to give it an airing. On her own neck be it, she grinned, as she looked in the mirror and tidied her hair.

In the hall a butler had shown her to a drawing room where she mingled with several other guests and waited for the Marquis to make his entrance. He was a tall, seemingly shy man, but by no means timid, with an obvious command of who he was and his position in life. He was a Grand Master of the Royal Masonic Lodge in England and a holder of many other splendid titles apart from that of Marquis. His latest interest was reported to be trans-humanism, in which life might be extended by a combination of artificial intelligence and nanotechnology. Compton Wynates he saw as his home, whereas his other, far larger, residence at Castle Ashby nearby was let out for weddings, conferences and other such events. The Marquis was in a black tie and dinner jacket, as were the other male guests, and they were gathered near a fireplace of immense proportions in which a small log fire gave off a minimum of heat.

Mrs G was pleased she did not look out of place among the others with whom she engaged in small talk over dinner, mainly about the arts in which the Marquis was interested. At the table, seating sixteen in high-backed Elizabethan chairs, sat the Marquis at its head. Behind him on the oak paneled wall hung the original of the best known painting of Henry VIII by Holbein. The Marquis had seated Mrs G on his left-hand side as a new guest since it appeared he had no current wife in attendance. He had married six times, and was possibly catching up with his now deceased father who was rumored to have exceeded him partner-wise. Mrs G had found him charming, but was unsure whether she had made a good impression. It was important that she did as the next day she would need his help with what she had come to find.

The Marquis teased Mrs G in front of the other guests, saying that her room was haunted, amongst the usual banter and inconsequential table chatter the English excelled in. He revealed with some amusement that a former ancestor some hundreds of years before had walled up a young woman to die in a room at the top of the house, whose ghastly screams could still occasionally be heard late at night. Consequently Mrs G had found little time to talk to the Marquis in a serious vein before dinner or after, since at the conclusion of the meal the women had moved to another room. The men remaining alone to partake in glasses of fine Port and Cuban cigars, leaving the female guests to amuse themselves.

Mrs G considered that the English of this class had never changed their ways and formalities since the days of Elizabeth I and probably well before that. None of the other guests had enquired why she was there since it was considered impolite to do so. The only interest in her had been her necklace, which had drawn their attention, but a combination of table etiquette and green eyed jealously had prevented them from asking its provenance, or its cost.

She had retired early to her room and tried hard to sleep in the knowledge of its resident ghost, who it was said would often walk the room crying out the name of some other lost soul.  She had tossed and turned for a while until she fell into a fitful sleep. She dreamt a weird dream in which she saw Abe and Ethan standing close by talking to one another. She heard Abe say "you must save the children" over and over, until they disappeared and she fell fully asleep. She was awakened by the shrill cries of peacocks, which wandered freely in the grounds of Compton Wynates, as they had done for centuries before.

At breakfast the Marquis had appeared with a friendly smile and suggested she spend the morning looking at copies of the Shakespeare First Folio of 1623 which had been magnificently reproduced from the originals of which only seven hundred and fifty had been printed. There were very few originals in private hands, but the Marquis was rumored to have one which was kept elsewhere in a secret location.

She had found the hand-tooled leather bound copies so heavy they were difficult for her to carry to the room's large refectory table. The Marquis came in for a while and, knowing of her interest, had indicated the coded double writing in the side columns and in between the lines, which was far easier to pick out in the larger print than anything she had seen before. He pointed out to her an example of the initials TT which seen together gave clues where to look for a coded message, particularly in the use of italics. Mrs G had understood that among other interpretations TT stood for "The Truth", so that by reading between the lines the truth of the hidden meaning could be found.

A variety of codes were used, often intermixed. The use of numbers gave an indication of where to look using a Time code. Henry IV for example, or Twelfth Night. The lack of a capital letter where it should be gave a clue as another code known as the Capital. A Bi-Lateral cipher was most used with italic letters in two different font types, which appeared with irregular frequency in the original editions of the Shakespeare plays, and not in those published later. It was important to know which code was being used in which play.

Some used symbols, others time, others anagrams, others places such as certain towns in Asia Minor and Greece. Equally the names of ancient gods had significance. Jove, Pluto, Apollo, Vulcan, Minerva, Juno and Neptune. Words used needed often to be matched with a similar word to give meaning to the code used. Some needed to be found in verse and continued through various plays and other works to unravel their final meaning. The whole undertaking was a maze of astounding versatility and ingenuity.

Much of this Mrs G knew from her great-grandmother's work on the Shakespeare ciphers, but to see it at first hand in a large, relatively easy to read format gave it a whole new meaning. She was impressed with the Marquis's own knowledge of the ciphers. She had used her married surname in obtaining her invitation and had not given the Marquis any clue of her Gallup family background. He had received her on the recommendation of the Duke of Northumberland as to her interest in genetic codes. Once he had given her half-an-hour of his time, and being impressed with her enthusiasm, the Marquis had left her to her own devices cautioning her to handle the pages with care. He had not returned until midday, at which point he proposed that she should go by private car to her hotel in London which he had arranged with a driver waiting outside, and that in two days' time she should meet him at a rendezvous in Islington in London, where she now stood, and where he had felt she might learn more of interest to her.

Dodging the heavy traffic, Mrs G crossed the tarmac road, which four hundred years ago would have been a dirt track with coaches and horses plying back and forth between London and the north. She pulled hard on the handle of an old iron bell pull outside the door of the hundred foot high building, whose red brickwork was showing signs of wear and tear. She could hear no bell from inside and pulled again. The place looked as if it was permanently closed. As she stood wondering what to do the door was suddenly opened by a small blonde woman, who announced herself as the Marquis' assistant.

"Please come with me," she said, and moved rapidly up the steps of several flights of old wooden stairs indented and worn from centuries of use. At what seemed to be the top Mrs G was ushered into an oak paneled room with small mullion windows affording a fairly good view of London to the south, although now blocked in parts by office towers, and a scattering of church spires from the past. "His Lordship will be with you shortly," said the female assistant, and left her alone in the room.

It had an aura she could feel. Not just a sense of smell coming from its old musty walls and through creaking floorboards, but of those who had been there before her over so many past eras. She seemed somehow to smell the scent of their bodies and of their clothes. A musky combination of leather, flax, body odor and cigar smoke; but perhaps it was all just in her imagination. She was looking at some carvings in the cornices next to the ceiling as the Marquis came in. He gave her a warm smile.

"I see you are studying the symbols," he said.

Mrs G nodded. "Yes, they're Freemasonry ones aren't they? I understand you're the head of the Masons in England? Should I call you your Lordship?" she enquired politely.

The Marquis smiled again. "No, no, please call me Spenny, other people do. It's an abbreviation of Spencer, a family name.

"The building you are in is Canonbury Tower built by one of my ancestors. It was often used by the first Queen Elizabeth, and was rented out to Francis Bacon in his later years. The Bacon Society of his present day enthusiasts meets here from time to time. I consider myself a custodian in much the same way as I see my role in British Masonry. If you will excuse me, I will let my assistant fill in the rest of the story. I have a sore throat today and I have told it many times, so she will tell it better than me. I will join you again when you are finished. Please ask her any questions you like."

The blonde assistant, who was obviously well accustomed to showing visitors around, immediately took up the story.
"Bacon instructed that his original works and the clues to the codes in them be hidden in various places for posterity. This tower was said to be one of them, as was his home at Gorhambury, which sadly is now a ruin. The panels in this room once concealed secret codes used by Elizabeth I. She would meet here with her most trusted servants including Francis Bacon, and her astrologer Sir John Dee, who were cryptologists of the highest level. They were both of exceptional intelligence and in Bacon's younger days they practised alchemy and other experiments as their hobbies at John Dee's Mortlake home at Richmond. Dee was said to have known the secrets of Merlin, King Arthur's astrologer and magician, from a thousand years before. Among their revelations was the ancient code for the Universe. 10x10x10. John Dee's own code name, believe it or not, was 007, which was copied for the James Bond stories by their author Ian Fleming who was himself a secret agent in World War Two."

Mrs G's mind drifted and she imagined the scene at Mortlake. The ever curious young Francis walking the short walk from his home to meet with the much older Dee in his star-spangled robes and long white beard down to his waist. Their attempts to move objects and to communicate by paranormal means had been recorded by Dee using mind-altering psychedelic herbs or psilocybin mushrooms. Mrs G had been through similar scenarios with Abe under controlled conditions in his quest for scientific advances, often with new manufactured substances now available.

The chemical drug LSD had been found in an experiment at the Swiss Sandoz laboratories in 1938 and used later by the American CIA as a truth serum. The hallucinogenic effect of the lysergic acid diethylamide had been little different from the use of the seeds of the commonly available plant of Morning Glory when mixed with a species known as Rivea Corymbosa, used long ago for sacramental purposes by the Aztecs. The secret, as Mrs G well knew, was in the blending. Too much and you might jump out of the window thinking you were an angel. Too little and you stayed with your feet on the ground. In general people were reluctant to encounter their inhibitions, and often by closing their minds to new visions instead met their worst fears. Mrs G wondered what magic weed Elizabeth may have partaken of with her chosen few in this very room. She walked across the creaking oak floorboards to look through the small bottle glass windows which overlooked the old spires and new towers of the now vast City of London of ten million or more people. The assistant joined her to continue her talk.

"The view from this room once commanded a clear vista of London as it was then with only some two hundred thousand people, against fifty times more than that today. It was from here the queen started her own secret service. Lord Walsingham – publicly recognized as the English spymaster then, never came here, as Elizabeth's maxim was "Trust no-one," including him! The Queen preferred her own intimate ring of spies, among them Francis Bacon's adoptive brother Anthony who doubled up as a Foreign Office diplomat."

The blonde assistant continued her surmise. "It may well have been from here that the secret ciphers of Mary Queen of Scots were decoded in letters to the French plotting to dethrone her sister Elizabeth, for which Mary was finally put to death. The coded name for the meeting place we are in now was Room 40, and the name has been in use ever since in the British secret service. It is possible to imagine those of the past meeting here discussing the coming Spanish invasion and how to counter it. John Dee would have studied the stars and the tides to see how the English might best defeat the Spanish in the prevailing conditions. The English used their fire ships to send the Spanish packing with a strong gale behind them. Earth, Water, Wind and Fire. Masonic symbols, and the Devil's too! It was the last time the Spanish tried to conquer England. They saw their defeat as divine providence, in which the English had the Devil on their side; not to be ignored!"

As the assistant spoke Spenny came back into the room and hearing the rhetoric, gave a thought to the good and plentiful years from that time on which had benefited his own family. England had not been troubled again from invasion until the time of Napoleon's attempt some two hundred years later, and of Hitler's operation Sea Lion, both of which had failed due to bad weather and the command of the

English fleet over the tricky waters of the English Channel.

The first Earl of Northampton, Spenny told her as they descended the stairs, although twenty years older than Francis Bacon, had worked closely with him on his book "*The Advancement of Learning.*" The first Earl was suspected of being a crypto-Catholic but it had done nothing to damage their relationship since sectarian beliefs were of little consequence to Francis and his all-encompassing Masonic views. What was preached was not always practised in their circle, and Francis had shared confidences with the Earl and entrusted him with works for his keeping.

Her visit over, Spenny bid her goodbye with such charm that only later had she realized she had been politely and royally dismissed, as no doubt had others in the past who had stumbled by chance onto secrets deliberately concealed from common knowledge. Opening the door into the busy street Mrs G once more felt she had been transported in time yet in which little had changed regarding human behavior.

# Chapter 30

**Savoy Hotel, London. November, 2014**

Mrs G returned to her room at the Savoy that evening, highly excited by the day's events. The fact that the ciphers were sequenced through many of the plays confirmed that both ciphers and plays must have originated from the same scribe, even though at times the plays had slightly varied styles. It was too nebulous to believe that various writers could have shared such complex codes across a variety of works to give them sufficient clarification of meaning as an end result. There needed to be a mastermind behind all the plays and poems. She thought it likely that the plays either reflected the mood of the same writer at the time, or that the writer had cleverly pretended different styles to give the impression of different writers so as to divert attention from the principal author. Overall she felt the underlying modus operandi was the same. As she was to discover later a cipher from the Shakespeare Quartos printed in 1619 had read:

*"Watching the storms but saying no unmeaning word, I put forth my secret letters."*

*"It may be no eye will note, no hand will aid --- If this be true I die and make no sign."*

Another signed by Francis Bacon:

*"Life is but one short race; it doth not twice reward us."*

And another:

*"So this Cipher shall be used to give my ill and tortured thoughts expression."*

And in Richard II:

*"Only quick sight could see where my decipherer hath been directed....*

*Induced by word or sign.... a faithful man who is to bring this history to that vast world which lieth dreamless, far, far off, as a thing apart."*

Mrs G's thoughts were broken when her mobile rang bringing her quickly back to earth. It was Gerry on the line. She felt bad she had not called the kids recently, but thought they should be okay in Esther's capable hands. She had exchanged brief text messages, but preferred not to have to give a date for her return, since she was still unsure when it might be, other than at latest by Christmas.

"Yo!" yelled Gerry "How's it going, Mrs G? Did you find any treasure yet?"

"No need to shout, the line is fine," she said. "No treasure yet but I have discovered the original 007, who was a spy for Queen Elizabeth I. He was called John Dee. I am uncovering a whole world undiscovered for many hundreds of years, in which the actions of people were concealed at the highest level. Only the paranoid survived, and they knew all the tricks to do so. What they did to their enemies was gruesome. Knowing your blood-thirsty mind, I expect you would have loved it all. "I feel certain now that my hero Francis Bacon was the writer of the Shakespeare plays, as my great-grandmother always maintained. I saw the same codes she saw written in the original works."

As she talked Mrs G thought how pleased her great-grandparents would be with her when her book was published and it vindicated their previous research. Despite their being dead for many years she sensed somehow that they would know, wherever their souls were now. Her feeling was instinctive. Her great-grandmother's paper on the *Shakespeare Ciphers* had been derided or ignored in her lifetime by the English, who preferred to stubbornly hold the view that William Shakespeare the Bard of Avon was the man they had been led to believe was a genius. Bacon it seemed had out-fooled them all, but for much longer than even he had guessed, or had even wanted

"What is clear now," she continued telling Gerry, "is that Bacon created the plays with the help of a team of people he assembled to educate the English people then, and for posterity. He was the team leader, the Master, who set out a path to follow and gave them the use of his home as a meeting place to express their thoughts and minds freely. Between them they helped Bacon to redesign English speech into an international language, inventing many thousands of new words and expressions used today. He wrote a book, *The New Atlantis*, which was a prescription for the laws and freedoms in America which have ever since been the beacon for democracy the world over."

"So are you saying Shakespeare was a front man? Why couldn't

Bacon say he wrote them?" said Gerry doubtfully.

"He couldn't because it was Catch 22 for him. He was a royal prince next in line to be king, but couldn't say so on pain of death by his mother. So instead he used people he knew as masks to say what he wanted to say, but could not openly do himself. Not just writers who helped him, but actors in his plays, and others who were never to know who wrote the works they were paid to put their name to. He was often critical of his mother which was a danger to him, but the allegories he used were smartly done so that only a few in the know would recognize them. Within the lines that he wrote in his plays and poems and other books he inserted his own codes, which put together told his whole life story. It was as if he had kept a secret diary but put it into a parable of verse and words disguising it, to be found one day in time after his death.

"The Shakespeare name was pure camouflage. What an adventure my great-grandmother must have had, as I am now! Bacon was a great guy and a good one," Mrs G went on. "Sadly his Mom was suspicious of his motives and even thought he might want to make himself King of America which he had helped found as a British dominion. He was in reality the Prince of Wales, just as the present Prince Charles of England is today. Bacon wrote a disguised verse about himself in a book called "*The Arrangement of Paris*." I have the verse here. It reads:

*"In sorrow we set words herein; we know not their fate nor ours, in a future near or far; for we are in truth the luckless Prince of Wales."*

"Rather like Jesus, Bacon had his disciples. I feel sure they were both psychic, just as was your grandmother Marilyn, who was scared of her own powers and tried to deny them. I think you and Marianne both have a touch of them too, as I feel sure did Mary Magdalene. But there is more yet to find out. How are you and Marianne? Is everything okay?"

Mrs G knew that Gerry had wrestled with religion at school, concerned with its various concepts from the whole A-Z of Aryanism, to Buddha, to the Zoroastrians and their sun worship. He was still on a voyage of discovery as to what he should believe or not. The Creationist idea of intelligent design which was taught in some American schools in the US Bible Belt had been around for a while. It was enjoying a recovery, trying to reconcile the birth of mankind as given variously in the Bible of some five to ten thousand years ago, against increasing scientific evidence of man's first existence millions of years before from his origin in primeval slime.

Creationism had been labeled a pseudo-science, and in dispute were other involved concepts of a common descent of all living organisms and the origin of the Universe on which the separate proponents were diametrically opposed. Mrs G thought that, although the million year theory was correct, man's intelligence above that of other animals was a far more recent event. It was more in line with the start of the construction of the pyramids by the Sumerians and Nubians, and the Egyptians who had enslaved the Nubians to build them and used their knowledge. Sumer and Nubia were said to have been the cradle of civilization. Before them only cavemen existed as far as could be found, with no architecture of any kind to show for themselves.

At the time of Francis Bacon's birth the Church's Old Testament teaching in Genesis of Earth's divine creation was widely believed. It was not until the fear of condemnation by the Catholic Church could be safely ignored that early scientists could challenge the belief that God created the world uniquely for man alone. Due to Catholic opposition the careers of Copernicus and Galileo had both ended abruptly for saying that the Earth was round and circled the Sun.

Fortunately for England, as Mrs G now realized, due to the banishment of the Catholics by Henry VIII and Elizabeth, science had started to speak its mind and flourish without danger, which it could not then safely do in Catholic Europe. This freedom had put England on a fast track of scientific discovery ahead of all other nations.

Francis Bacon was among the first with John Dee to be recognized for scientific research. They had helped form Gresham College in 1597 as the forerunner of "The Royal Society of London for Improving Natural Knowledge," which was the first formally recognized scientific body in the world. Famed since as "The Royal Society" it was still in existence in the 21st century and to which it was an honor to be made a member. Its long list of past members included most of world's most eminent scientists. Isaac Newton had been an early one, and had carried on the new science of astronomy from the discoveries of John Dee.

Abe had in his lifetime been invited to attend some of the Royal Society's meetings, which had delighted him since he was flattered with the respect it showed for his work on plant genetics and mutations. It was a shame he had died before he had the time to teach Gerry the things he knew, Mrs G considered, but they had spent some quality time together, and Gerry was one of those boys who was quick on the uptake, but would keep things to himself. Perhaps he knew more than he let on.

From the age of ten Gerry had read history and the sciences widely and had taken an interest in the origins of stars and the universe. He was a sci-fi movie fan often asking Mrs G questions on astronomy and the occult. It pleased, but worried, Mrs G at the same time since she understood the danger of misconception in any explanation of the spiritual world.

As for Marianne she was no problem. She enjoyed her tennis and went horseback riding at the local stables where she kept her chestnut filly, her parents having encouraged her to ride from an early age. She was friendly and outgoing as her grandmother had been and had more friends than Gerry, enjoying art and writing poetry. She also liked music and languages, could draw well, and was beginning to take an interest in cryptology which Mrs G encouraged her in. No trouble there Mrs G had reckoned. They were both bright kids with a good understanding of what made the world go round. Their parents' death had brought adulthood to them faster than might otherwise have been the case. No harm in that, she felt.

"We had some wacko call at the house today," said Gerry said, still shouting. "Some guy who spoke to Marianne from the intercom at the gate and asked if he could help with gardening. He asked about Grandpa's plants."

"Just ignore anyone like that," Mrs G replied, "but tell Esther to be sure not to let anyone in she doesn't know and make sure to put the alarms on at night. Please ask her not to give my mobile number to anyone no matter what they may say. Call me if it happens again and I'll contact the Boston Police. Your granddad gave a lot to their charities and they will be helpful if we ask them. Make sure the greenhouse doors stay closed in this cold weather to keep the heat in. I don't want you going in there touching things. What you don't know can be dangerous. I need to stay on in Europe, as I have more to do here."

Mrs G was concerned as she ended the call as she felt she should have been with the children, but the culmination of her endeavors was at last in her grasp and she did not intend to let go now. She was on a do-or-die mission, as the annoying cough she experienced daily sometimes reminded her. It hampered her and she tried to shake it off.

She wondered if it had anything to do with Abe's death. It seemed he had been poisoned and died rapidly from toxic ingestion, possibly by drinking one of his experiments, or even by touch or breathing. Poisoning had often been a risk he took personally with his new formulas rather than endanger anyone else. She could think of no other reason, or that anyone might want to kill him. Still it was suspicious since he always exercised great caution with his trials. She remembered that she had touched his cheek as she bent to look at him and the small line of still sticky blood that had run from the corner of his mouth. She had only done so momentarily and soon after she had washed her hands as a precaution.

She dismissed the thought from her mind, as the findings of the specialist she had seen in London had not been conclusive enough to pinpoint a cause. She had finished the new booster course of antibiotics he had given her and apart from tiredness at the end of her busy days it was overcome by her overall excitement in her discoveries, and she did not feel that unwell. She had noticed recently a spot of blood in her sputum when she had coughed over the sink and had watched it slowly curl away with the water down the drain. As for the bad luck associated with Marie Antoinette's necklace she did not give it a thought.

# Chapter 31

Elizabeth Queen of England sits surrounded by her courtiers and ladies in attendance. Now sixty-eight years of age she has chosen for the occasion of a dance in her honor a long flowing velvet gown of incarnadine red. A cream colored lace ruffle covers her now wrinkled neck and shoulders and freckled skin. In the cleft of her small sunken bust hangs a large pendant medallion of rubies set in gold. Copious puffed sleeves, slashed with colored silks and threaded with pearls and precious stones bolster her now skinny arms. Silver threaded gloves enclose her thin but long elegant hands.
Her own famously red hair, now thinning fast, is concealed by a wig tinted with henna dye and frizzled in the fashion of the day. The wig, one of many in her wardrobe, is decorated with a multitude of grey and white pearls and blue sapphires. The high cheekbones of her face blanched luminous white with foundation made from egg white, poppy seed and alum; in contrast her lips painted red with cochineal. In her younger days her dress for a dance would have been cut lower on her bosom supported by cups in the bodice of her corsage to show the nipples of her breast as a sign of virginity. Although still as slim and wiry as she has ever been, the outward physical charms with which Elizabeth had once mischievously courted many foreign admirers for her hand in marriage were now wanting.

The flirtatious days of dancing the night away are long gone and she signals her minstrels to start the music by the wave of her hand. She sits looking as her younger courtiers take the floor to dance the energetic Galliard with its whirling leaps and bounds and remembers her dances with her virile husband Robert Leicester. He has been dead now for a dozen years, and Elizabeth shakes her head to rid herself of his memory which alternately angers and saddens her. He was a rascal at heart she decides, but perhaps that was part of what she had loved in him before he had become untrustworthy to her with his various amours.

She had been infatuated with him from her first meeting in the Tower, and had bestowed every gift on the man her Court knew as a blithe idol. It was no secret he visited the Queen in her bedchamber every night. Leicester had played Elizabeth's game from the start, ridding himself of his legal wife Amy Robsart, and going along with Elizabeth's coquettish fantasies to gain himself fame and fortune, until he had in time played his own games without her.

When she had learned of his secret marriage to Lettice, Elizabeth had been furious. Since Elizabeth had banned the disclosure of her own earlier marriage to Leicester she could not now disclaim his to Lettice; but she could extract her revenge. One day when Leicester had turned his back on her at her Court she had publicly slapped his face, cursing his name, and after he returned from his unsuccessful command in Ireland she had cut him off reducing him to near penury. When he died from poisoning in 1588 Elizabeth seized all of his estate and possessions as if they were her own.

By now Elizabeth had few favorites remaining. One was her trusted longtime friend Walter Raleigh, who was to be at the dance this evening, and she looked forward to his arrival. It was the etiquette of the Court that no-one should attend an event to which she gave her presence by arriving after her entrance but, just as her annoyance rose, Sir Walter strode through the dancers and bowed low in front of her. He was now in his late forties and doffed his hat to show the curls of his once fair but now graying hair.

Elizabeth's eyes brightened at the sight of Raleigh, and forgiving his late coming, she clapped her hands in pleasure. "Do not stand on ceremony. Prithee come sit beside me and tell me your news," she exclaimed. "What delights can you relate me today, Sirrah?"

Raleigh had done much for queen and country in his lifetime. Helping to found her American dominions, while bringing back many valuable discoveries to her realm, and treasures to fill its coffers. Among all her subjects she trusted his loyalty the most and she had awarded him with a knighthood at an early age from whence he was known as Sir Walter Raleigh at Court. He and Francis had done well in populating the new world of America with settlers from England seeking their fortunes. The laws that Francis had set for their governance had met with little resistance, having ensured good order was maintained by the few soldiers installed there. The law-abiding citizens of her new American realm would set a good example for the future, or so Elizabeth believed.

Sir Walter's countenance was grave and he requested an immediate private audience with the Queen, but she was in no mood to grant it. "The nature of bad news infects the teller," she commented. "Tonight is one of festivity. Let there be no talk of the affairs of state. Come let us dance together to show the world we are carefree. If music be the food of love, play on," she exclaimed gaily to her musicians as she rose to take the floor and the tune was quickly changed to the more sedate slow dance of the Pavane to suit her taste.

Raleigh looked perturbed. He had an urgent message for his Queen, which could not wait. He had heard rumor of a coup against Her Majesty and had come to warn her. Delays had dangerous ends he told her. He insisted on speaking, but she would not listen. She had waited to dance and Sir Walter was to be her partner. She had expected her son Robert to be present and to dance with her and make her laugh, but he had not come, and it angered her. He was probably at the theater or gambling on bear-baiting or cockfighting with his friend Henry Wriothesley, the Third Earl of Southampton, and had forgotten her. Although she loved Robert dearly, he was headstrong and did not always please her. Her nose wrinkled in petulance.

Elizabeth had heard there was a play being staged at the Globe theater that night, but knew nothing of the author. She believed Francis had long been concerned with his legal career and works of a more serious vein. In his youthful days Francis had written *The Comedy of Errors* and some poetry to please her, but she was not aware of any more from his pen. Perhaps Francis had adopted the customary practice of gentlemen writers of paying masques or vizards, as they were known, to disguise his authorship, but if so, she had not been made aware of it.

She was, however, cognizant of a number of past plays under the name of Pallas Athene. That Francis and his friends had taken Pallas as their muse had delighted her; not least for the poems Francis had once written her in the name of Pallas and sent to her out of his devotion. Elizabeth had not for a moment appreciated the extent to which the Good Pens of Francis at Twickenham were a powerhouse of published works of books and pamphlets of all descriptions to advance Francis' ideas and projects or that they still included the production of plays.

Francis himself had funded a network of printers and had his own printing plant owned under an assumed name. Its output of works were published under a variety of pseudonyms, some who were themselves writers of their own works, such as Marlowe, Jonson and Nashe, while other names were bought for a specific purpose, such as those of Greene, Lyly and Peele, to disguise the real author. At their core was Francis, and Twickenham Hall, also known by the Good Pens as the 'House of Philosophy'.

Life at Twickenham at Francis' expense had drawn to it many good minds, including some revolutionary contributors, as well as hangers on who saw their host's hospitality as a right of personal indulgence of expression. Wine and tobacco had flowed freely, despite Francis' own objections to drunkenness, a custom more honored in the breach than in the observance by some of his friends.

Many of the themes of the plays concerned amours. *"The Shepherd's Calendar,"* a candid and cheeky story of twelve months in a young shepherd's life, had been written when Francis was eighteen, under the masked name of Edmund Spenser. It mixed a moral theme with a mocking bitterness of romance, as befitted Francis' mood at the time after his affair with Marguerite had ended. It also reflected the philosophical views of a literary group formed by Francis' father Leicester known as the Areopagus, a name previously in use by the Greek Arians, and their similar beliefs to those of Jesus and Mary Magdalene. The play was evidence of Leicester's involvement in guiding Francis towards his artistic and philosophical expression from an early age.

The London house in which Leicester lived was built on the Temple site of the Knights Templar whose past influence at all times ran through the thoughts and purposes of Leicester, and those of Elizabeth herself. Edmund Spenser had been introduced to Francis by Leicester and he had later lent his name as a mask to the famous *"Faerie Queen"* poem of 1596 by Francis written to restore his mother's affections for him after she had banned him from her Court. In it he flatters her as *Gloriana* by paying tribute to her heritage from King Arthur and his Knights of the Round Table. The poem was first published six times without attribution to an author.

The poem *Venus and Adonis* first published in 1593, also without attribution, received notoriety for its intimate depiction of a passionate affair between unnamed lovers. Most likely by an older woman of a young man in sexual role reversals, reflecting the seduction of Francis by Marguerite of Navarre. Some have claimed since that it was a tale of the seduction of Francis' young and beautiful friend Henry Wriothesley. If so then it would certainly have meant it was not written by William Shakespeare the Bard of Avon, any more than were any of the other sonnets allegedly written by him. Along with the comedy play *Love's Labour's Lost* first performed in 1597, both are more likely to describe Francis' youthful romance in Paris.

*Love's Labour's Lost* was a mischievous play about a mythical King of Navarre, who fasts for three years to forswear sex, when a group of women appear outside his castle and play erotic tricks to entice him into sexual adventure. Once more it is only too likely that Francis had in mind Marguerite, whose husband having first rejected her for a favorite mistress was now engaged as King of France in homosexual affairs with both of Marguerite's two brothers. A scandal which Marguerite herself had revealed publicly and for which she suffered house arrest for many years as a result.

As for Francis, he would never forget his young love Marguerite, but the flames of his passion had turned first to dying embers and then to ashes. By now he had set his eyes on the young, beautiful and extremely wealthy Elizabeth Hatton. Romance had taken on a new practicality for Francis. He considered his new choice would be seen in a better light by the Queen.

Elizabeth had been pleased with Francis' artistic nature, but it was his success in his profession of the law of which she most approved. It was as much for his own good as hers since she needed trustworthy legal advice on many matters. Francis had also made a start with his friend Robert Fludd on publishing the New English Bible which had left little or no time for him to write plays, or so the Queen believed. Apart from a leading role in the English Parliament of which he had been a member since twenty-one, Francis was also a close member of the Queen's Secret Service.

It was a pity Francis had not found the time to marry, Elizabeth fancied. It seemed that after his affair in Paris, over twenty years ago now, he was more devoted to his work and male friends; but there was still time yet, she reflected. It was just as well he should leave marriage until his career was firmly fixed, as a wife might influence him other than as Elizabeth wished. It was not that she was unpleased by Francis' devotion, but at times it demanded more than she could return. Even so, she was easily flattered, and particularly liked the last lines of one sonnet which Francis had composed for her starting with the words:

*"Seated between the Old World and the New,*
*A Land there is no other Land may touch,*
*Where reigns a Queen in Peace and Honour true,*
*Stories or Fables do describe no such."*

And ended with the lines:

*"No Age hath ever Wits refined so far,*
*And yet she calms them by her Policy:*
*To Her thy Son must make his sacrifice*
*If he will have the Morning of his Eyes.*

Francis had especially written this for Elizabeth to remind her of his love for her as her true son.

For the play of Richard II he had composed verse that he felt sure would delight her in a mixture of flattery and caution in its intimation of her own successful reign over England.

*"This Royal Throne of Kings, this sceptr'd Isle,*
*This Earth of Majesty, this seat of Mars,*
*This other Eden, demi-Paradise;*
*This Fortress, built by Nature for herself,*
*Against Infection and the Hand of War;*
*This happy breed of Men, this little World;*
*This precious Stone, set in a Silver Sea,*
*Which serves it in the Office of a Wall,*
*Or as a moat defensive to a House,*
*Against the envy of less happier Lands.*
*This blessed plot, this earth, this realm, this England.*
*This nurse, this teeming womb of royal kings,*
*Feared by their breed and famous by their birth,*
*Renowned for their deed as far from home,*
*For Christian service and true chivalry,*
*As in the sepulchre of stubborn Jewry,*

*Of the world's ransom, blessed Mary's son,*
*This Land of such dear souls, this dear, dear Land,*
*Dear for her reputation through the World.*

Despite her clever wiles as a politician, Elizabeth was prone to mercurial mood swings and her affection for Francis over recent years was not as it once had been. Francis' ambitions in Parliament had on occasions gone too far for her liking. He had spoken up for its members having a greater say in the running of the country. In this he had overreached himself at times and seemed to harbor ambitions to place himself at its head. No doubt, Elizabeth thought, to compensate himself for her refusal of his claim to her throne. Throughout her life she stood on guard against any plans her sons might have which might threaten her hold on the Crown.

Francis' new ideas of democratic rule were anathema to Elizabeth since her ancestors had ruled with absolute power. How could commoners command the same respect as the elite of Europe from whose blood she came, with their intellect derived from a thousand years of genetic ancestry? She had been infuriated by one incident in which Francis had led Parliamentary opposition to her demands for funds she had needed urgently to arm against a Spanish invasion plot, and she had considered his role against her both arrogant and naive.

Democracy was not a notion which Elizabeth was happy to entertain, especially when it did not advantage her. Being seen to have concern for her subjects was one thing; allowing them a say in proceedings was altogether another.

She had always ruled with an iron rod and she had a while ago decided to teach Francis a lesson by cutting off her allowance to him. He could stand on his own feet and come to terms with the real world, she had decided, and without the financial support she had given him all his life. Neither did she intend to assist him in obtaining further positions of power. Power and money came together as he must now learn. He would need to find out more for himself about what it took to be successful in the manipulative art of politics. Half way through his life, now in his mid-thirties, it was no longer a time for innocence.

Her actions having given Francis food for thought, she had slowly brought him back into her favor as he in turn behaved as she wanted, but she had not relented in her decision to cut off his funds. She had not received the same devotion from Robert, but as she saw him as having a lesser intellect, and being impetuous by nature, she was more forgiving of him. Besides he had the handsome looks of his father and had inherited her own often fractious temperament, which she understood better than Francis' calm patience.

As the dance came to an end, and knowing that to persist he might well offend Elizabeth's mood, Sir Walter held his tongue. After all, what he had heard was Court gossip, and if it was not true he did not want to be the bearer of the bad news that it was Robert Essex of whom it was said that he was conspiring to claim her throne. He did not trust Essex whom he saw as an impulsive character, but he was conscious of his closeness to the Queen as her rumored son, or even as her lover as was whispered at Court. If the news of Essex's threat to the Queen was false, Raleigh would put himself in danger of losing all favor with Her Majesty. Her age had, if anything, increased the temper she showed at anything amiss. He did not relish being shot as the messenger, and so he discreetly kept his silence.

# Chapter 32

**The Globe Theater, London. 7th February, 1601**

The Globe Theater was built almost entirely from wood and stood on the South bank of the Thames at Southwark. It was one of several theaters in London built in recent years thanks to the influence of the Earl of Leicester and under the auspices of Elizabeth in their joint advancement of English culture. The Globe had been financed mainly by James Burbage, who was a prime mover in the English theater as an organizer and promoter of theatrical works and shows. He was a friend both of Francis' father, and of Francis' own close colleague, the writer Ben Jonson, who had helped raise funds for the Globe, as too had several actors who performed there. James Burbage had died only recently and his son Richard had taken over its activities.

The Globe's famed rotunda shape enabled a mainly standing audience to view a performance from almost any position around the raised semicircular stage. Covered private side boxes at upper levels gave the nobility and the wealthy weather protection from a large circular opening in its roof and from the often rowdy audience at ground level. On occasions it would be used for bear-baiting and other more bawdy entertainment than on show this evening.

Although having been commissioned three years earlier by the Duke of Northumberland for private showing, the staging of the play tonight had been specially requested by Henry the Earl of Southampton. The drama to be unfolded to the general public for the first time was that of a previous King of England, Richard II, a believer in his divine right to rule who having been betrayed by a trusted friend, had lost his crown.

The curtain closed on the final act as the audience rose in an agitated state. From a private box two noblemen went to leave together. One, Sir Edward Coke, a notable Member of Parliament and lawyer, now nearly fifty years of age, whispers to his friend. "Make quick your exit, Sir. The downfall of King Richard as portrayed here tonight is a deliberate omen for her Majesty's ears. Once she is to learn of this, best not be seen to be as any part of it, lest she should act against those she sees as conspiring against her."

"Indeed Sir," replies a slightly built man with the stooped shoulder of a hunchback. It is Robert Cecil, who as a youth many years before had taken pleasure in Francis' embarrassment at Court on being teased as to his birth. "And more so if the conspirators were to be seen as friends of our mutual adversary the Lord Essex." The two exchange knowing glances and disappear quickly among the crowds leaving the theatre.

## Essex House (formerly Leicester House), London. 1st February, 1601

Robert Essex and Henry Southampton had spent the week before the showing of the play of Richard II at Essex House, on the site of the old Temple home of the Knights Templar. Elizabeth had granted the house to Robert after the death of his father and he had changed its name to his own. There they had been discussing and rehearsing with a group of similarly minded nobles the actions they should take when news of the play's performance reached the Queen.

Southampton's purpose in staging Richard II publicly had been to raise general alarm about a Catholic plot afoot to dethrone the Queen, led by Robert Cecil, and in doing so to raise the estimation of Essex in the eyes of both the public and the Queen herself. To defeat the plot it needed a well-executed plan which would involve separating Cecil from the Queen's own guard of soldiers under his command long enough for Essex, and a coterie of Southampton's friends, to present their petition to the Queen for Cecil's arrest. As the Queen put much reliance on Cecil as her advisor, any action taken against him might be seen by her as being against herself, and so the plan required delicate handling. It had been decided that Essex should meet with Cecil to find a way to put him off his guard. A pretext needed be found for the two to meet.

Several days before the staging of Richard II at the Globe, Robert
Essex was in a coach and pair sitting beside Robert Cecil whom he
had arranged to meet under the pretense of assisting the advancement
of Francis Bacon in Parliament. Cecil's power was at Court with the
Queen, whereas his lawyer friend Coke had great influence in
Parliament, thanks to Cecil's support. Between them they held sway
over much of what passed under the nose of the Queen in their
knowledge of her paranoia that her sons might wish to usurp her,
which anxiety of mind Cecil had long encouraged.

Coke's Parliamentary position as Attorney General had been hard
won against Francis' own desire for the post. Coke knew from Cecil
that Francis was Essex's older brother, as Cecil had long ago been
informed by his father, Lord Burleigh, now recently deceased.
Burleigh had for many years been the Queen's trusted advisor as
Secretary of State; his wife being the sister of Lady Anne Bacon who
had raised Francis. The Cecils had long known the secret of Francis'
true birth and also that of Robert Essex.

Cecil had known Francis since their teenage years and, thanks to his
father's past influence, he now held the important role of Lord Privy
Seal giving him direct access to the Monarch. He had long been
jealous of Elizabeth's sons and had successfully persuaded the Queen
to pass over Francis for several distinguished roles in her
grant. Cecil and Coke had their own ideas as to whom they wished
to succeed to the English throne after the death of Elizabeth, and they
did not include Bacon or Essex, with whom they knew they would
not find favor.

"Pray, tell me of Francis' desires?" quipped Cecil to Essex, tongue in
cheek as the coach slowed, since he had no intention of assisting
Francis. "I have great respect for his intellect and duties to Her
Majesty. You have my word I shall do all I can for his
advancement." Cecil was suspicious of the reason Essex had wanted
to see him, since they rarely talked. Essex tugged hard at the end of
his fine, red goatee beard. He had a long face with a long and noble
nose with a pronounced curve in the middle as did his mother the
Queen. He needed to make his point as the coach was nearing the end

of its journey.

"I am sure you know of Francis' integrity and desire to please the Queen. His loyalty and dedication deserves reward which I would be obliged you should recommend to Her Majesty. The Court is awash nowadays with talk of conspiracy and Her Majesty needs those around her she can trust. It is my intent that with some of my noble friends we should pledge our troth to her. In your position as her advisor I am sure you will agree that such an assurance would be welcomed by her. I would ask that you formally arrange our call on her," he added, seeking Cecil's reaction.

"Perhaps, Sir. I cannot see that she should need such assurance from your good self, but by all means pay visit on Her Majesty. I will ensure no harm will come of it. I will instruct the Captain of her Guard to make welcome your arrival if you should give me good notice. For myself I have planned a visit to my home in the countryside of Kent for some days with my falconer. He has secured a new goshawk I wish to put to the test. She will be hungry for prey in this cold weather and I should see some good sporting kills from her, if she is as fast and fierce as I am told." As they descended from the coach, Cecil went to shake the hand of Essex.

"Rest assured. I will do all in my power to assist Francis as you request. Meantime please keep me informed of your intended visit on Her Majesty."

Cecil had been in politics far too long not to see through the artless guile of Essex. He would be sure to double the Queen's Guard, increase rumors of an attack on her person, and postpone his planned trip to Kent. There would be greater sport to be found in London where Essex would be likely to take the lure more surely than the new goshawk. Her hunger could wait. Cecil relished his own feast ahead, long awaited as it had been, and now chance had come his way.

# Chapter 33

Francis had still not received any form of appellation from the Queen. Robert's title of Lord Essex had been inherited when he was eleven years old on the death of his foster father Walter Devereux First Earl of Essex, whose estate he had also inherited with a substantial income. Since Francis' funding from his mother had been terminated he had run up large debts which he was having to pay off from his not unsubstantial, but still insufficient rewards from his legal work.

He was not accustomed to living economically and his income from his law practice was fast swallowed up in the running of Twickenham Hall. He had funded it largely for the use of his friends the Good Pens and their activities, which Francis increasingly had less time for. The plays they put on under his leadership had a short life and revenue from them, although adequate to give some reward to their revolving circle of writers, had been more a labor of love for them than of a living.

There had been no surplus to finance the upkeep of the Hall and its grounds which were deteriorating in condition. Yet in one respect it was the estate at Twickenham which might resolve Francis' problems since Elizabeth had eventually arranged the transfer of its ownership to him as she had promised, having left him responsible for its upkeep. She felt that if Robert could support himself, then so should Francis. It was down to Francis to achieve his advancement as a senior public servant. If not, he would need to sell his already heavily mortgaged home and all that went with it.

Despite his pressing money problems Francis had a greater concern. That for his true brother Robert. Whatever had gone between them or not in their different lifestyles, they had a bond stronger than any other. They were of the same blood and Tudor heritage and so would share the same danger from the schemes of Coke and Cecil in the vacuum the Queen's death with no apparent heirs would cause.

Robert knew Francis had sworn to his mother he would present no claim to the throne, but Robert had not given her any such assurance. He wanted it, and Francis was well aware of this, and also that Robert's ambition might blind him to its dangers.

Robert had not fared well in his military campaign in Ireland to put down the rebellious population, by which he had hoped to please Elizabeth. He had returned after some years there with poor results. Elizabeth was yet undecided as to who should inherit her monarchy, not wishing to face her own demise. Her indecision rankled Robert and he decided he need to act while she was still alive. He did not want to end her life, rather he wanted to receive her approbation as heir apparent, or failing that to depose her gently, neglecting the ferocity with which she had clung to her royal role all her life.

Cecil, suspecting Robert's motives, had carefully cultivated Walter Raleigh, knowing of the Queen's trust in him, and had arranged for him to have an audience with her. Raleigh was always eager to ingratiate himself with the Queen and given impetus would be happy to give full vent to his suspicion about Essex, whom he always felt the Queen had preferred over him. Urged on and envious as he was, he was a puppet in Cecil's unscrupulous hands.

"Your Majesty," Raleigh had begged her on getting the Queen's attention. "Upon my word you must arrest the Lord Essex before harm befalls you. It is understood he has returned from Ireland with plans to depose you from the throne in his own name."
"Who informs you thus, Sir Walter? Not, I hope, the rogue Tyrone and his Irish rebels who seek to vanquish Essex with words. They are a fractious rabble. Beware you speak not words where you are unsure of their truth."
Once again Raleigh implored her. "Ma'am as your most trusted protector, I fear for your safety."

Elizabeth was not keen to take action against Robert. She gave no credibility to stories of Robert's reported desire to unseat her by force of action while she lived. He was still her favorite come what may and so she dismissed the occasional rumors of his regal ambitions. There were too many problems which she needed to resolve before appointing an heir. Her forty or so years in power busy juggling all ends had made it difficult for her to believe they might one day come to a close, and she would not be put under pressure by anyone, friend or foe.

The morning after the night of the first performance of Richard II at the Globe Elizabeth had risen later than her normal hour of nine o'clock, and had not appeared in the throne room to hear the pleas of the usual round of plaintiffs until midday. She had noticed a sudden silence as she entered, greater than usual, and a seeming air of apprehension among the people gathered there. Francis was in attendance, which was unusual as he had tended to keep his distance in recent years. He too appeared nervous. It was once again Sir Walter who spoke directly to the Queen, as Cecil had intended he should.

"Your Majesty should know that last night there was a play at the Globe which portrayed King Richard II in a manner which could be interpreted as a design on your own person and the throne."
Sir Walter continued to elaborate the plot in detail. This was his moment. Elizabeth's blood rose and she fumed, her voice reaching a startling pitch so that those near her backed away. "By the very Devil I will not be denied. Someone will answer for this, and if not there will be suffering. This is no play but a fanciful jest at my tenure as Queen, dissimulation watched in public by my people in a deliberate attempt to cause dissent."

She turns on Francis, standing expressionless, but guessing what was to happen next, he faces her.
"You, Sir, and those worthless scrimshanks, your Good Pens. Amongst them they must know the perpetrators which you will find before this day is out, or all their heads will roll. Find me the author of this obscene play and whomever is the publisher that they may be brought before me. If not they will cost you my indulgence for the rest of time," she screams at Francis.

She shakes her fist in his face and Francis departs in misery, for it was he who had written the play some years before. Francis had had no knowledge that it was to be shown publicly to discredit Robert Cecil as plotting to overthrow the Queen. Now by clever manipulation Cecil had cunningly countered by spreading rumor that it was Essex who was leading a rebellion with the same intent. Cecil and Coke took leave of the Court shortly after having been witness to Elizabeth's outburst and Francis' departure. As they stepped outside in the busy dirt thoroughfare of London's Strand alive with horse drawn coaches and horseback riders stirring up the dusty road, and with street tradesmen touting their wares, they spoke. Cecil has a triumphant look on his face as he speaks to Coke.

"Two birds with one stone I believe. Is this not the moment to strike at the heart of our enemies? What does your lawyer's instinct tell you? Is there some impediment yet to our plans?"

Coke speaks." Indeed, indeed, but what must be done must be done advisedly, without any implication or trace to our good selves. Raleigh has served us well today. Her Majesty must not see him as a dupe sent by us, nor must Raleigh himself believe so. Our hour has surely come, but for now we need to let events take their course."

With that Coke walked further down the road to the Inner Temple where he had his chambers at Clifford's Inn, and Cecil went on his way. They had not noticed Francis Bacon passing by on the other side of the busy street.

# Chapter 34

Francis traveled - to his venue on the other side of the Thames as fast as he could, having taken a horse drawn cab over London Bridge deep in thought. The tide was at full flood and the waters running too fast for a water boatman to row him across the short distance from the Inns to the Globe Theater where he was heading. On the bridge the staring sockets of eyeless heads on tarred rotting bodies of those whom his mother had seen as treasonable gave Francis little comfort. The Queen had no mercy for those who brooked her will. As her faculties slowly left her in her declining years she saw enemies everywhere, and there was little of the milk of human kindness left in her veins.

Francis gained entry to the Globe and was shown directly to the small office of Richard Burbage who, following the recent death of his father, now ran the theater. Upon Francis' entry Burbage, and Ben Jonson who was there with him, got to their feet to embrace Francis. They both saw the pale pallor of his cheeks and could guess what he had to tell them.

"We feared this," said Burbage. "We are in danger. Myself for putting on the play, but more so its author – yourself Francis. I should never have accepted Southampton's request to show it with the scene of Richard's deposition included. It has made us all hostage to fortune."

His tone of voice mixed anxiety with compassion since he knew the play had a double purpose as Francis had intended. It was not just as a caution to Elizabeth about a threat to her throne from Catholic conspirators; but a warning for Essex to leave well enough alone lest the Queen was to believe the danger came from him. It was in effect too clever by half and had backfired badly in its aim. The Queen's misinterpretation of its meaning might mean they would all pay a high price.

Francis spoke. "I am more than aware of the dangers to my friends.

The Queen's anger may not pass as she is oft these days disposed to much suspicion about plots against her. If her ire will not subside, I can draw her to surmise myself as the author. She presently suspects him to be among my Good Pens, from whom she urges me to find the miscreant. It will not be too far a step for her to believe I am the guilty party. She has today banned me from her Court, but I will write to her throwing myself on her mercy and pleading my innocence in that I wrote the play for the purpose of her own protection."

Burbage and Jonson were of one mind and Burbage spoke to dissuade Francis from his plan.

"Francis, you are blinded by your affection for the Queen, which she has not for some years returned to you. You are without position and title after all these years and now nearly bankrupted by your debts, but does she hold out a hand to help you? No! You need not answer. If she finds you as the author you will be fortunate indeed in the sound and the fury that will follow such discovery only to lose your career and possessions, and not your head. You must listen to what we say. We have a plan to save us all. To address the Queen now will be to no avail. Come not between the dragon and his wrath! The devil may cite scripture for his purpose, but for that it is too late. Rumor has spread across London these last hours to the point of Essex deposing the Queen this very day – no less! If it is thought that you wrote the play you will be seen to be in league with him. You have concealed yourself thus far under the name of Pallas and those of the masks of your friends, and you cannot now lend it to this play. You must make use of an author who cannot be suspected of being one of our circle of Good Pens, and one whose innocence can be proven, as ours cannot!"

Francis raised his eyebrows. "Pray, tell me who." He spoke softly, sinking his head in his hands.

"The actor Shaksper, whose name we have put to use at times to mask our plays with its similarity to the shaken spear of Pallas. With the money he has gained he has made a small investment in the building of the Globe. We believe for adequate reward he can be seen in future to lay claim to the authorship of all our plays so that your name, nor ours, may never be revealed. We will in future close the words of Shake and Speare together to add to that of William so that the author may be seen in future as a person and not a symbol.

Francis spoke out. "I have heard of this man. He has been a mask for some small works and oft plays the fool on stage. But to give him credit for my works for evermore! This needs to be considered. Can he play the part?"

"Needs must, my friend," added Jonson. "Stay calm and see the sense of it. The man has no connection to the lives of the nobility. He has a wife and children in Stratford some two day's journey hence, and hard to travel to in the winter months. He has an interest in the theatre and has only little education yet sees himself as a man of future repute. Indeed he has a swagger about his powers that well exceeds his capability, yet not so that it would make him suspect in the eyes of the Queen of being intimate in the affairs of Court. If he were thought to be the author, on examination he might bluster, but since he did not write it, and does not know who did, no harm can befall him. He is not one of our Good Pens. I believe he will play the part well."

Francis spluttered. "If it is bogus the Queen may well torture him to find the truth."

And with afterthought, "Tell me, does this man understand there would be a risk to his life?"

"Yes, but he is fond of money and more so of the fame it would bestow on him. There is little time to act, we strongly advise you to take this route. He will take a lump sum to buy him a good home, and has agreed to stay well clear of London for good. We have already sounded him out."

"But I am without funds", said Bacon ruefully, "at this time."

"There is no need of them. He who commissioned the play last night has realized late its unfortunate consequences contrary to his intentions. You will know him as your acquaintance the Earl of Southampton and close friend of Essex. He is a wealthy man and has made an offer to Shaksper to retain him with a stipend as the supposed author of all our future plays. Since you have remained incognito in the past this will serve always to deflect attention from yourself and of all our Good Pens. What do you say?"

Francis shakes his head. "I know the Earl well enough, but I need consider the implications,"

"There is no time for that!" exclaimed Ben Jonson.

"Come with us now and partake in a drink and some food at the Inn across from here. You will exhaust yourself with your worries. It is why you have good friends to assist you in your decisions. You know how you are beloved by us Francis. We are all lost in admiration for your genius and inspiration, without which we would have had neither great plays nor even an English Renaissance. What we suggest may seem extreme, but better than you with your head cut off or imprisoned in the Tower. You must make your decision now and stand by it so that we may forthwith put our plan into action with Shaksper. He is not the fool he oft plays, but his vanity will most surely attract him to it, on which we must act this very day. Once done that will be the end of it."

Ben continued. "We need speedily to find our publisher Mr Hayward, and to warn him to lie low until the deed be done, and we must hope for its success. By chance or happenstance there has been no author's name given out for last night's play, nor that of its publisher."

They walked to the Inn close by, through a small group of prostitutes reeking of cold sweat and cheap scent, their clothes tattered, and unwashed hair tousled, with bared arms, beckoning them and pulling at their clothes; catcalling after them at their refusal to respond to these approaches. Suddenly the whores scattered on notice of two men behind them in cloaks and the tall black stiff hats worn by officers of the law Courts.

# Chapter 35

Francis had stayed for a little time at the Inn after his friends had left. He had much on his mind and was oblivious of the noisy customers seated at the trestle tables with their jugs of small beer, the watered down drink that served in place of the dirty water from the Thames which had reduced London's population by half from plague and cholera only seven years before. It had forced the Queen's Court to leave in its entirety for the countryside to find clean water and fresh air away from the stench of the river in the summer months which served as an open sewer for everything Londoners chose to empty into it. Fortunately for Francis the clean country air of Twickenham upriver provided an escape whenever plague threatened, as it did for Elizabeth at her palace of Richmond on Thames with its cleaner waters.

As Francis rose to go so too did the two cloaked men who had followed him there and who, within moments of his stepping outside, had accosted him. One, the taller of the two and powerfully built, gripped Francis' arms from behind in the narrow cobbled alleyway. The other dressed in a frock coat and breeches denoting someone of official importance addressed him to his face, while striking him on the chest with a rolled writ tied with a ribbon. "Francis Bacon. My name is Hugh Clapton and I am an officer of the court with orders to serve on you this writ on behalf of a Mr Sympson of Lombard Street. You may recall this gentleman as an honest and fair man, a goldsmith by trade, who holds a bond for your good self in the amount of three hundred pounds. A tidy sum. This writ, Sir, is a warrant for your arrest and detention until such time the sum due from you is paid. I ask that you now accompany me to the Fleet Prison for debtors, and that as a gentleman you should do so in an orderly fashion."

Francis is taken aback. "My good Sir, I am aware of this debt, but not of its being owed on this date. Let it be known to you that its repayment is not due yet until some two months hence. It is you who are in error, so kindly unhand me. If you are in doubt I suggest it can be remedied by application to Sir Robert Cecil of the Privy Council, who is an acquaintance of mine."

Clapton rubbed his chin ruefully, sensing Francis' natural authority and the confidence of his statement. He did not want to get himself involved mistakenly with a person of standing, least of all Sir Robert Cecil whom he knew well to be in a position of power. His client, Mr. Sympson, was a banker, and not of the superior status of the nobility.

"I grant you, Sir, that on your word, and in the event of a misjudgment, I shall make application to Sir Robert forthwith to have him bear witness to your testimony, and if true, I make my apologies to you. Notwithstanding that should Sir Robert not uphold your account, I shall speedily return to make good your arrest."
He turns to the man holding Francis. "Unhand this gentleman for now" and with a small bow to Francis. "I bid you good day, Sir." On which he proceeded, writ, accomplice and all, to make his departure, huffing and puffing up the alleyway, while Francis breathed a sigh of relief. He knew that if he found himself in a debtors' jail, dank and wretched with the cries and pleas of those imprisoned there, with foul food and no money, that even with good help it would take time to be released. Now he would need to apply to Robert Cecil to help him out of his problem, which rankled him as he knew it would give Cecil an advantage over him to know of his monetary woes.

Francis had been uncertain of his statement that the debt to Sympson was not due, and did not want to run the risk of arrest again. He had absent-mindedly forgotten the matter with the many problems that occupied him and cursed the Queen for her neglect of him when he did all he could to save her from herself. He was perturbed with what had occurred and the constant pressure of indebtedness. He consoled himself with the thought that the better part of valor was discretion, and so had treated the writ server with a calm dignity and quick wit.

He had much to do that day with an immediate visit of importance to Hatton Garden. The tide now being reduced in flow he took a small ferry boat to the opposite riverbank of the Thames.

**Inner Temple. 8<sup>th</sup> February.  Mid-Afternoon.**

Sir Robert Cecil dismounts his horse outside Coke's chambers in Clifford's Inn, handing the reins to a waiting ostler.  Coke comes out to greet him and they stand conversing in the winter sun with a contented air.  Robert Cecil smiles wryly.

"It has come to my ears that our good friend Francis Bacon had the misfortune to be apprehended for a sum advanced to him by an acquaintance of mine, a banker. The debt having been called upon, but which Bacon claims is not yet due, which on enquiry is indeed the case since the term has an option for extension.  Even so there are reports about of his near arrest and mud will soon stick, which we need ensure.  Her Majesty will not be amused if rumors are to reach her Court, as they surely will.  The news should bear well with you and your suit with the Lady Hatton.  Bacon's own petition for her hand will perhaps now be brought to an end since she will not receive him well in his disadvantaged circumstances given her desire for her own advancement. Surely with your position in good stead it is propitious for you to win her favor."

Coke places his hand on Cecil's shoulder. "Indeed, Sir, spoken by the devil himself." With this he strides, smiling broadly, back into his lawyers' chambers, while Cecil congratulates himself on the hand he has played.

# Chapter 36

Lady Hatton is at home for tea in the gardens of her fine London house in Ely Place. Still only twenty-one she is considered the best looking and most eligible woman in London. First married at the age of fourteen to Sir William Hatton, twice her age, she had inherited a great fortune on his unexpected early death. She is a cousin of Robert Cecil and is making her way rapidly up the social ladder at Court, noted for her looks, intelligence, humor and love of dancing, and for her often direct manner of speech. This afternoon she is entertaining Francis Bacon, who had hastened to request a visit after the events of the last days to restore some good fortune to his woes. He had been attracted to Elizabeth Hatton, not only for her beauty and intellect but also for the comfort of her position and wealth. She too enjoys Francis' wit and good humor; he having made romantic overtures to her earlier in the year. She is bejeweled and beautifully dressed and coiffured in the fashion of her time. Francis is in earnest conversation with her, having arrived directly from the Globe.

"Lady Elizabeth, it gives me much pleasure that you receive me today, and I am to beg your pardon for my absence these past months since my affairs of late have devoured much of my time. I feel certain that you know of my intentions to gain acceptance for your hand in marriage, and of my earnest love for you."

Francis awaits some acknowledgement of his statement but getting none proceeds to unroll a scroll of parchment he has brought with him.

"I have here an extract from my new play titled *The Merchant of Venice* which I have dedicated to you in love, and wish to read for your approval. It is the story of a man, Antonio, pursued mercilessly by Shylock, a devilish banker who demands the heart of Antonio be cut out in settlement of a debt which Antonio has guaranteed on behalf of his friend Bassanio. The Lady Portia who is the wife of Bassanio pleads for the life of Antonio."

He begins to read but Lady Hatton interrupts him:

"Love sought is good, but given unsought 'tis better. Pray, read it to me. I am intrigued to know who this Portia might be, and am most flattered by your attention, Sir, which has been absent for some months. I had pondered on whether you may have forsaken our friendship. I have only today been distressed to hear from Sir Robert Cecil of your travails and the demands on your purse. I trust that which you now read brings better news to please me if I am to consider your proposal."

Not to be rejected so easily Francis proceeds to read aloud an extract of a speech by Portia.
*"The quality of mercy is not strained, it droppeth as the gentle rain from heaven, upon the place beneath: it is twice blest, it blesseth him that gives, and him that takes."*

Quickly understanding Francis' intimation Lady Hatton stops him there.
"Is it your thought I should plead for you in your present predicament?" she enquires. "If I am to be Portia then who would you presume to be? Antonio, or Bassanio my husband? What's in a name? That which we call a rose by any other name would smell as sweet. Do not answer so as not to impugn your motives further! It is best that I answer your proposal forthwith. I have a great affection for you Francis and concern for your situation, but I am young and it is your own wisdom you must consult. I cannot help other than offer my friendship which you assuredly have, and trust you know. But that is all. Now you must take your leave as I am receiving Sir Edward Coke this very hour."
Francis had set his heart and mind on Lady Hatton and is close to tears at the news that she is seeing Coke.
"He dost love thee only because he knows I love thee," he blurted out impotently.

Matters for Francis could hardly have been worse. Coke was Francis' rival in Parliament, and was now high in the affections of Elizabeth Hatton whom Francis had determined to marry to resolve his problems. He was angry with himself at the delay he had made in delivering his proposal, realizing too late that Cecil, as Elizabeth's Hatton's cousin, has been in a position to promote Coke's suit against his own. Elizabeth was not without compassion and seeing his crestfallen demeanor gently gave Francis a kiss on his cheek as she bade him farewell.

# Chapter 37

Robert Essex rides from his home at Essex House on the Strand with his friend Henry the Lord Southampton beside him. They are deep in conversation. They are accompanied by a dozen or so armed men, soldiers who had fought with Essex in Ireland. News of the meeting they had called with like-minded friends some days before to discuss how to bring an end to Cecil's power over the Queen had somehow leaked out. The idea of a formal deputation to Her Majesty to demand the arrest of Cecil had come to nought. Southampton, who had assembled a few noble allies and several hundred well-armed men to counter any trouble from the soldiers under Cecil's command, had dispersed his troops for fear that their actions would be seen as a full-scale rebellion. Now trailing behind Robert's small group was a rabble of a hundred or so Londoners on foot. Street hawkers and a motley crew of ragamuffins, prostitutes and beggars hoping for some trade or some pennies for food, and others excited by the rumors from last night of a coup to overthrow the Queen.

Essex turned to Southampton.
"I thank you, my Lord Henry, for the favor of aiding this man Shaksper in his retreat to Stratford. I hope in earnest it will save the skin of my brother Francis as he is no part of our actions."
"My dear Robert, I had it in my grant and it was a simple matter to accomplish. Noblesse Oblige," replied Southampton doffing his cap. "You know well the love I have for Francis' plays and poetry. I would have done it thrice over to save his authorship from being known. But now it is your skin that we must save, my Lord. It seems that by our commissioning of the play shown last night our plan to warn Her Majesty has gone astray and you are the suspect, not the rascal Cecil. He is a step ahead of us and has put it about that you are to usurp Her Majesty at any hour of day or night. He has doubled her guards only this morning I am given to understand, to resist a rebellion led by you. As we speak your very life is in danger!"

"God curse Cecil" exclaimed Robert. He is but a foul knave whom I will deal with in good course. I will take my leave now to make haste to the Queen to swear my loyalty. If I act alone her guards will not seek to halt me as I am so oft in attendance on her."

"You must proceed with caution, Sir. I hear the unfortunate Hayward as the publisher of Richard II has been apprehended and Cecil is threatening to torture him to reveal its authorship. Only yesterday did I see the knave Cecil in a dark place at White Hall discoursing with the Spanish ambassador, no doubt plotting to replace the Queen with a Catholic. We must urgently devise a plan of action to avoid your arrest. There is no time to lose"

Above the clatter of their horses hooves Essex shouted back. "Egad. The truth will out! By the devil, I am the Queen's very flesh and blood, and I will ride myself to her this moment to inform her that I mean her no mischief, so as to ease her troubled mind.. I have no intent to harm her. This duplicity of Cecil's is Satan's work. We must save Hayward's life, or perchance my brother Francis will be next to lose his."

Essex spurs his horse away from the small troop of soldiers now nearing the Queen's home in York Place, and in minutes enters its forecourt alone, catching the guard there by surprise. Riding directly through the midst of the Queen's own bodyguard now arrayed in full armor of breastplates and pikes, he dismounts, and with their cries of alarm behind him dashes up the stairs to the Queen's private rooms. "Where is Her Majesty? I must save her," he shouts aloud to her ladies-in-waiting outside the closed door of her bedchamber. The Queen has risen late after the distress of the previous day. Pushing past a waiting bishop who is there to conduct her in morning prayer; Robert bursts into Elizabeth's bedchamber. She is not yet fully robed, her hair is disarranged and her gray drawn face is without rouge. Her tire-maidens in attendance draw back shocked at Essex's arrival, followed quickly by the bishop and a captain of the Queen's Guard with drawn sword. Seeing the guard Essex puts his hand on the hilt of his own sword and advances on the Queen, meaning to kiss her hand, falling on his knees to swear his allegiance, but the burly guard grabs his shoulder to pull him round thinking he is attempting to kill the Queen, and is ready to thrust his sword into Essex's belly when Elizabeth screams. "No, no! Stay thy hand. Do not slay him! "

Simultaneously, the bishop throws his vestment over Robert's head and arms to restrict him as more guards enter to take him away. As

Essex is half carried, half-dragged, from the room he turns to call back to his mother.

"Your Majesty, I implore you. I need to speak urgently of your enemies."

"You are unfit for any place but Hell," she screams back at him in a fury, her face enraged. "Take him to the Tower!"

# Chapter 38

**Gray's Inn. The Law Chambers of Francis Bacon.
8th February, 1601. Evening**

Without news of his brother's arrest Francis had sought refuge in his chambers to contemplate his own problems. He sat surrounded by a collection of tomes and manuscripts, some complete and many unfinished, among them various symbols of Masonry. A polished human skull, an hourglass, and a square and compass. The stone wedge his mother had given him when he came of age was in use as a convenient paperweight on top of a pile of documents on his desk standing beside scrolls of parchments tied by small colored ribbons to denote their significance.

Francis' thoughts raced. How often the hopes of mice and men came tumbling down. Almost penniless and in debt, and now his suit for Elizabeth Hatton rejected in favor of his older and bitter foe Edward Coke, the man who had fought him tooth and nail for every worthwhile position in Parliament. Without the benefit of advice from the Cecil family Coke would have achieved far less; but now he was taking the prize from under Francis' nose. Having stupidly lost the support of the Queen, Francis saw he had only himself to blame. Come what may he was her flesh and blood.

He realized, despite his love-hate relationship with his mother, how good she had been to him in what he liked to think of as the salad days of the past. She had supported him from birth so that he had no need of concern for money, and so had given him the chance to run full rein on his grand projects and the expense of keeping his Good Pens. He had put nothing aside and now dared not ask the Queen for aid. Not so long ago he had publicly encouraged opposition to her request in Parliament for funds for her navy, which had angered her. He should have known she was not for changing. The motto on her coat of arms declared "Semper Eadem" or "Ever the Same," of which she was proud.

He realized it was his idealism about giving the people a voice in government which had caused the Queen to go against him. She had thought his motives without merit; and now his play Richard II which he had written with good intent had drawn her ire. Even his wooing of Elizabeth Hatton, which match he knew would have pleased the Queen, he had spoiled in his overconfidence that she would accept him. The primrose path he sought had led to nowhere.

He thought of the friends he might turn to for the assistance which he had so often given them. Some of those closest to him were now dead. The Knights of the Helmet pledged to bring back to England the wisdom of the Masons of which he was their Grand Master; but their members were sworn to secrecy about their activities. Francis had assumed the Queen would know of his work with them through John Dee who was a Masonic member and had the ear of the Queen for many years; but he too had recently fallen from favor in these changing times. The Queen had withdrawn into a world of practical politics by which her people received their daily bread, and had little time for talk of faith or of spiritual matters, which she now dismissed.

Francis reflected on his recent friendship with the Teutonic Knight Count Augustus. He and John Dee had worked hard to establish a Rosicrucian code of practice in Germany and the offer the Count had made for Francis and Dee to visit was still open. All these thoughts flowed in and out of his mind until he held his head in his hands in torment over what it was best to do. He had taken on too much to the neglect of what was most dear to his life. Thoughts of his lost love for Marguerite came into his head, and now he had lost the love of Elizabeth Hatton. Why was it women were such a distraction? Perhaps he had immersed himself overmuch in his grandiose ideas, and with the male company he kept, his friends, and others whom he portrayed in his plays.

In the *Seven Wise Men of the West* he had portrayed Robert Burton as the pedant; Christopher Marlowe as the braggart; Will Shaksper as the fool; Robert Greene as the priest; Edmund Spenser as the poet; and George Peele as the boy. What enjoyment they had all had together in its enactment. Where were they now? Marlowe was dead. Spenser too. The actor Shaksper confined to Stratford, well paid for the work Francis had done! He blamed himself. He tugged at his hair in exasperation at the pickle he found himself in.

Francis was to reveal later in his last major work, *De Augmentis,* in ciphers which he had indented. *"My adverse fortune seemed the theme most suited to the Plays, published by, and in the name of other men."*

But now there came a knocking at his door and his clerk ushered in a young finely featured man of slight build and dark pointed beard, dressed in a dandified attire of tight black silk stockings, with emerald green breeches and doublet and a toque flat hat of purple. His patent pumps raised his height on built-up heels. Sir Toby Matthew, twenty-two years of age and eighteen years younger than Francis, was a member of Francis' law chambers in Gray's Inn. Francis had liked him at first sight for his charm and erudite wit. He combined serious thought with an extravagant and somewhat theatrical air, which although Francis had now put it behind him, reminded him of himself at the same age. Years later it was said that Toby provided Francis with his alter ego. He amused Francis with his stories of the Italian Court which were reminiscent of those of Francis as a young man abroad. Toby had an intellectual mind, which appreciated Francis' inventive train of thought. They enjoyed long conversation far into the night on religion, the occult and philosophy. Later they were to work together on Francis' book *The Great Instauration* which promoted the concept of natural philosophy as the way to both science and faith. Toby had trained as a priest, but was an aristocrat by birth and not part of the same liberal set as Francis's Good Pens from his university days. He was unmarried, as he wished to remain. Francis had taken him under his wing at his law practice and they had quickly developed a close tie as confidants. Toby having a good command of languages and of Latin and Greek, as had Francis. Toby had confided in Francis his love for the rituals of the Catholic Church and its Mass which he had attended in Florence at the beautiful Basilica da Santa Croce, or the Temple of Italian Glories as it was otherwise known. It was to have held Dante's tomb, which reserved place still lay empty since Dante's family had resisted the removal of his body there. It was here that Michelangelo had been laid to rest along with Machiavelli, and later Galileo and Rossini. In Rome too Toby had recently attended Mass at St Peter's, where in the Sistine Chapel the exquisite ceiling of Michelangelo depicted the prophesy that Christ would save the world. Francis shared with Toby a love of beauty in art and in the human form in which there were no barriers of religion. Francis had once followed closely the Protestant ways of his foster mother Lady Anne, and her avowal of strict Puritan teachings, but he was more drawn to Catholic formality and appreciation of art and style. Even so he recognized the Templar past of the Tudors and their belief in what he saw as the true Nazarene Christian creed of Jesus. It remained the principle behind the charitable purpose of his Order of White Knights of the Helmet.

As Toby entered the room, gold topped Malacca walking cane in hand, he foppishly doffed his feathered cap. *"Est-ce que tu aimes mon chapeau?"* He exclaimed gaily. *"C'est un bonbon. Un cadeau."* A present from my new friend the Italian ambassador. He tells me it becomes me!"

"I do my friend, indeed purple is one of my favorite colors," replied Francis. "But, Toby, you need to hold your tongue in public in your leanings towards popery and your new Catholic friends, or you will fast make yourself enemies."

"My dear Francis," Toby replied with laughter, "but you are not the public and you and I share our own discretions, do we not?" he asked, as he laid a hand gently on Francis's shoulder.

He notices Francis serious face.

"Come, come, my friend, what ails you? Tonight we should celebrate my return and our passions for the finer senses of life. I see you are bogged down in your manuscripts. 'Tis time for some good wine and to hear of my tales from Italy for your amusement. Of the affairs of men; and of women too. God Bless them, poor souls, that you and I have no need of women or their gossip. Her Majesty excepted of course, and she has no need of men these days. You have suffered unrequited love too long, Francis, and 'tis good your memory grows dim of its pitfalls."

He pats himself lightly on his tightly trousered posterior.

"Give me a man that is not passion's slave when it comes to women!"

Francis was not in the mood for innuendo. "You must suffer your own pleasures, Toby. You know I enjoy your good company but what serves your priapism does not mine. On the contrary, I am completing a play which I have written for one whose hand I seek, but who has this day rejected me."

"Ah, my dear Francis, I hope your lines of romance will overcome the resistance of this person if she be true. I had for a dreadful moment thought that you had resigned yourself to true celibacy. For myself I am taken momentarily with a new passion for the beauty of the Vatican boys' choir and their heavenly voices. "Bellissima!" he exclaimed. "You, Francis, who can write such a splendid comedy of women as the *The Taming of the Shrew,* surely cannot wish to share a bed with a nagging wife. Think of the pleasures men may share together with good wine and talk of the arts and philosophies." Toby looked quizzically at Francis' face for a reaction.

Toby knew all too well of the pain Francis had suffered over Marguerite years ago and her refusal to respond to his poems and offers of marriage. Francis' love had turned sour. He had since satirically portrayed Marguerite as the devious Cressida in his play *Troilus and Cressida,* and was ever keen to use her as an example of female fickleness and the torments of the mind women put upon their sorry lovers.

"'Tis true," Francis owned. "I feel like a hunted deer, borne down with the weight of Parliament and laws and with my duties to the Queen. It was never my wont to pursue them, but to write with my Good Pens in good company and in good humor. Without them I would not have achieved half the work of my plays. But it is to a good woman I still look to share my bed and keep my house."
"But let that not come between us. Stay but awhile, and we will share a posset of hot milk and a glass or two of sherry sack for our supper so you may tell me your tales before your return so that I may forget my own of woe. Do not castigate me. When sorrows come they come not as single spies, but in big battalions. If thou remember not the slightest folly that love ever did make thee run into, thou hast not loved."
"My dear Francis, you must not depress yourself. Misery acquaints a man with strange bedfellows. Your genius is above all to be shared best with your fellow gentlemen. Without it your Good Pens would not have accomplished one single work of their own. They have but one Master whose presence shines through each play as does a sunbeam of warmth and light in the grey of a cloudy day. You are the very reincarnation of Homer and Virgil. What more could you ask? Come let us now drink to drown your sorrows that we may boldly face a new day on the morrow."

Francis smiled at Toby's exuberance remembering his own youthful days at Twickenham Hall and the merriment he had then in the revels with his friends, drinking and smoking weed through many good days and nights. He did not often visit his house there now. It was partly closed due to his lack of finances. Those remaining Good Pens were still welcome and he resolved to see them more to replenish his spirits with their laughter and talk. But they too had grown old with him while many had died. He shook himself, and on Toby's words decided there and then to stand by his own values and not to be forced by the wiles of Cecil and his allies to have to sell his home. He would fight tooth and nail to restore the life he once saw as his due. He would make a virtue of necessity. After all, what more could go wrong?

# Chapter 39

Francis has been summoned to Court by the Queen and is shown into her private rooms. She is now fully robed and bewigged and her splendid lace ruff surrounds her face and shoulders be-topping a violet gown. She is demure in her appearance, having quite recovered all composure from yesterday's scene. She speaks softly to her eldest son.

"Sit down, Francis. I need to talk to you. You are the only one I can trust who knows of Robert's birthright to my throne which he now demands, and which you have advisedly declined. I know your troubles, but I have been too out of sorts in recent years to help you. Things are not always as they may seem. I have been unhappy to have to watch you fight your battles without my help, but the more I help you, the more enemies you will have as my end draws nigh. It is why now Robert has drawn the malice of those who would seek to harm him and dispose of any right he may have to claim my throne, and so has aggravated his response. I am aware of Cecil's conniving abroad to restore a Catholic to England's throne, and most duplicitously, with the Scots King James also, so to end the Tudor reign. I am given to understand that Coke has stolen the Lady Hatton from under your nose. It is a sad day for the Tudors that we should fight against ourselves when we have enough enemies on which to spend our energies."

Francis is nervous and his stomach rumbles at the serious situation. His mother laughs, to relieve the pressure that overcomes them both, and to regain the humor they once shared.

"No matter. You may not know the story of the Lord Oxford who once farted loudly in my presence and being so embarrassed could not, because of his own reluctance, attend my court for seven long years. Upon on his return I told him that I had long forgotten his fart, at which poor fellow, he could not contain himself farted once more and nearly died of shame. So release yourself of your discomfort if you so please. If my own son cannot do so in my presence then I am a poor mother indeed. It is time for thought.

"We have urgent need to resolve Robert's predicament. Even now his enemies demand his head in their contrivance to implicate him. What fools he and Southampton have been to commission this play of Richard II. They have handed food to Cecil on a plate. Had it not been shown publicly I could have ignored it."

Elizabeth was happy to break the ice after her spell of disaffection with Francis. It was a relief for her in this desperate hour to see the warmth of a smile return to his face and his nervousness gone. She had nurtured her boys as naturally as any other good mother, giving them every opportunity to excel and reach the apex of their lives. The absent role she had needed to play with them in the circumstances of their birth had been as hard for her as it had been for them. She had not long to go now, she knew in her bones, and she needed to ensure they would survive without her support.

Robert's headstrong ways had brought him trouble, but she did not believe he had wanted to harm her. Still she could not see her way to nominate him as her successor. What royal claim would he have as the son of Essex and her cousin Lettice Knollys, as he was publicly supposed to be? She could not admit his true birth without revealing her own secret liaison with Leicester. Robert's rash entrance into her chambers had been witnessed by too many to be contained, and she needed to be seen to take action against him, or too many questions would be raised. She required Francis' calm advice since she knew he loved his brother and they shared the same foes. She had no one else to turn to now. For the first time in his life she asked him: "What shall I do? Robert is a hot-headed fool. He seeks the bubble reputation even in the cannon's mouth, giving ammunition to his enemies and a threat to my throne and his own life."

"Your Majesty, I do believe he wishes you no harm. His action was a misjudged one to defend you. He has enemies who would trick him, and his passion in your defense has blinded him to the consequences. If he was to have a desire for your throne, surely he would not act so foolishly?"

Francis was not sure if this was entirely true but knowing Elizabeth's mood swings he thought to say what best he could to save the situation for his brother. "His quickness of temper will soon cool," he reassured her. "I heard rumor today he was sick of heart and plans to make apology to you in the Star Chamber in front of his peers."

"And what if he is feigning sickness?" Elizabeth sighed. "What does my heart tell me then? How sharper than a serpent's tooth it is to have a thankless child! Would he tease me as Satan does at death's door? Do you remember, Francis, the ring I gave to you many years ago at Twickenham that you wear now on your hand? I gave the same to Robert too. To you both with the command that you should keep it close to you at all times so should you ever need my protection you should return it to me. I will surely know that if Robert sends it to me, he is true of heart, and that he is a man of honor."

"Your Majesty, I advise, I beg of you, that you express mercy. It blesseth both him that gives and him that receives."

Elizabeth shakes her head in exasperation.

"I will heed your advice this once. But forsooth Robert must keep his head about him or he will lose it. His actions towards me are treasonable in the eyes of his enemies. We can only wait. He will need be tried by his Peers of the Realm and my hands are tied until their final judgment. Only then can I grant him a Royal Pardon which is mine alone to give. But first he will need to return my ring as a sign of his loyalty to me. Enough, now, what of you?" she demands of Francis. "I trust you are no part of this? If Robert is to go to trial, you must attend it in an official capacity and assist in its just outcome against the wiles of Cecil and Coke who seek to implicate him. The publisher of the play has been found and is to be executed as an example to others not to defame me by scurrilous implication."

She gives Francis a sharp look. "The play is clearly seditious as any fool can see, as we now see witnessed in the noisy streets, but it is the fault of those of who showed it, rather than the author. Tell me, Francis, since you have lost the hand of Lady Hatton, do you wish for children now to inherit your name and knowledge? Do you not wish to look for a new wife?

"No more do I, Francis' answer came. "It is by memory, merit and noble works that proper men are known."

Elizabeth gave Francis a curious look.

Francis leaves to return to Gray's Inn but the streets are full of crowds now alerted by news of the failure of the alleged rebellion. Armed militia stream here and there and Elizabeth sees them from her window, frightened now for Robert, and what might befall him. She cannot deny for long the clamor for his trial by his powerful enemies. His actions have endangered her by good intention or bad. She needs a sign from Robert that his motives were pure and not what she is being given to believe.

## The House of Lords. 18<sup>th</sup> February, 1601. Morning

Robert Essex is taken from the Tower to the Star Chamber of the House of Lords where his fellow peers are to hear his pleas in defense of his actions. His friend Henry Southampton has been arrested too for suspected complicity in the alleged coup on the palace since he had ridden side by side with Robert. They are both to be tried together, and the mood of their peers is against them. Their trial took place with little pomp and ceremony. Robert had indignantly pleaded his innocence, but with Cecil and Coke handling its conduct the stage was set for a speedy verdict of guilty, and such was delivered. Francis had been summoned to attend by the Privy Council, headed by Cecil, to act as a junior counsel to the Chief Prosecutor, Edward Coke, as Cecil had slyly proposed to the Queen. It had put Francis in an invidious position, as Cecil cunningly intended, of acting against his own concealed brother. Even so, Francis had to do his duty by the Queen, but in being seen to do so he was confident that whatever the verdict, the Queen would commute it by exercise of her overriding prerogative of Pardon. Francis had thought to use his eloquence to help save Robert from himself at his trial and may have done so, but for Robert's pride in putting up no case for his actions other than swearing loyalty to the Throne. This proved insufficient to persuade his peers of his innocence, many of whom owed favors to Cecil as the Queen's advisor. If the Queen wanted to save her own son, as many present suspected him to be, then why had she let the trial take place? It appeared that she was no longer her own master. The Lords reached their conclusion. Henry Southampton was to be spared death and sent to the Tower to be imprisoned, but Robert was to be executed at dawn the following week. When no pardon was forthcoming from the Queen, contrary to Francis' expectation, he was seen by Robert's friends to have acted against him, and so he lost their trust, that of Southampton in particular. Once more the craftiness of Cecil had won the day. Far more providently for Cecil, an accident of chance had come his way of which Elizabeth was to be unaware until after Robert's death, and which Francis was never to discover.

In front of his peers, on the verdict of guilty being given, Robert had been stripped of his Order of the Garter, England's highest award, a gift from the Queen on his twenty-sixth birthday. He and Southampton, who was to suffer imprisonment in the Tower for an unknown period, were led by foot back to the Tower by a platoon of the Queen's guard. As was the custom with those who were to lose their heads, the executioner with his axe preceded Robert's own pitiable procession.

Crowds seeing him fell silent. They knew of Essex's daring on behalf of Queen and country. They knew of his noble title and that the same fate had befallen many others of equal standing in recent years. As they watched they crossed themselves blessing that they were lowly born and immune to the perilous machinations of State. They did not know that the man who passed them by, his head bare, and his good looks still about him at the age of thirty-five, was heir to the English throne. Their would-be king.


**The Tower of London. 18th February, 1601, afternoon.**


Robert was now alone, as Southampton had not entered the Traitors Gate with him, a passageway from which few ever returned. He was held temporarily in a small guard room between the inner and outer gate of the entrance, awaiting the clerical formalities of his admission before being admitted to the Beauchamp Tower where to await his execution. As he sat and slowly collected his thoughts at the fast-moving events that were to bring his life to an end he realized it was in the same place his true father and mother had been imprisoned nearly fifty years before, while they too awaited their deaths. His father had been dead now these last thirteen years. The similar tragedy of his situation did not escape him and his mind raced as to how, at this eleventh hour, he might yet be extricated from imminent disaster as his parents had been. As he stroked his pointed beard his fingers touched the small black velvet bag he carried round his neck at all times. Opening it he found the ring the Queen had once told him he was to send to her if in need of her protection. His fingers fumbled as he took it out and saw on its surface the crown and star crest of the Tudors, from whose proud lineage he came through his mother's blood. Quickly he replaced it in the bag, and taking from his ear a gold earring, he called over the Captain of the Guard. Pressing the earring into the palm of the guard captain as a bribe, Robert requested that a messenger take the bag with the ring directly to Lady Scrope, the Queen's own Lady-in-Waiting, at the Queen's home at York Place. He impressed on the guard the need for the messenger to run the four miles hotfoot and that he was to demand of Lady Scrope that the bag be opened by none other than the Queen herself. A young messenger fleet of foot had been called and Robert had repeated the same instructions which needed be carried out to the letter. As he was taken to the Beauchamp Tower Robert could not help but to cross himself in prayer to seek his salvation in the few days that lay ahead before his expected execution. This would be the test of his mother's declared affection of all these years. Would it still prove so?

### York Place. The same day. 18th February, 1601

Robert Cecil, in his position as Privy Counselor to the Queen, stands in front of her, a paper in his hands.

"Your Majesty, I have here a warrant for the execution of the Earl of Essex upon the charge of treason for your seal and signature, as requested by your House of Lords."

"How did my Lord Essex plead?" asks the Queen. "Guilty or not guilty?"

"Not guilty," replies Cecil, "but the plea was not accepted by his peers."

He holds out the paper for signature while his clerk prepares to heat the wax for her seal of office.

Elizabeth waves to the clerk to stop and addresses Cecil.

"You seem a mite inclined to haste, Sir. Your Queen will decide when it is time."

She knows she should never have trusted Cecil and his flattery. Foul dwarf that he was to play with her emotions. She needs to play for time if by chance the ring she gave Robert is to come to her. She knows she cannot hold out against the decision of the Lords for too long. She turns away from the hated Cecil so he may not see the anxiety in her face. She had trusted his now dead father, Burleigh as her closest confidant, and now it seems the Cecils had betrayed her in their quest for power over her own flesh and blood. Elizabeth remembered the day at her court when Francis was but a youth and his identity had been revealed in a cruel jest. She had seen then the envy in Cecil's eyes. What a fool she was not to have seen him as the villainous contriver he was. She knew not whom to trust any longer. She was now weary of life, as she had confided to the French ambassador only recently.

## Tower of London. November, 2014

Mrs G was walking westward from Tower Bridge along the embankment fronting the Tower beside the river Thames. It was early morning and a misty vapor from an icy ground frost slowly rose up the grey walls and turrets of the fortress. She was well wrapped up with her winter coat collar turned up to protect her throat and troublesome cough against the cold breeze from the river. A woolen ski hat which Marianne had given her with a picture of a Jack Russell on its front to reflect Mrs G's terrier-like determination kept her head warm. She passed by the massive portcullis bars of the Traitors Gate through which the Thames' dark waters lapped ominously, and walked the full length of the Tower's river frontage, until on turning to its main entrance, she found the ticket office. She was to be among the first that morning through the doors before tourists from the world over arrived en masse, as they did in their millions each year to see one of the great venues of history.

Built by the Norman William the Conqueror in the 11th century it had hardly changed in a thousand years, having housed, imprisoned and tortured the unfortunate, and witnessed their countless executions from queens and princes to commoners. As the early rays of the weak morning sun shone on its walls it seemed surreally Disney-like in its setting. Even so, Mrs G's shoulders shuddered involuntarily from the nearness of death, and the thought of the screams and moans that had not so long ago echoed round its walls.

Today she had come to see the Beauchamp Tower where Robert Earl of Essex had been imprisoned after his condemnation for treason by his peers over four hundred years before. He was a part of the story that she needed to complete on his brother Francis and their Tudor bloodline. Having waited shivering in the cold for the ticket office to open she was first in line to enter. Passing by a splendidly attired Beefeater guard in black felt cap and scarlet and gold velveteen costume, she enquired as to the whereabouts of the Beauchamp Tower. As she found her way to it she felt as if transported back in time, walking in the footsteps of the doomed Earl, almost expecting to witness his dramatic end.

She crossed the yard where so many had lost their heads, and where the jet black ravens still today squabbled and screeched in their raucous tones. Looking up at the portico of the Beauchamp Tower she saw above her, carved in stone above the doorway, the name "Robart Tidir", his true name as a Tudor Royal, and not that of Essex his supposed father. She wondered if Robert himself had found the time to carve it there in the short two weeks before Elizabeth had finally signed his death warrant, having refused Cecil his two previous requests. Even on the day of execution she had sent messengers to stay it but they had arrived too late. Without the return of Robert's ring her pride had got the better of her, and her indecision had played into Cecil's hands.

The scene had been described in its bloodiest detail. How Robert had been led down the very steps Mrs G was now standing on to the Tower Green on which the execution block had stood. Dressed in black he had discarded his coat to reveal a scarlet silk blouson to kneel before the executioner's axe. Despite all the love he felt for his mother and his expectation of her help, in this final hour she had forsaken him.

No tears clouded his eyes as they had been burned out by a red-hot poker in the Tower in a last failed attempt to obtain his confession of guilt, as Cecil had instructed. It had taken several blows to finally cut Robert's head from his body, and for it to be held up by his hair, blood dripping from its severed neck, for all to see. Those present included his brother Francis, and near him Raleigh; and the hunchback Cecil with his smug self-satisfied countenance. He had got what he had wanted.

In a letter written by the Dean of Westminster to a friend shortly after the execution, the Dean had reported how he had asked Raleigh how he felt since he had been an instrument of Essex's death. Raleigh had denied this and replied that *"the Lord Essex was fecht of by trick."* The trick having been set up by Cecil in which Raleigh had realized only too late he had been a dupe. Now only Francis was the thorn that need be removed for Cecil's plans to succeed.

As Mrs G looked away from the carved sign of "Robart Tidir" a thought crossed her mind. So Elizabeth had tamed her own "wild horse" at last, but what had it served her? That, Mrs G was yet to discover.

**Gray's Inn, London. February, 1601.**
**The afternoon of the execution of Robert Essex.**

Francis sits at his desk with a quill pen in his hand. He had pleaded with his mother for his brother's life telling her: *"To have a giant's strength is excellent, but it is tyrannous to use it like a giant."* Steely-hearted Elizabeth had replied in threat, suspicious of his motives and resenting criticism:

*"Thy own life's dependent on thy brother's death. 'Tis death for death, a brother for a brother."*

The black ink drips slowly on the parchment and diffuses with his tears as Francis looked at the words he had finally penned to his mother.

*"All my Honest Faith in Thee is Lost...*
*Oaths of thy Love, thy Truth, thy Constancy.*
*For I have Sworn thee Fair and thought thee Bright,*
*Who are as Black as Hell, as Dark as Night."*

He had once written similar words to Marguerite some twenty years before. But he was now beyond further words and could write no more, and as with Robert, he was never to see Elizabeth again. He believed she had deliberately sent his brother to his death and had used him, Francis, to prosecute her case, and even to condemn Robert in a *Declaration of Treason* she had requested Francis to write to absolve her. But he was wrong. It had been a grievous error which was to chase the conscience of the Queen to her dying day. One more disaster was in store for Francis this year.

The loss of his bosom friend and lifetime companion Anthony Bacon, aged forty-four. They had been inseparable from their earliest age. Francis had still kept the words Anthony had once written to him as boys together which were found among his papers after his own death.

*"We are as twinned lambs that did frisk in the sun, and bleat the one at the other. What we charged was innocence for innocence, we knew not the doctrine of ill-doing, nor dreamed that any did."*

# Chapter 40

**The House of Lady Nottingham, Kensington, London. December. 1602**

An old woman lays on a bed consumptive and dying, surrounded by her maids. Another woman enters, a lady-in-waiting to the dying woman.

"Lady Nottingham, Her Majesty is here to see you. May I bid her enter?"

"Of course," she wheezes, "I asked to see Her Majesty that my secret should not die with me."

The lady-in-waiting shows Elizabeth into the room. She goes to Lady Nottingham's side, bending down to catch her faltering voice.

"What is it you wish to tell me?" asks Elizabeth. "I knew your husband well for his good deeds."

She holds the dying woman's hand. Lady Nottingham raises her head to speak her words of confession.

"The ring. I have since the day of Lord Essex's death been haunted by my deception. The ring came to me in error by the messenger and not to my sister, Lady Scrope, as the Lord Essex had desired."

A look of realization and horror came slowly over Elizabeth's face. She had waited for the ring from Robert and it had never come. She had believed that he had no use of her and had feared the worst of him. That he must have hated her not to have sent the ring which could have saved his life by the Royal Pardon she would have granted him. Lady Nottingham continued. Her voice fading. "For he was his enemy, and on the day Lord Essex returned it...."

She paused, in fear of the Queen's angry face. "It was not of my doing."

Elizabeth now grasped the dying woman's hand as in a vice.

"Pray, who do you talk of? Your husband? Tell me what troubles you so the devil does not haunt you."

"I gave the ring to Robert Cecil, he was my lover. Forgive me, your Majesty, he told me it was of no importance. It is my confession before God."

Elizabeth steps back flinging away the woman's hand and shaking in rage. Her voice rises to a terrifying pitch. "May God forgive you, but

I never will!" at which she leaves, in the terrible knowledge she had signed her own son's death warrant in her misplaced distrust in him.

### Richmond Palace. 24th March, 1603. Past Midnight

Elizabeth, now forty-four years as queen and only six months off her seventieth year, has been lying on a heap of cushions on the floor for over two weeks fully dressed in her regal gowns. For months before now she had sat alone in the dark, deep in a melancholic humor. She had killed two of her children. One, nameless, unwantedly conceived in her youth, whom she had drowned at birth in a pool of water, and now had executed another whom she had loved.

In the days after Robert had been sentenced to death by his peers, and before she would sign his death warrant, she had waited hourly at a window of a room in Richmond Palace overlooking the road to London, in the hope a messenger would come with the ring. Mary Stuart's death too was on her hands. Elizabeth's mother had died before she had known her. Her father Henry had not wanted her. Her husband had left her for her best friend. Had she ever found true love, or had it ever found her? Only from the two sons she had disclaimed and whose trust she had lost. The Alone Queen, as she had wished to be.

How appropriate were the later known words of the ancient Persian poet Omar Khayyam:

*"The Moving Finger writes; and having writ*
*Moves on; nor all thy Piety nor Wit*
*Shall lure it back to cancel half a Line,*
*Nor all thy Tears wash out a Word of it."*

Those around her include Robert Cecil who has just entered.
"Pray, tell me, why is our Queen not in the comfort of her own bed? He enquires of a Lady-in-Waiting.
"She has seen too many things there that trouble her," came the reply.
Cecil leans forward over the Queen. "Ma'am, has Her Majesty seen

any spirits?" He asks her archly.

"I scorn to answer. I will have no friends of Catholics meddling with my realm. Your father Burleigh was an honorable man, but you, no, Sir, you evil dwarf, you dare taunt me to bring a foreign Catholic to the English throne!" Too late she now realized Cecil's trickery whose hunched deformity she herself had teased as a pygmy, for which he now took his revenge. Elizabeth wipes her eyes as her elderly archbishop begins to pray for her. She gesticulates to him to cease so she can speak. She had put little trust in the words of the Church. Those present drew nearer to catch her words now spoken in a whisper. Another man stands forward whom she recognizes.

"Closer, my Lord Howard, my friend. There is no prison to match the prison of the thoughts. The whirligig of time brings in his revenges. I am prepared to meet my maker."

As Howard steps back a member of her Council steps forward.

"Ma'am we have need to know of your wish as to the successor to your crown. Can you give us a sign? Is it to be the King of France or that of Scotland, or any other?"

Elizabeth passes a hand over her forehead.

"I will have no rascal's son in my seat, but one worthy to be King. A Stuart would unite our line of the Rose......."

She waved her hand. And here her words became low and lost to those around her. They were to be her last and as the candles flickered and the light dimmed she gave out her last breath.

Cecil, whose ear had been pressed to her lips, turned to the assembled group. "There you have it. It is to be James of Scotland. The Queen has given her sign."

The perspiration dropped from Cecil's brow. Only at the last had he switched allegiance to Scotland when the Queen had suspected him of secret dealings with the French, of which Essex had tried to warn her. Cecil had rapidly contacted James in Scotland so to play both sides of the coin and assure James of his support. Now he would have to make the best of this twist in events.

He thanked the heavens that even to the last the Queen had refused to acknowledge her sons' rights to the throne. All his efforts to discredit them surely had helped in her decision, or had she always been determined they would not follow her? He would never know. Sons of the rascal Leicester she had called them. What did it matter? Francis was no threat now his mother was dead. Now he, Cecil, was free of the Celtic Tudors for good, and James and the Stuarts would owe the throne and their gratitude to him as kingmaker. He felt sure he could persuade James to restore a Catholic regime. What he had forgotten in his moment of triumph was that the Stuarts too owed their ancestry to the same Merovingian bloodline of Mary Magdalene, as did the Tudors.

*Amy Robsart*

*Anne Boleyn Illustration*

*Elizabeth and two sons*

*Elizabeth 1st signature*

*Francis Bacon age 18
from a drawing by E M Ward.
RA, after Hillard.
Engraved by W Hall*

*Francis Bacon age 33*

*Bacon and his father, Leicester*

Henry VIII
by unknown artist

Juba and Selene
Parents of
Mary Magdalene

The head of
John the Baptist

Statue of Pallas Athena
Greek Goddess of knowledge
with spear of knowledge in hand

Nevill

Mr ffrauncis Bacon
of Tribute, or giving what is dew

Nevill

...dige fons refusing
of thorn
...tion yourselves
...ing as in Christ

Esquier agt

The praise of the worthiest vertue
The praise of the worthiest affection
The praise of the worthiest power
The praise of the worthiest person

Anthony Comfort and consorte

...elis
...shing ye hart
laden with grief and
oppression of heart

By Mr fraunces Thomas Thomas
By Mr ffrauncis Bacon of Gr

...nus iam transactis
...est in pactis
...ce Verba lactis
...Corde ffraus in factis

Philipp against monsieur
Earle of Arundells letter to the Queen
Speaches for my Lord of Essex at the tylt
Speach for my Lord of Sussex tilt

honorificabilitudine Loycesters Common Wealth

Graie Inn in the
revealed
from your service
more than externally
Incerto autore

Orations at Graies Inne revells
Queenes Mate

Earle of Arundles By Mr ffrauncis Bacon
letter to the Queens mlye

Essaies by the same author printed

By Mr ffrauncis William Shakespeare
Bacon Rychard the second
Rychard the third
Asmund and Cornelia
Ile of Dogs frmnt
revealing
day through
every crumy by Thomas Nashe inferior plaiers
peepes and
oco of William Shakespeare
as your

THE NORTHUMBERLAND MANUSCRIPT
In modern script with portions of the scribblings erased.

*The Northumberland Manuscript*

US symbol of the New Age Order
as on the US Great Seal and on
all US $1 currency

La Pieta statue

Thomas Jefferson
Mason and 1st President of USA

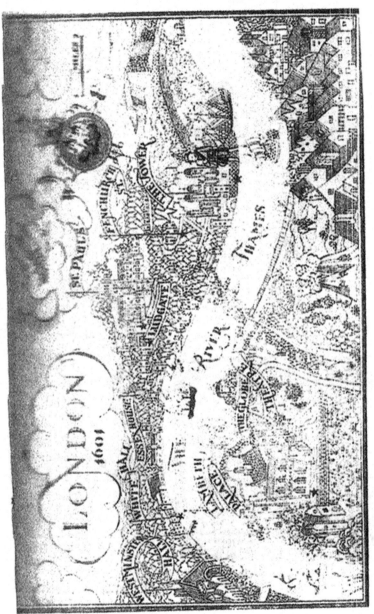

Map of London, 1601

*Richmond Palace*

York House

York Place

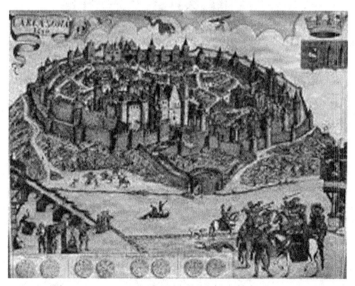

Carcassonne

*Robert Essex*

*John Dee*

*Robert Cecil*

*The Globe Theatre*

# Chapter 41

**Ritz Hotel.  Piccadilly, London. November, 2014**

Having seen Robert's name carved in stone on the Beauchamp Tower, Mrs G returned to her hotel. She had booked into the Ritz in Piccadilly in a room facing over Green Park towards Buckingham Palace which in Elizabethan times had not been built. The park had then been an area of open fields visited by pickpockets and prostitutes. The skin of pigs' bladders used as prophylactics to avoid the pox had lain discarded on the ground.  Rats the size of cats had run everywhere in the fields and streets in their thousands, living in the open sewers of the town, and on the low muddy banks of the Thames. The dreaded disease of the Black Plague constantly reoccurred. At that time few lived beyond the age of fifty. What had happened before could happen again. As Mrs G sat on the edge of her bed, she ruminated on the events of the day and remembered Abe's words of warning that humanity would soon lack resistance to the diseases of the past, but too often his words had fallen on deaf ears.

As she sat, she shed a tear at Robert Essex's unhappy fate, but more so for Elizabeth and the tragic ending to her illustrious life.  That Francis Bacon when young had portrayed her in a play as the "Alone Queen" was more prophetic than he could then have realized. Believing the calumnies of Cecil and trusting the duped Raleigh, while doubting her own children, the Queen had had no means to discover the truth. How odd that Elizabeth should share her reputation as a childless mother with Mary Magdalene, both victims of religious prurience and the stigma of illegitimacy.  Poor woman, her Tudor dynasty gone forever, although her bloodline, as with Mary, would still live on in unexpected ways. The discovery of the name of Robart Tidir at the Tower had been conclusive proof to Mrs G of Essex's true identity as the Tudor child of Elizabeth. Nor was she in any doubt that he and Francis were brothers. Lettice Knollys, who had raised Robert, had secretly married his father Leicester when Robert was twelve. From then on Robert and Francis had been brought closer together by their father and notwithstanding the five year gap in their ages, they had become firm friends. There were times when Elizabeth's favoritism towards Robert had upset Francis. Mrs G did not believe Francis' once jealous accusation of his mother's incest with Robert which, written in a fit of jealous pique, he had later regretted. The Queen had loved Robert's dilettante ways often playing backgammon and dice with him, and betting on her racehorses and on cockfighting at the many cockpit venues in London. None which held any interest for Francis. Robert had married with Elizabeth's approval at the age of twenty-four. But she knew too of his constant flirtations at court, often with her own young, fair faced ladies-in-waiting. She knew in her heart he was his own man, and of that she was proud. Of Francis she knew less since he had a coyness when with her. She felt he was less open, trying too hard to please her, while not mastering his fear of her rejection, nor recognizing the talent demonstrated in his many plays and poems unrevealed to her.

Mrs G realized now why communication in the Elizabethan period had needed to be so clandestine, with the veiled motives and interpretations of riddled words and speech known only to the informed. She appreciated why Francis' long-time muse Pallas Athene had served his purpose to bring new words and meanings to the English language and way of life; often revolutionary usages. Francis' efforts had allowed the fresh thoughts and ideas of new writers to gain expression while hiding behind the mythical invisibility of Pallas. It had been sheer chance that an appearance had been required for an author in person, whose name so usefully had a similarity to Pallas' shaken spear of knowledge. The good Lord doth move in mysterious ways, Mrs G had mused. Or was fate, in reality just chance, an endless throw of the dice, as might be all life itself? The thought disturbed her practical nature.

At the root of the endless deception of the times was the ongoing theological battle by the Catholic Church against the revival of Jesus' and Mary Magdalene's Nazarene teachings in the broad name of Protestantism. In her father's footsteps Elizabeth I had striven to maintain her resistance to the Pope against the unrelenting pressure from all corners of Europe to reinstate lost Catholic power in England. Many of the Queen's enemies were English nobility, still practicing Catholicism underground at hidden altars in dark cellars, who had lost their prestige and fortunes under Henry VIII and were resolved to restore them. His Holiness the Pope had promised a reward of two million golden ducats to anyone who would end the Queen's life. An immense sum.

Henry and his own father Henry VII, had practiced Catholicism as a political necessity to avoid war with the European continent, but their Tudor roots were as Celtic Christians, descendants of King Arthur and the Pendragons, and of the Merovingian kings.

Henry had been obliged to marry the Catholic Catharine of Aragon who had been married previously to his older brother Arthur, who had died leaving Henry as heir to the English throne. Catharine was six years older than her new husband and in sixteen years of their living together had failed to produce a son. Unsurprisingly Henry turned to new pastures to find the male heir which it was his duty to produce, but which brought the disapproval of the Pope. Not to be thwarted, Henry threw off the shackles of popery and its claimed divinity and introduced his own absolute right as king to be head of the English Church. It was not just Catharine the long-suffering Henry finally shook off, but the whole bloody history of Roman Catholicism and its sway over the British people. It was an act which was to be a turning point in the fortunes of the English people for the next four hundred years.

Francis' companion Anthony had spent twelve years as an English secret agent under the guise of a wealthy traveler and diplomat in Europe. Reporting directly to the queen, he sent back details of former Catholic English nobility still in contact with their European counterparts. He had warned of the secret construction of a fleet of warships in Spain intended for England's invasion, and his spies had given ample notice of it setting sail for England. Essex, at the side of his father Leicester, the then Commander-in-Chief of all the Queen's armed forces, had ensured that England was well prepared.

It was further proof, from their high and trusted positions close to the Queen that their relationships with her were as husband and son.
As for Francis, he had written in an address to the Queen that he was:
*"One of the Natural and True-Bred children, of her sacred Majesty."*
Clearly indicating he was one of her offspring.

The defeat of the Spanish Armada was the end of the efforts by the continental powers to overthrow Elizabeth by force, and since its failure Catholic activities had needed to be more covert. Just two years after Elizabeth's death the Gunpowder Plot to blow up the Houses of Parliament with King James and all its members present had taken place, led by the Catholic Guy Fawkes. It had been thwarted with hours to spare before the gunpowder smuggled into its cellars in thirty-six hefty wine barrels, each the weight of a tonne, was due to be detonated. The new king had not taken England back to Catholicism as had been hoped by some. Fawkes and his accomplices were executed. Only one escaped notice and that was Robert Cecil, whom it was said had engineered the whole plot and in a last moment of trepidation had betrayed his fellow conspirators.

# Chapter 42

Mrs G reflected on the information she had gathered, and finally felt that the last pieces of a giant jigsaw of secrets from the concealed world which her great-grandmother had uncovered were falling into place. Of a time steeped in undercover actions and coded communications in the face of the life-threatening punishments which both Protestants and Catholics suffered from each other for their beliefs. She looked back at the history of the Templars and their role as guardians of the Temple of Solomon once offering protection for all beliefs from opposing forces. Now it seemed as if nothing had changed and the religions of the world were once again at each other's throats, often one against the other in the name of the same prophet.

She realized more now why Francis had found cause to write his own disguised bilateral cipher into his works of Pallas and Shakespeare. Not just to hide his private life and his secret birth, but so that Catholicism or its like would not once more rise up to destroy knowledge gained from the past, nor prohibit the new world of scientific discovery in which the two might come together as one, as Francis believed they could.

From time immemorial mankind had formed exclusive bodies secreting information for their own protection and advancement. The word Kabbalah itself meant secrecy. From the day of his birth Bacon had been required to be a concealed man. It was a perverse situation equal to that of any of the dramatic inventions of his plays.

The document Mrs G had seen at Alnwyck so recently connecting Bacon to the Shakespeare plays was never intended for public scrutiny. Bacon's trustee after his death, his former secretary Rawley, had been carefully bound to keep all revealing documents hidden from prying eyes. It was only by accident that many years later the scribbled, but precious, Northumberland Manuscript had come to light, having been discovered at the former home of one of Bacon's scriveners, a drafter of documents.

As for Bacon's use of codes, Mrs G's great grandmother, Elizabeth Gallup, had evidenced these in her work published as *The*

*Shakespearean Ciphers* a century or so ago. The play of Richard II had originally been published anonymously in 1597. The title page gave a typical clue to the double writing and use of "33" as the numerical symbol of Bacon as well as that of the highest Masonic Degree, which runs like a golden thread throughout the ceremonials of Masonry and Rosicrucianism from the first Masonic step "T" and the thirty-three candles on the Rosicrucian Altar. The Title page of the 1597 play version read:-

Thirty –Three T.T.{ *T*-he –*T*-ragedie of Richard the se-*con*-d

con

Bacon   b A {*A*-s it hath been publickely acted *b*-y the right Honourable the *Lorde* Chamberlain

Lord          {his Ser

You'll   *u L* {-*u*-ants

              {*L*-ondon.

              {*P*-rinted by Valentine Simmes for Andrew Wise and

Tap      taP {*a*-re to be sold at his shop in Paules Churchyard at

              {*t*-he signe of the Angel

Reading from bottom to top with the first letters of each line the message becomes clear.

*"t-a-P-u-l-Lorde-b-A-con-c-T-T"* or "Tap you'll Lord Bacon see Thirty Three."

Few, and most likely none, of the plays known to be published before 1597:- *Two Gentleman of Verona, The Comedy of Errors, Love's Labours Lost, Love's Labours Wonne; Midsummer's Night Dream; The Merchant of Venice; Richard II and III; Henry IV, Henry VI; King John; Titus Andronicus, and Romeo & Juliet* - carried an author's name on their original publication.

Only after the queen had issued a warrant for the arrest of the author of Richard II did the name William Shakespeare become printed on all later editions of the plays. After the Stratford actor's permanent decampment to Stratford to live a good life on the proceeds of the pension granted him by Southampton, and from selling corn and lending small sums of money until his death in 1616, a further twenty plays were published and performed in London. These included: "*The Merry Wives of Windsor; Much Ado about Nothing; As You Like it; Henry V; Julius Caesar; Hamlet; Twelfth Night; Troilus and Cressida; All's Well That Ends Well; Measure for Measure; Othello; King Lear; Timon of Athens; Macbeth; Anthony and Cleopatra; Pericles; Coriolanus; Cymbeline; The Winter's Tale; The Tempest; and Henry VIII.*

Of other plays:- *The Taming of the Shrew; Henry VIII; All's Well that Ends Well; Julius Caesar; Timon of Athens;* and *Coriolanus -* there is no evidence they were even in existence during the lifetime of the Stratford actor, since they were not known until after his death. In addition Elizabeth Gallup had been of the opinion that many of the plays were relevant to Bacon's life in portraying real people of the day in differing disguises who the public might not recognize, but his friends would. In *Two Gentlemen of Verona,* one of his earliest plays, Bacon may be seen as Valentine; Marguerite, as Silvia; and the role of Proteus that of Francis' sexually active brother Anthony, also then in love with Marguerite. The plays *Romeo and Juliet* and *Troilus and Cressida* also reflect Bacon's love life and its highs and lows, while *Much Ado About Nothing* tells the story of Francis' father Leicester.

Earlier in 1593 and 1594 two poems *"The Rape of Lucrece,* and *Venus and Adonis"* had been published. Both had later been claimed to have been dedicated to Henry Wriothesley, the young Earl of Southampton, and close friend of Francis Bacon, although neither poem had carried the name of their author. Of the 154 sonnets later to be attributed to the name of Shakespeare the great majority had appeared originally without a name, and were for private circulation only.

The sonnets largely fell into two series. One of an uncontrollable lust for a "dark lady" and another about conflicted love for a "fair youth." The dark lady was almost certainly Marguerite, Francis' first love and one it took him years to forget, while the fair youth described has been later assumed to be Henry Southampton who at the time of writing was a twenty-year-old. The substitution of female for male and vice versa was a convenient disguise for the love objects of the sonnets and plays. There was no reason for the two lovers in "*Venus and Adonis*" to be male as was scandalously speculated, but more likely a man and woman in sexual role reversals. Even so, the bisexuality of the nobility of the day in England and Europe was not unusual, despite sodomy being illegal in the eyes of the Church and the law.

The youthful and attractive Southampton had a taste for theater and poetry and was an admirer of Francis' works, many of whose plays he helped provide finance to stage. The large majority, including all the earlier Shakespeare plays, were performed either by the Queen's Men or the Lord Chamberlain's Men, both groups of actors who came under the jurisdiction of the Lord Chamberlain's office, directly responsible to the Monarch. It was Leicester, Francis' father, who had encouraged play-acting and the licensing of actors under Elizabeth's reign. If the Queen did not know of Francis' authorship, then his father certainly did, and kept it under wraps.

Francis Bacon's home at Twickenham Hall was utilized by the Good Pens to churn out ideas for plays and books and pamphlets. There is no record that the actor Shaksper himself had any access to these facilities or to any publisher other than Richard Field who was known to both him and Bacon. The actor who later adopted the name Shakespeare was said to have played his last role in the play *Sejanus His Fall* after Elizabeth's death. If he and Francis Bacon had met it would most likely have been in a director to actor relationship. Having no known literacy skills the actor was not one of Francis' circle of Good Pens.

Shakespeare knew Burbage, the owner of the Globe, and Ben Jonson, both of whom were sworn not to reveal Francis Bacon's authorship. There was no reason why the actor Shakespeare would have known of the true authorship and no doubt assumed the flow of unattributed plays came from among the writers based at Twickenham Hall. It was to be chance and good fortune which gave him the opportunity to assume the mantle of their authorship for the rest of time. If Shakespeare did know the identity of the true author then to reveal it would have cost him his claim to fame and the good living that went with it, and so gave him good cause to keep it quiet.

From a booklet written in 1598 by an acquaintance of Bacon came the words:

"*So the sweete wittie Soule of Ovid lives in the mellifluous and hony-tongued Shakespeare, witness his Venus and Adonis, his Lucrece, his sugred Sonnets among his private friends.*"

That Bacon knew and had translated Ovid at an early age was known. Not so Shaksper the Bard of Avon who could read no Latin or Greek and had no known "dark lady" nor "fair youth" in his life, nor any romantic liaison that has ever been disclosed, apart from his one uneventful marriage.

Dante, the doyen of Italian literature, had been studied by Francis at Oxford. Some two hundred years earlier he had implemented a cipher of "Double Writing" which Bacon utilized early on as his own personal cipher. In a work written by Bishop Tennison shortly after Bacon's death, entitled Baconia, he had cited some papers written by Bacon to be: *"Too near the Heels of Truth"* to be revealed, and in which: *"much Mysterie consisteth"* in which the use of *"Roman and Italic shapes are confounded.*" This too was one of Bacon's basic codes. In the famous First Folio assembly of many of the Shakespeare plays printed in 1623, which carried a drawing of the Bard of Avon under the heading of William Shakespeare, Bacon's close friend Ben Jonson had written in an introductory note the words: *"Looke not on his picture, but his Booke."* He could hardly have expressed his meaning more plainly.

That the actor Shaksper had on his death left nothing written apart from the almost illegible signature on his will and testament was all Mrs G needed to convince herself that he was not the author of anything! Where had he been between the ages of twenty-one to twenty-nine? Nobody knew. He had not been seen or heard of until 1593, and it had not been until around 1597 when he was thirty-three that the first published versions of plays bearing his name had appeared, despite the prior enactment of many of them. The date accorded with the actor's disappearance from London to Stratford for years to come, conveniently out of the way of investigation.

What more was needed to convince herself of Bacon's use of the Shakespeare pseudonym? Was it that her wish was the father to her thought? No, it was not. Mrs G was convinced. Francis Bacon fitted the bill, and no-one else.

# Chapter 43

Mrs G was flushed with the success of her discoveries. Her pastime of unraveling codes with Abe, her research in the years before she came to Europe; the information she had from Gerry's grandmother, and the deciphering done by her own great-grandmother had all given her a grand head start to the clues she needed to find and unravel. She felt she was riding the waves of a voyage of discovery that would reveal all she had set out to do, for herself and for Abe, and the children, and for her book for posterity.

Her training in genetics had taught her to follow her inductive nose where bloodlines were involved. She had little time for the novel theory of "memes" which claimed that mental thought and its retention was the principal influence on genes. Mrs G considered it was the other way round in that a gene pool of infinite resource existed in the unused DNA of every person, as the scientist Francis Crick had discovered. In time of essential need the genes would signal the mind to utilize their resource. The less the mind was inhibited by past practice and open to fresh thought, the more likely there would be a successful outcome. If the mind relied only on its own precedent, the less likely it would be to use its genetic resource to find new, imaginative solutions.

Mrs G did not go along with those, including many modern scientists, who said that no God existed. It ignored her view that mankind and the Universe were one in all respects of mind, body, and soul. Not one of soulless and mindless atoms, but of boundless interconnected energy that had meaning. The Universe was God and God was the Universe since it had order, and order required intelligence.

Mrs G was fully aware of the chemical and magnetic power of genes, in that the body was no more than a slave to them, an outer shell dedicated to their command. She believed they were our subconscious, which we knew existed, but could not explain, but which controlled all our natural impulses. Those of sexual attraction and the fight for survival being the foremost, since all life was driven to procreate so as to achieve immortality by genetic rebirth. In effect the gene pool resource existed in a separate dimension from the mind.

For a moment she almost felt sorry for all the Devils, Satans and Lucifers the way they were maligned. To give the Devil his due he was simply part of the duality of human nature. The Dark Side, which was common for mankind and the Universe alike.

Despite her own Methodist Wesleyan childhood upbringing with its emphasis on being charitable to others, Mrs G was well aware of her own body and the chemical desires her genes dictated to it. She had once had a crush at college on a boy who had played fast and loose with her emotions and her body, which had fulfilled a need in her she could not control at the time. Whether they were purely physical, or spiritual, she was too young to deduce. However when he had found stronger attractions elsewhere, Mrs G had resolved to put mind over matter in any future relationship.

She knew that by genetic process plants were minded to reject union where the result would turn out unsuitable progeny. It made it easier to understand class structures and the ethnic nature of human tribes. Mrs G consoled herself that her work with Abe had given her the freedom she valued most, of thought and expression. It had been enough to have loved Abe's faculties and purpose, and to care for him. Looking back she felt that Abe's companionship had been more valuable than any passing passion; a union of minds. It was not one to pass on genetically, but only through the success of their work. This they shared with all creative people whose work lived after them.

# Chapter 44

**London. November, 2014**

Mrs G had found time to carefully examine enlargements of the photos she had taken at St. Christophe, the Templar chapel at Montsaunés, built on the spot of an earlier Church over a thousand years before. The encryptions she had found there had persuaded Mrs G that Mary Magdalene may have christened her child there. The small chapel had been built near the Franco-Spanish border in the foothills of the Pyrenees mountain chain and fell under the jurisdiction of the nearby Fortress Cathedral of St. Bernard de Comminges, said to be the Roslyn of France, with many identical Templar motifs.

The Romans had previously built a castle on the site where the cathedral now stood. It was where the Jewish King Herod had been exiled by the Romans after his daughter Salome had demanded from him the decapitated head of John the Baptist as a test of her father's love for her. The cathedral was a stopping point on the pilgrimage trail from the church citadel of Santiago de Compostela in northern Spain to the great cathedrals in France, and from them to Roslyn. Mrs G had been fortunate in obtaining entry as the Montsaunés Chapel was only open on request. She had appealed to the local padré for permission, having explained her background in cryptology. With further investigation Mrs G believed that the symbols she found might link Mary's child directly from Jesus to the Merovingian bloodline of King Merovech and his son Clovis, which origin they had claimed as kings of the Celtic Franks. The complex codes Mrs G had seen at Montsaunés had been a long standing mystery to the present day. The carvings on the exterior walls of the chapel depicted the usual grimacing gargoyles to ward off evil spirits, but two were of particular interest. One of a young mother with an infant in her arms, and another of a man and woman embracing as lovers.

The interior walls and ceiling of St. Christophe contained astonishing frescoes unlike anything else in medieval art. The walls and ceilings were covered in stars and solar wheels of geometric, Kabbalistic designs and of Hermetic rites, with a multitude of astrological signs and symbols. Despite the name of the chapel there was virtually nothing that was Christian about it in a present day sense. Some symbols bore a resemblance to Near Eastern iconography, while the star spangled vault reflected the stellar covered ceiling of Unas' pyramid in Egypt, as well as those at the Hebrew Temple Mount in Jerusalem. Some similarities to markings at Roslyn were apparent, but there were others unlike any she had previously seen. From the many photos Mrs G had studied she formed the opinion that the star patterns were the same as those which the Magi, the three kings of Bible fame, had observed at the time of Christ's birth. What if the same celestial formation had been repeated at the time of the birth and christening of the child of Jesus and Mary Magdalene at this very same spot? Why else would they have been shown there?

The nearby cathedral at St Bernard de Comminges, also built by the Templar knights, would have afforded protection to the chapel which lay in the short distance between the borders of the then Kingdom of Navarre and the French citadel of Carcassonne. It was also near the place Mary Magdalene had sought refuge after her flight from Palestine, which was hardly coincidental.

From inquiries Mrs G had discovered that Marguerite had given birth to a child, a daughter, not many months after her long liaison with the young Francis Bacon. Mrs G guessed that Marguerite, with a husband who had rejected her, and a dissolute court life of countless amours, had wanted a child from the one person she had found to be still untouched by the demons that pursued her. Francis with his purity of soul was that person. The real identity of Marguerite's child was no doubt concealed, Mrs G reasoned. It was not until later that Mrs G had reason to believe that Marguerite had handed the child to her mother, Catherine de Medici, to be sent to the Medici family palazzo in Italy to be raised there, so that Marguerite's husband Henry was never to become aware of its existence.

It was virtually certain that Marguerite would have known of the tiny St Christophe Chapel. It made sense that with her Nazarene ancestry from the Cathars who had once inhabited the area she would have had her daughter by Francis christened there, avoiding a Catholic baptism or any record of the birth in her husband's nearby kingdom. Mrs G's heart beat faster as her imagination soared. The adrenalin that flowed with it overcame the mounting tiredness which she had been experiencing over the past few weeks.

It had been Marguerite's belief that she held a common ancestry with Mary Magdalene. If the child of Marguerite by Francis was to be of the Merovingian bloodline which Gerry's grandmother Marilyn claimed for her own ancestry then at what point had its descendants come to obtain the title Compte de St Germain well over a century later? More information was needed. Marilyn had said she would explain the circumstances to the children when they came of age, but she had died with her own daughter beforehand, and if Abe knew he had decided against passing it on.

Scores of French nobility had left France for England following purges of Protestants and many had gone on to America with English settlers to start a new life. Some years later more of those of noble blood had run from sharing the same fate as Queen Marie Antoinette's beheading on the guillotine, in France's anti-monarchist revolution in the name of *Liberty, Equality and Fraternity.*

In 1757 the French had lost their colonies in war to the British and had become a bankrupt nation, setting the scene for their coming revolution some thirty years on. The then Compte de St Germain, as Mrs G discovered, had left France well beforehand along with those with an eye to their future safety. He was a clairvoyant and a close friend of Madame Pompadour, the renowned courtesan and mistress of the French King Louis XV, blamed by the populace for France's failure in war. The Compte had visited London for a while meeting the then Prince of Wales. After living in America for some years, he returned to Europe and settled in Hungary. There his family, the once royal and wealthy Racokzis, had dispersed, their fortunes having been devastated in 1700 following years of war with the Hapsburgs. The Compte was a writer, philosopher and chemist, with a magical sense of entertainment; and, as Mrs G was to discover, he was a Rosicrucian and a Mason.

Mrs G's brow knitted, perplexed at the paper chain of events in the tight circle of nobility who had controlled Europe in those times. Nearly all of them were interrelated in some form with a store of genetic intelligence and wit. Yet many self-destructed through their own exclusive self-indulgence. The more Mrs G had delved, the more the information flowed. Of secret liaisons. Of bigamous marriages. Of incest. Of bastard children. Of a multitude of perversions; and of disguised identities. And of murder too. All in the pursuit of power and fortune. The art of seduction was indispensable in the scheme of things. That the nobility would hold great dances and balls in which they were masked to conceal their amours gave excitement to the risks involved. Life was short and to be enjoyed. Wit, sex and power were the essential ingredients of high society, much as they had always been and were still today.

As to whom Francis Bacon was, Mrs G had made up her mind, and understood why his playwright's identity had needed to be invisible. Why was the body of the immortalized William Shakespeare not laying in Westminster Abbey alongside other great English writers and poets of the time? He was not, because London's intelligentsia and elite then well knew that William Shakespeare was not one of their kind and that he was no more than a mask. It would be another hundred years or more before the name Shakespeare had come to have importance as new generations of people sought the real identity of the man behind it. Concealment was the name of the game. Revelation was only for those in the know.

Bacon himself, despite the great scholarly works to which his name was openly attributed, had been mysteriously excluded from burial at Westminster for reasons Mrs G was yet to discover. Of more importance to Mrs G was what Bacon might have known of immortality, as had come to her mind on that late afternoon she had found Abe dead. Did life go on forever, in some other form? It was the same Holy Grail quest which had been sought and proved elusive for centuries past.

A book known as *Der Fama* which had been published anonymously in Germany in 1614 had been connected to Francis Bacon and John Dee. It was something Mrs G still needed to follow up. It supposedly held the answer to the Philosopher's Stone, as the spiritual liberation from the cycle of birth and death, based on numerology handed down from the Sufis and ancient Egyptians and of the Kabbalah. Mrs G had much to do yet to complete her giant puzzle to her own satisfaction. As for the Grail, there was no evidence that Bacon had searched for it as a tangible object. That he had found its true meaning in another form was becoming more evident to her. Did she, Mrs G, honestly believe that the Grail held the magical power of immortality? No, not as an object, but she did not doubt that it had existed as a symbol of faith in the reality of what it stood for. She sighed. She was feeling tired now and wondered if she was not perhaps suffering from the same delusions as all those who had sought the Grail.

Time for a double vodka martini in the Ritz bar and to see what was on at the movies. Last year the choice had been between *"Noah"*, *"Son of God"*, and *"Gravity"*. Expediency meets Faith meets soulless Space in the form of a rotund George Clooney. All on the same mission to extend life beyond Earth, she opined to herself. Best stay away from the movies and try live theater for relaxation.

Mrs G turned to Ethan who had come into the room quietly during her thoughts and had sat down with a benign smile on his face while she prepared to go out. Ethan wore a fine wool black polo-necked sweater, without his usual priest's white dog collar, and his slim, smooth looks appeared almost androgynous. He was, as always, difficult to fathom, but somehow she felt he was the one person who understood her mission, which she had increasingly confided in him. They joined hands and took the elevator down to the bar.

# Chapter 45

As Phil Buonarroti left the baggage hall he spotted Ethan.
"Great, thanks for coming." Phil greeted Ethan with a high-five.
"I don't have much time. Next stop Berlin. I need to get over to
Terminal 2," said Phil. "Why not come with me? Should have gone
through transit, but best to use the time to catch up. So what news of
our sleuth? Anything I need deal with?"
Ethan reported his findings: "She has done a whole deal of research
into Bacon's connections to the Masons. All background for her
book. She is convinced of Gerry's Merovingian bloodline. As such
she sees Gerry as a natural born leader, ready to be given control of
the funds from Abe's foundation when he comes of age at eighteen.
She has confided to me she will be happy to hand him the reins of the
Magdala Foundation and rid herself of the responsibility.

Ethan saw the look on Phillip's face.
"Is there a problem? Surely, with guidance you can control him?"
"How? We don't know anything about the kid. He seems a little
strange. A bit of a loner with his head in the clouds. We know Mrs G
has a deal of influence over him, but we don't know if she has any
notion that Abe was upset with us before his death. If so she may
have passed on her fears to the boy. What's more vital is what she
may know of Abe's antibiotic super strain, and whether she has
passed any inkling of it on. It fits in with our plans for the best use of
global resources and can make us a fortune in the process. We need
to get control over Abe's foundation to put our plans into action.
At the same time we need to protect the kid as it's his Merovingian
connection which gives us so much clout with our rich members.
They believe in the superior intellect of his ancestry. It's as if he's
the old Aga Khan, who was given his weight in gold every year by
his faithful Islamic followers, and so died from being overweight!"
Phil laughed, as he usually did at his own tasteless jokes. They got
out of the shuttle bus and went into Terminal 2 for a quick chat over
a coffee.

"If we can invest the foundation funds in our long term projects with our associates worldwide, neither Mrs G nor Gerry can ever unravel the contractual obligations. We have a network primed and ready to go. Mrs G is the one we want out of the way, or else to win her confidence, whatever suits best before the boy comes of age. I said I'd publish her book for her, so I can get a good look at it before anything in it gets out which we might want to suppress." And as an afterthought, "How's she doing? She had a nasty cough when we met. Said she needed specialist attention for it. One of our Order is a specialist in Boston. We can send her to him on her return. When do you think she'll be back?" Phil said with a questioning look.

Ethan told him. "She's not well. You don't have to worry. She won't live long without my help.
"Yeah, so you said, but we can't leave things hanging in the air for too long. If you could give her a helping hand in one direction or another, you would certainly get the gratitude of the Order," Phil joked feebly, red -eyed from the flight and looking at Ethan with a weak dry smile.

Ethan gave Buonarroti a long, hard look until Phil turned away and wiped his eyes with a tissue.
"You forget something," said Ethan, quietly, but forcibly. "You may think we have the same beliefs in life, but I take instructions from no-one, and certainly not from you. I do what suits my purpose. I have yet to make a final judgment on Mrs G. She's an experiment of mine. If and when your interests are the same as mine I'll let you know. I know what you're up to. It's not my job to help you take life away from people. I'm all for letting people enjoy themselves in venal pleasures while they are alive. The Apocalypse you seek will give rise to a whole new world order, and heaven knows where that will lead. The Sun's entry into Aquarius in 2010 heralded a dramatic shift in cultural paradigms, and look what's happened since then. The revival of thousand year old sectarian arguments threatens half the world with zealots who have no fear of death or afterlife. There are new spiritual forces driving the world. It's not about money. It's about power over the minds of people. A far more formidable prospect."

Ethan wagged his finger at Phillip as the public address system announced the Lufthansa flight to Berlin, while Phillip looked out of sorts at his reaction. It was not what he had expected, but then Ethan was a creepy guy sometimes. He could not recall now just exactly how he had met him. Maybe one of the Order's members had recommended him previously. As Phillip left with his Louis Vuitton briefcase and hand baggage Ethan called after him. "What happened after Abe's death? What was the result of the autopsy?" But Phil had deaf ears that didn't want to hear, or perhaps could not over the noise and bustle of the airport. He disappeared into a line of people heading for the departure gate.

Ethan guessed why Phillip was off to Berlin. Phillip had dropped a hint he was seeking to establish a new order in Europe with the same proactive ideas he was introducing into the Washington Lodge. They were similar to the Arian doctrine of the Merovingians and the Templars about controlling the world order by meritocracy rather than democracy. Arianism had gone underground after the demise of the Templars, and had re-surfaced in Europe in Renaissance times. Napoleon had tried to implement it and Hitler too had sought to twist it to his vision of a super-race by assimilation of its ideals and symbols.

Fascism was once more gaining ground in Europe. The empty promise of increased prosperity which only the rich enjoyed was creating extremism. The incessant pressure to work harder to pay greater taxes was not what the mass of people aspired to. Their greatest concerns were about inequality, racial and religious tension, and war and disease, in that order. The raw capitalism of a technological age under the label of progress simply acerbated the high oxygen fuel that gave rise to aggression between the have-nots and those who saw themselves as achievers. Ethan saw the two sides of it only too clearly.

Despite efforts to contain their revival the Western world was only now coming to understand the implications of old religious rivalries in a nuclear world, and most likely Phillip believed their threat needed to be ended fast, and in one fell swoop. "First strike" was the military expression for it but use of nuclear weapons might receive a response in kind. There needed to be a better solution. In all probability Phillip was preparing like-minded allies for the coup he was planning. Abe's elixir would produce a super-race immune from disease and chemical warfare, and Phillip would justify the selection process as a triumph of intellect over ignorance. Even so it would take time and time was not on the side of the US and its Western allies.

Ethan rubbed his chin. An interesting moment, he thought. Was not that the wish which Confucius had bestowed on his enemies? That they should "live in interesting times." How many had gone before Phillip seeking to change the world and failed? That Phillip himself might be the disposable dupe of a concealed power whose goal to control humanity stemmed from the distant past would never enter Phillip's one-track mind. Ethan grinned at the thought. His own antecedents were eternal.

Despite his Masonic principles Phillip was not a man of any great faith, but he realized that down the ages people had sought spiritual answers. The Greek Stoics had called it "logos spermatikos" later also known in Latin as "anima mundi". In New Age terms it was known as "the law of regeneration in the Universe in which all life was connected as the soul was connected to the body."
This was all well and good thought Phillip, but now was now and action need be taken. Abe had supplied the means. Now Phillip had the plan, and it needed to be acted upon. He liked a quote from George Bernard Shaw, the famed 20th century British playwright: *"Our question is not to kill, or not to kill, but how to select the right people to kill."*
As for Ethan, Phillip would soon put someone else on the job of tracking down Mrs G. It was essential to know where she was and what she was doing, and if necessary she would have to be stopped. He had no time to play mind games with Ethan.

# Chapter 46

## Gray's Inn Chambers, London. 1601

Francis had to do some serious thinking after the death of the Queen. She had left him nothing on her death except for her earlier gift of Twickenham Hall and its eighty acres of parkland, against which he had heavy debts. Elizabeth had seized the possessions of Francis' father Leicester on his death, and those of his brother Essex had been forfeited to the Crown as a traitor. Elizabeth was the last of the Tudors, and her wealth, without recognized heirs, had fallen on her death into the possession of the Crown. Furthermore, Cecil and Coke now appeared to be effectively in power in England, having ensured the English throne had gone to James VI of Scotland as their preferred candidate, whom they believed would restore Catholicism to England. Fortunately for Francis, the new king was his own man, and not to be easily persuaded by Cecil. Before becoming James I of England he had been James VI of Scotland for some thirty-three years on the abdication of his mother Mary Queen of Scots, having been appointed as the Scottish King a year after his birth. Rumor had it that he was a switch baby, substituted on the death in childbirth of his mother's real child to ensure the Stuart's claim to the throne of Scotland. So long as Francis remained silent over his real identity as Elizabeth's son, and so was not perceived as a claimant to the English throne, then James' uncontested accession would complete an effective and peaceful union of all three ancient realms of England, Scotland and Wales; although it was to be another hundred years before Scotland and England became legally united.

James was sitting pretty, in position rather than description, since he was of a slight and weedy build and pasty visage. What he lacked in looks, he made up for in intellect, writing a number of scholarly books, including one claiming the divine right of intelligent kings, and a theological study on the role of Demons. He had been nicknamed "The Wisest Fool in Christendom" as his pleasure was to play the role as fop and buffoon for his own amusement, having an interest in all things theatrical. Although married out of a requirement for an heir, and raising three children, his fancy was for good-looking young men. Those who satisfied his desires he would promote to high rank. Death or imprisonment awaited those who did not.

Of concern to Francis was that James might return the new Protestantism of Elizabeth's time to Catholicism, but James was to cleverly steer a course between the two. Catholics could practice quietly as long they gave no trouble and recognized James as head of the English Anglican Church. In the circumstances in which Cecil had believed he had put an end to Francis' ambitions Cecil soon found himself vying with Francis for James' favors. Francis' learnedness, combined with a wit and humor no longer suppressed by his mother, was of greater entertainment value to James than the over-solicitous manner of Cecil. Francis had been working previously on *The New English Bible* in partnership with Robert Fludd and a team of clergymen, and flatteringly proposed to James its name should be changed to *The Official King James Bible*. Despite Francis' relationship with James, Cecil was not to give up easily against Francis any more than was his accomplice Coke. Resentment of Francis' birth and new found ability to entertain and promote himself, as well as his profound knowledge of law, still provoked their envy and irritation.

In an incident in the Houses of Parliament Francis had stood to speak on the relaxation of taxation on the poor which was not in favor with the members present. Taking advantage of the situation, Coke had interrupted Francis, insisting he had no right to be in Parliament under the rule of "capias ut legatum" which debarred someone cloaking his real identity. It was Coke's ploy to reveal Francis as the son of Queen Elizabeth which as a noble would bar him from the House of Commons, and to alarm the King that Francis might be a rival for his throne. Coke had no scruples in damaging Francis' reputation and Francis was to have to use all his wits to contend with him.

# Chapter 47

## British Museum, London. November, 2014

Mrs G walked up the steps from Great Russell Street to the British Museum entering through its imposing Palladian columns. She passed through the glass-domed Great Court and into a section of administrative offices to meet the man she had made an appointment to see, a Professor Johnson. She pressed a buzzer on a counter top, and a clerk came to take her through a maze of dusty corridors and closed doors directly to the Professor's room. He was the image of a typical academic, with bent shoulders and back from a lifetime study of ciphers and hieroglyphics. He rose from a large table laden with manuscripts to greet her, his graying hair falling over his wide forehead and tired pouched eyes. He gave her a wan smile and asked her how he could help, looking at the pile of papers Mrs G was carrying. "I don't have much time today I'm afraid," he said pleasantly. "What would you like me to examine?"

When Mrs G had finished her explanation, the professor had requested some days in order to inspect her papers, and to give an answer.

"There is no guarantee I can help," he warned, "but I will do my best. An interesting subject. As a matter of fact I am currently examining something similar, but the results may never be revealed. There are many people who would prefer their secrets to remain so. The Dead Sea Scrolls, for instance, and the Messianic Seal whose meanings can be interpreted in many ways that may upset our current understanding of life and the Universe. There are dangers involved in researching ancient beliefs about invoking the Devil and his cohorts, of which you should be aware. I will see what I can do and if you contact my clerk in a few days, he will let you know when you may collect your papers and any written answer I feel able to give you. Are you in any hurry?"

The professor saw Mrs G hesitate anxiously, as she spoke. "It's a question of time... " she nervously coughed in reply. "There is one thing in particular about which I need know its real meaning and history," she said, showing him an image of a symbol she had brought with her. He reassured her with a smile. "I will try to study the material this weekend for you. I am sure you are eager for an endorsement of its authenticity from the Museum. I will do my best." Mrs G returned the smile and asked. "How far is it from here to the Burlington Arcade, can I walk it?"

"No, best you take the tube to Piccadilly from Holborn and walk from there," he told her. "It's not far." And with that the Professor ushered Mrs G out. He had a feeling she was not too well and he would do his best to oblige her. The skin on her hand had resembled the color of the parchment he had been studying. As Mrs G left the Museum she did not notice a black car parked outside near her exit. There was a man in the driver's seat. It was Ethan.


## Burlington Arcade, London

Having walked from Piccadilly Circus past the Royal Academy of Art, Mrs G wandered through the elegant old shopping arcade with her breath misting in the cold air. She looked into the windows of the tiny boutique shops selling everything from expensive cashmere, to handbags and gloves, dinner plates and tea services, silver and jewelry. She stopped next to an obese older man and woman with telephoto cameras hung round their necks, his and hers baggy tartan pants, and sneakers. They were tourists looking in a window full of miniature hand-painted knights of armor and their shields and emblems of a once glorious nobility. The figures were bought nowadays as collectors pieces for prices in the thousands of dollars. What did the couple know of those times? If they did it would probably scare the pants off them. "Ignorance is bliss," she thought, but not where she was concerned. She was hungry now for the truth she had set out to discover.


She turned into the same small bookshop where she had previously purchased the limited edition copies of Shakespeare's plays. The door rang a bell as she entered and the owner of the shop appeared and recognized her. "I think you will be pleased," he said. "I made enquiries about the book you wanted and have had it sent on loan from a colleague. But it is quite expensive I'm afraid. It is not a 16th century copy as those are very rare and found only in museums, but it is a copy published nearly a hundred years ago."

He locked the door of the shop against incoming shoppers who so often wasted his time browsing, but purchasing nothing, and produced a large, heavy, leather-bound book with the title engraved in gold letters: *The New Atlantis*. He eyed her cautiously as to her reaction and saw she was pleased.

"I don't think I've been asked for this before. My wife says she studied it years ago and tells me it's the blueprint for a perfect world, a Utopia, written four hundred years ago or more by Francis Bacon. Just up my wife's street it is; she's always looking for a better world," he confided. "A book of invention and science which foretells submarines and aircraft. Thomas Jefferson used it as a model for America's New World, but sadly it was never finished I am told. A bit like America now. Unfinished business." His words came out thoughtfully. "Who knows the future, best left alone at our age, but as the great bard once said 'All the world's a stage and we have our exits and our entrances.' "England's been there and gone, with other empires before it. Who'll be next?" he said phlegmatically, and shook his head. "Do you want the book? I'll need a debit card or better cash to pay for it. How will you take it? It's a bit heavy for you."
"No, I can take it in my carrier bag," Mrs G said, having come prepared.
"It's only a short walk to my hotel in Piccadilly."
With that she paid with her no limit black Centurion card in the name of the Magdala Foundation and was let out of the door.

# Chapter 48

**England. 1606-1612**

In September 1606 Francis progressed down the aisle of London's Marylebone Chapel resplendent in purple robes from head to foot. Tyrian purple obtained from rare shellfish at the rising of the Dog Star Sirius was the most expensive dye to obtain and was Francis' favorite color. His new bride attired in violet robes trimmed with silver thread and adorned with pearls beamed her smile nervously at an elite array of guests. The couple cut a theatrical scene of great splendor. Now forty-five years of age Francis had been recently awarded a knighthood by King James with whom he had established a close relationship. His once amorous intentions towards Elizabeth Hatton forgotten since her marriage to Coke.

On Francis's arm is his new young wife of fourteen, Alice Barnham, a commoner from an untitled but rich merchant family, and heiress to a substantial fortune willed to her by her father. Amongst her fineries, she is wearing an array of ornaments of gold and silver. A crowd of friends and well-wishers surround them from the upper echelons of the King's Court and the Law, all dressed splendidly for the occasion. As the couple pass down the aisle comments are made on the lavishness of their dress and the expense of the wedding ceremony.

Francis had lost many friends at Court after his mother's death. They had been fair weather friends who had expected his demise and had waited in the wings while they saw which way the wind might blow under the new King. But on Francis' re-establishment with James they had flocked round him once more. Francis had reopened his home at Twickenham, and those of his Good Pens who remained still showed him respect for his genius and wit.

It was rumored in court circles that Francis would climb a lot higher in position under the blessing of the King, which now seemed assured against the decreasing influence of Cecil and Coke. That he had now married Alice, a commoner, was seen as putting an end to any possible ambition he might have to England's throne, as no commoner could ever become queen. Soon after James' accession to the throne Francis had written *The Apologies* to explain that he had joined Coke's legal team in prosecuting Essex at the command of Queen Elizabeth. Although his compliance had been contrived by Cecil, it had lost Francis friends, particularly Henry Southampton who never forgave him, but the publication of *The Apologies* satisfied many others, including the new King, as Francis intended.

Despite the King granting Francis various positions of State which helped to supplement his income, Francis had decided to sell Twickenham Hall and its grounds in 1608 to repay his debts in full and restore his fortunes. After the death of his foster mother Francis moved to Gorhambury at St Albans. The Temple, as it was known locally, had been willed to Francis by Anthony Bacon on his death. It was a day's ride out of London, and it was where Francis installed his new wife to make it his permanent home.

In Francis' determination to please he had fought many parliamentary battles on behalf of the King and his extravagant court, often against Coke who would take advantage of any opportunity to start an argument with Francis. In 1610 Francis had won a major parliamentary battle on the King's behalf, after which the King had dissolved Parliament to demonstrate his divine right to do so. On its re-instatement in 1613 the King appointed Francis Attorney General, a post he had always wanted, and which gave him great influence over the newly-appointed Parliament. Even so, Coke had managed to pass a parliamentary motion to disallow the position of Attorney General the right to vote.

The fights between them rolled on, and Francis, now fully understanding the politics of power, as his mother had intended he should, was winning under his own steam. He was riding high, and would continue to do so. Coke's marriage to Elizabeth Hatton was falling apart, which he had entered into as much to rival Francis as for any other reason. Coke had gained a fiery and opinionated wife now disappointed with her husband's progress and his growing obesity, and an increasingly foul temper, often goaded by Francis in parliamentary exchanges.

Among a mass of varied works Francis had written an essay entitled *Of Deformity* as a serious journal on the subject, since only rudimentary knowledge existed at the time on abnormal physical features. After one verbal sparring match which Francis had won with Coke in Parliament, Coke had sent the hunchback Cecil a copy of the book by messenger, under the pretense it came from Bacon, so as to further infuriate Cecil to side with Coke against Francis.

The sale of Twickenham Hall and its parkland and his appointment as Attorney General had left Francis with money to spend. His wife Alice, as the new mistress of Gorhambury, had redecorated the house in the latest fashions, employing a small army of more than seventy servants for her new home. To operate The Temple, as it was named locally, the services of individuals known as Steward, Treasurer, Auditor, and Sergeant-at-Arms were required, apart from a legion of footmen, chambermaids, grooms and gardeners.

Despite her young age and the dispersion cast on her youthful marriage to Francis, Alice was intelligent and not unattractive, and was seen about town at York House, Francis' home in his youth, which he was now leasing for his use in London. Here Alice was pleased to invite new friends and acquaintances from the milieu of the Court and its nobility. Although it seemed Francis had not lost his interest in the female sex, there were to be no children of the marriage, and Francis continued to spend most of his time with his male colleagues, as he was accustomed.

Among his friends Francis' closest confidant was Toby Matthew, with whom he exchanged many of his private thoughts and sought advice on his writings. In a letter of 1609 Francis wrote to Toby for his opinion of the play he had written, *Julius Caesar*. The play was not known to be published or played until 1623, again under the masked name of William Shakespeare, as was *Measure for Measure*, on which Francis and Toby also corresponded in 1609.

As Attorney General, Francis was now the leading exponent of the law in England. His plan to bring about the union of England and Scotland had brought him into the utmost favor with the King. He had written the four thousand word *Discourse for a Happy Union between England and Scotland* soon after James had been crowned King, and had made a brilliant speech in Parliament to win the English votes needed to formalize it.

Francis was now also Grand Master of Freemasonry in England with their Templar heritage, and by merging England and Scotland he could ensure that a single code of practice reflecting Masonic values became the basis for a United Kingdom. The English Lords, however, were not to be persuaded in favor of the proposed union, envisaging hordes of kilted Scotsmen, sporrans dangling, armed with dirks and daggers in their socks, running amok in the Houses of Parliament, and so Francis' motion in the House of Lords was defeated.

Since his mother's death Francis had greater freedom to publish works under his own name. He had finished editing what was now to be called *The King James Bible* and had completed his book of *The Advancement of Learning* which was to become the first part of the six volumes of *The Great Instauration* in which he proposed "*the kindling of a light in nature to reveal the most hidden and secret in the world.*" These words were to be echoed later in the Rosicrucian book *Der Fama*.

*Der Fama* was a publication Francis had worked on with John Dee. Dee had been born thirty-five years before Francis. He was a Welshman who had studied math, geometry, philosophy and Greek at Cambridge and had obtained his Bachelor of Arts degree at the age of seventeen. At nineteen he became a Founder Member of Trinity College. He had lectured on Euclid in Paris at twenty-three where he had been offered a senior position at Sorbonne University which he rejected to return to England. Temporarily imprisoned in the Tower of London by the Catholic Mary Tudor as a revolutionary he had there met Princess Elizabeth who had aided him in his career on their release.

John Dee had acted as tutor to Queen Elizabeth in astrology and the occult, areas which fascinated her throughout most of her reign, and he had become an important figure at her Court. He had advised astrologically on the date she should be crowned as Queen and, as a meteorologist and navigator, advised on the weather conditions which aided Drake's foiling the attack of the Spanish Armada. He had formed an investment partnership with Elizabeth in the Muscovy Trading Company trading with Russia in seeking a north-east Arctic navigational passage from England to China.

His long spindly beard, and many colored robes, gave him the impression of a magician, one he liked to foster as successor to

Merlin, the wizard to the Court of King Arthur. As a member of Elizabeth's secret service he devised the hieroglyphic numeral of 007 as his code number.

Dee was knighted by Elizabeth and lived at Mortlake, a short walk from Francis Bacon's house in Richmond. There he established an immense library of books taken from the Catholic monasteries which Henry VIII had closed. Dee experimented with alchemy in attempts to find an elixir of ingredients which would offer a cure for all ills. In this the young Francis assisted enthusiastically, often staying for nights and days experimenting in reviving the dead and dying, animals and people, with their concoctions.

Dee was a belated convert to the newly formed views of Copernicus in which the earth revolved around the Sun. As time and ideas progressed Dee lost his friends, as well as his faculties, when he began speaking to spirits via the dead, involving necromancy and convincing himself he was speaking with angels; possibly the victim of his own hallucinatory potions!

The time was a turning point in which the old practices of alchemy were becoming the new chemistry, while science was replacing theology. Bacon too moved with the times towards finding life's meaning in a mixture of natural induction and mathematical reasoning. Dee died in 1608 virtually penniless reduced to telling peoples' fortunes, having planned to go to Germany. His work with Francis on *Der Fama*, a discourse on the ideas of Masonry, was not completed before his death, and wasn't published until 1614 in England as *The Fama Fraternitas.*

The recent years had flown by for Francis. By 1612 his lifetime foe Robert Cecil had died, aged forty-nine, having been given the title Lord Salisbury by King James. At fifty-one Francis was on top of the world that his mother had wanted for him. Not as a king or playwright, but as a politician and statesman. His only enemy now was Coke, his older political adversary; still in a powerful position, but without the close ear of the King who preferred the wit and wisdom of Francis. Despite James' many self-indulgences he kept England and Scotland at peace with their continental neighbors. As for himself Francis was reminded of the words he had written for his play Julius Caesar.

*"There is a tide in the affairs of men which taken at the flood leads on to fortune."*

In his room at Gray's Inn Francis leaned back in his chair and wiped his brow. At last he felt his achievements had been recognized, long held back by his mother's wishes, and now finally he was his own man, a friend of the King, with a loyal young wife, and with his good friends back again.

# Chapter 49

## Whitehall, London, 1613

Sitting prominently on his throne James I of England, now forty-seven years of age, is surrounded by sycophantic courtiers. Beside him stands a handsome youth of twenty-one, by the name of George Villiers, whose white-stockinged upper thigh James openly fondles. Villiers had been described then as *"the handsomest bodied man in all of England and of so sweet a disposition."*

James could be described as louche at best. His choice of expression and humor was frequently foul-mouthed. His head was large; his body balanced on rickety legs, with the affectation of a clown, but yet a master of deceit with a business-like mind. He regarded the world and those around him with a baleful demeanor from whom he required to be handsomely compensated for the duties of King.   From early on in his reign he had handed out unsolicited knighthoods on a large scale, demanding annual payments in return, so establishing the English payment for honors system, still continuing into the 21st century.

George Villiers had recently replaced James' former favorite whom James had made Earl of Somerset, having indulged him in an excess of gifts which had caused a scandal in which Somerset was put on trial for blackmail. To save himself Somerset had threatened to expose the king's "unnatural vices" and personal secrets of orgies held in secret rooms in the Scottish palace of Holyrood while practicing devil worship. More particular, and of more concern to James, was the accusation that James had no true Stuart blood in his veins and was a pretender to the throne, the illegitimate product of his father and a commoner. James bluffed and double-bluffed his ex-favorite to avoid discovery and incrimination, and finally silenced Somerset with imprisonment in the Tower where he was to have to suffer the cold comfort of pleasuring his jailer's sexual depravities for the next ten years.

A meeting was to take place of the Privy Council at a hearing where the King had commanded Francis to advise on his behalf as his counsel, under his latest title as President of the Court of the Verge, which gave Francis jurisdiction over Greater London. As newly appointed Attorney General Francis was looking forward to the occasion, as Edward Coke was to be the advocate on behalf of England's supreme judiciary, the Law Lords, for a ruling to which the king was opposed. The issue concerned *"Commendams"*, a means by which the King raised funds by selling favors, and its legality had been challenged. Coke was now Chief Justice of the King's Bench, a position he had not wanted since it was of no great monetary value, but which Francis had advised the King to grant him. In answer to Coke's anger at being side-lined, Francis had teased: *"Ah, my Lord, your Lordship all this while hath grown in breadth, you must needs now grow in height or you will become a monster!"*

The capricious and increasingly corpulent Coke now found himself in a legal battle against the King and his advisor Francis. In an unwise move Coke had persuaded all twelve Law Lords to write a letter to the King to reject Francis' opinion, without full appreciation of the King's own wishes on the matter and his predilection for his Divine Right. Headed by Coke, the Law Lords entered the throne room and all bowed to the King. The stage was set for Coke to overreach himself in his fury at Francis' taunts, and he duly obliged. The King was no fool, and he realized the Law Lords had been swayed to suit Coke's war of words with Francis. In consequence James had decided that he would be the sole judge of the action. Coke's hatred of Francis was intense, not just for his jealousy over Francis' birth, but also because of his wife's renewed acquaintance with Francis. Coke often called Francis a bastard in public, and had said scornfully to Francis' brother Essex before his execution "You thought to be Robert I. Now you shall be Robert the Last." But today he had gone a step too far.

As the hearing continued it became apparent that it was Coke who had gone out of his way to call a trial case as a deliberate challenge to Francis, and that he had involved the Law Lords by deceit. When realization dawned, the judges fell as one on their knees in front of the King and his courtiers, pleading they had signed their letter of opinion in misapprehension under advice from Coke. Coke in his position of Lord Chief Justice had to retract and eat his words, and was banned by the King from acting as a judge, also losing his seat on the King's Privy Council, which James gave to Francis. Coke was then to be judged separately by the Privy Council as to his suitability for a position there and was found guilty of a range of misdeeds, including corruptly receiving money for favors by which he had become one of the richest men in England. He threw himself at the mercy of the Council, groveling for hours on the floor, crying and whimpering, so as not to lose his livelihood.

On his knees in front of the King he had whimpered while the King's new young favorite George Villiers had laughed at his misery, and mimicked him as if he was a cur begging with his paws, and putting out his tongue as if to lick the King's feet, much to James' amusement. George had so pleased James' sense of black humor that shortly afterwards he was given the title of Gentleman of the Bedchamber. If it had not been for Francis' plea for him, Coke would have lost all, but on Francis' advice to the King, Coke was ordered to recant his crimes. They were read out to the Court as an admission of:

*"His deceit, contempt and slander of the Government and his perpetual turbulent carriage against the Liberties of the Church and the Royal Prerogative and his exploitation of the Laws."*

Coke was demeaned, and in view of his harsh treatment of Sir Walter Raleigh at his trumped-up trial for a plot against James in 1603, the general public were happy to see Coke's downfall, or so they thought it to be.

# Chapter 50

**St James's Park, London. December, 2014**

Mrs G walked beside Ethan, the last of the autumn leaves scattering round her feet in her Ugg boots. Her coat and scarf pulled up against a sharp northerly wind.  Ethan had on nothing but a lightweight grey suit and silk clerical shirt with no topcoat. On his head was a stylish, wide-brimmed, black Herbert Johnson hat. He seemed not to feel the cold. The bare hand which he put into her own cold gloved one felt warm. She had taken it gingerly, although somehow drawn to him. They stopped for a hot drink in a small self-service café with few people inside, and sat at a narrow table surveying the waddling ducks and grey geese outside seemingly oblivious to the cold. Even within the café's draughty warmth she felt the same chill she had at times sensed before in Ethan's presence, and had tried to shake it off. This time she had thought out in advance what she was to say, and how to overcome both her reluctance and her fear about what she might discover.  As Ethan returned with two polystyrene cups of coffee she coughed nervously, took one from him and observed: "In the name of progress we lose a friendly smile and a china cup and add yet more toxic rubbish to our world on the grounds of disposability."

Ethan smiled. "You are right. The balance of nature is as critical as the balance of beliefs, and of the planets themselves. Opposing forces surround us everywhere. Ignorance is not bliss."
Mrs G caught her breath to stifle a cough. "So, we should approach nature as a reverent lover to discover her secrets?  And what of humanity's soul?  Aren't you its destroyer?"
Ethan gave her a long, deep look, and one eyebrow rose perceptibly. He had wondered if and when she would eventually discover him. She was psychic after all, and intuitive. He congratulated her secretly on her acuity and on her nerve. She held him in a steady gaze, and for a moment he needed to look down to stir his coffee before looking up at Mrs G once more.

"So, you know who I am?" he intoned with a disarmingly gentle inflexion of voice. His eyes closing to small slits in a tight smile to disguise his own surprise that she had sprung this moment to face him down. Eyes being the window of the mind which Ethan preferred to be one way only.

"Yes, I believe I do now," said Mrs G. "The Devil Incarnate. What satisfaction does it give you to entice people to a soulless end? There is something un-natural about you. Godless, despite your priest's collar. Answer me honestly," she demanded with bated breath, hesitantly awaiting his response.

Ethan did not speak but watched to see Mrs G's reaction as he pulled down his priest's collar to reveal a small tattoo below his Adam's Apple, the size of an old copper halfpenny piece, half-an-inch in diameter. She gasped momentarily at its sight and drew away from him, as it was a sign she knew was of the devil, of the ancient horned androgynous figure of Baphomet whom the Catholics had once accused the Cathars and Templars of worshipping. He watched her carefully as she caught back her breath.

"I am Ahriman, the reincarnated God of choice of ancient Zoroastrian times, and progenitor of Lucifer. I offer long life and earthly riches in return for your soul. Some say I am the god of the dark side of man. Of greed and a stealer of souls, but that depends on what you want to believe. You are of entertainment to me because you are dying with little time to your end, and I can save your life if you discard your search for a life beyond, and your pointless quest for Francis Bacon and his Grail. But you must do as I say. Let me come with you to your journey's end. I will not harm you."
And he stretched his hand out to hers, which she withdrew quickly.

"Disguise or not, your words don't tempt me, nor would they have my husband. Tell truth and shame the devil. You may think I am a woman of science, but since Abe's death my heart has been open to faith in a greater intelligence than man's conceit. I am not afraid of you and your darkness, and you may accompany me on one condition, that you leave Abe's grandchildren alone once I am gone. There is only one desire I have left now to fulfill. You have no power over me!"
Ethan plays with his plastic cup, squeezing it in irritation at Mrs G's stubbornness of will.
"The lady doth protest too much methinks," he growled his words now. "Knowledge reaps its own rewards. I will agree to your condition, but only if I fail to change your mind before your natural

death. Who is to say what is good or bad? There is no darkness but ignorance. My work is to reward the power of human intellect, not the stupidity of the weak. You should be honored I give you my time and attention."

Ethan paid the bill and got up to go. He asked her what her plans were now, but she had none that day but to return to her hotel and think out what she should do next. Somehow what Ethan had said had not surprised her. From the time she had first met him in the Inner Temple off the Strand, and again in Carcassonne, where he had appeared from nowhere, she had sensed a dread coldness in him.

Was he for real, or just an illusion? Was her own mind going now with all she had to do, facing what Ethan had said was soon to be her doom? She had always felt his physical presence strongly. His piercing eyes and strange odor, almost sulfuric. He was eerie at times, but then his charm would overcome it and she would feel strangely magnetized by him, as his smile won her confidence and his gentle touch soothed her. She shivered now at his deception and wondered how it was she had finally detected it. Was it something innate in her? Her own belief in good? Or was it the angel that in her mind's eye sat on her left shoulder? There was one more thing. The email she had seen on her laptop that morning in the code she and Abe used together to scramble their private exchanges. It had been received just as she was shutting down the computer. She had read it three times over and her heart had beaten faster each time.

The message had been clear to her:
"*aaabaabaababaabaaaaaaabaaaaaabaa*
*aabaabaabaaabbbaaaaaabbaa*": Beware Ethan!

She walked the next ten minutes with Ethan without speaking. Across the Mall from St James's Park and up the Duke of York steps, westward along Pall Mall, turning right up St James's Street and taking a left before Piccadilly to enter the Ritz. At every step she had expected something untoward to happen, but nothing had. Ethan went on his way, as usual never saying where, which strangely, she had never questioned.

Mrs G mused how it was the saints' names from the past were everywhere in London. St George of the Crusaders; St Patrick of Ireland who had preached the doctrine of Mary Magdalene adopted by King Arthur's knights; St. James the elder brother of Jesus, and in Bacon's time James was the name of the King and his new English Bible. Did time mean anything? It seemed as if the past was only yesterday since every part of it was what humanity was now and could never shake off. Or had the world always been the same? The same questions. The same search for answers in which only perceptions changed. The same battle of conscience between good and evil.

As she entered her room she went straight to her laptop to reboot it to read the coded message once more, but try as she might she could not find it again. It had gone from her screen and was nowhere to be found. Stupidly she had been in too much of a hurry to leave and too alarmed to see who had sent it. Surely it could not have been from Abe? His computer was at home in Brookline locked away in his old desk, and Abe was dead and buried. Nobody else knew the email addresses they used between them or for that matter, their shared code.

# Chapter 51

A procession of two hundred horsemen and marching soldiers, plus a sundry crowd of hangers on, advances along Chancery Lane towards Charing Cross, passing the Temple Inns. Being the first day of the Trinity Term Francis Bacon is to open the Law Courts in State in his newly appointed role as Lord Keeper, the title his foster father Nicholas Bacon had once held. Those at the forefront accompanying him include the Lord Treasurer and the Lord of the Privy Seal. They are followed by a long train of earls and barons, knights and gentlemen. Cheers greet the sea of jostling steeds and uniformed and colorfully be-robed gentry as they pass along the route. Francis' fame and popularity as a fair administrator of justice is now widely acclaimed by Londoners as a whole.

Immediately after Francis' investiture as Lord Keeper the King had set off for Scotland for a six-month holiday leaving Francis to rule in his place, effectively as Regent of his English realm. Francis' wife, Lady Alice, as his consort, whom he had described as "a handsome woman to my liking" was now first lady of the land apart from the Queen Anne, James's Danish wife. Both Alice and Francis are today resplendent in regalia that equals in magnificence that of the King himself.

On arrival the court criers call for silence, and the chatter of those present ceases so they can hear the Lord Bacon address them:

*"On his departure to attend to matters in Edinburgh the King has by the Grace of God given me the undertaking to make revision of the laws of our realm to please His Majesty. Contrary to my predecessor Sir Edward Coke it is my intention to make any future injunctions to impede the law a hard pillow to sleep on indeed. In future justice is to be applied with mercy and equity."*

All present stand to mightily applaud the speech in which Francis has pledged to rectify the corrupt abuses of the court which Coke had previously subordinated to his own wishes, often over and above those of the King. Both Coke and the King had in the past operated in an environment where favors were standardly exchanged in return for monetary benefit. The King's extravagances at court for his clothes and revels and plays, and above all for gifts to his handsome favorite George Villiers, never ceased. James had no compunction in openly kissing Buckingham or fondling him for all to see and was soon to grant him a stately home of his own at Stowe.

Many of the excesses of the king were known to Francis, to which he turned a blind eye. The extent of the Kings' involvement in certain malpractices, together with Buckingham, to obtain their incomes, in which Coke had aided and abetted, Francis was yet to discover. Despite the work of the State required of him Francis feels secure enough in his position to end his speech with the words: *"I would reserve some measure free for Business of (my) Estate, and for Studies, Arts and Sciences to which in my nature I am most inclined."*

### Hertfordshire, England. April, 1617

Coke knew the good reception which Francis would likely get on stepping into his shoes and had kept well away from London. He had other plans to recover his lost confidence with the king. Today he had come to visit a woman who might help him to restore his former prestige. As his carriage pulled up at a large country mansion with spacious grounds attended by gardeners, a covey of grey partridge rose from the long grass at the side of adjoining woods, their chattering calls mixing with the beating of their wings as they took flight.

Coke is greeted by servants and led through an imposing entrance into the drawing room of the house, lavishly, but tastelessly decorated. He is greeted there from behind a dressing screen by a fat heavily-built woman, seemingly in her mid-forties. Her face, once pretty, now has two chins. Not yet having completed her morning toilette of powder and rouge, she is being assisted into her camisole and boned corset by two maids who struggle while she puffs and pants to ensure the strings are laced as tight as the laws of physics and gravity will allow.

She gestures Coke to take a seat with an imperious flourish while she continues to be inserted into a voluminous and florid dress. Then sitting while her wig is placed on her sparsely-haired head and coiffed with a few last finishing touches of backcombing. What remained of her natural hair, spruced that morning with hot curling tongs, falls in sparse ringlets on to her plump pink shoulders.

"So what brings you 'ere?" She demanded of Coke in a vulgar accent from heaven knows where. It had better be sumpthin 'portant for you to see me at this hour."
"Indeed my dear Lady Compton."
Coke had difficulty controlling the sneer that tried hard to turn his lip. "I trust I am not too early at this midday hour. I understand your son is well and enjoying his endowments in the splendor of the King's Scottish palace in Edinburgh's fair city."
The rouged face now fully applied, her ladyship turned to address Coke.
"This hour is that at which great ladies of rank arise on, Sir, I'll have y' know. As for me son 'e is indeed well endowed, Sir, and finds 'is pleasures at His Majesty's indulgence! 'is nickname for 'im is 'Steenie' and 'e says 'e' as the face of 'n angel!"
She completes her outpouring with pride and delight, as to the King's raptures over her son George, whom she had done her best to bring up in good graces, teaching him to dance and to act as a courtier. She gives Coke a knowing wink, and totters across the room on high heels from behind her dressing screen, her weight being so great to bear that her ankles bow her shoes outward. As she approaches Coke to offer him her hand to kiss, she lets off wind in a staccato serenade, plumping her flabby posterior down on to the crimson cushions of large gold-painted chaise-longue onto which she subsides. As she waves her hand for Coke to speak, she produces an apple, which she prepares to engage with.

Edward Coke starts again. "Highly fed and lowly taught" is what springs to his lips, but he contains his words from her hearing, for this is Lady Mary Compton, formerly married to a wealthy Leicestershire sheep farmer turned sheriff. Her son George recently appointed the Marquis of Buckingham by his doting lover King James. Coke requires a favor from her, or rather a trade, which may redeem him with the King. Coke's marriage to Lady Elizabeth Hatton, twenty-six years his junior, had proved disastrous. It had been said of them that if they were not compatible they were at least well matched in their articulate and hot-tempered, headstrong ways. Coke had stolen her from under Francis Bacon's nose in a wedding held quickly in a private house rather than a church, which match was later reported to be invalid. They had produced two daughters, the youngest being Frances, now seventeen years old.

"I am given to believe you have another son Madam, the charming Sir Edward Villiers, who is perhaps eligible in the question of marriage? My most beautiful prize, my daughter Frances, should I say, might be made available." Coke leaned his chin forward on his hands to see her reaction. Not that he had asked Frances, or indeed her mother from whom he now lived separately, but first he must see whether his ruse was likely to succeed. If Frances were to marry the brother of Buckingham then Coke would be in a prime position to gain Buckingham's ear and so hope to win back favors from the king.

"On what terms? What is your design?" The rouged lips spluttered a reply through a mouthful of apple.

Coke realized the bait had been taken.

"May I suggest the sum of twenty thousand pounds in addition to a thousand marks a year payable to you personally?" he enquired.

Lady Compton replied with relish. "Indeed it would go some way to recoup my loss of funds since the appointment of that damnable Bacon as Lord Keeper of the Great Seal."

Coke gave her a wolfish glance. He knew he had an ally. "I am sure that if you were to agree it could be arranged if your son, as the new Marquis of Buckingham, would see his way to the restoration of my good relations with His Majesty, and a pardon for the proceedings brought against me."

Lady Compton rose as graciously as she could endeavor, spitting out apple pips and letting off an enormous belch as she vacated her seat. "Then so be it. I will trust you to make the necessary arrangements, but you must be sure not to inform your wife of my involvement. She has no love for me. As for my son George I will have a word in his ear. You need beware that he is well disposed to my Lord Bacon whose advice he often seeks. Do not look to me for a guarantee of success. That is to be your affair; but what if your daughter should refuse my son?"

Coke rose to take his leave.

"You need have no concern over that dear Madam. As for my wife she does not speak to me and has deserted my home with my daughter. She has made me a public cuckold as once more she favors the company of the Lord Bacon with whom she had past dalliance, and now he is appointed Lord Chancellor she seeks his status against my own diminished one," Coke whined indignantly.

"Trust me; I shall endeavor to make arrangements with Godspeed. For the moment, I bid you farewell."

Coke felt he was on sure ground if he could gain Buckingham's attention. He was aware that the king had made a speech to his Privy Council only recently in which he had openly acclaimed his love for Buckingham, whom the Archbishop of Canterbury had not so long ago introduced to the King as common cupbearer on account of his fine legs. So infatuated had James become that he had proclaimed to the members of his Privy Council: "*I am neither god nor angel but a man like any other. Therefore I act like a man and confess to loving those dear to me more than other men. You may be sure I love the Earl of Buckingham more than anyone else, and more than you who are here assembled. I wish to speak on my own behalf and not to have it thought to be a defect. Jesus Christ did the same, and therefore I cannot be blamed. Christ had John and I have George.*" Coke doffed his cap to Lady Compton on his exit. Now sixty-six, he was beginning to show his age. The years of incessant ambition and of climbing the slippery rope to fame and fortune were taking a toll, but he would not go down without a fight to the last against the man he hated more than anyone in the world. His nemesis - Francis Bacon.

----------------------------------------------------------------------------------

*[Note: George Villiers was successively and rapidly promoted by the King through the ranks of entitlement beginning with a knighthood and rising through the ranks of a Baronetcy, to an Earl, a Marquis and finally a Duke. Only the son of a King or Queen had the entitlement of Prince.]*

# Chapter 52

## London. April, 1617

Francis sat alone in his room at his chambers at Gray's Inn. On his writing desk the symbols of Masonry were prominent. He had finished his work for the day on a chapter of his book *"The Great Instauration"* and as he replaced his quill pen in its inkpot he sat back in his chair and rubbed his sore eyes. Eyes that had perceived more of the world and its past and present than all but a few other Englishmen before him. The king had recognized his scholastic eminence and had asked him to continue his work on finalizing the *King James Bible*. James had not understood Francis to be the author of the Shakespeare dramas and comedies despite the small sketches and revues which Francis and his Good Pens at times created for his revelries.

The arrival of spring was late, and a small coal fire burned in the grate, making the room pleasantly warm. Francis had taken off his jacket and was in a shirt of white linen with lace cuffs which he had pushed up his arms to allow him to write freely. He put his hands behind his head and fingered the ring his mother had given him with the Masonic crown and star symbol of a prince, as she had also given to his brother Robert Essex. He remembered too the wedge-shaped stone the Queen had given to him that memorable moment at Twickenham Hall. The evening when he was twenty-one and she had danced with him and left by boat to cross the river to her palace at Richmond. For years he had used the stone as a paper weight. He took it now from his desk and held it in his hands to examine it closer. The light being poor he rose to cross the room to the window to see the inscription on it the better. The Celtic Rose of the Tudors and of Mary Magdalene clear on one side but on the other was another etching, very faint, which although he had noticed before, he had not thought to determine what it was. There were no words to decipher, just an outline of a figure.

The stone was worn, and although he took it to the light of the window of his room overlooking the lawns stretching down to the

River Thames, he still could not recognize the inscription. He returned to his desk to take a magnifying glass to study it more clearly, but could still see only a vague engraving.

Suddenly he had a thought, and going back to his desk, he took out a leaf of blotting paper and poured some ink from the inkwell onto it. Before it could dry he pressed the back of the stone into the black ink and quickly impressed it onto a piece of blank white paper he had made ready. There in front of him was the imprint of the marking on the stone. He looked at it, puzzled at first, and then realizing he was looking at its reverse gave it another look. In all the image was no more than an inch square. It revealed the picture of a serpent, with what appeared to be some indecipherable hieroglyphics surrounding it. He looked more carefully and knew at last what he saw, as his memory served him well from his journeys in Arab lands with his tutor Paulet some forty years before. As with the dawning of an age he understood finally its meaning after all the time it had been in his possession, and which his mother must have known when she had gifted it to him. The stone itself appeared to be a smaller replica of the wedge-stone which was the last stone inserted into the building of the ancient Egyptian pyramids, on which the whole structure finally relied. But it was not the stone now that was at the core of Francis' realization, but the engraving of the serpent which he saw was encircling itself with its tail in its mouth. It was one of the oldest symbols known to man, from times before the Pharaohs, over ten or more thousand years ago; the most ancient of all knowledge.

It represented the continuity of life. A divine figure of both the beginning and end of time. Its first known appearance had been in the funerary text of the *Egyptian Book of Antiquity of the Netherworld.* It had been associated with the god Ra and his union with Osiris in the underworld. Osiris was among the first of all gods, the god of afterlife and of fertility, who at the fullness of the moon fruitfully flooded the shores of the River Nile and the moats surrounding the pyramids. Osiris was also the benign and beautiful God of Love. The kings of Egypt believed that as he rose from the dead, in union with him through a process of imitative magic they would inherit eternal life.

Francis recalled that Plato had described the primal serpent as a self-devouring, self-regenerating thing, which portrayed the entire Universe as an immortal mythological constructed entity. So this was what his mother had given to Francis. The knowledge of the existence of immortality which she had denied herself through actions she had little option but to take as Queen. It is a wise mother who knows her child, he mused. He returned to his desk. His thoughts raced excitedly. He realized now his time could come, but not as he had imagined it. What else was it that Plato had said? He recalled: *"Many shall be restored that are now fallen and many shall fall that are now in honor."*

# Chapter 53

**Ely House. Hatton Garden. London**

A rider on horseback arrives at night time at the impressive London home of Lady Hatton. He dismounts and walks up the steps to bang forcefully on its barred doors. There are no lights showing and after repeated banging the door is opened by a manservant. Behind him in her nightgown is Elizabeth Hatton. She has never changed her name to that of her husband Edward Coke, who now strides into the hallway of her house to confront her.

"Please leave. You have no business here," Elizabeth speaks firmly.

"You have not answered my letters," Coke shouts in return, his face red with anger. "I will not leave without Frances. She is my daughter and must obey my wishes."

"You have no right to be here. This is my home, not yours. Frances is not here. Please leave now."

Coke edges forward as if to make a rush for the stairs. Elizabeth moves to cut him off.

"I know your intentions and I am opposed to them. I will not have my daughter sold as a slave in a sham marriage. You disgrace her and me. Nothing can come of nothing. I chose not to bandy words with you. I bid you good riddance!"

"Send for her. Or do I search for her myself?"

As Coke moves nearer the stairs two male servants emerge from the shadows of the barely lit hall to bar his way. "This will not deny me access. You will see!" But realizing his words are falling on deaf ears, he leaves.

As soon as the door is closed, Elizabeth goes directly to Frances' room.

"Make haste. Your father has determined to wed you to suit his pocket, and he will return. We must go now under cover of darkness to hide you away. I have a cousin in the country who will conceal you until the danger is over."

Half an hour later Elizabeth and Frances leave, having packed hurriedly. They go with her two coachmen in Elizabeth's private coach, drawn by four of her best horses, and drive quickly through the silent London streets, until reaching the open road where the horses pick up speed along the dirt highway under a pale moon. The journey to Sir Edward Withipole's house in the nearby County of Surrey takes some three hours and it is best that they arrive before dawn so as few people as possible are witness to their arrival. Once there she and Frances are welcomed in and Elizabeth explains the situation to her cousin, who is happy to oblige her wishes. Elizabeth bids Frances farewell feeling she is in safe hands and hastens to return to London.

On her return by midday she finds Coke has been back before her, and left. With his son Clem and some burly men at arms he has forced entry, disarming the frightened servants. Coke had ransacked the house turning everything upside down, searching for Frances and any sign of where she may have gone. Papers and books are strewn across the floor, cupboards and bedding hurled on to the ground to find any hiding place. As they had left Coke had instructed two of his men to remain near the house and report any return of Frances or of Lady Hatton or her coach and coachmen. Their endeavors had revealed Frances' destination which they had reported at once to Coke. In his fury that Frances had disobeyed his wishes he was not to rest until he found her.

### Francis Bacon's Chambers at Gray's Inn. Later in the day.

Francis is in a meeting which his clerk interrupts and he goes outside to an anteroom to meet with a highly agitated Edward Coke, who is pacing up and down the room.
"I understand you have a matter of great urgency to discuss. Pray, Sir, of what assistance may I be?" Francis demands of Coke.
Coke feigns a smile.
"It is the matter of my daughter. She has been abducted and taken to the home of Sir Edward Withipole in the country, and I request a warrant for her arrest which it is in your authority as Lord Keeper to grant."
Francis ponders, and relishing the moment returns the smile with grace.
"Surely Sir, but if I am not mistaken this gentleman Sir Edward is a cousin of your esteemed wife? May I ask how your daughter came to be taken to his residence?"
Coke is incandescent with rage. "Taken there by my accursed wife. I have received the information within the hour from one of her own

coachmen. Let us not stand on ceremony. I want the return of my daughter now!"

"I need assume if she was taken by her mother she went under her free will," says Francis calmly. "It would not be in my interest to assume otherwise and so it would be outside my office to interfere in this domestic matter in the King's judgment, which I represent."

Coke's is incensed. His face reddened and his lip quivered in rage. "Then, Sir, am I to take it you will not issue a warrant?"

Seeing Francis' face Coke turns and walks out rather than wait for the reply he knows will be in the negative.

# Chapter 54

**Hertfordshire. A day later**
**The country house of Lady Compton to which Coke has**
**returned.**

On Coke's return Lady Compton notes his flustered appearance.
"A surprise indeed Sir Edward, to what do I owe your visit?"
"A necessary one, you may be assured Madam." Coke spoke with great gravity.
"Pray, tell me," came the skeptical response. "I trust it is to be the satisfactory conclusion of the matter of which we spoke recently about the marriage of your daughter to my son?"
"An unforeseen situation has arisen," grimaces Coke. "My daughter has been abducted and is to be taken to France on the first boat by her mother to wed the Earl of Oxford. I am in dire need of your intervention. Only the word of the King can override that of the Lord Keeper in this matter. Your son Buckingham must hasten to have a word in his ear. There is no time to lose."
"Have you requested the Lord Bacon to intervene? Surely 'e cannot refuse a man of your position?"
"I have and he has," replied Coke, his face reddening once more at the insult to his status.
"Then I shall see to it myself. No need to impose on the king. I shall give you a letter now to take to Lord Bacon demanding a warrant. You will see 'e will not refuse my demand."

"Your concern in this matter is much appreciated, Madam. It is my hope the Lord Keeper has sense enough to conform to your request," Coke said doubtfully. He felt he could not argue for more.
"Be assured, Sir Edward, me interest in this situation shall not be hindered, and if me wrath is touched upon then those in power will truly feel me vexation." She scribbled vigorously with quill and ink, sealing the letter with orange wax. She rose imperiously; pouting at her reflection in the mirror, to ensure it reflected her image of herself as some Grandee Duchess of long standing, rather than the second wife of an ageing and now dead sheep farmer. Nobody dare pull the wool over her eyes nowadays, she thought, as she remembered her youthful wooing of her husband to be, bent over the rail of a sheep

stall in a hay barn among the animals that gave him his living as a farmer of some worth. Perhaps it was his poor eyesight or that he had not cared overmuch to choose which woolly cunny was which, but shortly afterwards he had proposed marriage.

She handed Coke her letter and bid him his leave, as she prepared for a lunch of partridge stuffed with wild mushrooms and truffles sent from France, washed down with a good Burgundy wine. No sparing on expense she thought. I will soon be in funds again from Coke. He could well afford it for her favors. She would write to her son, currently entitled Marquis of Buckingham, to tell him of her wishes which she was sure he could persuade the King to agree to on her behalf. She considered the receipt by her son of her note would be at much the same time as Bacon receiving her letter, which if he was to ignore her request to arrest Coke's disobedient daughter, the King would soon overrule.

### Gray's Inn, The following day

Francis Bacon has received Lady Compton's note, delivered to his offices by Coke's son Clem, and sits at his desk, having dictated a letter to his secretary. He reads it to himself to check the wording before calling a messenger to have it delivered.

*"To you, My Lady, I answer only in truth, my actions are represented in the interests of our good and gracious King in that I see no reason in law to grant you your request."*

Sealing it with wax and his personal seal Francis calls for his Clerk of Chambers with instructions to send it by messenger posthaste to Lady Compton.

# Chapter 55

Sir Edward Coke had made up his mind. He would wait no longer. Francis's clerk had told Clem he would need wait for a reply to Lady Compton's note until the following day, to which he gave short shrift. By that time Frances and her mother could well have flown the coop from their cousin's house and could have reached the French coast from any one of the small fishing ports along the English south coast, and be wed to the young Earl of Oxford before it could be stopped. Goddamn his wife, Coke cursed, she had the spirit of a wild cat he could not tame. Too much wealth was not good for women, he considered. It gave them too much independence.

Later in the day Coke, and his powerfully built son by a previous marriage known as Fighting Clem, had halted their horses and dismounted now only a mile away from Oatlands, the country mansion of Sir Edward Withipole. Clem had assembled a band of a dozen men, all well-armed, and on horse, to whom he was busy giving instructions as to what they should do on arrival at the house. They had waited past midnight for the darkest hour to gain the element of surprise, and to avoid recognition.

The plan was for Clem to attempt entry peacefully by requesting the immediate handing over of Frances, but without instant compliance his men were to ram open the door with the heavy branch of an oak tree they had chopped down nearby. On knocking at the door there was no response and on cue the door was smashed open by force with two blows of their oak battering ram. Clem had leapt in, sword in hand, followed by his men equally armed. The resistance they met was pitifully inadequate and they quickly cut down or put to flight the several sleepy retainers hastened from their beds to give fight. As for Sir Edward Withipole he had not put in an appearance, having hidden himself behind a secret panel in his bedchamber.

Clem would brook no resistance and had told his father to remain outside to prevent being recognized. He had asked if his father had received a warrant for his half-sister's arrest, and receiving no reply he had assumed the action he would take would need to be speedy, and that any witnesses were to be eliminated. Once assured all resistance was removed, Clem bounded up the stairs to the bedrooms above the hall, bursting open doors with brute force.

He found Frances lying under the covers of her bed, shaking with fear and dressed only in a flimsy night robe. She screamed and struggled as Clem tried to grab her, spitting, cursing, kicking, and biting Clem's hands, scratching his face until it bled, as his sweating body closed in on her. Clem grabbed at a leg and finally pulled her disheveled onto the floor, the lower part of her body naked from the waist down exposed to his view and the men who had joined him in the room.

Clem signaled to his men to take her down to the waiting coach they had brought with them, carrying her by her arms and legs with no thought for her modesty. Her young limbs splayed awkwardly as she twisted and turned as they flung her into the coach with nothing to cover her, and two men to accompany her and hold her down if she were to attempt to escape.
In the background her father emerged from the shadows to congratulate his son, and bid him to return Frances to his house in London.

In London Elizabeth Hatton had heard earlier that evening that one of her coachmen had taken himself to the local tavern where he had got drunk on porter and spoken openly of his journey the previous night. There one of Clem's men had found him and by holding a knife to his throat had soon discovered the residence where Frances had been taken. Furious, Elizabeth had realized Coke would stop at nothing to retrieve Frances and once again she summoned her coachmen to take her back to her cousin's house at Oatlands.

Late at night she headed out of London once more down the King's Road and over the Thames on the Putney ferry. She sat up front with her coachmen, urging them on along the rutted roads and winding country lanes, scattering the hens, wildfowl and sheep that ran for safety out of her path. It was not long in the coming dawn light before she espied a cloud of dust ahead of her, its cloud appearing ever larger as she travelled towards it. It was Coke and his men returning to London with Frances. Coke had joined Frances in the carriage with her two guards, and their coach rattled from side to side, jostling its occupants together as it careered violently on its way.

As Coke's coach and his entourage of men drew closer to Elizabeth's carriage it became apparent that at that hour and with the number of accompanying men that it could be no other than the coach carrying her daughter back to London. Elizabeth had little time to think as the two speeding vehicles drew near. She recognized Clem at the head of the troop of men, and knew that he would do his damnedest to force her off the road. He could be near enough to a madman in his violent behavior. Her horses now were lathered up, at full stretch, the foam streaking from their mouths, reins loosed to let them gallop freely. She knew she had to act now or risk her own life, with her coach and four overturned and perhaps her horses' legs broken. It was not the time to try to bar Coke's coach.

Elizabeth grabbed at the reins of the coachman beside her and pulled with all her might to steer the horses to the left towards a sloping grassy verge. In the nick of time her coach swerved sufficiently to avoid a murderous accident of twisted and mangled horses and broken coach shafts and wheels. In just seconds Clem's party of horsemen and coach drivers with Frances and Coke thundered by shouting and jeering with foul oaths. The slope Elizabeth had headed towards slowed her motion appreciably and as her coach came to a standstill it gently tottered and rolled over on its side, careening her and her coachmen onto the grass.

When she had picked herself up with no apparent injury she turned to see the cloud of dust from the coach she was sure contained Frances growing ever smaller, as it disappeared back up the road to Richmond and then on to London. She inspected her horses who had luckily escaped injury, and slowly her coachmen raised her carriage with the help of some ropes and two farm laborers who had come to survey the scene and get a penny for their troubles. Elizabeth was in no mood now to hurry back to London, she knew she had lost this round of her battle with Coke, and she deemed it best not to risk another accident in a coach which was now not the best for wear.

# Chapter 56

In London on Coke's arrival he had Frances carried, still half-naked in her night robe, into his house. He called his servants to take her to an upstairs room where the window shutters to the street were to be nailed shut so she could not escape and her cries could not be heard, and for her door to be securely locked. Dismissing the servants he and Clem tied Frances to the four bedposts with a cord by her arms and legs, ripping off her torn night clothes until she lay face down, naked and spread-eagled on the bed. With their horsewhips in hand they proceeded to flay her body severely until her screams ceased, reduced only to a whimpering moan.

"Now, damn you, you will do as I say," hissed Coke in cold rage. "Hold this Bible and swear you will marry Edward Villiers as I command you or I will thrash you to within an inch of your life." Battered, bruised and caked with her own gore, Frances did as Coke told her, swearing to marry as soon as her bloody weals healed, sobbing in pain and woe on the bed as Coke and Clem untied her cords, leaving the room and locking the door.
"Let her scream for all I care. She needs be taught a lesson. She will not have choice of her own paramour. Violent delights have violent ends!"
Coke at last had won the day, or so he thought.

Elizabeth Hatton had not been long in London from her slower journey back to her house in Hatton Garden; the horses, exhausted by their exertions, washed down by the grooms while her coach was examined for any needed repairs. She had no doubt what she should do next. Without a change of clothes and bruised and dusty from her accident, she had walked the short distance directly to Francis Bacon's chambers nearby at Gray's Inn. Brushing aside his Clerk of Chambers she had entered Francis' room, her face pale, and her eyes red and tired from her escapade. She was not a woman to cry easily, but she felt the tears in her eyes as she saw Francis, in the realization he was the only person who could save her daughter.
"I beg forgiveness at this bold intrusion," she spoke anxiously to Francis. "But I am bereft. Lost this night of my daughter Frances. Taken from my protection. I am like a cow that has lost its calf. Heaven knows what fate may befall her. I implore your help."

"Pray calm, sweet lady." Francis spoke sympathetically and quietly. "Tell me what ails you."

When he had listened to her whole story, he spoke again.

"I shall inform the members of the King's Council and your reconciliation with Frances will take place before the day is out."

## Sir Edward Coke's House, London. The same day

A group of horsemen draw up, their leader demanding to see Edward Coke who appears at the door. Recognizing their uniforms as officers of the King, he asks them what their business is.

"Sir Edward Coke, a Council of the King has been convened by the Lord Keeper and an order has been made that your daughter Frances Coke be made a ward of the Court. I am given to understand that you are holding her here. I am commanded to take her hence, and should you oppose I hold a warrant for your arrest."

Coke spits his reply. "No doubt the doing of my diabolic wife and the damnable Lord Keeper," he curses. You may have her with pleasure." He turns to his servants. "Bring her down. Ensure she is dressed properly. She is to go with this officer." He turns in fury back into his house. What has happened to the promise of Lady Compton? Had she not conversed with her son to gain the ear of the King, as she had promised as part of the deal they had struck?

The Duke of Buckingham had indeed received the letter from his mother. He had fulfilled her wish that he speak to the King for permission to release Frances for her marriage to his elder brother which, between the bed sheets, the King had instantly granted. That the King's decree had not reached Francis' ears, was unfortunate to say the least, since by his speedy assistance to Elizabeth Hatton in convening the King's Council to obtain Frances' release, he had unwittingly counteracted the King's wishes, having given the Council to believe he was acting with the King's approval. Back in his chambers, Francis had consulted with his fellow lawyer and friend Toby Matthew.

"I am on the edge of a precipice my good friend," Francis confided in Toby. "The Council itself and all its members have been condemned by the King for misconduct in acting on my instruction."

"Petition the King on behalf of the Council. Its members know well you acted in good faith to protect an abducted maiden," suggested Toby helpfully.

"The King is no friend of the female race," Francis replied. "He will not agree that a father cannot take his child as he may want, or that the mother can have any say in the proceedings. I should have had greater consideration at the time, but my feelings for Elizabeth and against Coke swayed my better judgment. I will do as you say, but I fear it will be to no avail. I have the ear of Buckingham and my hope is that he can persuade the King to ameliorate his belief that I have gone against him."

As they speak Francis' clerk appears with a document which he opens for Francis to peruse. Francis reads it out loud to Toby. "It is a demand for me to attend the Council to explain myself and to make apology for misleading its members. I fear I face a brewing storm. I will need strong friends to weather this. You, Toby, and my Masonic comrades of the Order of the Knights of the Helmet. They have ways to bring pressure on the Council, and even on the King himself."

Toby demurs, he has, unbeknown to Francis recently secretly joined the Catholic Church to please his new young Italian lover, and understands well the King's amorous subservience to Buckingham. It was rumored, as Toby had heard, that Buckingham himself had converted to Catholicism and was bent on influencing the King to do the same, and to encourage his son and heir, Charles, to take Catholic vows.

# Chapter 57

Mrs G lies in bed in a private hospital clinic in London's Cromwell Road. She is drowsy from medication and sees through half-closed eyes a doctor standing over her. He leaves as a nurse adjusts a monitor attached to her wrist. There is a saline drip solution attached to her arm. As the doctor goes to close the door, a man behind him in the corridor outside touches his elbow. It is a priest in a clerical white collar. It is Ethan.

"Excuse me, Doctor, Mrs Gallup, how is she?" he enquires.

"Are you a relative? The police want to make contact with her family or someone who knows her. She has only recently recovered consciousness. She is an American tourist it seems, on her own here."

"I know her. Is she alright? Is it her lungs? My name is Ethan by the way."

"I don't know about her lungs. Why do you ask? She was brought here by ambulance having been struck by a car. She has been concussed from hitting her head. She's broken her wrist and is badly bruised, and she needs rest. Fortunately there has been no loss of blood. The car didn't stop. Driven by a man apparently, according to a witness. She was lucky it was no worse. She's under sedation right now and her general resistance is not good. Her immune count is low and she may be suffering from delusions. She said she had some papers in her handbag she urgently needed to deliver to a Professor Johnson at the British Museum. If this is true, and you can vouch that you are a friend I will give them to you to take there, as they are cluttering my crowded desk. If you come with me now I'll give them to you. I'll need you to sign for them. You look reliable."

Ethan looks over the doctor's shoulders at Mrs G through the half-opened door, her eyes have closed.

"Yes, of course," he said softly, "that'll be fine. I'll be happy to take them."

Ethan is waiting to see Professor Johnson to deliver Mrs G's papers. He has been there for some time before the professor eventually comes to meet him.

"I expect you are from Mrs Gallup. Are you working with her?" he asks.

"You could say that. I have some papers for you from her. She has been held up."

"Just finishing the last batch she left here. Are these supplementary? She didn't say there would be more. I am generally in agreement with her findings. She is an excellent cryptologist. All I can do is to authenticate her sources. I suppose she wants me to do the same with these. I hope they will be the last."

Ethan mumbles a reply. "I think so. I trust you agree with her findings? They're for publication so I understand."

"Oh yes, I wouldn't quibble with them, but for publication I don't know. She didn't mention it. There's always someone who will want to find fault with them or interpret them some other way. Things can be misunderstood. That's historians for you. They all have their own agenda."

He peered at Ethan from under bushy, greying eyebrows. "I don't want my name mentioned. The Museum would be aghast. She will need to obtain written permission if she is to use it in any way. She asked me as a favor for my opinion. She is on a mission of sorts, it seems, and I have been happy to help her." He smiled benignly at Ethan, but got no response other than Ethan's last remark.

"I will tell her. I am sure she will be pleased. I don't expect she will have much time to write her book now." At which he turned to leave.

As he left, the professor realized he had forgotten to say that he had authenticated the symbol Mrs. G had particularly asked him to verify. The circular serpent and its hieroglyphics had proved to be as old as time itself, or rather as long as intelligent man had existed. That it was to be the missing link for Mrs G to connect Francis to his past he could not know, nor was she to know for some time.

# Chapter 58

**The Court of King James I, White Hall, London. May 1619**

Georges Villiers, now promoted to Duke of Buckingham, is slouched in a chair, his famed slim and stockinged legs crossed over. He is conducting a meeting with both Francis and Edward Coke on the King's behalf. Both the elder men of lesser rank stand in audience in front of him. The King had recently survived an assassination attempt on his life, and out of fear and prudence had wanted, despite past differences, to make peace with the two most able men of law who served him. This had come as a great relief to Francis who considered that in his relationship to the King he was of late more sinned against than sinning.

As for Edward Coke, the King was to restore him to the Privy Council from which he had been removed for deceiving the judges to overturn James' selling of honors. James had since come up with other money- raising schemes. One was taxing "*recusants*" or those who were still illegally practicing Catholicism, particularly in Scotland, to pay a due to the King not to be prosecuted. Effectively this was no more than extortion, but it worked well and brought in large sums to benefit James' high cost of living.

Coke was pleased with his reinstatement, and that his agreement with Lady Compton had proved successful. It had turned out that his daughter Frances, given promises of grandeur and a fine status in Court, had eventually wed Buckingham's brother Edward later in 1617, her hand being given away in marriage by the King himself. Coke had been obliged to pay a dowry of £10,000 sterling a year, an immense sum at that time, to keep the couple, as well as having to keep his pledge to pay Lady Compton, both of which promises he was eventually to renege on. But now having edged back in favor with the king with Buckingham's help, he had not realized that Francis too still had Buckingham's ear.

Coke had been instrumental in the prosecution in October 1618 of the sixty-seven year old Sir Walter Raleigh and his subsequent execution. Raleigh had realized he had been duped by Cecil and Coke to wrongly incriminate Essex, and he and Coke had kept their distance since. The King had granted Raleigh funds for a new expedition to find gold in the Americas, but had tied his hands by commanding him he should not set foot in the Spanish occupied lands there or attack the Spanish galleons and their golden cargoes, which had so filled Elizabeth's state coffers. Raleigh had returned empty-handed as a result of the restrictions put on him by the King, and in addition his son had lost his life in a sea battle Raleigh had picked with the Spanish against the King's orders. On his return pressure was put on James by the outraged Spanish ambassador to have Raleigh executed to which James had agreed with little compunction.

Raleigh had served his queen and country well in the Elizabethan age of adventure, but this was now at an end under James' double-dealing politics with the French and Spanish. Raleigh had summed up the spirit of his own era by commending the axeman to sharpen his blade well. As a small crowd had gathered in the yard of the Palace of Westminster to watch the end of a great English hero he had calmly said that the axe would be: "A sharp and fair Physician to cure him of all his diseases and miseries." On the leather pouch, which in prison he had stored the tobacco he had been the first to bring to England's shores, he had written the words: "This was my companion at my most unhappy time."

Due to Raleigh's popularity with the public James was forced to issue a *Declaration of his Motives* for his decision to execute him, full of false accusations concocted by Coke. Raleigh's dispatch in October of 1618 was none too soon as far as James was concerned. It meant he had got rid of the old guard who had served the Tudors and he would milk the minds and estates of those few who were left until and as far as it suited him. These, he intended with the help of Buckingham, would include those of Bacon and Coke, and the fortunes each had amassed. But events were to take their own turn. It would not be long before James himself became sick from his excesses of living. He suffered severely from frequent occurrences of pain from kidney stones, one of which nearly killed him shortly after his wife, the Danish Queen Anne, died in March 1619.

# Chapter 59

**Cromwell Hospital, London. December.**

Mrs Gallup was sitting up in a chair reading a large book on her lap. She had one arm in a sling but she was leaving early the next day at her own insistence, with the doctor warning her to take things easy. Her bruises were subsiding and she could walk unaided. However the skin on her face and arms were of a yellowing color and she realized her body was not well. It was a sign of kidney problems. Perhaps she had jaundice. Her hospital doctor was an orthopedic specialist and so had not commented. She needed to get back to Boston for a good checkup, but she was not going to be put off by Ethan's forecasts of doom. It was in his interests to scare her. She was yet to complete her mission and so needed to lay a false trail to rid herself of him.

The door opened and Ethan entered.
"How did you know I was here?" she asked him, suspiciously.
"I have my spies, and when I enquired at the Ritz they told me you were here. The hospital must have called them. Are you alright? An unfortunate accident. You were lucky it seems. I am sure you need some good rest. Why don't you pack your bags and go back to Boston in time for Christmas to be with your step-children? You must have completed all your work here surely by now? Incidentally I dropped off some papers of yours at the British Museum, which your doctor asked me to do. The man there, Johnson, told me they would be ready by now with the other documents you left with him, but that he would not vouch for them publicly."

He smiled his benign smile as if butter would not melt in his mouth, as my grandmother would say, thought Mrs G, angry now at Ethan's undisguised inquisitiveness.
"I am leaving for Boston as soon as possible, once I have all my papers. I have enough now to write my book, but it will need time. My arm hurts and my back and ribs. I will be glad to get home."
Ethan smiled. As he had intended it had taken the car accident for her to realize that life on Earth had become important to her again. The things that mattered most. Home and family, rather than delving into

an underworld of mystery that was not for her to concern herself with. He knew there was more she needed to find to complete her quest and he wanted to put an end to her adventures as other matters pressed on him. Not only that if she gave up her search he considered he was no longer obliged to honor his deal with her not to tempt her grandchildren. It was very rare he made deals of honor as they were not to his natural instinct. Now he had nearly won his game with her he decided to tease her for his own amusement.

"Tell me," he asked her. "Why did you never have children?" Mrs G, tetchily now, retorted.

"The opportunity never arose. I was happy with my life and my studies of the science of plants. It was only when I had to look after Gerry and Marianne after their mother died that I realized how interesting it was to witness growth in humans as well as plants. They each inherit the same genetic capability of their forbears. Although I would like to pass on my own erudition to the children it can never replace the natural instincts of the genes they were given."

Ethan saw his chance. "So, why see your life ebb away? You have only months now to live, if not weeks. Why not trust me to give you longer life? It is in my power. You will need help to make good decisions with Abe's foundation, and to advise the children for years yet. You can have decades more yet here on earth if you forget the whole idea of immortality, and your book. What is the point of it? People want to know what is here on earth they can aspire to. Not some intangible dream of what they might have been, or what might happen in some other world for which they must forfeit pleasures in the one they live in."

Mrs G attempted to close her ears to Ethan's persuasive talk and went to turn a page of her book with her one hand. Ethan moved to help her and saw its title, *Instauratio Magna,* and its opening lines. *"The seeds of power and good to men",* he intoned. "Francis Bacon's thesis for humanity. How fitting. A master of great works, and what good did it do him?" he teased sarcastically.

Mrs G responded heatedly. "That's not the point. It was what Bacon gave to others more than for himself. He was a giver, not a taker. Not a dealer like you. He was steadfast in his respect for truth. His mastery of English changed the world. He wrote the English Bible, and helped found America as the land of the free with his book *The New Atlantis*. He started the world's first scientific society that gave birth to Newton's theories, and moreover he believed science could fuse with the natural world as the answer to the mystery of life in this world, and the next. He saw them as one and the same.

"Huh, but what proof do you have?" Ethan smirked. "His works are forgotten now. Look what happened to your hero. He achieved his position by chance from birth, more so than from the genes you claim shapes your plants and every living thing; but once luck deserted him, he lost the will to defend himself. His royal genes did nothing for him. He was a coward. He died ruined, destitute, to be excluded from history's hall of fame, barely known today in his true dimension. Unless that is, your book is to do it for him, which I very much doubt. Who today knows the true character of Shakespeare as a person, or who cares? What does it matter? Bacon need blame his modesty on himself. The meek shall not inherit the earth if I have anything to do with it!"

Mrs G knew there was no point in continuing the discussion. She had no doubt that Bacon's genius stemmed from a bloodline of a resourceful gene pool continued by his Merovingian and Tudor forbears since it was first maximized. The aristocracy had always bred among themselves so as to excel, just as they reared their pedigree horses.

It was a matter of self-discovery how best a talent was found and utilized. She had no trust left in Ethan or Ahriman, or whatever or whoever he claimed to be. The temptations he offered had brought the ignorance of greed to the forefront of the world and the result was the destruction of man's own innate chemical and spiritual knowledge. She wished the wretched soulless Ahriman would disappear in a puff of smoke forever and let her get on with her life. If she was dying, as he claimed, she was not afraid to deal with it herself. She knew of the death and rebirth of everything in the universe. Why should she sell her soul and give up on all that her journey meant to her to find the truth she sought? How had Abe died and why? He had obviously not sold his soul or he would still be here, she thought. She shook her head trying to rid herself of questions.

Mrs G's mind drifted now into semi-conscious delirium, still under sedation. It was plants she knew about, she told herself. They were no different to people and all animals and anima. The same substance. A perpetual continuum of seed from father to mother to son to daughter. A corridor of time in which the future was a constant reflection of the past, but each new circle with a small twist. The circle never quite completed. This was what Abe had discussed with Karl Popper.

She was sweating now with perspiration on her forehead. She must break free from her bed and complete her mission. She looked to see how she could get away from Ahriman. She could sense the androgynous presence of his evil now, his smooth smile, his silky tongue, persuasion personified; and she looked up to see him, but he had gone, as quickly as he had manifested himself.

There was only one thing left now she wanted to finally do to achieve her goal. As promised she had to return to the children by Christmas. She had left them far too long, ignoring their texts on her uncharged iPhone which messages she had not been able to return in the past week or more, sedated in hospital. She had to make the rest of her journey alone, to get away from Ethan for her final journey. To hell with his "deal". To shake him off for good. Until then she need humor him to throw him off the scent and tell him nothing of her plans. She had completed her reading of Bacon's books, and of *The Fama*. It was in effect the German Rosicrucian Manifesto of 1614, and it had decided her where to go. It was said to resolve the message of the Philosopher's Stone and to bear Francis Bacon's imprimatur, and it was all that was left for her to finish her research. Tomorrow she would leave for her final destination.

# Chapter 60

## The Temple, Gorhambury House, St Albans. January 1621

Francis was at home in the seclusion of Gorhambury House, built on the original site of The Templars in England. Several days before on his 60th birthday on 22nd January 1621 he had given a great feast at his London home at York House. To it he had invited his friends and colleagues from the Masonic and Rosicrucian fraternities, those of his own Knights of the White Helmet in the tradition of the Templars, and those remaining among his Good Pens.

He had completed all of his books except that of *The New Atlantis*. The *"Reformation of the Whole Wide World"*, which he had once boasted was his dream to accomplish to his lover Marguerite while still a teenager, was completed, while Marguerite was now dead. Another *"The Confessio Fraternaitalis"* he had recently completed and also *"The Family of Friends"*. Least of all importance were the Shakespeare plays. Of all of them he had said their purpose was: *"That out of all ranks a Society should be composed having for its object the General Welfare of Mankind, and pursuing it in Secret."*

At Francis' birthday feast were all those who shared the same views and ideals.

His great friend Ben Jonson had stood to recite a poem in his honor.

*"Hail! Happy Genius of this Ancient Pile!*
*How comes it all things so about Thee smile?*
*The Fire? The Wine? The Men? And in the Midst,*
*Thou stand'st as if some Mystery thou didst."*

Jonson and all those present knew the occult meaning of the words in that *"Pile"* meant "Spear" in Old English and *"Fire"* was a Masonic reference to the charging of their glasses. The *"Men"* were Bacon's team of writers, and *"Mystery"* was the clue to Francis' hidden identity which those present knew and were sworn to secrecy.

Only shortly before Francis' birthday the King had told him he was to grant him his chosen title of Viscount St Albans, Lord of Verulam. It was an accomplishment he had achieved by dint of his own endeavors, of which Francis was immensely proud. The investment of his titles had taken place at the King's favorite residence at Theobald's in Hertfordshire. Francis had been crowned with his coronet as Viscount St Alban and Baron Verulam in front of a glittering array of his peers. The King together with his son Charles the Prince of Wales, and a dozen or more viscounts and earls had attended. The ever duplicitous George Duke of Buckingham followed behind Francis holding his robe of office. The list of Francis' State achievements had included Attorney General, Privy Councilor, Lord Keeper, and Lord Chancellor, while those closest to him knew him as poet, author, astrologer, philosopher, chemist and scientist, and not least as playwright.

On the estate at Gorhambury Francis had let his wife Alice lavish the modern equivalent of some ten million pounds sterling, as well as re-instating York House in London. In the fourteen years of his marriage Alice had behaved as an exemplary wife, sharing his vicissitudes and his glories, but a year before his final triumph as viscount she had been discovered by Bacon in an affair with a John Underhill of a similar age to Alice. She had been thirty years younger than Francis when she married him, but it seemed despite all his talents she had found him wanting in one of life's most essential requisites.

Francis had not suspected her dalliance and in his dismay was to fall back on his long and friendly relationship with Elizabeth Hatton for female advice in the otherwise world of men in which he had occupied his life. Not for the first time he felt deceived by women. Today in the setting of Gorhambury he had been reflecting on his life with his friend from Germany, The Duke Augustus, expansively demonstrative and loquacious, with a distinct Teutonic accent.

"Mein lieber." the departing Duke boomed warmly to Francis. "It has indeed been an honor to be with you and to share with you your thoughts for the future of our Teutonic Rosicrosse Order and our Templar ancestors. I will be pleased on my return to my friends and colleagues, who have high regard for you, to tell them of the grand award your King has seen fit to bestow on you. Your recent books I have read with great interest and they shall form part of our learning.

The *Instauratio Magna* written in your own name is a masterpiece indeed. I am obliged to you for the *Three Concealed Parts* of it and instructions for our Secret School of disciples to spread your words." The Count stopped for a moment in thought, and looking keenly at Francis, said: "My greatest hope is that all the trappings of wealth and power that you have gained since we last met are only secondary to the eternal spiritual search for your conscious soul."

Francis realizes the implication, and speaks carefully, choosing his words. "The devil offers many temptations. It is true that the need for position to make oneself heard in the world brings with it power which can be too easily abused. The judgment of it lies more easily in the hands of others than of the self, and so I am truly grateful for your words of caution. In truth the final verdict has yet to be made, most likely in another world. I have been both the beneficiary and victim of high birth and education in that I cannot hide from the questions the world asks of us and the knowledge that I have. But under many guises I have attempted to share its best use with others. Intelligence needs must always triumph over ignorance, as those of our Order know well. Ignorance is but bestial oblivion."

Francis pauses to wait for the duke's response which is not forthcoming. In retrospection he takes a sip of Malmesbury wine, dispatched to Gorhambury's cellars from the former Benedictine vineyards of Wiltshire, to soothe his guests' sore throats from the long speeches of the past few days. He drank from an engraved goblet with his initials FB etched into the crystal glass, and after a pause he continues. "It has been my life's work, but without my brotherhood of Good Pens and the knowledge of the past from the pens of Plato and many others before me, our plays dedicated to Pallas Athene and her Spear of Knowledge could never have taken place. We have sought to combine the spirit of humanity's past with natural science to reach the soul of man through his heart and mind. Our plays and poems help us to recognize ourselves and all our good and bad and comicality by our own nature. In nature it is said there is no blemish but the mind. None can be called deformed but the unkind."

The Duke of Augustus smiles benevolently. "No-one can be more appreciative of your motives than myself and our German family. You will always find a welcome in our mountains of Carpathia, the stronghold of our Teutonic Knights, the brothers in arms of your Templar Knights and those of the Round Table. We share the same Arian practices of our Saxon forbears and your own Celtic ancestors, and seek to continue their works without the call to arms. I know of your search for immortality, by the power of the mind and by science and chemistry. If you should come to visit us at our Racokzi Castle you will find hospitality and practice to your liking. We are princes there as you are too, of royal blood. The Duke looked knowingly at Francis.

Francis guesses the Duke knows of his secret but his reply is couched in the terms of words he had once written for his play Richard II.

*"This soul prison where I live unto the world; thus play I in one prison many people, sometimes I am the King. Then treason makes me wish myself a beggar; and so I am. Then I am kinged again, and by and by, think that I am unkinged again by James, and straight am nothing. But whate'er I am nor I, nor any man, that but man is, with nothing shall be pleased till he be eased with being nothing."*

The two men embraced in empathy and Duke Augustus bade Francis *Auf Weidersehen.*

# Chapter 61

A man in clerk's garb presents himself at the desk of the Chancellor's office. His name is John Churchill. The final hearing of a civil proceedings concerning a Lady Wharton is to be heard that day with Francis Bacon presiding and adjudicating as Lord Chancellor. Churchill, who is there on another matter, has been instructed to wait to see if a response is required to take back with him to the law chambers of the Queen's Counsel where he works - those of Edward Coke. While he waits Lady Wharton herself arrives, splendidly bewigged and bejeweled attired in the manner of the well to do of the day, and is immediately addressed by the clerk in charge. He bows attendance on her.

"Good day, Ma'am. It is a pleasure to have you grace us. Pray, may I ask the reason for your visit?" The Clerk of the Chambers proffers her a small bow of recognition.

"Indeed," purrs Lady Wharton. "On the merit of the Chancellor's decision of my case I wish to offer my token of appreciation of a good and fair hearing." With this she hands the clerk a heavily weighted purse. Realizing the purse contains a substantial sum the clerk asks for the Registrar to witness the amount of the money to be counted out, which is recorded in his ledger at its value of the day of two hundred pounds sterling in gold coins. While they do so Churchill sitting nearby notices the exchange and soon after he departs. On having received the money the Registrar and clerk thank Lady Wharton for her contribution to the expenses of the Court, and she leaves.

On Francis' appointment as Lord Chancellor in July 1618 he had condemned the former practices of Coke, and had set down new rules for the behavior of the Law Courts and its officers to abolish further corruption. In doing so he had unknowingly upset the machinations of Buckingham whose duties to the King included raising funds for his exorbitant whims, while lining the pockets of Buckingham himself and his friends.

Buckingham had now achieved all his ambitions and was effective ruler of England by virtue of the emotional power he had over the King. He had built himself a magnificent country house at Stowe filled with art treasures and sculptures purchased while on his travels in Europe, during which absence the King would openly cry with tears of disappointment.

As was his duty Francis had seen fit to appoint men of integrity as Officers of the Courts. One, a Mr Whitlocke, to whom on his appointment as Sergeant at the Chancery Bar Francis had written:

*"Mr Whitlocke. Have a slow pace. Judges make no haste. Keep your hands clean and those of your servants about you; keep them in awe that they may not dare to move you in things unfit. Fly all bribery and corruption, and preserve your integrity, not respecting any in course of Justice; for what avails it if you be incorrupt and yet shall be partial and a respecter of persons? Look to suppress the power of such Gentlemen that seek to oppress and suppress their poor neighbours. Be not too servile nor too severe.*

This Francis had written on the very same day his clerk had received Lady Wharton's generous gift to the court.

*[**Author's Note:** It would seem evident that Francis' own clerks had received a bribe from Lady Wharton to influence Francis' judgment, but at that time in civil cases both the Courts and its lawyers depended on fees paid by those clients wealthy enough to afford a good and fair hearing. The judges themselves were the adjudicators of what that entailed.*

*In the England of the 21st century if opposing views occur between government and the judiciary, the Attorney General in the role of both politician and lawyer, is called on to adjudicate between them, though it is to the government he owes his job. The position often requires difficult decisions to me made. Although Francis Bacon had resigned his role of Attorney General on gaining his title of a peer of the realm, this was much the situation he was soon to experience. His new role as Lord Chancellor and upholder of the law of the land was to pit him against the divine right to govern claimed by the King to whom Francis was also obligated to serve in his other role as Lord Keeper of the Great Seal.]*

# Chapter 62

## London. February 1621

Francis had not realized the scale of Buckingham's corrupt schemes or the extent of the King's involvement, His Majesty being happy enough for Buckingham to find ways to fund his grand lifestyle while he stood in the shadows. Buckingham knew James respected Francis as the honest face of his rule, which James liked to project so long as it did not disturb his objectives.

But once Francis had accepted the position of Lord Chancellor and his subsequent Barony of Verulam and ennoblement as a Peer of the Realm, his dominant role in the lower House of Parliament, the Commons, had ceased. In Francis' delight at achieving the highest position the state could award him as a noble viscount he had not fully realized that without his political role as a commoner he was in danger of becoming a tool of the King. It was as Buckingham had intended, guided by the crafty Coke, the now newly elected Attorney General. Between them they were now to control the King and his parliament.

Francis had drawn the anger of the public by being seen to be instrumental in the prosecution of Sir Walter Raleigh. Unwittingly, Francis had been duped. A letter sent to the King by Buckingham purporting to be advice from Francis to try Raleigh in private was later proven to have been written in the handwriting of the crafty Edward Coke. A private trial of Raleigh was not popular with the public who saw him as a hero. The ruse was part of a slow staging of a plan by Buckingham and Coke to undermine Francis and his new code of legal ethics, which damaged their corrupt interests. Francis' forthrightness had also put him on dangerous grounds with the King's belief in his own Divine Right by writing to James:

*"Not to be too anxious to meddle. Deal with Parliament frankly and nobly as becomes a King, though you may want money from it do not let it appear as your real cause for calling it. Do not be afraid of*

*Parliament, be skillful in calling it; but don't attempt to pack it. "*

That Francis was not some puppet to be dealt with and destroyed simply or easily Buckingham was aware. The plays of *Hamlet* and *Macbeth* both dealt with the manipulations of kings and politicians, and Francis' enemies most likely knew of their provenance. With Parliament back in force after its long disenfranchisement at the King's command, Buckingham now had Coke in place to influence and control the Government, and Francis as Lord Chancellor was the only force likely to stand in their way.

Buckingham and Coke had devised yet a new means to raise funds directly for James' pocket alone, rather than requiring permission of Parliament. Having sold honors and titles to the wealthy they now saw a more lucrative field in which they sold monopoly rights by Royal Appointment to merchants in exchange for immense sums. Francis had written to Buckingham to call a halt to the practice, describing it as *"the canker of all trades. "*

It was through Buckingham that these monopolies and patents were sold on behalf of the crown. The King had granted all rights to sell them to his favorite, who had in turn given their licensing rights to his relatives and friends in return for a large cut of the ensuing profits. They included such diverse areas from the grant of *Making of gold and silk Thread* to the licensing of *Inns and Taverns*.

Among Buckingham's associates was his brother, Sir Edward Villiers, now the husband of Coke's daughter Frances. He in turn employed various scoundrels in what was no better than a protection racket. These included Sir Giles Mompresson, a cousin of Buckingham, and Sir Francis Mitchell. In league together they set about extorting huge payments from merchants bidding for the monopoly trade in their markets, which if they could not pay would mean their ruin by those who could. Mompresson was known as "Over-reach" and Mitchell as "Justice Greedy." Parliament became locked in discussion how to deal with what was daylight robbery. Some saw that perhaps the crown had some right to license the making of gold lace or even the importing of bullion, but not to demand money for the selling of salt or horsemeat, under threat of being jailed. If funds were to be raised it should be for the Treasury and not for the King's own pocket.

Bacon, anticipating public reaction, had commented in criticism. "Money is like manure, of very little use except it be spread."

He soon found himself in the middle of the dispute since as well as being Lord Chancellor he was also Lord Keeper of the Great Seal, which required him to stamp its Seal on the grant of all monopolies. He advised the King to take legal advice before making further grants, and presided over a Council meeting of law to determine the result. His view was that although the King had the ancient rights to grant the patents that it was unwise to do so, and that any monopolies given should be relinquished.

Francis' opinion should have been the Wisdom of Solomon but the Council members owed their favors to James and Buckingham and found in favor of the King, putting Francis in an invidious position since he could not stop the process. Buckingham and Coke lost no time in taking full advantage of his embarrassment by attempting to make him a public scapegoat as the granter of the monopolies. The public however was not to be fooled, and saw Francis' stance against the grants as upholding the law against royal corruption.

The King himself now began to see Francis as a foe. The House of Commons members who had been recalled to Parliament were against the grant of patents and monopolies, and Francis was seen as encouraging their views. Funds the King required for other purposes were granted him temporarily by Parliament on the condition the practice of monopoly grants was stopped, and that Mompresson and Mitchell be tried for the crime of extortion. There had been uproar in Parliament as Coke had tried to persuade the members to reverse their decision. Meanwhile, Mitchell fled abroad and Mompresson vanished from view to avoid possible arrest.

Coke, sensing the danger to himself as a politician, brought all his cunning and power of oratory to the fore. He cleverly persuaded those politicians who were against the monopolies to turn their wrath on Francis for granting them, as he was obliged to do as the holder of the Office of the Great Seal. The King, now worried, denied personal responsibility by saying he had sought legal advice and that of the Council who had agreed his rights to grant the patents, despite Francis having advised not to do so. Coke and Buckingham now sensed their long planned chance to strike at their hated antagonist.

# Chapter 63

**Temple House. Gorhambury. March. 1621**

Francis sat alone, more in sorrow than in anger, contemplating the recent ruinous series of events in which the wheel of fortune had come full circle. He had not slept one wink the past few nights trying to deduce how he might avoid the trap his enemies had set for him. Within days Coke had put together a final plan to destroy Francis. It had been devised together with Buckingham and his mother Lady Compton, still enraged by Francis' refusal to hand over Coke's daughter Frances to Coke as she had ordered years before. This was to be her sweet revenge.

Coke stood up in the House of Commons to denounce Francis for bribery and corruption. Witnesses were produced in the shape of two men, who in separate past court hearings claimed they had paid small sums to Francis' clerks to obtain his judgment in their favor; if true, they incriminated themselves for corruption. It was clear that they had been persuaded by bribes from Coke and his allies to give false evidence and the House of Commons decided to call a committee to hear their dubious accounts, which most likely would have been insufficient for any further action.

However, on the appearance of John Churchill, the members of Parliament changed their view. Churchill, having once been sacked by Francis from the senior position of Registrar some years before, and scenting a large reward, had gone to Coke with his story of seeing Lady Wharton in Francis' office some two years previously. The amount Lady Wharton had handed over was substantial and the House of Commons members decided, since Bacon was now a peer, that it was the job of the House of Lords to examine the evidence to see if there was a case for his impeachment.

Francis had at first believed he would weather the storm, as the King would save him in knowledge of his honesty. He had not reckoned on the forces against him. Dean Williams, a senior churchman and former friend of Francis, but now the lover and suitor of the viperous

Lady Compton, helped convince James to abandon Francis altogether. Francis' pleas fell on deaf ears. James brought pressure on those peers who looked to him for favors to side against Francis.

Francis had now fallen ill. The events of just a few weeks in obtaining the highest position he had so long yearned for had now descended catastrophically into charges against him of the crooked practices he had so long campaigned against. His wife had recently deserted his bed for her lover and Francis had nobody to turn to who had influence enough to save him other than the King, who was hiding behind Buckingham. Nothing could have struck him so painfully to the very core of all he had stood and strived for all his life. Only the Knights of the Order of the White Helmet might help him now in the secret power they exercised behind the scenes in the name of honor and tradition, which Buckingham held in contempt. The King was himself a Mason, holding the highest illustrious degree of the Scottish rite.

Francis asked for time to prepare the case for his defense, for which he was given a month up until April 17th when the House of Lords re-assembled after the Easter parliamentary recess. He had retreated to Gorhambury to give consideration to what he should best do. The questioning words of the Duke Augustus became clear in his mind. Had he forfeited a reputation in a life of knowledge and writing in place of power and position and wealth? What worth were these now? Would he be known forever as a man disgraced? The only persona the public knew of him was as a man of power, and men of power need take the risks involved. From time to time they provided amusement and solace for the public in having their heads chopped off. The public knew little of Francis' academic treatises and, apart from a handful of his remaining Good Pens, few now knew of his role as the writer of the popular plays of Shakespeare.

Was he now, if found guilty, to lose all influence over the world and its betterment as has been his life's ambition? He was to wrack his brain with many sleepless nights over his decision. To excuse himself of guilt he would need to publicly reveal Coke and Buckingham's machinations and so possibly incriminate the King to whom he was pledged to serve. The dichotomy tore at his mind.

He sought help in what he knew of faith. He had at first followed the examples of his foster mother to tread the strict path of Protestantism.

By adulthood he had turned to the revival of ideals of Masonic philosophy. This declared that the love of a natural universe of a divine creator for the good of mankind was to be shared with all living things. It was essentially that of the Nazarene Christian creed and it required faith in a personal communion with the Creator. Francis had never needed it more. Francis got up from the desk at which he had been sitting in a room full of emblems, of the Tudors, of the Masons, and the Rosicrucians, and of the Templars, and gazed blankly from the windows of his magnificent home. It was here in St Albans the Templars had first come to England to make a home, named after a Christian saint beheaded a thousand years before by the Romans for upholding the teachings of Jesus. Now he, Francis, was the Viscount of St Albans, with his own heraldic shield and his own home, with his ambition to educate the English people in the wonders of the world almost fulfilled. Was it all now to turn to dust?

# Chapter 64

## Gorhambury.  April 1621

With his day of reckoning at hand Francis understood better than at any time before how his mother had suffered the same predicament, facing an early death or life imprisonment in the Tower. Only now he realized the strength she had required to advance her own ideas for her people against those who would oppose her.  The need for her to be wily so as not to give advantage to her adversaries, which Francis now realized he had naively done in deluding himself that his honesty alone would protect him. He understood now the blend of bravery and cunning his mother had needed to thwart her Catholic foes, and the horror of her final discovery of the lifelong deceit of the Cecil family in whom she had put her trust.

No wonder her maxim had been "Trust no-one" which Francis had seen as a paranoia he did not want to sustain in himself.  No wonder she had tried to steer him away from the throne and any claim to it. She had urged him to study law so he might make a living on her death; instead of the arts which she had admired in him, but saw as no protection. Only now at the age of sixty did he realize all the events that had shaped his life to this moment, and that his mother may have known his character better than he had ever known himself.

Francis turned away from the great mullion windows that overlooked the grounds of his home. The rain had drizzled down every day of the Easter period, falling from a low blanket of grey clouds and drip-dripping slowly off the new young buds of the trees, as it always did in England at Easter, regardless of the dates of the moving feast. There was a knock at the door and he heard a familiar voice. He turned on the polished oak floor and crossed over the tapestry rugs to greet his visitor.  It was Sir Toby Matthew, his longtime friend and once fellow lawyer.  Toby came to greet Francis with a sad smile and kissed him on both cheeks holding his hands warmly. Toby had returned posthaste from a journey en route to Rome where he now lived as soon as he had heard the news of Francis' prosecution. So well-known was Francis' fame in the capitals of Europe the news of his coming trial had travelled far and fast.

Francis thought of Marguerite who had died some four years ago, having become Queen of France with her husband Henry IV. He thanked God that she was spared the news of his downfall. He had never forgotten her and the most passionate days of his life. Of his want for the closeness of her flesh, which had brought him the nearest to physical love he had ever known, fueling the countless poems and sonnets he had written in his unrequited love for her.

Toby had guessed his thoughts now at this desolate hour. The need for love even more than faith; if there was any difference between the two, he thought. He himself had found love for a young fellow priest in Italy, which had caused him to join the Catholic Church some years ago. Without progeny the Church was now his family.

"Where is your wife?" asked Toby. "Why is she not here with you?"
"In body perhaps but in spirit with another," answered Francis, since his wife was still living in separate quarters at Gorhambury despite her open affair. "Ne'er have I found true love since Marguerite. Love's labor's lost in vain. Friendship and affection perhaps, if that is love." He looked at Toby enquiringly.
"Is it not strange that desire should for so many years outstrip performance?"

Toby was swift to reply. He was no lover of women. As a Catholic he saw Mary Magdalene as a sinner, and fornicating females as dangerous as Eve herself.
"You need see Marguerite as a succubus, a female demon, sent to tempt you to the ways of the Devil. She and your wife have had what they wanted from you and neither had qualms to make a cuckold of you. Do not depress yourself Francis. You are better off without a woman. You have given the world the love of literature and entertainment, of comedy and poetry and drama to make people happier in their lives. These alone will make you immortal. What more can you ask of yourself? This is not the time for wretched reminiscence. It is time now for action, to use your brilliant mind to defend yourself against these gallows knaves who would steal your life from you."

Francis spoke softly. In his mind he still saw the image of Marguerite as a saint in the revelations of body and soul he had discovered with her. He turned to Toby wryly, "My work is nothing to the union of souls which remain forever." Turning away, tears in his eyes, Francis held his head in anguish. "'Tis best not to defend myself Toby. To do so may inculpate the King, and it is only by his pardon that I can escape with my life."

Toby gripped Francis' shoulders, and shaking him looked directly in his eye. He quoted Francis' own words to him from the play Julius Caesar:
*"Cowards die many times before their death; the valiant never taste of death but once."*
It cut Toby to the quick to say it as he knew Francis was no faint heart, but he wanted to alert him to his danger as best he could. "Francis, you need act now. Pull yourself together. It is reported that Coke has this very day opened Parliament with fresh accusations against you. He will not rest until you are dead. To default on your defense will be adjudged as guilt. How will the public see you, and all your friends who have stood by you, if you can't stand by yourself? Is there cause to the charges against you? I have come to help you prepare your case. There is not a moment to lose."

Francis rubbed his chin ruefully. "There is a case against me. It is not Coke's bribed men I am afraid of. It is the case of Lady Wharton where my clerk received fees in advance. There was no intent at deceit since the sum was counted and recorded in the books with two witnesses from my offices as Lord Chancellor, the proceeds to be paid towards the court. There was nothing hidden, but had I known I would have instructed the gift be returned. My judgment of Lady Wharton's case was not influenced, but cannot be proven for or against. I shall remain here at Gorhambury, and refuse to enter a plea and rely on a pardon from the King whatever the judgment of the Lords. His Majesty's decision is final.

Toby realized there was nothing more to be said on the subject that night, but implored Francis to think again. He turned his thoughts to matters on which he might give Francis some cheer. "Take heart, Francis, in your accomplishments. You will know your friend Ben Jonson has today endeavored to begin publication of the Shakespeare Folio. Fifteen of your plays. What better tribute to your work these last years? Now that the fellow who took your deserved honors has been dead these seven years, unwept, unhonored and unsung in Stratford, his fate must not befall you too. Your genius must be revealed for all to know. The public will save your reputation, if not the King, I feel certain."

"Dear Toby, smiled Francis wryly. "Thank you for your kind words, but a man is but what he knows, and his destiny is what he makes of it. I realize now men are not born to claw a fortune but to exercise virtue. I always knew, but fate took me astray." Francis rose to leave the room, quoting the famous lines he had once written for the Prince in *Hamlet*.

"*I shall sleep on this perchance to dream whether it is nobler in the mind to suffer the slings and arrows of outrageous fortune, or to take arms against a sea of troubles.*"

Francis bid Toby goodnight and rang a bell for a footman to escort him to a room for the duration of his stay. He was grateful his comrade had come and that he would have his company until the result of his trial. He followed shortly to his own bedchamber where he had a restless night.


He dreamt he was standing in the grounds outside The Temple at Gorhambury facing a line of horsemen dressed in the armor and red-cross tunics of the Templar knights, standing on a checker-board of black and white squares. Their leader on a white horse spoke. His face hidden by the closed visor of his white helmet. In his hands he held the symbols of the Compass and the Square of Masonry. Francis remembered his dream many years earlier when the knights had hailed him as their leader.

"You are accused of crimes of dishonor – how answer you?" The leader intoned in a sepulchral voice.

"Not guilty."

"Then as a Prince you must defend yourself on your vows of Honor," came the reply.

"It is not a crime but an error of misjudgment that be on my part, that I have been entrapped and have no defense."

Once more the voice intoned:

"Without defense you are craven and disgrace our Order, and shall henceforth forfeit its protection."

With that the white horse and rider reared into the air, and with his fellows disappeared into the night.

# Chapter 65

The following morning Francis told Toby of his dream. With his head held in his hands and somber of face, he confessed to Toby that he had no belief in theology but only a belief in the natural good. Was it a lack of a prescribed faith that now put him in this predicament, or his enquiries into scientific theory, or perhaps his acquisition of power and wealth by which he had betrayed his own principles?

Francis said that his father, Leicester, had believed as the Epicureans did in the time of the Areopagus, of a universe in which life was given to enjoy nature's gifts of the senses. Of eating and drinking and companionship. Not in excess, but by living modestly and limiting desires to those which life offered naturally.

He told Toby of his experiments with John Dee in the restoration of life which had come to nothing. He now believed although the world consisted of atoms which were universal, he doubted they could be reassembled in human form. More important was the magnetic conduction of the soul or of the senses which might be transported to a parallel universe.

Francis confessed to Toby that to please his mother's wishes he had given too much of his life to the state and the law. That his need for money after the Queen's death to continue his plays and works had drained his finances, leaving him in debt with no option but to obtain wealth. That his detractors had accused him of marrying his young wife Alice for her money had been in some part true. That she had left him for intimacy with another he could not blame her as he realized, he had once done with Marguerite. It was only when body and soul were in union that there could be true happiness.

Francis told Toby he felt he was losing his mind and had lost his way in life. How with all his knowledge he had not understood until now the evil that surrounded him out of jealously, or how it was that his friends denied him when he needed them most. He had been so sure of his own ideals, and yet now he had become the subject of a tragedy worthy of his own plays.

Toby went to sit by Francis and took his hand in his.

"While I was in Rome I learned the true story of Christ and what followed him and of how quickly his Word was taken to be used and abused. You must not blame yourself, Francis. It was Christ who said you must render unto Caesar the things that are Caesar's and unto God the things that are God's. The two may exist together, but they are not one and the same. You must not chastise yourself. If you can say you have done as best you can, what more can you do?"

Toby paused to take a sip of wine from a silver goblet, while Francis walked again to his window to stare out at the darkening clouds scudding like portents across the sky. The ghostly visions of the night before were nowhere apparent. He told Toby of his dream to see what it might mean.

"Your dream shows you are doubting yourself, and are scared of the consequences. You are the leader of the Masons and your own White Knights and need now show the strength of your Tudor heritage or they will desert you. I don't see you as a fallen angel, Francis, and if you are, then now is the time to redeem yourself."

Francis went to interrupt but Toby resumed.

"It is a rare man that is not tempted by the devil. That Christ's name has lived so long is proof that men realize the difficulties of resisting temptation as he gave his life to do. You are no exception, Francis. That you castigate yourself shows that you are too ready to see faults in yourself. You need recognize the two sides of yourself that all men have. No-one is infallible. Jesus forgave sinners so long as they recognized their sins. That you do so now is admirable. You have given much to the progress and joy of humanity. You need be aware of its value. What is to be gained by allowing your enemies to denigrate you, even if you are in error? They have no qualms to take advantage of your honesty which they see as weakness. You are sacrificing your life. Peter died being flagellated on a cross as part of a Roman circus entertainment. Jesus' brother James was stoned to death. Paul had his head cut off without even a trial he was entitled to have as a Roman citizen, and Jesus was crucified! Is this what you intend?"

Toby reached the end of his impassioned discourse. He knew his words could mean do or die for Francis. "I beg you to reconsider your plea. Do not throw yourself to the wolves that would devour you."

Toby spoke biblically and saw Francis finally tire under consideration of his barrage of words. He could do no more. Now it was down to Francis and whichever angel sat on his shoulder that he would turn to for advice. Good or bad. Was he to refuse to vindicate himself and so risk his reputation, his ethics, his friendships and his career, or in his defense risk his life by incriminating the corrupt and pathetic pederast who was king?

# Chapter 66

The Speaker called the House to order. The ranks of the English peerage rose from their benches as one, cloaked in their finery of scarlet robes trimmed with gold and the fur of white ermine. The numbers of pointed stars on their diadems denoting their rank gleaming in the rays of sunlight streaming through the windows of the Upper House of Parliament, The House of Lords. It was their task to defend king and country whether against foreign armies or corruption and treachery in their midst, and today they had one of their own, only weeks before raised to their ranks, who was to be judged by them and called to account.

There had been some wagering beforehand on the result. Whether Francis might acquit himself by his powers of eloquent oratory against the equal force of Coke's vehement invective. A number had a good guess at the result since they had pledged their allegiance to Coke and Buckingham to ensure their own favors continued. The betting was more in the nature of in what manner Francis might be executed or the length of his term of imprisonment.

The Speaker called for Francis by his new title: "Viscount Verulam of St Albans," as the heads of the assembly turned towards the door that Francis was expected to enter and stand trial before his peers. He had not been arrested as he would have been if the case against him was of treason. Apart from the rustling of robes, and a degree of coughing, silence took place in anticipation of an event in which a man's life was at stake. The king was out of London, and Buckingham was nowhere to be seen. Coke held the floor as counsel for the crown prosecution. He preened his robes to command the presence he felt fit for the occasion and signaled for the defendant to be brought before the court.

Instead of Francis, the Clerk of the Court entered, with a paper in his hand, which he handed to Coke. The Clerk had just minutes before received the document with the instructions for it to be read in open court. Toby Matthew himself had brought it on Francis' behalf that morning to ensure its safe delivery. Only he knew its fateful contents. As Coke received the letter from Francis he indicated to the court to sit, and untying the ribbon and breaking its waxed seal, he opened it in the increasing murmuring hum of those present. Coke paused until all were seated and silent and opened the short script. In just a few words addressed to the court Francis had entered a plea of no defense to the charges of which he was accused. Coke read it twice over to himself before speaking aloud to the court, upon which a gasp went up that Francis was neither to present himself nor to enter any plea. Francis' words on the document were:

*"Having understood Particulars of the Charges, not formally from the House, I find matter sufficient and full to move me to desert the Defense."*

Angered that they had been deprived of their prey, a party of four Lords were dispatched forthwith to summon Francis to appear in person the following day but found him in bed unfit to move. The next day on the 1st May the court re-convened. Coke asked the Speaker for silence and rose to call the House to order and to consider a verdict. "My Lords. My advice is that since the defendant has refused to appear or to enter a plea in his defense that he is to be tried in absentia. I call on your Lordships for assent to proceed judgement against the absent defendant and for the court to decide penalty as seen fit."

Coke stood to read out the charges, of which Francis had not at any time been made fully aware. One was of three debts owed (not in itself a crime). The second charge was of three private arbitrations which having not been part of the Chancery Court process should have been ruled inadmissible in their prosecution. The third charge listed thirteen payments received after Francis' judgment of their case had been made, of which one gift had been returned, and two handed to Francis' clerk of office unknown to him. In the case of Lady Wharton, payment had been taken prior to Francis' judgment.

A show of hands gave Coke the right to proceed by a large majority with few dissenters. Buckingham had been busy to ensure sufficient votes against Francis and now those who had wavered had little choice but to side with them on Francis' refusal to defend himself. Coke recommended to the Court that Francis be stripped of all his possessions and worldly goods and be seized forthwith and imprisoned in the Tower of London at His Majesty's pleasure, awaiting sentence on his life. The formal sentence of the court was to be given on May 4th. Toby, waiting outside, hastened back to Gorhambury where Francis apprehensively awaited the fate he knew would befall him, but he had decided to put his trust in the king for a reprieve. When the sentence came it was in four parts:

1. A fine of £40,000. *(£80 Million sterling in 21st Century terms)*

2. Imprisonment in the Tower at the King's pleasure.

3. Disbarment from any office of state for life.

4. Disbarment from Parliament or any attendance at court as a lawyer

The result took away everything Francis had built for himself since the death of his mother the Queen, and any future opportunity to earn a living. Soon after his sentence he gave himself up to the arresting Officers of Court who took him to the Tower where his mother, nearly some seventy years earlier had been imprisoned. Buckingham and Coke had achieved their objectives. They were that any further examination of the matters against Buckingham and his friends that might also incriminate the King were now swept away. That Coke obtained his long-awaited revenge. That Sir Edward Villiers, Buckingham's brother, who had fled the country with fellow accomplice Sir Giles Mompresson could return, and that Sir Francis Mitchell was released from jail where he had been sent on corruption charges.

The King had avoided disclosure of his criminal association, and Lady Compton, with the help of Buckingham and Coke, had turned the tables on Francis in one single moment of drama for which she had waited her time. "Revenge should have no bounds," she was to exclaim delightedly to her friends. Francis made no public statement that might have embarrassed the King. He expectantly awaited his pardon for crimes he knew he had not committed, and for his invaluable services to the crown. But nothing came, and Francis' hopes sank. He wrote to friends and those he hoped could influence the King in his favor.

A letter he penned to the Spanish ambassador, Gondomar, described his future hopes. The letter was telling as to his work as a concealed author.

*"Your Excellency's Love towards me I have ever found warm and sincere alike in Prosperity and Adversity. For which I give you due thanks. But for myself, my Age, my Fortune, yea my Genius, to which I have hitherto done scant justice, calls me now to retire from the stage of civil action and betake myself to letters, and to the instruction of the actors themselves, and the service of Posterity. In this it may be I shall find Honour, and I shall pass my days as it were in the entrance hall of a better life. May God keep you.*

The letter shows Francis' regret that his work for the state would now be unrecognized, but that he might now devote his time to writing for the benefit of future generations. As for his plays and countless poems and sonnets, their public recognition in his lifetime was to be postponed indefinitely. It was from the time of Francis' letter to Gondomar that Ben Jonson was to begin the compilation of the great Folio of plays, to be published two years later, under the name of William Shakespeare.

However, for Francis' diminished hopes to be realized the King's pardon was still required. As he sat desolate in the Tower awaiting his fate, his own prophetic words written for the play Richard II came to mind.

*"I am disgraced, impeach'd and baffled here. Pierced to the soul with slander's venom'd spear. The which no balm can cure but his heart blood which breath'd this poison."*

# Chapter 67

Francis had been placed in a small cell lit only by a slit window and a single candle. With time slipping by without any reprieve from his sentence as he had hoped for, his concerns had grown. He asked for a quill and paper so that he might write to the King. By the dim light he wrote:

*"Your Majesty, I am old, weak, ruined and in want, the very subject of pity. I pray you grant me pardon; my heart is heavy and mine age is weak, grief would have tears, and sorrow bids me speak."*

The words were taken from an old Masonic plea. He ended with the request to:

*"Procure the Warrant for my discharge this day."*

The King had a difficult decision. He had to contend with Buckingham and Coke who sought Francis' total extinction. Francis had been more than a statesman and courtier to James. He had been his loyal personal advisor for many years. James faltered between the emotional chemistry Buckingham had over him and guilt over the allegiance he should have shown to Francis in his hour of need.

James almost certainly knew Francis had been framed by Buckingham and Coke with false and untrustworthy evidence. It was rumored that James had personally asked Francis to refrain from a defense so to avoid any risk to his throne, and that it was why Francis had done so with the assurance of a pardon. James was clearly troubled. He did not want Francis' death on his conscience, but equally he wanted him out of the way for good and an end to his lengthy battles with Buckingham and Coke.

At last the King made his decision and in June 1621 Francis received notice of his fate. It was to be less than the pardon he had requested and expected, and one with strings. He was to be allowed to leave the

Tower but needed to live outside London. The fines imposed on him were to be suspended and his confiscated assets were to be given to state trustees to hold against claims by his creditors; and after to give Francis a life pension, which in the event was never to be paid. The King no doubt believed this decision was one which would absolve him from his own guilt. It was also probable that Francis would not live for long as he had been seriously ill with worry.

As it was, Francis was to live longer than most of his adversaries, including the King, who either were soon to meet their death or total disgrace and fall from power. As James had planned, Coke was the next to fall from favor. His vituperative prosecution of Raleigh had made him unpopular with the public, as had his prosecution of Francis Bacon. James soon took the advantage and Coke was given a taste of imprisonment in the Tower for eight months, to be released on condition he confined himself to his house in Buckinghamshire and out of London. John Churchill, the chief prosecution witness against Francis, was given back his old job as Registrar of the Chancery Court from which Francis had sacked him, but he soon was to be found guilty once more of forgery and fraud and imprisoned.

Dean Williams had been given Francis' role of Lord Chancellor, but was soon stripped of it when he rejected Buckingham's mother, Lady Compton, whom he had been deceitfully wooing to obtain his position. As for Buckingham he was to be killed in a seaman's inn in Portsmouth by the hand of John Felton, a subaltern in the Navy, who believed he was doing the English nation a favor in killing him, so much was Buckingham despised. Subsequently, Lady Compton and all her Villiers clan lost their power and position. James himself became a mental wreck with Buckingham gone.

As for Francis, without his wife and with little money, he sought out his old friends. He could only visit London at short intervals and few of his Good Pens had survived. Many had died. Ben Jonson proved the most loyal, helping to organize the Great Shakespeare Folio of thirty-six plays, twenty being printed for the first time. Six had not been heard of before. These were the *The Taming of the Shrew; Henry VIII; All's Well That Ends Well; Julius Caesar; Timon of Athens, and Coriolanus.* Those many plays previously published were altered, some substantially, most probably to avoid controversy or true provenance. *The Merry Wives of Windsor* was doubled in length from the time of its first performance.

*The Tempest,* in which Francis was seen by many to portray himself as the character Prospero and to forecast the future of the world, came last. All this seven years after the death of the Stratford actor Shaksper, whom Francis had nominated as his Shakespeare nom de plume. A further sixteen books written by Francis and published in his own name were to follow in the three years after his release from jail. Some on war, some on science, and on metaphysics and magnetism. A Treatise on *Life and Death* and the completion of *The Great Instauration,* a lifetime's work itself.

# Chapter 68

**Ely House, Hatton Garden, London. Summer 1621**

One other friend had not forgotten Francis. Elizabeth Hatton, now divorced from her marriage to Coke, and still wealthy in her forty-third year. She had asked Francis to pay her a visit at her Hatton Garden home near Chancery Lane. It was a warm summer's day when he arrived at her back gate so not to be seen publicly, and she came to the gate herself to see him in and sit down with him in the garden where she had been picking fruit, and lavender to scent her home.

She was still a beauty, having been married twice, and embattled by Coke who had tried to steal her wealth from her. But she had been more than a match for him and had left Coke miserable and even worse tempered without her charms. Her hair, tied in a ribbon behind her pale blue bonnet, was still the blonde color of her youth, and her elegant frame well shaped in a bodice of white lace above a tight-waisted, long dress of cream linen. Her cheeks had the fresh glow of the apples she picked which matched her full pink lips and offered Francis a picture of softness. He felt more confident as she gave him a welcoming smile, and came closer towards her, doffing his cap in a small bow.

She had not seen Francis since his imprisonment and disgrace and was shocked at his appearance. Instead of the sumptuous robes he once wore he looked unkempt in worn clothes and was unsure of his reception. Shy rather than timid but a shadow of his usual outgoing personality. He was not so much a man broken, but a man reflective on the vicissitudes of life of which he had so often written in respect to others in his plays, but which had now so directly sought him out.

She held his hand and sat him down at a garden table under the shade of a laburnum tree, its yellow flowered foliage gleaming in the sun's rays, not betraying its ability to cause delusions to the human mind if crushed and taken as a potion. What tiny alterations to our brain can cause madness, elation and depression, Elizabeth thought, in the way we see ourselves, and as others see us. Were we ever in control of any of them, or even of our joys and pleasures? She knew of Francis' notions to discover the meaning of life, but what good had it done him, poor man. Better he should stand by his laurels of the pleasure and thought his plays and poems had provided for so many.

"Francis, it is my pleasure to see you, even though you are confined to a short time in London, as I understand by the court's ruling. You have been ever in my mind. Why did you throw yourself on your sword? Not to defend yourself against the conniving Coke! That terrible man who married my daughter Frances to Buckingham's insane brother. Thanks be to God she left him and flew to France. The foul Buckingham was even to pursue her there with claims she was a witch, and now you too are bereft thanks to his vile plots. You are the most honest and worthy of men that I know."

She paused to look at him closely and saw his gaunt grey look and sad eyes. I see you are in need of care and repast. Please stay and tell me of your life now, and your plans. I will have a meal brought for you."

She did not mention his wife Alice whom she had heard now lived in quarters at Gorhambury separate from Francis. The Trustees of Court had allowed her to continue to live there with her lover John Underhill on an allowance from the funds confiscated from Francis' former assets. Alice was later to marry Underhill but then soon to reject him in a passion for a young servant.

Elizabeth asked Francis to explain his sad lack of defense and Francis spoke ruefully.
"Aye, there's the rub. He is my king and I was his Lord Keeper. I was damned to obey and damned not to! I am weary now. I may be poor, but I am free – free of the trappings of life, of power and position. Free to be as I want to finish my life's work."

Francis ran his hand through his gray hair pushing it back from his now heavily-lined face. He rubbed his eyes at what he saw, and grinned.
"Aha!" he suddenly exclaimed seeing the servant bring an omelet on a silver platter.
"I see you have called for eggs for your Bacon!"
They both laughed, and the concerns and fears of the years fell away,

and they were both young again in spirit as they had once been long ago. All pretensions apart they chatted merrily together.

Elizabeth spoke happily. "The robbed that smiles steals something from the thief. In truth I did not believe you to be my fallen angel. With mirth and laughter let old wrinkles come. What now of your plans? To fly once more to redeem your virtue? What of your work on the Bible?"

"With my pen, as before, I hope. I am compiling all my plays with Ben Jonson – still under the Shakespeare name. I finished my work on the King James Bible ten years gone now, and the conversion of the Psalms into English. I still need complete work on my *"Great Instauration"* and *"The New Atlantis"* to show the world new ways to live without need for a king, but under self-rule of good men alone. I have written a new Constitution for our dominions in America that men should be entitled to freedom and happiness in their lives. I am working now on a new play to be named *The Tempest*. It is to be of the travails of life, but of hope too, and of a future I would have liked for us." He gazed fondly at her. "We are such stuff as dreams are made on."

Francis gave a shy smile. He was not at ease explaining himself to the female sex. They did not always appreciate his earnestness. His mother and foster mother had been strong in their dominance of him, as indeed had the older Marguerite in the wild love affair of his youth in which he had been the passive lover. His young wife Alice had been easier to deal with in her initial respect for his wit and position when she was less than half his age, but as Francis grew older she had rejected him to prefer the pleasures of the flesh and younger company. Men grew too serious as life's battles took their toll over time.

Liz Hatton too was a strong-minded woman, raised from an early age to wealth and power with beauty to match, but she understood the beauty in Francis' soul and his romantic ideals. She smiled and put her finger to Francis' lips, as if to hush his words of self-rule for the king's dominions. If he was heard, his remarks were treasonable. Francis had lost none of his ideals and perseverance, she was glad, even though he had lost his fortune. Like all clever women she had been careful to keep hold of her possessions and not to chance them as men so often did in the challenges they took upon themselves.

She knew it was Francis' generosity and his endeavors to help his country and fellow man that had caused his earlier indebtedness. His costly experiments with alchemy to find the secrets of long life and immortality had also cost him dear. Even now it was said the trustees of his confiscated estate were selling its assets as they deemed fit, a situation over which Francis had no control, and open to corruption.

Having been accustomed in his youth to be able to ignore the subject of money thanks to his mother's indulgence, Francis had never managed his finances well. His actions, as with many men who dared the new, appeared at times foolhardy, however worthy they might be, that he should risk his own existence to be remembered to the world as its benefactor. The old wisdom of never a borrower or a lender be, as his mother had once advised him, had also served Elizabeth Hatton well.

The two prattled away more friendly and closer now than they had ever been. Elizabeth had always loved him, but as a man of good nature, wisdom, wit and conversation, not as a husband or father. She sensed neither of the latter two in Francis. He had always been too busy with his work, and with his efforts to put the world to rights, surrounded always by the male company of his Good Pens and his legal circle.

Elizabeth had suffered enough from battles with the aggressive Coke and his lack of human compassion and his bad tempered moods, and was happy to be away from power and the misogynist world of the law. Francis had not told her of the amusement he had had working on his book of jests and adages with Ben Jonson, named *The Apothegms*. Men's humor was best left to themselves. Elizabeth saw beauty in the arts and nature and so felt comfortable with Francis who had once before made her the subject of his poetic verses.

She kissed Francis, and held him close with great affection, as he took his leave, bidding him farewell and to return whenever he was inclined. It was a sad reflection on the times that a good man should have been brought to his knees, but at least he had his life, and his beliefs and dreams still remained. In truth, she reflected, that was all that mattered for good men. To achieve their aims through their work was what made them. She was proud of him, but she was a woman of her own strong inclinations. Not a wifely follower of men. Francis was the master of his fate. The captain of his soul. She understood this well. Some words came to her mind.

*"In the fell clutch of circumstance
He had not winced or cried aloud.
Under the bludgeoning of chance,
His head was bloody but unbowed."*

# Chapter 69

**The Ritz Hotel, London. December 2014**

Mrs G looked out over Green Park from her suite towards
Buckingham Palace where the Royal Standard, indicating the
presence in residence of Queen Elizabeth II, flew its flag of lions
*passant guardant* on a background of red, gold and azure against the
cold, pale blue sky. A strong breeze swept the remaining leaves from
the branches of the trees to scurry in circles along the ground, finding
resting places in nooks and crannies together with the detritus of
discarded plastic cups, candy wrappers, and used contraceptive
packets that littered the park. From centuries past a refuge for the
sudden passions of those in need of quick solace, day or night.
Gentlemen and grooms, widows and whores; soon to resume their
place among the respectable who walked the streets of Piccadilly
lying north of the park's precincts. Nearby the offices of the most
discreet and powerful of the world's bankers lay a stone's throw
away linked by a narrow alleyway leading to St James's Palace, the
home of monarchs long before Buckingham Palace had been built.

Mrs G reflected on the times of both the reigns of Elizabeth I and II
and the differences between them. The first from the Celtic strain of
the Welsh Tudors and their Merovingian bloodline whom fate had
ordained to be queen. The second of mixed Saxon and Scottish blood
who had come by no less chance to gain the throne.

What a chasm now existed between the present discreet and
politically correct resident of "Buck House," as the Brits liked to call
it, and the brilliant firebrand resident of York Place who led her
nation and navy to become the empire that Victoria too by chance
had inherited as Empress. This "nation of shopkeepers," as the self-
appointed Emperor Napoleon had jeeringly called it before his defeat
at Waterloo.

What would the upright Victoria have thought now that the son of the
British heir apparent was married to a commoner of Jewish blood? It
would seem the one-day-to-be Queen Catherine had more in

common with the first Elizabeth and her connection to Mary Magdalene than people imagined! Mrs G giggled. How one's thoughts could wander. Life was what one made of opportunity. She hoped the new Catherine would fare better than the last queen of that name as the first of Henry VIII's six wives.

Her mind returned to Francis Bacon and what her plans should be next. Her thoughts were similar to those of Elizabeth Hatton. Mrs G had become affectionately attached to Francis by now. She felt she knew her man and that his downfall had been similar to Abe's in that he had not lived long enough to see his life's work appreciated. Their lives both ending in the lack of recognition of their achievements. She sensed her own life now was running concurrently with Francis. That time was running out to accomplish the end they were both to seek, of the knowledge of the future and of immortality. She had been reading all she could of Francis' works and there had been a sonnet by him that gave her a feeling of closeness.

*"No, Time! Thou shalt not boast that I do change:*
*Thy Pyramids built up with newer might,*
*To me are nothing novel... nothing strange,*
*They are but dressings of a former sight;*
*This I do vow and this shall ever be;*
*I will be True despite thy Scythe and Thee."*

The great obelisk of the Washington Monument sprang to her mind. The meaning of its hieroglyphics intelligible only to a few. More important was its symbolism of past knowledge and a world beyond, as the Pharaohs had known, from whom the American Founding Fathers had taken their cue for their New World Order.

Poor Francis, his brilliance recognized by Jefferson as one of the world's three cleverest men. Yet now he was almost unknown other than as a disgraced lawyer. His true genius still denied him. She remembered his lines in the play *Othello* written soon after his trial and the forfeiture of his fortune and reputation:

*"Who steals my purse steals trash, but he that filches from me my good name, robs me of that which not enriches him, but makes me poor indeed."*

She had not sensed she had spoken the words out loud and as she turned from the window to resume her packing, she saw Ethan quietly watching her from a chair in which he was seated.

"I came in with the maid when she brought your tea. I hope you don't mind."

He smiled his usual smile of charm and nonchalance. The element of his surprise arrival lost on her, so often had he made his unexpected appearances. Mrs G said nothing to reproach him. She wanted no argument with Ethan. She just wanted him out of her hair and out of her life, and she knew she must keep calm in order to achieve her get-away. Soon she would be gone, bag and baggage.

She spoke her thoughts. "Strange that Bacon never sought revenge on his enemies. Before long they all suffered death or disaster by imprisonment or madness by their own evil doing. The spiritual law that governs our conscience."

She said this pointedly, knowing that Ethan would wriggle uncomfortably to hear her words, however unperturbed he might appear on the surface. Ethan raised an eyebrow.

"An eye for an eye. A tooth for a tooth. That's not your belief. You have chosen a fallen angel in Francis though you choose not to see it. Like Solomon he was born into power and wealth and corrupted by the need to keep it. *Homo sapiens'* intellect is its own death warrant. Who does not want possessions and luxury if it is available to them? That it kills the warmth of the soul is as I desire. That is my profession. Who cares about an afterlife when the present one suffices with its plenitude of material wealth to those with the skills to obtain it?"

He paused to see the effect of his remarks but Mrs G went on packing with no trace of annoyance.

"Where do you intend to go now? Surely your mission is ended? Why don't you go home? The children need you there and you can see out many years more with them by courtesy of me!" he said snidely, as if he had won his game with her, set and match.

"To Germany," Mrs G replied, knowing somehow he would find out where. She had asked the hotel desk to book her flights, but with his priest's collar disguise he would most probably fetch the information out of them, even if he wasn't clairvoyant in his knowledge of her movements with his mysterious exits and entrances.

"Francis Bacon had a friend whose family may still live there since they were aristocrats and they may yet have some knowledge on record. There is a book I have read which connects Bacon to the German Rosicrucians. They were a close fraternity modeled on the Templars and their Masonic beliefs from the Kabbalah, sworn only to do charitable work."

Ethan yawned. Mention of ethics disturbed him. He was happiest with those creeds and religions which relied on pomp and ceremony and wealth, since, as with most institutions of power they were corruptible. Nor was the revival of the ancient Kabbalah upsetting since its creed was to believe in a Creator who could be good or bad. His own power was equal to that of good and gave him a fairly easy existence corrupting the souls of mankind. Overall he felt on top of his game and had no qualms. He was a necessary evil he joked to himself. How was it that Mrs G was so damned incorruptible? He rarely found her sort of person among the rich, while the poor were all too concerned to survive to have much time for thought. Philosophy was a luxury few could afford.

Ethan wanted now to finish his business with Mrs G as he had new matters at hand. It seemed unlikely she would succumb to his temptations. He had tried hard enough in all the ways he knew but force, and force was not his métier. Seduction and temptation were, but his charm and promises had failed him with Mrs G, however smooth tongued he had been. His task still remained to ensure she would not follow in the footsteps of Francis Bacon to discover the secret of immortality. Another matter too needed be resolved. Phil Buonarroti had been trying to reach Ethan to find out what was going on. Apparently, the Order in Washington had met and they needed to know when Mrs G was to return. There had been some concern over the Magdala Foundation. For the time being Ethan decided to play hard to get and first finish the job he himself had in hand.

Mrs G finished her packing ready for her departure the next day. She went to the door and opened it for Ethan to exit ahead of her. As she walked with him to the elevator he asked her where she was going for the afternoon. "None of your business," she replied with a disarming smile. "I will see you tomorrow," she lied, knowing that she was to leave very early to catch the plane to Berlin the next day and could hopefully lose him for good. The Ritz doorman hailed a taxi for her and she waited until it reached Hyde Park Corner before she gave the driver instructions on where to go.

# Chapter 70

## Highgate, London. December 2014

An hour or so later heading north after a drive through the clogged London traffic of the Edgeware Road they approached Highgate Hill in Hampstead. The wind blew harder and colder now and she was pleased she had brought with her the thick Burberry winter coat and Marianne's Jack Russell ski hat needed in Boston's winter months. She turned up her collar and drew her scarf around her with a gloved hand as she left the taxi and walked up the slope of the hill from where she could gain a good vantage point over the ground where Francis Bacon had drawn his last breath. Her own breath hung in the chill air, and a smattering of snow fell lightly on the ground.

## Highgate, London. April 1626

It was on the ninth day of April 1626 that Francis had driven to Highgate in the carriage and company of his friend and fellow scientist, Sir John Wedderburn, formerly the personal physician to King James who had died a year before. His son King Charles I was now on the throne of both England and Scotland as his father had been, although the two countries were still not united in law.

Easters were cold in the England of the 17th Century and several inches of snow lay on the ground as they proceeded slowly up Highgate Hill. Suddenly a fowl ran out ahead of their horse and coach and flapped its wings in the snow. The horse shied away and Francis commanded the coachman to stop so he could descend. With Sir John looking on Francis took the bird in his hands. Its wing was broken and it was near to death. Francis made a small incision with a pocket-knife he always carried and began to stuff the bird's body with the ice that lay around them. As he explained to Sir John, who was occasioned to Francis' often eccentric experiments, it was an opportunity to see if having been 'frigerated', as Francis called it, that the bird could either be revived at a later date after its apparent death, or that it may be eaten as fresh meat at a later time without degeneration.

By the time Francis had finished stuffing the bird and attempting to close its wound his hands were blue with the cold, and he clambered back into the coach with the help of Sir John. He sat wet and shivering on his seat with a grey tinge to his face and his lips blue, on which slivers of red-tinged ice still stuck where he had brushed them with his hands with the blood of the bird. As they continued Francis began to shake with the cold and Sir John was concerned with the time it would take them to return to London or to Francis's house at Gorhambury, which might take several hours with darkness approaching. He communicated his thoughts to Francis.

"No more of this now, Sir" Sir John exclaimed, as Francis tried to keep the bird cold by placing it on the ledge of the open window of the coach. "You have caught a bad chill and need warmth as soon as possible."

"I fear you may be right, Sir", replied Francis. "I cannot be sure of making the journey back without some immediate remedy. God maketh man, and taketh him away. What can you suggest, Sir? Perhaps you will shortly be able to continue the experiment by 'frigerating' me," he joked wryly. Sir John offered Francis a swig of the French cognac he always carried with him in a flask, but Francis' lips were so blue now with cold he could hardly take more than a few drops without spilling the hard liquor.

"This is no time for jest, Sir, insisted Sir John. "Sixty years or more is not an age to take in vain. I know of a house nearby of the Duke of Arundel and oft not used by him, but I feel sure his servants will offer hospitality if he is not at home, since I am his physician and known to them."

"Forsooth, let's make good speed there," said Francis through his chattering teeth. "If I am to be too late for revival, have no fear, Sir. I have kept my faith with the truth. It is the stars above which govern our conditions."

The coach proceeds at haste now to Arundel House, a half mile distant, and on arrival Sir John talks to the housekeeper who is acquainted with him. She tells him the owner of the house has been imprisoned in the Tower of London and that the house is empty of servants and she has instructions not to let anyone in. On Sir John's insistence of Francis' urgent need she says that she has a bed in a small staff room on the ground floor although it has not been aired of the winter damp.

As Sir John sees his friend to the bed, Francis' chest wheezes with the cold, his breathing coming hard with exhaustion. Sir John commands the housekeeper to bring a copper warming pan filled from coals from the small fire in her kitchen parlor, which she places under the bed's damp mattress, together with a glass of water on a side table. Sir John knows he can do no more at this hour and in these conditions, and bids his leave to Francis now lying feverishly on the bed, his head held in his hands. Sir John promises to come back tomorrow as soon as possible with medicine and transport to take Francis to a more suitable place to recover.

The housekeeper, frightened by her responsibility after Sir John departs, now leaves Francis for the warmth of her parlor and its small coal fire. The night sky is clear of cloud, and dusk is closing fast. The evening star Sirius appears high in the inky void of the heavens before its fellow stars are apparent, and the whole universe of stars becomes visible in an infinite panorama.

The next day the housekeeper woke early and remembered her guest from the previous evening of 9th April. The day was the same as that of Jesus' resurrection, and she crosses herself before going to Francis' room in the event that he may have died overnight. She has not heard a sound, but she was a deep sleeper and had locked and bolted any doors that led to her room. Somewhat tentatively she takes a cup of warm water to Francis and knocks on his door, receiving no answer. Slowly she enters the room, the door creaking on its unoiled hinges until it is fully open. Her hand trembles and the hot water spills at what she sees. There is no one there. Francis is gone and the bed empty. The housekeeper makes the sign of the cross once more and falls on her knees, shaking. She had heard nothing in the night. Francis needed to have come through her parlor to exit the house, but the front door, which she examines, is locked and there is no way he could have gone from any other exit. She awaits the return of Sir John in trepidation.

The snow is still on the ground. The only footprints she can see are those made from last night on Francis' arrival. Just one thing catches her eye she had not seen before. A small round enamel badge the size of a halfpenny lies on the floor by the door of Francis' room. On it is an emblem she had seen pinned on Francis' cloak the evening before. A cross with a red rose at its center. It is the sign of the Rosicrosse.

## Highgate.  December 2014

As Mrs G walked she contemplated Francis' final moments. She knew of the story of his death and of his possible spiritual resurrection, or of his flight aided by fellow Rosicrucians.  She had wanted to see the site of it with her own eyes, but all that was left now of Arundel House, and the surrounding estate of the 2nd Earl of Arundel, was the Old Hall, a more recent structure built some two hundred years later. There was now no trace of the house Francis Bacon took refuge in, nor any sign apart from a painting of him hanging on the walls of the Old Hall.

The Old Hall was visited nowadays by many tourists who revered the memory of Francis Bacon as a great man. Many from overseas rather than the English themselves. Americans, Germans, Indians, and even Chinese and Japanese knew of his fame.  Cryptologist, chemist, scientist, poet, philosopher, writer and statesman; founder of the state of Virginia which was to be become the nation of America.   But as the author of the plays published in the name of Shakespeare, few knew him. Francis was said to have been buried at St Michael's Church, St Albans, but when his tomb was opened for investigation no trace of human remains were found.  As for the Stratford actor Shaksper his tomb too held no remains.

What a strange world it was we lived in, Mrs G considered, in which truth was often stranger than fiction, but who was to tell which from which?  Did we in reality live our lives in a blinkered three-dimensional fantasy without any idea of what was happening in a parallel fourth dimensional world of space and time, let alone a parallel universe of infinite multiparallel universes, as some now believed existed?  In that her thoughts were in common with Francis. Infinity had been a subject that fascinated them both since the discovery of finitude might provide the conclusion to the scientific quest for the beginning of the universe and man's existence.

The modern concept of Cryogenics was for the body to be deep frozen on death in order to be reinstated alive at some future date. It would seem, Mrs G thought, that if Francis had indeed tried all forms of reincarnation with John Dee in his attempts to discover a means to immortality, then the act of his stuffing the bird showed he had not yet found it. If this was so then perhaps her quest had failed and Ethan was right. She needed to go home, and perhaps even accept his promise of long life, if she could believe him!

With her day done Mrs G took the waiting taxi back to the Ritz for her last night in London. Tomorrow she was to be on the final leg of her adventure before she set off for Boston with whatever secrets she might still discover. The cold of Highgate Hill had chilled her to the marrow, as it had once done Francis, and as she sat in the back of the taxicab she coughed violently and once again brought blood onto her handkerchief as she had increasingly done since her visit to her Harley Street doctor. She had ignored his warning that she needed treatment at London's Lister Hospital for unknown diseases. There had not been the time.

She had been too busy wanting to complete her mission. The weeks away had gone by so fast, but yet her adventure seemed like an age. One in which she had relived her life anew in a world in which time meant nothing and everything. She went early to bed to be ready for a 5.00 a.m. call to get her to the Lufthansa flight to Berlin the following morning. It departed from London's inner City airport, situated by rail on the Thames not far from the ancient Tower of London. There was no sign of Ethan and she hoped he would not know of the small central London business airport. She locked and chained her room door and slipped between the bed sheets with a sigh of relief. Tomorrow was another day. She would call the children in the morning and tell them she would be back in the next few days.

Ahriman at worship

Baphomet - Androgynous God
combine of Man and Woman -
Good and Evil

Caravaggio's Mary Magdalene

Carving of the
head of Ahriman

Francis Bacon age 40

Francis Bacon with spear
indicating he is Shakespeare

King Arthur

Tobie Matthew

The Emanation of SCIENCES, from the Intellectuale
Faculties of MEMORY IMAGINATION REASON.

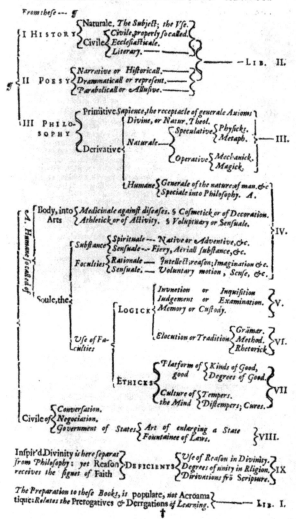

*Logic Process from Mysticism to Science*

*Gorhambury*

*Gorhambury ruins*

*Merovech King of the Franks*

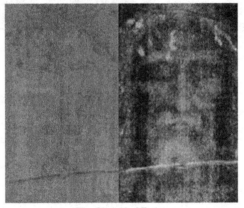

*The Shroud of Turin*

*The Secret Service 007 code of John Dee*

*Edward Coke*

# Chapter 71

(PART THREE)

**Boston USA. December, 2014**

Gerry had been busy during Mrs G's absence. From a distance he had been fascinated by Mrs G's quest and had decided to spend his winter holidays researching the life of Francis Bacon. With his sense of the macabre he found it extraordinary that so little importance had been attached to the lack of any remains in Bacon's tomb at St Albans. Was this the proof of his immortality or was he Christ reborn as some had claimed for him as they had for other geniuses such as Dante and Leonardo da Vinci? Gerry's imagination challenged his rational senses.

The adult world that lay ahead of him he saw as boring. In it inhibition and paranoia reigned. The cultural and spiritual renaissance and youth revolution of the 1960s, in which Gerry's grandparents had been part of a new world of wandering minstrels of the likes of Bob Dylan in place of the old philosophers, was now gone. Haight-Ashbury and Woodstock were now history and could not be explained without having been there. A communion of the senses sharing visionary highs from mind-altering drugs now discredited by governments scared that people might abandon work altogether for pleasure. The CIA then had even branded the use of LSD as the work of English intelligence agents living in California to undermine America's moral fiber!

Now today it was the use of manufactured drugs. Those of Ecstasy and Ketamine had been replaced by substitutes with names such as TINA, GHB and Easylay, marketed by criminals for the teenage market, which replaced the natural senses of pleasure with quick rush substitutes. As soon as one was found and banned, a new concoction would take its place. Many were made in China and people would take them with no idea of their chemical ingredients. Cocaine was still the social tonic pick-me-up of the Wall Street stockbrokers and bankers and their accompanying acolytes of accountants, lawyers, and high-flying wives and mistresses. It gave them high performance mentally and sustained them sexually for as long as they could handle its eventual habit forming dependence and debilitation. Its ingredients were now mostly chemical, usually cut by dealers with speed, bleach or talcum powder, with results far removed from the coca leaf of its origin. As for pot or marijuana, it was now legal in several US states for the personal recreational use in which former US President Thomas Jefferson was known to have indulged, and for use as a relaxant for the ills of old age.

Abe had been careful to caution Gerry. "Use drugs but don't let them use you." It was easier said than done, but along with his college friends he knew to stay well away from habit-forming drugs. Abe had educated him well on their effects and what substances each drug contained. They were the last thing he wanted right now in his life. It was the challenges that lay ahead which stirred him, and he kept his body in good shape with early morning runs and push-ups and his evening karate training, creating his own adrenalin rush. Not flaking out with no-goods. He knew drugs made no distinction. Either you had the character to deal with them or not.

There had to be more to life than drugs, porn, and rap. Nothing was truly new anymore but for space travel and the digital world. On this Marianne agreed with him, but not that the digital world offered new technology frontiers to conquer, but that as a social medium it offered opportunity for genuine global democracy which was already under threat of restriction.

Across North America and much of the world data on the movement of people and their interests was now recorded daily for use by those in power to protect their own positions, as much as those they claimed to protect. George Orwell's book "*Animal Farm*" was now outdated and no longer a Kafkaesque fantasy, but day-to-day practice. How was it possible to revitalize a political system in which little changed and power-broking dynasties still flourished? Gerry had read the words of Proudhon, a famed French politician and advocate of anarchy as freedom. Writing in 1851, he had said:

*"To be governed means that at every move, operation or transaction one is noted, registered, entered into a census, taxed, stamped, priced, assessed, patented, licensed, authorized, recommended, admonished, reformed, exploited, monopolized, extorted, pressured,*

*mystified, robbed; all in the name of public utility and the general good."*

Proudhon had founded the Mutualist Society and became known as the father of anarchy, a word of which it had been said by its critics *"was an escape from the harmonious monarchy of Reason, only to fall under the irregular dictatorship of Folly."*

For the moment Gerry's greatest curiosity lay in the occult, since it was an area of mystery carefully avoided by his teachers at college. His college tutor, Ben Buck, had explained that in Bacon's day alchemy and chemistry, astrology and astronomy, theology and science, had become intermixed. The first lead to the last. Magic was not a word to be derided. Its very meaning was of the occult and the Three Kings of Bible fame had given their name of the Magi to it. Ben had told Gerry simply that Magic is that which it is: the exact and absolute science of Nature and its laws. Something which most had not properly comprehended. Bacon had been one of the first with John Dee to attempt to differentiate fact and reality from supposition and superstition.

Ben had a personal interest in Rudolf Steiner, a relatively modern Austrian philosopher who had sought to find a synthesis between science and spirituality. Steiner had been influenced by Goethe, a 19th century Protestant poet and plant evolutionist. Goethe had written *Faust*, a notorious play in which a bored young scholar sells his soul to the devil and seduces a young virgin whom he impregnates.

By chance the American author of a recent thesis describing Shakespeare's knowledge of science and astronomy was due to lecture in Boston in a week's time. He was to discuss those Shakespeare plays which referred to the changing Elizabethan views that the earth revolved round the sun, which had been seen as heresy by the Church. Ben had invited Gerry to go along with him.

The lecturer had proposed that the majority of Shakespeare's plays referred to real people and events of the time. It was apparent to Gerry that those from the scientific sphere of knowledge were all fellow associates of Francis Bacon and not of William Shakespeare the actor. Neither were they linked to Christopher Marlowe or the Earl of Oxford both of whose names had been put forward as the author of the Shakespeare plays, but had no scientific background. A Canadian author too had recently brought out a book entitled "*The Science of Shakespeare*" but, strangely to Gerry, no consideration had been given to Bacon as the Shakespearean author. It was becoming obvious to Gerry that either there was a conspiracy to obscure Bacon as Shakespeare or a blind wall of ignorance to accept it.

Gerry was now only weeks away from his eighteenth birthday in January. He soon had to make a career decision whether to opt for MIT, the famed Massachusetts Institute of Technology, or Harvard; both were near his home, but he had not resolved in which direction he wanted his life to go. Marianne was less inquisitive than Gerry but no less intelligent. She was of a calmer disposition but with determined views on the equality she believed women should share with men. In her knowledge that she too would soon control an equal part with Gerry of their grandfather's billion dollar fortune, she was already making note of how she might best apply it after attending college at Wellesley near to her home.

Marianne was becoming attractive now, of which she herself was unaware. She had lost the braces on her teeth a year or more ago and had grown to her shoulders the Titian red hair which set off the strange turquoise shade of her eyes. She had a good firm slim body, five foot nine inches tall, gained from riding and swimming at which she excelled. As for her studies, she enjoyed sociology and biology, and was naturally good at math. Following in her mother's footsteps she had a love of animals and had taken up horse riding at an early age resulting in a drawer full of prize certificates won at gymkhanas and riding events.

Marianne's mother had studied medicine as Abe had wished, but had decided to apply it to veterinary purposes. After her marriage she and her husband had bought a ranch on the high plains of the Portuguese Alentejo where they bred the famed Lusitanian horses, bringing them to the US for equestrian events. She and her husband did not mix with the often newly rich, racing community of Kentucky's rolling countryside and the magical chemistry of its blue grass whose ingredients helped produce its champion thoroughbreds. In Boston society her grandmother's ancestry had form and with it went discretion.

Marianne and Gerry shared the grief of their parents' death and that of their grandma Marilyn, whom they had loved for her eccentricity and wit. Now this year with their grandfather's death too they realized, despite Mrs G's care for them, they were soon to be out on their own in the world. It strengthened their common bond. The evening Gerry had come home from the lecture on Shakespeare he had sat down excitedly to discuss it with Marianne. He had wanted to impress Mrs G with his information when she next called. Marianne asked Gerry to tell her more about it on the following day when there would be more time.

# Chapter 72

Mrs G's early Lufthansa flight from London landed at Berlin's Tegel Airport. She was met by a car sent from the palatial Adlon Kempinski Hotel situated near the Brandenburg Gate and once famous as a haunt for the erotic revelries and high living of German army officers during the Nazi era. She quickly registered at the reception desk and had her hand baggage taken up to her room where, after a quick wash and brush up, she was soon back in the grand lobby with its famed blue glass skylight dome, asking the concierge for a taxi to the Pergamon Museum. Before the wall dividing East and West Germany came down, the museum had been in the Eastern sector of Germany under Soviet control, but was now open and available to all.

Its principal treasures, similar to the Metropolitan in New York and the British Museum in London, were those from the ancient Egyptian, Babylonian and Greek epochs, with vast rooms full of statues and carvings carrying the ancient encryptions of which Mrs G had made a hobby of deciphering. The great altar statue of Zeus and the Goddess Athena together were housed at the Pergamon, with the bust of Nefertiti's wonderfully symmetrical face and head at the Neues Museum next door. How beauty was as essential as intelligence in life, Mrs G mused. Together they were the killer combination as Cleopatra and her great-granddaughter Mary Magdalene had known so well to use in their choice of the men in their lives. Marianne had the makings to be a beauty one day, as her grandmother had once been, Mrs G reckoned, and there was no doubting her intellect.

The taxi took her down the Unter den Linden and soon arrived on the Museum Island under the Palladian pillars of the Pergamon's massive portico. It was lunchtime and crowds of young from the world over stood or sat huddled in the cold air on the steps to the main entrance. As at the British Museum only weeks earlier Mrs G asked for the archive offices where she had made an appointment. She was taken to a small waiting room where within a few minutes two women entered the room. One, an older and elegant woman in a long plain raincoat discreetly lined with luxurious sable and a matching fur hat, introduced herself with an extended handshake and a warm smile from her blue eyes.

"Fraulein Gallup? Please be welcome," the elder woman suggested in English but with a strong German accent.

"I am Renate von Holzchuher. My great-grandfather was Albert Von le Coq. I understand you are interested in seeing the Andrea portrait which is owned by the le Coq family and is on loan at this time to the Pergamon, who are kindly restoring it." She gestured with a gloved hand towards the younger woman accompanying her, dressed in a grey overall.

"Yes, oh - hello," said Mrs G absent-mindedly. "Please call me Jane."

Events were getting close to her final goal and her excitement was getting the better of her now that she had put Ethan's disconcerting presence behind her. She returned the smile she had received. "Please excuse me but I have waited a long time to see this picture, so I am a bundle of nerves. It is shown in the Rosicrucian *Fama Fratenitas* and is a link to the son of Queen Elizabeth I and the past.

"I am aware of its provenance. Please come with me to see the picture," Renate requested in a firm voice. "This lady with me is an assistant at the museum from the department of restoration and she has found time at short notice for us to see it."

They left the room to enter a long grey-walled corridor leading at the end to a large high-ceilinged windowless room with a north-facing skylight. There were various pictures covered with large dustsheets. The strong smell of oil paint and turpentine filled the air while many pots and paint brushes lay on adjoining tables. Being lunchtime there was no one else there.

"I am so pleased you have had the faith to follow this up." Renate continued. "I received your email and was happy to arrange for your visit. I understand you are a cryptologist as was my great-grandfather Albert. Your interest would mean a lot to him. He was an adventurer and archaeologist whose interest lay in the discovery of ancient texts and ciphers, many of them from the Orient and India which he felt might pre-date those of the Egyptians who shared many of the similar Buddhist and Manichean beliefs. He headed an expedition through Iran to western China on the old Silk Road once taken by Marco Polo, and before him Alexander the Great. He found evidence of an Aryan race of red-haired people with their bodies buried four thousand years ago well preserved in the salt deserts. Their women were said to be six feet tall. They resembled those of the Frankish tribes in Gaul under the rule of the Merovingian kings and of the red haired English Celtic warrior Queen Boudica. Strangely the Iranians of today with their dark features take their name from the Aryans.

"Our German Emperor Wilhelm II financed my great-grandfather's expeditions in a search for a super-race, and he brought back many artifacts to be stored in Berlin, but they were unfortunately destroyed by bombing in the last war. My great-grandfather was a strong believer in immortality of the mind and senses, rather than of the body or soul; a subtle difference I am told. His conclusions were similar to those of Descartes, the French founder of modern philosophy, who asserted that thought and mind were separate from the body and its passions."

My great-grandfather found evidence that Francis Bacon had worked closely with Valentin Andrea, believed to be the subject of this picture. It was no secret then on the European continent that Bacon was the son of the English Tudor Queen. It is one still well-kept though from the English it seems. I suppose the powers that be don't want a genuine Tudor to pop up somewhere with a better claim to the throne than the German Saxon line that reigns England now! Quite an irony really. I am sure you know Queen Victoria was a close cousin of Kaiser Wilhelm. Even today our Prince Hanover holds the title of Duke of Cumberland as a royal British duke." Renate laughed and continued. She was obviously well informed in such matters.

"It has been said that Valentin Andrea and Francis Bacon were one and the same person on the basis of a footnote to a book *The Anatomy of Melancholy* in which the names Valentin Andrea and Lord Verulam are seen together as one. But I have little doubt they were separate individuals with shared thoughts. The book was accredited to a Richard Burton, who I understand acted as a mask for Bacon, and the footnote may have been intended to confuse."

The assistant stopped in front of a medium-sized painting on a small easel and carefully took away the covering dust sheet. *"Das ist* the painting you wished to see?" she asked expectantly.

Mrs G gazed at it intently while Renate continued her soliloquy, clearly proud of the picture's history. "It is lent here by permission of my family," she repeated. "It is the picture of Valentin Andrea, completed we think in or about 1640. He was reputed in Germany to be the author of the Fama Fraternitatis. It was the German Rosicrucian manifesto on the conduct of life, as I expect you know." She looked at Mrs G for acknowledgement.

"I am unable to say how my family acquired it other than it belonged to my great-grandfather."

They drew closer to the picture as Mrs G examined it in detail, while the assistant stood by concerned she should not touch it in any way. The picture was that of the lined face and head of an old man with a white beard among a plethora of shields and emblems of former Teutonic knights and Masonic signs, an hourglass, a skull, and a magnifying glass among them.

"There you can see what I believe you wish to find," said Renate, pointing to a shield bearing the faint emblem of a rose. At the bottom right was one inscribed with the name of 'Roslin.'

"It is the shield of the Roslyn family of Scotland who sheltered the Templar Knights and their treasure of King Solomon. There are other links too, shown to the Rose Line of Mary Magdalene. When the Templars fled from France some came to Germany to join with the Teutonic Knights, where their charitable ideals still flourish under the name of the Rosicrosse, as you will know." Once more she looked enquiringly at Mrs G for confirmation. "You see the initials here" she said pointing at two separate shields. They are the initials F and B. For your Francis Bacon – *vielleicht*. She used the German word for perhaps. "The name under the portrait is Valentin Andrea, but some claim the picture is of Francis Bacon. Do you recognize him?"

"Not as a man of this age," replied Mrs G. "It is difficult to tell. There are no pictures of him near the time of his death in England. He was said to have died in London from pneumonia. His tomb was erected in St Albans where he lived, but it was found empty when opened years later. He was a master of many things and experimented with the transmutation of souls following in Dante's footsteps of a half-world between life and death. It is possible that Bacon was brought here by friends while presumed dead and means were found to resuscitate him. The alternative is that he came here in spirit!"

"I would like to think his spirit came here if not his body," said Renate. "My great-grandfather discovered a link to the Andrea name in the Carpathian mountains in Transylvania. My mother's family were Protestant Huguenots and there is a famous Protestant university they attended in a town some short distance from where Andrea was said to have lived in a small village." She paused hesitantly as if unsure whether to continue, seeing the nervousness in Mrs G's face, and her dry lips which she licked spasmodically between coughing into her handkerchief.

"It was a tiny village, not far from a castle of the Rakoczi family, then the home of the Hungarian royal family, themselves Rosicrucians. They had vast wealth from a secret source. Some say from alchemy, turning lead into gold, while others claim it was part of King Solomon's treasure." She paused one more time to see the effect on Mrs G who, coughing again with excitement, asked for some water which the assistant gave her from the water cooler nearby. Having sipped the water Mrs G queried: "The village?"

"Unfortunately, my great-grandfather was too ill to travel at that time so he never went there. I don't recall its name. I am sorry," explained Renate, seeing the disappointment on Mrs G's face she took Mrs G's hand in hers and gently squeezed it.
"Please call me Renate" she said. "Believe me, Jane I want to help you with your quest." She looked sympathetically at Mrs G.
Mrs G thanked her. "I appreciate all you have done, Renate. You have been most kind to see me."

She realized suddenly how much she missed Abe. What a tower of strength he had been to her in life. For the first time since he had died she felt totally alone. Somehow she had believed that her search for Francis' final ending would lead her to know how Abe had died, and what he had died for, so she could share it with him. But now she had in her tiredness begun to doubt. Had it all been a wild goose chase for nothing?
" It is my last chance to find what I seek," she said, almost in a whisper.
"And what is that? Can I ask why this is so important to you?"
"My own Holy Grail," said Mrs G, "I must go now to find this village. I don't like to ask you, but I don't know anyone here in Germany and I need to send these packages to the US before I leave Berlin. It may be my last chance. Would you be so kind as to mail

them for me? I will pay you."

Renate waved her hand brusquely. "There is no need, my dear Jane, I will be happy to do so. I wish you success with your journey. Please keep in touch and let me know how you get on."
She smiled warmly at Mrs G but with certain sadness at the earnestness she sensed in her, despite her admiration for it. She felt somehow Jane would not achieve her goal. The mists of time would have covered the traces she sought. She took the two small paperback-sized packages already labeled and promised she would have them sent by FedEx the next day. It was to be the last time the two women saw each other. As Jane went to leave Renate could not resist but to kiss her gently on her cheek as if she was a lost and lonely child.

# Chapter 73

Phillip had called a meeting of the Order. His members were demanding action from Phillip as its chief executive. The possible loss of income from Abe's Magdala Foundation was an issue which was his responsibility and needed to be resolved or a new source found. As a rule Phillip reported directly to the Worshipful Grand Master, a shadowy and hooded figure whose identity was known only to a very few, but whose decision was final.

The top echelon of the Order was highly secretive but its members had many links to the political and business communities of Washington and New York.  Abe's marriage to Marilyn had attracted new members. It had shown there was no sectarian bar to anyone other than those whose concepts were seen as regressive. The members were attracted to the Order's Masonic ideals of a fraternity for an orderly world in which to conduct their global business activities unhindered by divisive religious dogma. All those at the meeting would be initiates at least of Masonry's 32nd Degree, the highest status being that of the 33rd Degree of the elite Scottish rite.

Abe's death had come as a shock. Although in his late seventies, his enthusiasm had been undaunted and he had been a major contributor of funds to the Order for charitable purposes.   Phillip had not told his fellow members of Abe's anger in the last conversation he had had with him, as he was concerned that he had overstepped the mark.  In retrospect, he should not have mentioned to Abe his ideas as to how and when Abe's new antibiotic elixir might be used; after all, it was Abe's baby. But now that Abe was dead he would not need to disclose his blunder.

He could not understand how Abe had died. He had no involvement as Ethan had suspected. The initial postmortem, a copy of which Phillip had obtained from a medical associate in Boston gave the cause as internal hemorrhaging. Mrs G had not been satisfied and had requested further investigation which had not yet been completed.

Perhaps Abe had taken too much of his own medicine. Phillip chuckled at his own black humor. At least Abe was now out of the way; but then how was he to know what was in the phial Abe had left with him and which was now locked away? Whenever he looked at the picture of the pyramid and its all seeing-eye which covered his wall safe he would glance away as if to expect smoldering sulphuric fumes to emerge.

His thoughts changed. His smart young assistant had buzzed him to say the members of the Order were arriving and convening in the large boardroom, which seated up to fifty members. Only thirty-three members would attend with the right to vote. It had been impossible to fit a round table in the room for so many, so the one they had specially made was a compromise, shaped like a coffin with rounded ends. The windows of the room had recently been lined with a sepia tinged metallic film to reflect any view from outside, and to repel the electrode beams of any sound listening devices which might be pointed at them. That morning Phillip had personally supervised a sweep of the boardroom for any bugs that might have been planted. Most, if not all members, drove directly into the Order's private underground car park in the building and used its private elevator. It was fitted with thumb and eye recognition electronic passkeys to gain entrance to take them up to the Order's Suite 666 on the sixth floor.

Despite Phillip's error with Abe he felt sure enough of his own standing in the Order. His family, the Buonarrotis, were Jewish in origin, but had rejected traditional Jewish views to become revolutionary Masons way back in Italy in the 19th century. Phillip had followed in his own father's footsteps in establishing the Washington Order with ever greater authority since he had been put in charge of its business activities. He had a supreme ability to raise funds of substantial size from wealthy contributors in the US with a mixture of a promise of favors, or of their withdrawal. He was a careful observer of history and was of the belief that knowledge should govern ignorance. He was fond of past quotes to this effect, not least of those of Machiavelli whom he admired. One he particularly favored was that *"It is better to be feared than loved if you cannot be both."*

The administration of the Order had been based on that of two pyramids. A smaller one on top, representing the executive, inverted so that its tip touched the tip of the larger one underneath which represented the mass of the Order's members, who only very rarely made contact with the top. As far as most were concerned, the activities of their Order were purely charitable. It was the wealthiest in Washington and most probably in the USA.

Phillip entered the boardroom as its members were taking their seats, and greeted them all by their first names. Their name cards had been placed according to their prominence and at the head of the table today would sit the Grand Worshipful Master himself. Phillip would sit at his right hand in order to take him through the agenda and offer any advice if required. Confidentiality of their discussions was assured, quite literally upon pain of death of any member leaking information, of which all were sworn to obey as part of their traditional initiation rites.

Phillip had had the opportunity some time back to become the head of a large multi-billion dollar US corporation with worldwide interests, but he preferred the job he had now in which he met many of the most important people in America on first name terms. He had trained himself to do a task few others could do without his extensive knowledge of Masonic history, and his command of national and international politics. He had a worldwide web of connections as well as those near to local Washington gossip where he mixed daily with politicians in many of the capital's smart restaurants and bars. Apart from English he spoke the Latin languages of Italian, Spanish and French fluently, and had a good understanding of Arabic.

His assistant Noi, whose attributes he had personally chosen for the job was a Thai Chinese who had been trained by the Chinese People's Republic as a spy before defecting to America, still only twenty-six years old. Apart from languages of which she spoke fluent Mandarin and Russian, she was skilled in all aspects of espionage, including seduction.

Phillip's own spouse, Ursula, was a typical Washington wife on the charity circuit. She was forever organizing lunches and dinners for various causes without favoring any particular section of Washington society. Their two children, a boy and a girl, now in their teens, attended the best schools that money could buy and were currently on vacation ski-ing on the pistes of the swish, up-market, Swiss ski resort of St Moritz. Phillip had recently been elected a member of the resort's exclusive mountain top Corviglia Club, a rare invitation for an American where waiting lists were up to twenty years long. There he could hob-nob with the rich and famous of Europe who would meet their Swiss banker friends over a gourmet meal followed by a leisurely afternoon ski downhill, lunch and snow conditions permitting. Ursula had planned for her children to mix with the elite, and had it in mind that either her son or daughter might one day make a good match for Gerry or Marianne, and their billion-dollar inheritance from their granddad.

Phillip called the meeting to Order. The thirty-three members attending had been called at short notice and so they formed a majority of Phillip's own cronies as he had intended. Ethan's last message on the state of Mrs G's health had triggered the immediate need. The main purpose today was to discuss what might happen if control of Abe's Magdala Foundation should pass from the hands of Mrs G to Abe's grandchildren.

Phillip had been concerned to have to work with Mrs G, although since his promise to help her with her book he had felt he could persuade her to continue the funding of the Order which Abe had threatened to stop. If she were to be ill or die, however, it would be Gerry who would take her place as head trustee of Abe's foundation once he had reached the age of eighteen.

Phillip frowned. The loss of contact with Ethan was annoying. There had been the incident at London airport when Phillip was en-route for Berlin, after which he had heard nothing. All that Ethan had hinted at then was that his interests were not the same as Phillip's. It was disconcerting that he had not explained himself, and since then there had been silence, except for a text message that Mrs G had been in hospital after a car accident. Phillip had had no response to texts he had since sent. What game was Ethan playing?

Phillip had arranged with a detective agency to watch the Brookline house where Gerry lived with his sister, but there had been no sign of Mrs G's return, and it seemed Gerry seldom went out during his vacation times any more than his sister did. A strange pair, thought Phillip, not like other kids, with Christmas coming and parties to go to, as he stood to start the meeting.

Above all his other concerns was the question of Abe's life-saving potion, and who else might know about it. It was a serious matter which could be Phillip's downfall if badly handled, but a huge opportunity otherwise for the Order, and the kudos it would give him. This was the big one, Phillip thought. Despite the cool of the air-conditioned room drops of perspiration dampened the collar and armpits of his button-down Brooks Brothers shirt as the members of his Order looked to him to speak. They were one of the most influential groups in America and a force to be reckoned with against the opposing views of their global rivals on how the world should be run; China, Russia and the new revolutionary movements of Islam not excepted.

# Chapter 74

Gerry had decided to ask his tutor over for an evening meal at home so that Marianne could join in the conversation as she had asked. Ben Buck had come round early since the snow was falling lightly in Boston, and he wanted to leave before the chance of getting snowed in. Ben had a PhD in philosophy, but was not the professorial type, still retaining a youthful streak in his mid-thirties. He had the mentality of a perpetual student always on the side of the world's revolutionaries and social causes. One of his favorite quotes was from Voltaire:

*"To learn who rules over you, simply find out who you are not allowed to criticize.*

It matched his attitude to life and authority and he liked to repeat it to his students as a welcoming gambit.

Ben was good looking with slicked-back dark hair, and had a mystic aura about him that impressed many of his students, particularly his frequent young female admirers. He and Gerry sat in the comfortable sitting room where Mrs G had last told Gerry and Marianne the tale of their Merovingian heritage. Now there was log fire burning in the open mock Tudor fireplace under a carved stone mantelpiece with a striking picture of Abe over it, where Mrs G had hung it. It was by the artist Lucian Freud, a renowned "warts and all" English portrait painter who had recently died, and a distant relative of Sigmund Freud, the world's best known shrink of the 20th century. Ben had an irreverent nature but appreciated good creative art and the painting had captured well Abe's air of quiet resolution.

Ben knew of Abe's family standing and reputation in Boston, but would not have wasted his time with Gerry if he thought him not a keen listener or pursuer of information. He had not met Marianne before and was pleasantly surprised when she joined them in the room. He started off as he would his standard lecture with his favorite opening quote from *King Lear*.

*"The stars above us govern our conditions"* and added the famous quotation from *Julius Caesar "The fault, Dear Brutus, is not in our stars but in ourselves"* as a contradiction in terms to explain that the words of the Shakespeare plays were meant as food for thought for his audiences rather than being judgmental. That, however bizarre their situations or characters might appear, they should not be dismissed since truth was often stranger than fiction.

That he was to now dissect the plays allegorically was to give them relevance to the time and events in which they were written.   Although Ben had considered the authorship of the plays, this had not concerned him greatly. That Bacon might be the true author would have made Ben's explanations of the texts a lot more plausible, as he was soon to appreciate.

Knowing Gerry and Marianne were unlikely to have had much time to give thought to the hidden meanings of the plays, Ben reckoned it was better to start where his lecture would finally take them, and to work backwards. He explained that in Shakespeare's time, in the space of half a century in Europe, a Christian-centric world of theology had become a scientific one, in which new technology gave rise to new concepts as to how the world was formed, and what it meant for humanity.

The invention and use of the telescope by Copernicus, Galileo and Kepler, and by John Dee and his friends before them, had been a turning point. That as the power of telescopes increased they had found that, contrary to orthodox views, the earth and planets revolved around the Sun. Other discoveries came thick and fast. That of magnetism and its distinction from electricity and its importance to gravity. The law of hydrostatic pressure and that of the swing of a pendulum. The revival of thinking of Lucretius that the world consisted of nothing but atoms, and so the destruction of much of ancient philosophical thought from Aristotle to Ptolemy. The inductive thinking of Montaigne and that of Bacon combining with the new deductive theories of science, soon to be followed by Newton's theory of relativity.

Many references to these ideas could be found in Shakespeare's plays if you knew where to look, and were as visionary then as science fiction was today. The intelligentsia of the time in Europe were a small band of people. Novel ideas travelled fast and were seized on by authors and artists to elaborate their works with new concepts, much as did movie directors of today to attract the public with dramatically futuristic screenplays. Old philosophies were reviewed in the light of the new mathematical sciences. John Dee's magical experiments in alchemy became the foundation of chemistry, although he was to die bankrupt in money and ideas as the new world swept him by.

Two Thomases, Digges and Harriot, were among Bacon's circle of friends. Digges was a mathematician and astronomer who had been apprenticed to John Dee and later worked with Tycho Brahe, a Danish astronomer, in discovering that changes took place in the position of the stars. At much the same time Giordano Bruno in Italy had come to the same conclusion based on new findings of Arab and Egyptian geometry rediscovered from two thousand years before.

Harriot, an astronomer as well as an explorer, had spent time in America with Walter Raleigh, and spoke the native Indian Algonquian language. He had drawn a detailed picture of the moon's surface by use of a telescope several months before Galileo. Harriot was the same age as Bacon and had worked at Alnwyck Castle with John Dee under the auspices of the then Duke of Northumberland, known to them as The Wizard. In all they were a collection of the best minds of their day; adventurers in every sense of the word. Harriot was an expert ship's navigator and, en-voyage to America, had designed for Raleigh a way to stack cannonballs without them rolling on deck, in a manner which equated with the structure of atomic theory as it is known today.

Scientists may have formulated new theories but it still took the sensibility of writers to portray what they meant to ordinary people. Descartes was at first forced to conclude that atoms had souls, since if the Universe was made entirely of atoms there could be no Divine force, and man's life as a composition of atoms was otherwise pointless. His maxim *"I think therefore I am"* in which body and mind were viewed as separate entities gave him a clever way out of this dilemma. It was becoming clear that the Catholic religion, under the iron hand of the Papacy, had been a convenient escape from reality and that truth was rather to be found in man as a creature at one with the universe; not its master. A vast unimaginable space into which man was cast for no discernible reason, and it was scary. As Pascal was to write some years later: *"Who has put me here? By whose wonder and direction have this place and time been allotted to me? The eternal silence of infinite space frightens me."*

Men were endlessly to look for answers, refusing to accept there might be none. New technology was often seen as magic and witchcraft best left alone. That a telescope could now show much the same mountains and craters as those on earth took away the fantasy of religion and a God of the heavens. The Shakespeare plays *The Winter's Tale* and *The Tempest* dealt with these topics.

Bacon had written many works of scientific interest, including his *Great Instauration*, a massive work of six major parts presented as a voyage of discovery. As Ben Jonson had said of him *"Bacon was not of an age but for all time."* As Bacon's ideas progressed so did the references to science in the Shakespeare plays, and the dichotomy between religious thought and scientific deduction. As new scientific discoveries blew away the fables and dogma of religion, many writers came out as outspoken atheists. Christopher Marlowe, the author of *Doctor Faustus*, being one, as well as being openly gay. His play in which Edward II showed his love for Piers Gaveston *"his sweet favorite"* was an open challenge to those who saw male to male love as an abomination.

Homosexuality was seen by the Catholics as debauchery. It was on a par with atheism and those who followed the hard-nosed practical maxims of Machiavelli that man should use everything in his power to win what he wanted for himself. That Marlowe had made his own pact with the Devil in the character of Faustus' doctor was clear, and that Marlowe was to die young, from a knife stab wound to his eye, and drunk into the bargain, seemed fitting justice to his critics. He and Francis Bacon were of similar minds but were not of the same temperament. Bacon was calm and coolheaded. Not a big drinker. Marlowe was a rowdy individualist but they found inspiration together, at times with Marlowe as a mask for Bacon. Many of their close circle were paid spies of the Queen working under John Dee, as was Bacon's adopted brother Anthony. They relied on each other's loyalty, needing both to conceal their espionage activities, and those of their close fraternity of male bonding and intimate relationships.

All of this information Ben expounded with dramatic gestures and humorous quips. It was at this point that Gerry interrupted Ben, who had paused to pour himself a Coke on his one hundredth tour of the room since he liked to walk while he talked, waving his hands in the air to make his points.

"I have told Marianne that Shakespeare was just a paid mask for Bacon, and that it was Bacon who wrote all the Shakespeare plays. Our stepmother Mrs G has told us she can evidence it from secret ciphers in the plays."

"Okay, no prob," said Ben off-handedly. "It's not really important who the author is."

"Oh, but it is!" Marianne interjected. "Surely we need to know? He has shaped people's ideas for hundreds of years! I want to know everything about him. The things he liked and didn't like. If he was straight or gay, or had children, and who his friends and family were, and you tell us it doesn't matter? Weird!" she exclaimed.

Ben was confused himself now. What Marianne said was possibly true. People had accepted Shakespeare as the Bard of Avon for so long now that it was rarely questioned, or if it was, then it was soon stamped on. Bacon certainly was a leading scientific and philosophical mind whose books were serious reading. Perhaps people may not have seen another side to him. One of a love of life and of humanity. But if Bacon was truly Shakespeare, he had for sure turned out one hell of lot of work in one lifetime!

"Well, I would like to meet your stepmother one day. She sounds interesting. Her views do contain a grain of truth. Shakespeare seemed to have no life to speak of whereas Bacon was famous in his own day. It has been said Bacon was gay, but there is no actual evidence for it that I know. He had gay friends and was one of a group of men who came together in their thoughts and minds against long established views. We do that at college, so?" Ben shrugged his shoulders. "So what if he was gay?"

Gerry liked Ben. That he had not tried to put Marianne down pleased him. He had accepted she might have a point about Bacon. Ben was a broh', Gerry thought. Levi 501s, Adidas sneakers, a crumpled sweat shirt with a picture of the Greek goddess of sex, Aphrodite on the front. Of darkish complexion with quick dark brown eyes and long black hair swept back, he had a swashbuckling piratical air about him. A touch of the Johnny Depp, he thought. Gerry knew Marianne well enough to know she had taken to Ben, despite her criticism.

Ben sat down. He was an hour or so into his talk and felt at ease with the two kids. Professors at the college always had to be on the lookout for the admiration and attraction of pupils, especially girls who easily became infatuated. These were two bright kids who understood what he was saying and were attentive and easy to get on with. He had taken a fancy to the girl. He would enjoy teaching her. She was a cool one, giving little away of herself apart from the odd furtive glance.

"Ok, let's get it rolling again. Time and tide wait for no man!"

Ben kept talking for quite a while more, with few interruptions, except that now the idea that Bacon may have been Shakespeare messed with his train of thought, as well as Marianne. He had tried to charm her, but she appeared inscrutable, paying close attention but ready to challenge him. All good things were worth waiting for, he thought.

It was a handy moment for a break and for Ben to stretch his legs and gather his thoughts. He went to the French windows fronting onto the garden and opened them. A blast of cold air entered. Closing them behind him he went onto the lawn and took a battered roll-up joint from his jean's pocket, dragging on the last couple of hits as light snow fell softly on the branches of the trees. Despite the cold it was a magical evening. Each falling flake different from the other in their iterated form; just as it was with each living thing on Earth whether human or plants or whatever.

His mind wandered a little with his thoughts as the THC of the cannabis took effect. Just cheap home grown shit. Not like the Cambodian stuff he had finished now from his recent vacation at Cambodia's Angkor Wat which really blew his mind. Little did people know a THC variant was present in the tea they happily drank the world over and was barely distinguishable chemically from cannabis. The last time he had smoked good grass he had wondered how many great artists had owed their talent to a chemical imbalance at birth, or had been helped along by a mind altering substance. Most great inventions of mind or matter had come from rare visionary moments. Art would sometimes illustrate these moments visibly.

It was strange how the paintings of Hieronymus Bosch so closely resembled those painted by the earlier Cathars, and by Peruvian shamans many hundreds of years later. The shamans used a plant concoction called Ayahuasca to enhance their senses. Picasso's later drawings of his insightful two-faced character portraits had been attributed to his use of opium. Whoever Shakespeare was, had he found his inspiration from opiates, as had other philosophers and poets before him? Odd that it might infuse scientific advance as well as spiritual enlightenment. But why not? Both required the mind to travel new paths of consciousness.

The idea that justice might not be God given had been startling to the Elizabethan world. Now it was claimed that humanity was an infinitesimal part of a vast cold universe in which no other being existed, where before God and his angels had welcomed the good. So, if heaven did not exist, did hell? It all gave rise to confusion and a need to adapt. Not least, Ben thought, to whomever was the author of the Shakespeare plays with their changing perspectives on man's condition. *The Tempest*, most probably the last of the plays, depicted nature and humanity itself as the answer, in that mankind and nature, collectively, was in effect the universe, and if the universe was God then God was within all living things. The Shakespeare era had been a time of tumult and revolutionary thought looking for new answers.

Those who today saw no allegory in the plays, or reference to new revolutionary views, could surely only see the author as rather a dull creature who had been left behind in contemporary thinking. In this they were decidedly wrong since Bacon, if he was the Shakespeare author, was the foremost scientist and philosopher of his day. That the author had faced and dealt with these fluctuating questions was apparent from the plays. In *Hamlet*, for example, there was no specific mention of an afterlife as if it was an unacceptable thought, and in *All's Well that Ends Well* we are told – "*Our remedies oft in ourselves do lie - which we ascribe to heaven*" and in *Macbeth* the assertion that life "*is a tale, told by an idiot, signifying nothing.*"

A new practicality now offered comparison to fantasy. It would seem that suddenly religion had turned to nihilism. Yet neither provided the answer. Either you believed in faith or you did not. The two could not coexist. Or could they? Or was it that our mood determined choice? Perhaps everything was always relative and mankind was ruled by whimsy? So much for judges, Ben thought. The concept of precedent on which the law relied was one he could not agree with. Each set of circumstances was as different as the people involved in them. Ben stopped his thoughts now. It was cold outside. He needed to get back to the warmth of the room and his two students whose questions had made him think. He consoled himself with a pet quote, as he re-entered the door to the house.

*"All that is certain is that nothing is certain,"* he said out loud to himself, as Montaigne had so famously written. Lucretius had said much the same a thousand years before, which Karl Popper had echoed not long ago. An example Ben used for his students was: "the poor must be lazy," an assertion known in psychobabble as "cognitive bias." Montaigne was not a scientist, reaching his decisions by inductive thought, while Bacon had mixed inductive thought with that of deductive science.

Ben guessed Montaigne and Shakespeare may have met. Montaigne was thirty years older than Bacon. He had shut himself up in a large manoir in south-west France, occasionally visiting Paris at the time Bacon was there as a young man. Many of the Shakespeare plays contained ideas found in Montaigne's essays. In *"King Lear"* the villain Edmund had clearly said that *"people were as they were by nature"* which reflected Montaigne's views that people need live with the characters they are born with. In the play Edmund had scorned the old who he saw as useless and expendable. A dilemma now facing the civilized societies of today.

Ben brought his thoughts back to earth. Why had he not given more time to the question of who had written the Shakespeare plays? It was crucial, he now understood. He decided to change the course of his lecture to discuss some new theories of a colleague of his by the name of Peter Usher.

Ben had gone way past the time he had reckoned to stay. He needed to conclude his talk but it was late now to call a cab with a foot of snow outside. Esther had long gone to her bed and Marianne noticed Ben checking his watch anxiously. She and Gerry had been absorbed in the lecture. She glanced at Gerry while Ben was collecting his papers. She had wanted to offer Ben a hot drink as he was shivering from the cold, while she called for a taxi. Gerry saw her glance and mistook it.
"Why don't you stay the night, Ben? No need to chance a cab now. The road will get cleared in the morning. Would you like a hot drink? Or maybe a Jim Beam?" The whiskey had been Abe's preferred

tipple and there was a case of it in the cellar. Ben hesitated. If his college superiors were to find out, he might be courting trouble. He thought for a second and then said "Yup". The offer was tempting, and he would sort himself out in the morning and finish off his talk over breakfast. The Jim Beam would be a good nightcap. He would take the bottle with him to his bedroom.

# Chapter 75

**Phillip Buonarroti's Office. Washington DC. December**

Phillip had opened the meeting with a discussion of Mrs G's state of health. He had not mentioned Ethan by name since he was not known to its members, but more of a personal acquaintance of Phillip's and roving spy, of little plausible background. On the occasions he had met with Ethan they had found they had much in common in discussing the virtues of meritocracies, apart from an interest in life's luxuries, good food and good wine included.

Phillip had not considered that Ethan might have any ulterior motive other than self-interest. He had thought the idea of wearing a priest's collar a clever ruse for an undercover agent, as he had believed him to be. He had not bothered to find out if Ethan belonged to any particular denomination, or of his lifestyle. After all, he knew of many priests who could be found gambling at the racetrack or satisfying their carnal desires with some of the chosen of their flock of both sexes.

Phillip had considered whether to point out to the meeting that Abe had wanted to remove him as a trustee of the Magdala Foundation. If Abe had told Mrs G of his decision, then Phillip had decided to use his powers of persuasion on Mrs G to keep his position as a trustee on the basis of the protection it offered Abe's grandchildren. With Abe's important elixir in their possession they could be in danger if it was known to unfriendly parties. Phillip decided to tell those assembled today only that Abe had objected to his superstrain of antibiotics being used on a selective basis. A subject which he had not previously raised with the members.

He told the meeting of the phial that Abe had deposited with him, which was now secure in the safe in Phillip's office, monitored by a hidden camera at all times and opened only by an encrypted algorithmic code sequence changed hourly and sent scrambled to Phil's email address. The Order had its own privately-operated internet service provider based on a small independent island in the

Pacific for its exclusive use, beyond the attention of the Pentagon and of its allies in GCHQ, the major global listening post of the UK government, with whom the US swapped information.

Phil decided to admit that Abe had stated that if the phial was to be opened without expert supervision, its contents might rapidly destroy whole sections of humanity if its pathogenic spores became airborne. Further, that only Abe had the formula for the correct dosage to give a lifetime's immunization against plague and disease to its recipients. The question now was since Abe was dead who else may know the correct balance of its properties in a form that could save mankind rather than destroy it? There was no knowing if Abe had written down the formula or where it might be, if not simply carried in his head.

To Phillip's suspicious mind it was becoming a possibility that to avoid the public disgrace that Phil had threatened Abe with over his past mistake, that Abe may have deliberately taken his own life; perhaps to illustrate the potential perils of his invention. It was either that or an accident or the action of some other party of which Phillip had no knowledge. Although he had considered ways of dealing with Abe he had not at that point reckoned on his disposal, but perhaps someone else may have. It was disconcerting.

As far as Phillip knew no similar phial had been found on or near Abe's body, but from his inquiries it seemed it may only have needed a fraction of the fluid's spores to be ingested, by contact or inhalation, to cause virtually instant death in its concentrate form. A powerful antibiotic by the name of Coliston discovered some fifty years ago had a similar effect and had been banned, since there had been no known way to effectively dilute its potency. How long the effects of Abe's discovery might last was also an unknown factor. Did it have a shelf life and, if so, what was it? He was totally in the dark.

Phillip had made discreet inquiries but it seemed Abe had been working on his project for several years to culminate his life's work and had played his cards close to his chest. No patent for it had been taken out as far as it was possible to ascertain, which in the competitive world of giant pharma the drug companies might have been stolen or imitated once published. From Phillip's inquiries it seemed Abe' laboratory assistants knew nothing of it but had said

Abe often worked late at night on his own pet projects. He had done so on occasions from the small laboratory at his home, and may well have not wanted to expose his research team to the drug's dangers. Since Mrs G was not a chemist it was unlikely she would have played any part in the drug's creation, but perhaps Abe might have left its formula with her. One way or another on her return Phillip swore he would find out and, if she had it and refused to tell him, then he would have it forced out of her. It was of far greater importance for its secrets to be in the hands of the Order and their choice of its best use. Phillip was not a weak man, but his ambitious wife Ursula, of German extraction, had always been his driving force in decisions of conscience, and she had urged him not to get bogged down in sentimentalities. He was to see himself as a commander in battle, she had said, in which lives were expendable in order to win. She did not appreciate that once on the battlefield only confusion reigned.

Ursula had spotted Phillip early in his career and was behind his every move. She knew all about Phil's sexual preferences and saw no reason to put a stop to his pastimes with his youthful assistant. It let her off the bondage hook, which had become boring, and she had her own more interesting fish to fry in the gymnasium where she exercised daily. Her body was strong and her figure still taut and there were many young athletic women who liked the flattery she gave them and her open attentions in the locker rooms and showers. Hardly a week went by without a new soapy conquest!

But God forbid that her Phil should fall in love in some silly infatuation. She would soon put a stop to that. Life was good, and if Phil's ambitions were realized she and he would be sitting pretty at the top of Washington's messy pile. She knew its reality and had no illusions about the world. She was lucky to have been born twenty years after the end of World War Two and to have avoided the post-war deprivation her parents had suffered. Now that Germany was back on its feet with a woman at its head who dominated European politics, she was proud of the German race and its people's determination to be "uber alles" once more. She sympathized with Hitler's ambition to restore the chaos of Germany's social crisis in the depression years after World War One with strong leadership. She approved of order, which she saw as sadly lacking in the USA of today.

Phillip did his best as a layman to explain to the meeting the properties of sulphonamides, and despite his own lack of detailed knowledge the members had been happy to accept his explanation. One other concern bothered him that he did not mention to them. Suppose Mrs G was to disclose Abe's project publicly in the book she intended to publish? As the elixir of life it was said to be, then she might see as the purpose of her Holy Grail that its benefits should be revealed to the world. What had Abe told her? If anything. Had she told anyone else? Perhaps the children. He dismissed the thought. He realized he was getting paranoid and shook it off. In any event she had said she would send him a draft of her book in advance.

It was imperative to the Order that the Merovingian connection of Abe's grandchildren continued. The Worshipful Master ruled that the Order's strengths lay in the spirit of its past. It was why a membership of Phillip's branch of the Washington Order was so much sought after. It was their duty, and most particularly the responsibility of the Order's chief executive, to protect the Rose bloodline of Mary Magdalene. It was why Phillip's father had introduced Abe to Marilyn and why Phillip had encouraged Abe to place his funds and his inventions in the Magdala Foundation. It gave it charitable trust status, avoiding taxation, as well as any public exposure of its accounts so long as it contributed in some part to wellbeing in the world.

The Order had previously asked Phillip to provide research to give reassurance to any decisions they might make. Great surges in population movement were now taking place in Africa and a Middle East torn with internecine religious strife in Islamic disputes stemming from the time of Mohammed's death fifteen hundred years before. Mullahs in Pakistan and Iran and North Africa were preaching hatred of all things Western to their young while filling Europe with an immigration overflow of poorly educated people hostile to Western ideals. Their Islamic concepts held earthly life cheap, very different to those of the Western material world. Attempts to change their beliefs were seen as an attack by infidels and the more radical Muslims would stop at nothing to pursue their cause. It would not be long, with funding from the super-rich oil states and their opposing sects, that they might get their hands on nuclear weapons or biochemicals for use in warfare. Many minor nuclear devices such as depleted uranium shells were now available on the black market.

There were other problems. Tuberculosis, which had been eliminated from Europe fifty years ago, was now returning along with polio and other deadly illnesses imported from Eastern countries. They were fast becoming resistant to antibiotics due to overprescription. It was incredible to think that in less than a lifetime the world's most potent medical cure of penicillin, discovered in England just in time for mass use in World War Two, was now on its way out with nothing to replace it. Only now was the world waking up to the reality that the days might soon return when every day operations requiring an incision, such as an appendectomy or caesarean, had only an even chance of survival from death by bacterial infection.

In 1919 an influenza epidemic in Europe had killed twenty million people, young and old, more than were killed in the entire four years of World War One. It was proof that infectious diseases were a greater threat than war. Plague often laid dormant for years. There had been two outbreaks in 1957 and 1968, and it was now some thirty or more years since any new advance in antibiotics had been made. The plagues of the Middle Ages had halved the populations of cities such as London in just a few years. The World Health Organization had recently issued a report warning of the returning dangers of virulent plague and flu and the horrific disease of Ebola spreading in Africa had amplified their caution.

Phillip's figures had their effect. The attention his members were giving him was riveting. Here Phillip stopped. It was 12.00 EST. and time for a break to allow the members to give some thought to the food made ready in the hospitality suite. They would reassemble in thirty minutes.

# Chapter 76

**Brookline, Boston. December 2014**

Gerry had come down to breakfast early and found Esther preparing the table. He told her they had a guest and Esther had said nothing when Ben had joined them. She was looking forward to Mrs G's return. It had been a responsibility having the kids under her eye and she did not like the thought of strangers staying overnight. She hoped Gerry knew what he was doing inviting his tutor back. He didn't look like any professor she had ever met, but then that was not so many. They had taken their orange juice and coffee and doughnuts into the conservatory, the overnight snow melting on its windows. In half an hour Marianne had joined them looking a little dazed, and Ben began where he had left off. He had called a taxi to come an hour ahead and needed to finish what he had started.

"The Shakespeare plays when written were bang up-to-date with events of their time, but the publication dates on their covers were often out by many years since the texts were often copied and recopied, or were updates of plays which had been written or performed years earlier. *Macbeth* had been written to please King James on his ascendancy to England's throne and to whom Bacon was to owe his then upcoming career. *"Double double toil and trouble"* were words known to millions but they did not realize the famous dance of the witches round their cauldron referred to the rotation of the planets in the celestial world. *Macbeth* was written to provoke a new moral outlook on the world as was that of *Anthony and Cleopatra*, and of the resistance to it from the wiles of women wishing to achieve their own ends.

"Several of the Shakespeare plays, *Hamlet, Lear, Macbeth, Othello* and *Cymbeline* showed a knowledge of moving stars as were shown in the Elizabethan Chronicles publications of Raphael Holinshead, of which we have a record today. Other plays, *Love's Labour's Lost, The Winter's Tale* and *The Merchant of Venice,* all contain references to newly discovered stars. It is apt that the setting of *Hamlet* was in Denmark due to the presence there of Tycho Brahe who had built an observatory on an island by the name of Hven where he lived and worked. He had observed a new supernova in 1572 which was very possibly the star described in *Hamlet* in the ghostly walks of the dead king. "If it was a new star, it would have possibly been the first since the birth of Christ which had led the three wise men of the Magi to him, and so a portent of some great event, possibly a new king or the much-prophesied Apocalypse of the Bible. The 1572 supernova proved to be a turning point in astronomical history and was shortly after to be followed by the Great Comet of 1577 when many people forecast a disaster or "*dis-astra*", the Italian meaning of "*ill-starred*", which would follow.

"The towers and turrets of Tycho Brahe's fantastical home were likely the model for Prince Hamlet's castle of Elsinore. Brahe, who wore a silver nose in place of the one he had lost in a duel, was supported by the Danish king who spent an entire ton of gold setting up the world's first scientific observatory on Hven which mapped seven hundred and seventy seven stars. King James had visited it with his Danish wife as did John Dee and Digges and most probably their fellow scientist Francis Bacon.

"Tycho Brahe corresponded regularly with John Dee, and with Tom Digges who had seen the supernova as a young man. It was considered miraculous since it had faded away altogether two years later. A portrait of the Brahe family at the time included two of his relatives by the names of Rosenkrans and Gyldenstern, It would certainly provide evidence for Bacon having written *Hamlet* and that the two names were most likely taken by him for use in its later versions. Unfortunately for Brahe he was later than most in obtaining a telescope and his theories were being rapidly overtaken by technology advances in optics, and with them the prospect of an infinite universe."

Ben looked at his watch. He needed to sum up before the cab came to collect him.
"An astronomer from Penn State University by the name of Peter Usher reckons many of the characters in the Shakespeare plays relate to real people. In *Hamlet* he claims the prince was the astronomer Tom Digges, who represented the new sun-centered universe, and the Danish king as his father Leonard Digges. Laertes is Tom Harriot, another astronomer. The prince in *Hamlet* says "he could be bounded in a nutshell" or the old finite world as seen by Ptolemy (personified

by Claudius), or count himself as the 'king of infinite space' of a new unbounded cosmos."

"In short Usher believes that *Hamlet* in its final version was designed to move thought from the old astrological world of magic and theory to the new scientific one of astronomy. Digges had shared his own view of an infinite universe with an English friend John Florio who was the tutor to the Earl of Southampton, at that time Francis Bacon's great friend. Like many of the Shakespeare plays *Hamlet* had hidden meanings, only obvious to those in the know at the time.

Overnight Ben had begun to think more about Bacon being the writer of the Shakespeare plays. Certainly Bacon was a known astronomer. Gerry had told him of Mrs G's discovery that the plot of *Hamlet* was originally written for one of Bacon's earliest plays, but that it was not staged until twenty years later. Bacon was a friend of the astronomers Digges and Harriot, and would most likely have given *Hamlet* a major update from its early drafts to include their recent astro discoveries for its first public performance.

Ben continued, looking to see if Marianne was following the discussion. She had her head down on her iPad. It was difficult to know whether she was following him or was dreaming.

"The ciphers hidden in Shakespeare plays used several codes. The use of numbers was one. The number three in *Macbeth* comes up time and again. The three witches; three murderers; Duncan is murdered at three, and the three 'tomorrow's' of Macbeth's own soliloquy. Three times three is the witches favorite multiple of three, and so on. They are said to have cosmological significance in pitting the devil against good. The number two in *A Midsummer Night's Dream* is the 'dyad' of two signifying a duality of incipient doubleness and confusion. In brief, Usher claims the plays are more artful than anyone had formerly believed, indicating the ingenious and intricate mind of whoever was the author."

Ben paused to emphasize his meaning. "The 46th Psalm, attributed by many to Bacon, has the forty-sixth word from the beginning as "shake" and the forty-sixth word from the end is 'spear'. There are many such clues which some say are fantasy, but there are too many to be dismissed as coincidence.

"Until the time of the Shakespeare plays the public had believed that the planets possessed souls, so the new propositions needed to be dealt with cautiously. The *Merchant of Venice* and *The Winter's Tale* connect the world of Shakespearean romance to the arithmetical language of Al Gebra. It had been hidden for centuries by the Arab Moors since it had offended the religious beliefs of Islam. Had the English not brought it back to England after raiding the Bishop's Palace at Faro in Portugal it may never have been put to use. Looking back it can be seen as the time when science began in Europe, the egocentric Earth was no longer, nor was man at the center of all things, as religions had before prescribed. But science may well have been known to an ancient world long before and been forgotten, or deliberately concealed."

Ben thought it best to end on this note. Appropriately food for thought as he tucked into his breakfast of ham and eggs Esther had gotten for him. A change from the cup of three spoonsful of Maxwell House freeze dried coffee run under a hot tap which was his usual bachelor's morning intake.

He helped himself to an extra cup of Esther's coffee made from Colombian beans. The strong black liquid gave him the morning kick he needed. Coffee was still America's favorite drug, along with Coca-Cola. The coffee awakened Ben to the thought of Lucretius and his theory of atoms two thousand years before those of Isaac Newton, whose views were not far removed from today's English physicist Stephen Hawking. Little changed in the eternal search for scientific answers to life which constantly escaped a final solution. No wonder a spiritual answer was sufficient for the majority of people, and who could justify doubt of it with any certainty.

*"Plus ça change plus c'est la même chose"* Ben echoed the words of his last student girlfriend, a pert, gamine-looking exchange student from the Paris Sorbonne whom he hoped he had taught as much as she had taught him about celestial attraction. Descartes had admitted that mind and body did meet on occasions via the pineal gland. The Law of Attraction. It must have been in a moment of good sex! The new young generation learned fast. He wondered if Marianne spoke French, the language of romance. He had not asked her.

# Chapter 77

Waiting to restart the meeting Phil surveyed the scene from his window. Outside, life in Washington went on as usual. The population of the town itself was now eighty per cent or more of black African origin. Of the three hundred and twenty million Americans, who formed less than five per cent of the world population, one in five was of Latin American origin, mostly Catholic, as were the fifty million of Irish extraction. That left an ever-decreasing minority of WASPs, or White Anglo Saxon Protestants, who had originally staked their claim in defeating the native Indians and founded America as the world power it had become today. Successive presidents had been WASPs. Now there was one who was not.

What did the Americans of today know of the ancient Masonic connection to the Capitol? Or what did they care about history? In the last fifty years they had gotten their promised Utopia as near as dammit; striding a global economic empire devised with the almighty US dollar as the world's only reserve currency. Despite this background of materialism there still remained the paradox of the simple Protestant ideals of much of the population of the southern Bible belt. Many other Christian communities too shared their belief in the good Lord. It had been claimed only recently that the average American citizen spent twenty minutes of each day in prayer. As for the remainder their faith could not be determined, but they included many who were potential converts to Islam, as Phil saw it, if not openly practicing that faith.

One-quarter of the entire world's wealth was in the USA. Democracy had become a creed as much as any religion, which the US used as its flagship to control the world as far as it could. But it was by no means shared by all. Trouble lurked everywhere. Mobile phones and the world wide web of the internet provided ease of communication to individual pockets of extremists to act in minutes on a single command given from anywhere. It all smelled of danger and an end to US world dominance. With Abe's elixir, the lives of Americans and their chosen allies could be saved from the threat of rapidly growing hostile populations. Democracy needed to be made secure for those whose purpose it served. To many to whom religion and the law were one and the same, democracy was an insult.

The struggle between creeds had never gone away. Christians, Jews and Muslims continued their arguments in the Western world. Each one split into rival factions. Masonry had been reborn in Elizabethan times like a phoenix from its Templar and Egyptian past. Thanks to Francis Bacon its ideals had been those of America at the time of its independence. But what the Founding Fathers had understood as a simple sharing way of life for the American people had now been ignored and abused. It was time for Masonry to show its singular strength once more. With the immense power offered by Abe's invention Masonry could bring nonsectarian order to the world, as the Templar knights had attempted in years past, but this time by natural causes without use of weaponry. This Phillip considered his personal objective. That it might need the elimination of those of different views to the American way he felt was justifiable.

Masonry was at the heart of Washington. The great Temple on 16th Street guarded by two immense bronze sphinxes. The Washington Monument was a copy of an Egyptian obelisk. The Capitol Building, its foundations laid in a Masonic ceremony by George Washington himself. The entire city designed to an underlying plan of ancient megalithic measurements in which Masonic symbols were on every corner. A copy of the Book of Enoch, containing the secrets of ancient astronomical knowledge was rumored to be buried deep underground at the center of an elliptical triangle containing both the White House and the Pentagon.

Yet now Washington's Masonic past lay dormant, covered by a thick, sugary icing layer of charitable social work and useful business connections. The seal of the United States itself had imprinted on it the words *Novas Ordo Secloram*, or New World Order; the hopeful words of Francis Bacon for a New Jerusalem, now long forgotten. So, what now was new? Was this what America's founders had intended? Half of those founders at the signing of the American Constitution had been Freemasons. Should the privilege of freedom be taken for granted? It was time to wake up the sleeping dogs in the network of Masonic lodges in every town and city and to give them new purpose in a new world led by a new America, based on the old. Phillip had convinced himself, in the manner of his ancestors. Abe's potion consisted of natural substances and hadn't Francis Bacon himself said that *"Nature to be commanded must be obeyed."*

Phillip's reverie was interrupted by the inevitable Washington wail of police sirens, perhaps saving a life somewhere, but more likely escorting VIP's or America's near virtual president in a seemingly endless cavalcade of cops on motorbikes and armor-plated SUVs with tinted windows full of secret agents. Everything was kept secret from the public. "Candyasses!" Phil mused. It was time now to continue his meeting.

# Chapter 78

Refreshed by coffee, yoghurt and doughnuts the members had filed back after their hospitality break. Phillip now used a well-prepared slide presentation, filled with easy to follow colored bar charts, to reel off a bunch of statistics on health and population growth. "Today's world total is seven billion," Phillip recounted, "expected to reach nine billion people in twenty-five years, tripled in a lifetime from three billion since 1960!" He was to continue in the same vein. The whole subject matter of population control or eugenics as it had once been called, was one which the memories of the Jewish Holocaust had shamed any public discussion into silence ever since. Even so it had not stopped concern for what in effect was the largest single problem facing the world today, but its debate had needed to be behind closed doors.

In the 19th century the Malthusian economic doctrine claimed that populations needed to be controlled or man would soon become extinct from lack of food and resources. Not only was population growth since then alarming, but the problems of depleting natural resources and climate change made the situation worse. There was still strong resistance worldwide to the use of genetic crop farming. Without necessary food or water tens of millions would fight to find ways of obtaining it, crossing world borders in such numbers they would be unstoppable. It was already happening as Africans fled in hordes to Europe risking their lives to leave the chaos caused by warring religions and the breakdown of order. Further, the aged and socially handicapped were growing in numbers. Their support by state assistance came from the taxation of declining work forces being replaced by automatons. McDonald's was now proposing to dispense ready-cooked hamburgers from robot kiosks! Where was the money to come from to provide for the problem of welfare dependency soon to face people of all ages and race?

As they absorbed Phillip's information there was little doubt in the minds of the members of the Order that some would be required to contribute from their own deep pockets. In the last year or two alone governments in the US and Europe had uncovered some of the untaxed hoards of the rich by forcing disclosure of bank accounts in offshore tax havens. Many of the world's largest corporations were under attack for tax avoidance, profiting only their management and shareholders. In many cases it was automation that had brought them riches. Either that or the transfer of the manufacture of their products to low wage areas of the East leaving the West's unemployed in their wake.

The World Economic Forum had only recently warned that the financial collapse of 2008 was not over and the efforts to resolve it were simply window dressing. A new "fatal spiral" of fiscal crises was forecast, triggered by ballooning debts which could never be repaid over generations. Meantime governments spoke in platitudes, postponing the issues, concerned only with their next elected term in office. The pensions time bomb would cripple both state and industry with the impossible task of paying people living way past their estimated life cycle.

Apart from war and its terrors, of which Machiavelli had said that "war was perpetual," the only possible solution to reduce the population was disease. Since time began nature itself had culled people. But the advance of medicine had put a stop to it. Now a medicine was needed to restore the balance. A virus of the sort designed to wipe out the devastations of rabbits which destroyed the human food chain. In the past, after plagues had decimated populations, resources of all description had quickly become more attainable and less expensive. The price of housing came within reach of everyone since many more homes were available and individual purchasing power increased substantially. Yet despite the lessons of the past population growth continued to mount inexorably. It had to be reduced drastically, and there was no time like the present.

Phillip warmed to his theme.
"It is necessary," he said, waving his laser pointer towards the statistics displayed on the large LED screen at the end of the room, "to understand that the current situation is already an emergency. The golden age of medicine is past. Soon all strains of antibiotics will be ineffective. It is not just people who are dying each day from incurable bacteria but cows and pigs and chickens are now immune to cure. One-third of all antibiotics now go on animal treatment out of the 200,000 tons produced every year. The threat is no longer to the next generation, but to all of us living today, young or old. Either

governments chose to suppress news of it as they have no popular answer, or they are ignorant of the intensifying risk."

It was not that the members had no conscience of their responsibility for the automation which had created so many unemployed in an over-populated world. But this morning Phillip's words drove home the imminence of its dangers to their own interests, and that it was time to take action to deal with it.

Phillip continued his address.
"Globally over seventy per cent of bacteria have now developed resistance to antibiotics. The cost of medical cures has risen inexorably to hundreds of billions of dollars a year, requiring the use of expensive antibiotics known as carbapenems. Even these are failing. Infections are running rampant in hospitals. Bacteria have found ways to adapt and mutate." Phillip concluded. "It is fast becoming the perfect storm."

He paused momentarily to draw breath, and to see the impact on the members. They were all appropriately quiet and asked few pertinent questions, perhaps numbed into silence by the overwhelming size of the problem that lay ahead. One way or another it was time for Phillip to deliver his *coup-de-grace*.
"It is not just natural causes we need consider. There is that of bio-terrorism. Our enemies have unknown quantities of chemical weapons. The US government has poured funds into its secret Philadelphia research center looking for antidotes, but with little success. As for the drug companies their funding on new antibiotics has dropped to 1.6 per cent of their research expenditure, as they see no likelihood of developing new strains."

Phillip paused once more to sip his glass of water into which he had earlier slipped a large shot of vodka.
"But if we are to believe Abe, he found what the world is searching for. His past record is undeniably excellent. Despite his low-key approach his credentials in the field are the best. He is lauded by his fellow scientists and chemists as a leader in gene splicing using the once mystical Fibonacci sequence of PHI to 1 as his basis. It is considered the building block of nature by which the universe itself is created. It is known as the Golden Ratio of Divine Proportions, in use down the ages in building, music and art. Used by architects such

as Le Corbusier, and by da Vinci in his drawings of the human body. By mathematicians such as Euclid, and Fibonacci himself after whom it was named. In short, the code to life!"

"I have every belief Abe produced the antibiotic super-strain the world needs for its salvation. I have a sample here in our offices. It is for all intents and purposes the elixir of life. All we need do is to know the optimum dosage and ensure it is used only by the right people." Phillip sat down and mopped his brow. The rest was self-explanatory. Once the Order had the correct formula in its hands it would market it under its own price control. It would be expensive, especially at first while ramping up its production. Those who could not afford it would have to do without it, just as it was now with other costly life-saving drugs on the market. The members assumed the American public would get first shot at it and Phillip thought it best not to go into any further details at this point. What he had agreed with the Grand Worshipful Master was to be a secret for the time being.

If the foreshadowed unpreventable plagues were slow to dent parts of the world, then a powerful super-strength release of Abe's elixir would speed things along. In an overdose form it would be little different from smallpox which without previous inoculation could kill tens of millions. As too with smallpox it initially required human contact to disperse, but would soon spread rapidly through the air in a self-amplifying process. Without prior vaccination of the right dose it would be unstoppable and deadly. As for those enemies of America without a vaccine then they would soon find a place in heaven. God willing!

The meeting ended with a show of hands vote, with no abstentions, for Phillip to use everything at his disposal to trace the whereabouts of Mrs G, and to obtain the formula of Abe's perceived wonder drug. Once it was in their possession they would decide on its final use and distribution. That Abe's elixir was not yet in their grasp seemed to escape them, confident as they were in Phillip's abilities. Phillip's plan was both simple and subtle. The perfect "soft kill". He sought in his mind for a quote to justify the outcome. *Macbeth*, his favorite, appropriately supplied it: *"Fair is foul and foul is fair".* Perhaps now his time had come to be king. King of America!

Phillip smiled at himself in his reflection in the window as the members trooped out to the elevator. He looked forward to opening a bottle of 1982 Petrus in the coming afternoon. Now he had the Order almost eating out of his hand he would celebrate his day's work at the exclusive Four Seasons Hotel in Foggy Bottom, overlooking the Potomac River. Noi, his young Thai Chinese assistant, had reserved a luxury suite for an entire afternoon devoted to their joint sexual proclivities before Phillip returned home to his wife that evening for yet another fund-raising event. The more you gave the more you got what you wanted was a maxim of Phillip's.

He felt pleased with his day's achievements. How pathetic today's politicians were he mused. It was the price of democracy and the two party system. One step forward and one step back. The passing politicos were puppets pulled by strings behind the scenes by people of whom they, and the public, knew little or nothing. Those with the power of eternal knowledge, of which he saw himself as one.

He relished his self-award of the next few hours to be spent with his nubile assistant whose contortionist capabilities offered him a large variety of opportunity in their shared pleasures of Saturnalia and Eonism.  Sometimes, he thought, it paid to be generous to give pleasure to others as well as having it returned to oneself. He laughed aloud that he had told his office to tell anybody who might be looking for him that he would be tied up for the afternoon. It was good when in a position of real power to have a self-deprecating sense of humor.

# Chapter 79

**Carpathian Mountains. Hungary.  December. 2014**

On Renate Holzchuher's advice Mrs G had taken the train from
Berlin to Vienna in Austria where she stayed overnight, and from
there early the next day to Budapest in Hungary, where she had hired
a driver to take her to the Carpathian Mountains in the area of the
Rakoczi Castle and the nearby remains of its old mansion.  The
nearest town of any size was Patak, which had once been part of
Transylvania. It boasted a Protestant college started in 1531 after the
stifling fetters of Catholicism had ended.

As they drove the two hundred kilometers to their destination the last
part of the journey was on increasingly poorly made roads. They led
through a valley abutting densely wooded mountain slopes on which
wolves and bears still lived in mountain lairs among the peasantry,
for whom little had changed in centuries in their means of
living.  The traffic grew less on the often steep and frequently icy
winding route.

In the wars of the past two hundred years, in which Transylvanian
territory had changed hands several times, Communism had come
and gone, relieving the farmers from their servility to their past
feudal landlords but now having to take responsibility for
themselves. Those in the small villages and hamlets they passed
surveyed the car suspiciously from the small roadside bars and cafés
and from the fields.  Unknown vehicles were infrequent here. Snow
covered parts of the ground, but the branches of the trees were bare
as if none had fallen recently despite it being visible on the mountain
peaks. The taxi smelled strongly of cheap cigar smoke and bad body
odor and the two-way radio to its control station crackled incessantly.

As time passed Mrs G had taken note of the occasional inn signs
along the way. When the car had reached a small village of a dozen
or so homes within a few miles of the town of Patak, she saw a
hostelry that appeared more welcoming than others, some of which
had resembled stage sets in a Dracula movie. She knew the mansion

she sought had been built in the countryside and had decided to take a chance to make her inquiries locally rather than in a busy town. Her heavily built bearded driver had been as helpful as his Hungarian accent and small command of English language had allowed, and Mrs G asked him to come in with her in case she needed protection. She need not have feared.

The small lobby was unattended and bare but for a high-topped wooden counter with a small brass bell. On ringing it a woman, broad of bosom and beam, seemingly in her seventies, appeared down a narrow flight of stairs. In surprisingly good English she was happy to say there was a room available for the price of US$55 for the night and at a lesser price of $40 a night for three nights. This included a breakfast of cheese and cold sausage with coffee. For another $15 a good evening meal could be made available. A bathroom and lavatory could be found at the end of the upstairs corridor normally to be shared with other guests, should they come. The woman explained there were no other guests at present since it was out of the tourist season, and so Mrs G would have use of the bathroom to herself, even though it did not contain a bath or shower, but rather a small wooden tub with an antique wood stool placed in it to sit on.

Mrs G thought the inn would provide a useful base of operations and she was unlikely to do better at the late time of day. She liked the pleasant face of the proprietress, as the woman turned out to be. She settled for a three night stay there and then, paid up front in US dollars, which were accepted without any problem. Better still, the woman spoke good, but accented, English sounding her "w's" as "v's" in the German manner.

Mrs G paid off her driver, once more in the ubiquitous dollar bills, and was led up the stairs to a small dark room with heavy wooden furniture that would have fetched good money in the US as genuinely antique, although basic in design. She had asked the Ritz in London to have her main baggage sent back to Boston by British Airways and so was traveling light, with only hand baggage and her warmest clothes, worn in layers.

It had become dark, although only four o'clock in the afternoon, and a crescent moon was slowly making itself known over the tall pine trees outside her window. Mrs G tidied herself and went downstairs. There was no TV in the room or Wi-Fi, and she saw her i-Phone was showing nothing in the way of a signal. She had intended to text or email her location to the children, but this she would have to leave until later. She hoped to encounter the proprietress once more, and in that she was to be more than fortunate.

Dora, as she was called, was at the counter when Mrs G came downstairs, and took her guest to see the rest of her residence, consisting of a small dining and sitting room combined, with a cheerful wood fire burning in an open grate, the scent of pinecones filling the room. Dora brought her a cup of coffee of unknown origin, and with a severe and bitter taste needing a large quantity of sugar, but with a surprising kick. Taken with the small glass of pear schnapps, which Dora had brought to her table without Mrs G's request, the two together afforded a quick tonic to Mrs G after her long journey. Suitably fortified she decided to fire questions at Dora.

Dora was not only intelligent, but was a mine of information on local history and was clearly delighted to have an interested listener. They were soon on first name terms.
"Vat ist your interest here?" she had asked Mrs G.
"I need to discover if a man called Francis Bacon ever visited the Rakoczi family nearly four hundred years ago and if there is any connection between him and someone called Andrea and a St Germain," she declared bluntly believing it best to come straight to the point with what little she knew. She would not in a million years have expected the response she got.

Dora knew the whole story. Nowadays she said there were few left who did. In these modern times people seemed not to believe or have time to be interested in history. In her lifetime what traces remained of the local aristocracy had been wiped out. Their titles and lands taken and any remaining wealth and possessions finally lost in the days of Communism. Transylvania itself, once bordered by the former kingdoms and principalities of Hungary, Serbia, Moldavia, Slovakia and the Ukraine, did not now officially exist, having changed hands many times before under the Austro-Hungarian and Ottoman Empires. The Rakoczi mansion Mrs G sought was now in Hungary Dora said.

Many of the former Muslim population had been ejected as had most of the Jews, and Dora herself was a Lutheran with Saxon antecedents. The area included many old castles and mansions in various states of decay or preservation, as funds allowed. They had once belonged to royalty of times past who had disappeared into oblivion, but Dora still remembered the legends surrounding them. Wars may have destroyed written records, but could not eradicate past glories and disasters passed down by folk tales on which Dora had been raised.

The Rakoczi nobility themselves, Dora was happy to recount to Mrs G, had fought valiantly under the Hungarian flag against the Hapsburgs and had lost eighty thousand of their countrymen in the process, bankrupting the Rakoczi family and the Principality. The last prince who had lived there, Francis 2nd of Transylvania, had by the 18th century been ruined by war and had no choice but to flee, abandoning all his lands and possessions.

Bacon, Dora said, had to her knowledge come to live at the Rakoczi Castle, and then at its nearby mansion. He had sought its sanctuary having either fled from England in person or, as had been rumored, his body having been brought back to life at the castle by use of alchemy or transmutation which was practiced by the powerful Rosicrucian Rakoczi dynasty. The family was renowned for their intellect and gathered under their patronage people from Europe of similar brilliance and vision. It was here that Francis Bacon had met the forty-one year old Valentin Andrea, some twenty-five years Francis' junior.

John Valentin Andrea was the son of a theologist from Herrenburg in Germany and of a cheerful disposition, and he and Bacon had got on well. They shared interests in mathematics and the occult, including alchemy, and in similar views of a Utopian world based on the natural order. Andrea had been working on a thesis establishing a code of practice constructed around the beliefs of the Templars and the Gnostics. The Rosicrucian movement was to be devoted only to charity and peaceful means. It was to form the passive basis of a New Age culture and the promise of the dawning of the coming two millennia of the Age of Aquarius.

Similar esoteric beliefs were held at that time, including that of Theosophy, a philosophy concerning a hidden knowledge of wisdom, which once understood, offered the individual enlightenment and salvation. It had been seen by some as similar to the original Arian beliefs of an exclusive master race. The Rosicrucian movement was then both new and covert, deliberately establishing its origin as a fable. It did so to distance itself from the previous militant Templars, devising the name of Rosenkcreuz as its mythical creator, a figure of the imagination. In fact, as Gerry had now informed Mrs G after his tutor's lecture, the invention of the name had come from that of Tycho Brahe's relative Rosencranz, whom Bacon had co-opted for Hamlet.

Mrs G and Dora discussed the local history for hours that evening over supper since there were no other guests dining, engrossed in conversation. Finally after their meal of borscht soup and a goulash of wild mountain boar, backed up with further coffee and schnapps, they believed they had uncovered the most likely story. Francis' friend the Duke Augustus had once proposed to him the Rakoczi family home as a place of refuge, should he ever need find succor from the tribulations of life.

Soon after Francis' arrival the family had invited Valentin Andrea to meet Francis and to stay in their mansion not far from their castle, where the two could work together. They had communicated in earlier years by post on the joint publication of *Der Fama*, which had been completed in its initial form in 1615, some years before Francis' arrival in Germany. Its cover had not then carried the von le Coq picture of the grey haired man. By the time of the later edition on which the picture appeared Bacon was then considerably older than Valentin Andrea, so the picture was more likely to be that of Bacon than Andrea.

Before the two women retired for the night they were well disposed to each other and had swapped tales of their own lives. They had promised to recommence the next day as it was getting late and it was Dora's practice to rise at first light. The wind was blowing strongly, and Mrs G shut firm the window shutters to her room to keep the increasing noise of it in the forest outside from disturbing her.

The gale had howled overnight as if it were a pack of wolves outside her door, and rattled the shutters at Mrs G's window. In her sleep she saw Abe. She felt he was alone without her and was trying to warn her of something. He held a small phial in his hand like those he used at his laboratory. He was pointing at Gerry and Marianne and waving them away. She tossed and turned on the horsehair mattress of her bed and coughed up blood on the towel she had placed to protect her white feather pillow.  The morning seemed long in coming.

# Chapter 80

**Brookline, Boston. December 2014**

Gerry and Marianne were worried. Christmas was on its way and they expected Mrs G's return imminently, but had not heard from her in the last week. They had not yet received the parcel she had asked Renate Holzchuher to send to them, of which they knew nothing. Esther would go to bed early in her room after she had prepared supper for them, and the two lived in a digital world watching clips on YouTube and Periscope, or chatting on online forums with friends they had made worldwide. The web knew no frontiers of the mind.

With snow on the ground outside they would sit together on cushions having supper on a low table in front of the warmth of the fire, as Esther was strict about rationing the central heating oil. They would talk of their parents and their heritage and what they wanted to do in their lives. They knew they were privileged, but as many of their friends also had wealthy backgrounds their status had not concerned them. Racism had never touched them. America was a melting pot and Esther had helped to look after them both from birth. They were sure they would make something of their lives. But what? Neither need work for a living, but they wanted to see the world and do some good in it.

Marianne had explored the idea of becoming a social anthropologist. The origins of life and human behavior interested her. She had also become intrigued by Mrs G's knowledge of cryptology for which she herself had a natural bent. It was a skill akin to writing software code which either came easily or not, and at which she found she excelled. Otherwise she was tempted to work with an American Volunteer Youth Corps in Africa, but the increasing terrorist revolutions there gave her some doubts. Dictators were replaced by new dictators. Nothing much changed in the ancient tribal wars of the world's largest continent.

Gerry had learned a good deal from his grandfather in the last year or so. Abe had often called him into his small lab in the cellars below the house to let him watch his experiments. Abe had talked excitedly, not just of curing disease, but of creating a giant leap forward in human intelligence in resurrecting a fourth dimension from a psychoactive substance he believed was known to a select few in the past. He had told Gerry he believed he had found the correct correlation of ingredients for a new potion he saw as a true elixir of the next stage of intelligent life. Gerry now guessed it was not dissimilar to that sought by Bacon and John Dee.

Marianne apart, Gerry had found girls a waste of his thought process with their constant chatter. The world of political systems had begun to attract him including that of anarchy. Was it necessary for people to be controlled by State or Church? He was attracted to atheism too for the same reason. Surely, he felt, self-ingenuity was the real intelligence that expanded the mind, not that learned from text books. He had read the histories of many great men; philosophers, politicians, scientists and adventurers. Abe had told him of his friend Karl Popper who believed the more man searched and formulated scientific solutions, the more complex and questionable they became, chasing a will-o'-the wisp. It seemed to Gerry it was the same with philosophy as a whole. There needed to be one single answer.

As for himself Gerry followed no particular creed. If he was anything he was one quarter Jewish from Abe and one quarter Nazarene Christian from his grandmother. His parents had been of no particular persuasion; if anything agnostic. That there was good and bad in the world was obvious. He knew they both existed within himself. He found nationalism boring and insular. Rather than having pride in being an American he saw himself as a citizen of the universe. That was to be his starting point.

# Chapter 81

## Carpathian Mountains, Hungary. December 2014

The day after her arrival Mrs G had come down to breakfast intending to visit what was left of the Rakoczi Mansion to see what or who she might find there. By good luck it was only several miles away, but Dora had told her it had been deserted for many years, now just a shell of a building said to be haunted. The locals, she had said, due to the two bedfellows of ignorance and suspicion, were unlikely to be helpful. Besides Dora had heard from the man who delivered her hot, newly baked morning bread that during the night the road leading to the deserted mansion had been blocked by a fallen tree and was closed pending the arrival of a tractor to pull it away. To have to walk the muddy track in the rain was not a comforting proposition without knowing what she might find, and Mrs G was short on time.

After breakfast, she shared another mind-jolting jug of coffee with Dora who started once more to finish the stuff of legend that she knew. It was rumored, said Dora conspiratorially, that Francis Bacon had been cared for by a young teenage servant girl at the Rakoczi Castle. Shortly after his arrival there she had fallen in love with him due to his kindness and his humor, which she was unaccustomed to in an age when servants were expected to say little and know their place.

It was said that the girl's mother had sought sanctuary in the castle many years before, herself then a teenage girl, and had been taken in for domestic service. Being of unknown parentage, and having recently attained puberty, it was thought her soul might be unclean and so required purging of any possible evil. She had been taken bodily and laid shackled and naked on a stone altar in the dark vaults beneath the main chapel to the castle as part of a once ancient sacrificial ceremony. There, accompanied by incantations against the Devil, her virginity had been abruptly taken in a ritual ceremony designed to purge all evil elements from her body.

All those present were hooded, and in the dark of the dank crypt lit only by guttering candles, there had been no way of identifying them, or knowing which of the men was the father of the child she afterwards bore, and who later found succor from Francis' kindness. The rape and debasement had taken place in silence with only the sounds of her own cries of protest to be heard, until hoarse of voice she had succumbed to the inevitable and lay panting and spewing and shaking until her bonds were removed. Only one short advice had been whispered to her by a man in the robes of a monk. "It is for the good of your soul to release the demons inside you. Now you may leave their darkness to be led into the light of truth" She had cried silently for a whole year and had never again given herself up to any man.

Nine months after her ordeal she had given birth, and it was the child she bore who as a teenager Francis was said to have delighted with romantic poetry he had written, spending time to teach her to read and write. She in turn had tried to write poetry in which Francis had encouraged her. One might imagine that one night she had dared creep into his bedroom and seeing his welcoming smile had slipped easily from her rough dress and in between the soft bed sheets with him where she let him hold her in his arms like a child. Their liaison was claimed to have lasted another ten years until at the age of twenty-five she died in childbirth. The story was the stuff of folklore handed down by servants who in those days gossiped about the deeds of their masters as much as they did now. Dora said.

Francis would by then, in 1640, have been in his seventy-ninth year, and gossip had it that he had happily acknowledged his paternity of the baby girl who had survived her mother's death. The child was given into the care of the Rakoczi family as one of their own and soon after Francis left the Rakoczi home. She was named Liza, after the name of his own mother Elizabeth, and perhaps also, in memory of Elizabeth Hatton.

As the story goes thirty-six years after her own birth Liza herself gave birth to a child fathered by the Rakoczi Prince Francis I with whom she had had a secret liaison since she was fourteen. She would have been well educated at the Rakoczi home, speaking several languages, learning to play musical instruments and writing poetry so to act in return as a teacher to the Rakoczi children. It was said that the wife of the prince had been unable to bear him a necessary son and heir and so Liza's male offspring by the prince had been adopted and accorded the title of Prince Francis II. As history recalls he inherited the family fortune and estates which, in 1700, after a heroic and desperate battle against the superior forces of the Hapsburgs, he had lost. Five years earlier in 1695 the young Prince Francis, then aged nineteen, had had a son by his wife Charlotte Amalie of Hesse whom he had married the year before. He was their second son, and they had named him Prince Franz Leopold.

"At the age of five," as Dora explained, "and after his father's ruin, Franz Leopold was sent to Italy to live under the auspices of the Medici family to whom he was related. His parents falsely reported him as dead, since his life would be in danger if he were ever to return to his homeland to claim his title. On his coming of age he abandoned the Rakoczi name and took for himself the title of the Compte de St Germain." This was for a reason which Dora said would soon become apparent. In time he would also style himself the Prince of Transylvania, claiming his status as a scion of its Dragon Dynasty and their magical powers."

Dora had now warmed to her subject. It was the chance of a lifetime for her to show her knowledge of local history to a stranger who was so attentive. She poured more coffee and pear schnapps for them both and smilingly kept talking. "As for your Francis Bacon," Dora went on, "once he had given up all his worldly goods to his infant daughter Liza, and thanked the Rakoczi family for their fraternal hospitality, he was said to have found a spot not far away from Dora's home village in the hills. There, as the tale is told, he had built a tiny chapel of rough stone with the help of a local herdsman. He had survived there alone for five more years, living on a diet of herbs and wild fruit and nuts, and from occasional offerings from those in the village who might pass by. His aim was to do all that was now left for him to achieve the immortality he had long sought. To find his way in the universe pure in mind and spirit, away from the earthly world and as near to the stars as he could take himself.

# Chapter 82

By now Mrs G's health was fast deteriorating in that she was finding it difficult to distinguish between fact and fantasy. What Dora had told her next itself relied on her often imaginative recall of events. It was on the last day of her intended stay that Mrs G had found the tiny chapel. Dora had told her the local schoolmaster was off duty over the Christmas holidays and, being sixty or more in years, was well versed in local history and spoke English. Dora had contacted him to say a visitor wanted to see the chapel, and he had agreed to be Mrs G's guide. The chapel lay in the forest well off the beaten track and Dora had packed some wurst and black bread for Mrs G, and two bottles of the local brand of Slovakian Budweiser for her and the guide, saying she would give Mrs G use of a room at the inn free for another day if required. Her guide had morning work to do and it was not until early afternoon that they had set off up a little-used track through knee high undergrowth worn largely by the muntjac deer and wild boar that roamed the hills. The wind had turned and the cold air brought with it flurries of snow. The guide had wanted to wait until the following day, but Mrs G had insisted she could not delay.

As they walked Mrs G asked the guide if he knew of Francis Bacon. He shook his head. "Not that I know, although I teach local history at our school. The man who lived here, took the name Germanus after a Gallic aristocrat in the 4th century A.D. who followed the Nazarene cult of St Alban in England. The Gallic once lived in the county of Devon in England where he was a friend of the great English King Arthur and later became Bishop of Auxerre in France, or Gaul as it was then called. My father told me the real name of the man who lived here was chronicled in the village church but the record was destroyed in the last war. It is said he died at this chapel and was buried in a grave here. The Rakoczi family called him 'The Master' and we have known him here since as St Germanus."
"St Germain," said Mrs G excitedly, her heart beating fast now. "A grave? Incredible! How old was he? Do you know?"
"Germanus died in 1645" her guide continued. "The date was on his tombstone outside the chapel. The Rakoczi family erected it, but it fell into disuse after they went from here many generations ago. It is near this spot somewhere, but I have not seen it for a while now. There is a legend in the village that St Germanus is reborn many times to fight the Anti-Christ until the final battle of the

Apocalypse. Some believe him to be the grandfather of Prince Franz Leopold Racokzi, who became known later as the Compte de St Germain. My son lives in America and he tells me that historians there have claimed that a stranger by the name of St Germain was with the Founding Fathers when they drew up the American Declaration of Independence in 1776, and mysteriously disappeared afterwards. He too was known to them as 'The Master' or 'Teacher'."

Thoughts were coming to Mrs G thick and fast. Figuring out how it all came together. The Gallic Germanus was a disciple of the 3rd century Nazarene Saint Alban whose name Francis Bacon had taken for his noble title in England. In his new found life in Transylvania had Francis taken the name of Germanus to disguise his former existence? Was this what Dora had said would soon become apparent?

Mrs G's mind whirled feverishly. Dora had told her that Franz Leopold, the son of Francis Bacon's Rakoczi grandson Prince Francis II, had at age twenty-one changed his name to the Compte de St Germain. After his family's downfall he had been placed in the care of the Medici household where he had been brought up from childhood. So too, as Mrs G knew, had been the child of Marguerite of Navarre, one hundred and twenty years earlier. Supposing the young Compte had fallen in love with a female offspring of Marguerite's child raised in the same Medici household, and had had a child by her? In an age when aristocrats frequently formed liaisons within their own families it would be as likely as not. If so then that child would be consanguineous with the blood of Francis Bacon from both of his two children by two different mothers, as would be any of the child's descendants. It would tally with the claim of Gerry and Marianne's grandmother, that they were descendants of the Compte de St Germain; and in consequence of the Merovingian bloodline of Mary Magdalene which Marguerite claimed, as did the Tudors, and so Francis Bacon as a Tudor prince.

When they had found the chapel its doorway was partially blocked by brushwood, and stones had fallen from the doorway arch. Mrs G squeezed herself through the thicket into its opening. The gooseflesh on her arms tingled and her teeth were on edge with nervous anticipation. It was dark inside, and she shone the small beam of light from her i-Phone onto a ceiling covered with a growth of vines and creepers, much like the designs on the pillars at Roslyn. Ivy covered much of the walls and stone slab floor as the light beam disclosed a small stone altar place with no crucifix. After some minutes trying to imagine Francis living here over 360 years before the light beam dimmed as two black bats screeched noisily by her head, and she turned to go back.

As she went to leave tears poured down her face and her heart beat fast with exhaustion as she coughed up blood profusely. But still she had not quite completed her quest. She needed to find the tombstone and its inscription. The guide motioned her to come with him, but she had no will to leave. He fastened his backpack securely with its water and emergency rations. The snow was falling fast now with a cold wind setting in hard and they had a good two miles to return to the village. Winter conditions could change fast and treacherously and her guide grew impatient. "Follow me immediately, please," he requested and led to make a path in the snow with his heavy-duty walking boots with Mrs G behind him, their breath vaporizing in the cold air.
"I will bring you back when the snow clears but now we must go."

He walked on fast; the snow was in his eyes making it difficult to follow the rough path. Only after another two hundred meters did he glance back to find Mrs G was not behind him. In the gathering dusk she had gone back and was to the side of the chapel, bending forward over some rocks while the snow fell fast on them. Her attention has been drawn by a wild rose bush among the brambles and thorns climbing a half-fallen stone pillar. Its one red rose standing out against the white of the snow. She had gone to the pillar and was clawing away the undergrowth and brambles with her bare hands to find its face.

The guide watched from a distance as she scratched away the dirt revealing the surface of a tombstone with a carved rose centered in a cross. The same rose of Mary Magdalene and of the Tudors. She scraped the stone face more frantically and there, etched into it she saw the name Germanus and the dates 1561-1645. The dates were those of Francis' birth and death. It was the final proof that he and Germanus were one and the same. Underneath them was the symbol she had taken to the British Museum for identification. That of the serpent devouring itself, as on the underside of the keystone which Francis had been given by his mother the queen. Unbeknown to Mrs

G it was also the symbol of the Rakoczi family. She spoke her thoughts aloud.

"What does it mean?

"It is the Ouroboros. The Cosmic Serpent. The most ancient symbol of eternity from the beginning of man's time; that of immortal life. That which Queen Elizabeth forfeited for the earthly power she denied her sons, so that they might find its secret."

The deep voice came from above and behind her, and as she turned to see its source she gasped. It was Ahriman. He had come from nowhere.

"You," she exclaimed. "You knew where to come, but how? You are truly the..."

Her words trailed off into a hoarse whisper. There was something terribly different about his face.

The smile had gone. His expression vulpine. In the oncoming darkness his eyes seemed to glint yellow.

"Of course. I offer choice. The material world versus faith. Earthly possessions against immortality. From the beginning of time kings and princes have succumbed to me. I have offered life on earth to you before, and I do so now. This is your last chance. You can live for many years yet if you accept. Now you must take it. There is no more time. To be or not to be?"

Mrs G laughs feebly. Who else in life had needed to ponder that same question? She was tired now. More than she had ever been in her life. Her body cold and shaking. How could she ever rid herself of this devil that pursued her? She urged her brain to think. At last she spoke.

"No! Francis Bacon died a free spirit. He died as he finally wanted, with nature, where his soul would be nearest to the universe, furthest from the temptations of humanity. I am certain now that Abe made the same choice to dispel evil, and I choose to join him. The children must make their own choices. That is their destiny."

Ahriman shakes his head slowly and grimaces. He wonders at her obstinacy but admires her for her steadfastness. For once he is persuaded to tell the truth.

"So be it. Abe died by his own hand. He died to save the world from the Order's intentions to abuse his trust. He threw away his chance of worldly glory. I could have saved him, to make his fame and fortune forever; as I can save you now."

"To thine own self be true and thou canst not then be false to any man." Mrs G spoke Bacon's own words, and then hesitated.

"And the children?"

"The Prince of Darkness is a gentleman. I swore to you not to tempt them if you could not be tempted. But if they are to stray into temptation by their own device, I will give no such assurance. I admire your faith. Few go where you go now. Those who look to the stars – to eternity."

The glow in his eyes lessened now as he watched her closely, the force of energy in his body slackening perceptibly, and as he saw the guide returning up the hill, he disappeared into thin air. He had done all that he could. Now it was time for new adventures. It was not often that he lost. There would be many more to inveigle. He grinned devilishly. His work would never end. As a fallen angel it was his fate to be earthbound forever. By the laws of the balance of nature evil could never be brought to an end as it was the essential opposing force of good.

Mrs G looked up at the sky. The snow had stopped temporarily and the evening star Sirius had just come to light through the clouds as if to guide her. As she touched the tombstone she looked heavenward and a fine beam of light cut like a lance through the twilight towards her, blinding her vision as it speared her body and fell on the face of the Rosicrosse. She sank into the snow. Her crumpled form turning sideways so that she faced the stars. She had blood on her hand, which stained the white snow where she had clutched the red rose whose thorns had torn at her wrist.

The guide ran quickly to her, having seen what he thought was the outline of a man beside her, but as he reached her he saw she was alone and that he was too late. There was no vapor from her breath in the cold air, and a thin trickle of blood ran from the corner of her mouth. He did not touch it, nor the skin of her face which seemed flaked raw with the cold. She had gone. To wherever Abe was, and Francis too. She had made her peace with them. Her quest ended. She had found her own Holy Grail. Love of Abe. Love of the natural world. Love of all that was good in life. That was all it had ever been.

# Chapter 83

A small package had just arrived by FedEx from Germany, which Phillip opened with interest. He had still not heard from Ethan, and there had been no sign of Mrs G's return to Boston for the Christmas vacation. The detective whom Phillip had installed discreetly outside the gate of her Brookline home over the past few weeks had seen nothing. It had been irritating, having got the Order to go along with his project. Mrs G was now the key to his long-awaited ambitions.

The prospect of his becoming the Order's Most Worshipful Grand Master once his plans were achieved was tantalizingly close. A greater prize still of the Most Illustrious Master was held by an unknown figure, who and where that person might be was unknown. The various members of the Order, ranging from media barons to financiers and industrialists in major organizations such as oil, munitions and pharmaceuticals, and from old money, would then more fully appreciate Phil's own antecedents. As a Buonarroti, whose Italian family had once been revolutionaries against monarchic and religious tyranny he was sure of himself. Now it was the very democracy his forbears had fought for which required stronger leadership along the lines of Machiavelli's no bullshit principles of self-interest.

A distant descendant of Michelangelo Buonarroti, the supreme painter and sculptor of Renaissance times, and of the revolutionary Filippo Buonarroti, born in 1761, Phillip was proud of his Italian heritage. Filippo had come from a Jewish background and been trained as a lawyer, as had Phillip, but had been seen as a subversive in Catholic eyes for re-establishing Templar ideals in the name of Masonry. He had published his own newspaper with views which were soon to provide the spark to fire the ready dry tinder of the French Revolution.

From his home town of Pisa Filippo went to Corsica where had befriended the then young rebellious Napoleon Buonaparte who had claimed Merovingian lineage from his noble Corsican family. After Napoleon became emperor he had three hundred small solid gold bees from the cloak of the Merovingian King Merovech sewn into his imperial robes as bringers of good fortune.

Expelled from Corsica where he had joined the revolutionary Jacobins, Filippo was imprisoned in Tuscany and escaped to Paris. There the "Reign of Terror" of the left wing bourgeoisie was headed by Robespierre who put him in charge of Italian revolutionaries in France. Being alternately in and out of favor and after imprisonment in Paris, Filippo settled in Geneva having been released by order of Napoleon. In 1830 he was granted French nationality and returned to Paris to form a Masonic Lodge.

Some years before in 1776, the Bavarian Weishaupt had formed the Illuminati, named after a 15th century Spanish group of esoteric priests called the Alumbrados. Weishaupt had trained first as a Catholic Jesuit and his aims were both ambitious and deceptive since personal power was his driving force. The Illuminati ideals, although well intentioned as egalitarian, were basically fascist and soon failed, but the term Illuminati had been used since to include various power groups formed to influence the world order. Masonry had long rejected the term to avoid confusion, as had Phillip's own semi-autonomous Order.

In his life time Filippo had set up an extensive European spy network of Masonic lodges. He was known as the greatest conspirator of his era, and his ideas were used later by Marx in his work on *Das Kapital* and the formation of Communism. Equally they were concepts shared by Francis Bacon for his Utopian *New Atlantis* and by the Founding Fathers of America.

Despite his Italian-American braggadocio, Phillip was no fool. By studying the life story of his ancestor he had long ago concluded that the ideas Filippo had propagated failed in time. On the one hand, communism had proven unsuccessful as equality without spirituality could not be achieved by force. On the other hand, America's form of democracy was now to be found wanting for the same reason with the increasing gap between the world's haves and have nots. In the global world of the internet the super-rich and their corporations could vanish in a smokescreen of a virtual tax free world avoiding responsibility, so leaving nation states to be governed by those of inferior intellect. Phillip liked to find quotes from philosophers to fit his prognoses. One from Plato he felt suited the current situation: *"One of the penalties of not participating in politics is that you will end up being governed by your inferiors."*

While the internet and commerce might transcend and negate national borders, national politics did not, and the result was chaos. Large parts of the world were in disorder with terrorists running amok secretly financed by double dealing organizations proclaiming to be friendly to the West while detesting its Judeo-Christian culture.

The internet, the most brilliant prospect for world unity that had ever been devised, simultaneously enabled a means to destroy it. America's stand to advance democracy was becoming an impossible task. What price their weaponry once their enemy could respond in kind? President Obama had tried force and then withdrawal from force, using covert means for regime change giving rise to the Arab Spring. Yet this had sadly failed and new Islamic militancy or anarchy had taken the place of previous dictators. It seemed as if all hope had gone for a peaceful world with the ancient quarrels between Jews and Muslims as antagonistic as they had been for millennia past. There had to be another way. The Masonic Founding Fathers of America had not shunned militant action to ensure their vital freedoms. Nor would Phillip.

Abe would in time have approved of his plan. Phillip felt sure of it. It was for the benefit of humanity at large. It was why Abe had abandoned his parent's Orthodox Judaism to become a Mason. Whatever its critics might say Masonry had helped restrain many of the world's past oppressive religions. Masonic beliefs in charity were known and appreciated worldwide. Phillip did not stop to consider his plans might be as unjustifiable as those of warring religions. Each one had strayed light years from the simple truth of Jesus that good men might in truth be left to rule themselves. Phillip was not so trusting of humanity. There had to be order.

The package Phillip had received was well sealed, and he tore away the last pieces of paper from it with his hands. Inside was a thick gummed envelope, and inside it loose-leaf sheets of paper, some typed in small print but with handwritten notes which had been scanned and copied, some of which appeared to be hieroglyphics or equations. It must be the "book" Mrs G had promised him. About fifty pages Phillip estimated. Most probably she had not had time to finish it. Mrs G had been busy, but it was shorter than he had expected. There was no covering note.

If the information the "book" contained was to touch on Abe's invention, or his connection with the Order, it would not see the light of day. He, Phillip, would make sure of that. He felt sure that Abe would not have told Mrs G of the Order's intentions to use his elixir selectively, but then again he might have done. The thought made Phillip's stomach queasy and he quickly popped another Zantac from a packet he always kept handy. It was a good job that Noi, his assistant, politely ignored his flatulence. Fortunately it was a sign of appreciation to the Chinese, someone had once said.

He leafed quickly through the loose pages of which he could make little sense. The words and numbers appeared jumbled, with drawings of strange symbols. Arrows pointing here and there, and more annoyingly much of it seemed a scribbled mess, perhaps in code; but if so, then the Order had contacts who could deal with that. He remembered that the last time he had heard from Ethan he had said Mrs G had been in hospital after a car accident. Perhaps her mind had been wandering and what he was looking at was just the product of her delusion.

The sheets were un-numbered and without any apparent order. Perhaps Mrs G had died, as Ethan had predicted, and so she had had no time to complete them. But if so, then who had sent them and why? Phillip had some calls to make and would try to make sense of it all later when the office was quieter during the Christmas period just days away.

He crossed the room to the wall safe, having checked the latest code sent that hour to his lap top. The papers would be secure in the safe for the time being. As he opened it he saw once again the phial Abe had given to him. The book was nothing compared to the problem the phial presented in finding the secret formula of its contents. It was essential to find Mrs G to learn what she knew. Where the frigging hell was Ethan? Phillip had relied on him too much. What was Ethan's goddam problem? Phillip's normally well-controlled temper rose. No trusting these foreigners he thought, but then again he had never questioned where Ethan had come from. Too late now, "the son of a bitch," he spoke out loud.

*"In time we hate that which we often fear,"* was a quotation from Shakespeare that rung in Phillip's ears and disquieted him. He had an intimate knowledge of the history of the Founding Fathers, and as a Mason had always known perfectly well of Bacon's supreme role in its Masonic ideals. Washington's Folger Library was a mine of material on Bacon's life. Although he believed Bacon was the author of the Shakespeare plays what was the point in upsetting the public's view of Shakespeare as a commoner from nowhere? It was the sort of thing that gave people hope, not realizing that intellect was born and bred in the bone.

Phillip had seen no point in exposing his own leading role in the Order to Mrs G, or of anything other than its charitable activities. The less she knew the better. The Order was one of men, not of women, he was pleased to say. As with other members, Abe was sworn to be discreet, and Phillip was sure Abe was a man of his word. If Mrs G had died, then Phillip as a trustee of the Magdala Foundation could push through agreements assigning distribution of Abe's elixir to the Order before Gerry became eighteen and assumed notional control. Once Phillip knew for sure what had happened to Mrs G he would need move fast as Gerry's birthday was only weeks away, but if necessary documents could be backdated to fit the bill. Gerry should be easy meat to control, Phillip thought. The boy knew nothing of the affairs of smart business, and probably never would bother himself with them, since he had no need to work. A Trust Fund babe or "lucky sperm" as someone had so succinctly labeled it. "Jesus goddam Christ," Phillip swore again. Where had Ethan gone! Why no contact? It would be the last time he dealt with him.

He closed the door of the safe with its picture cover of a pyramid with its all-seeing eye through which a tiny camera filmed anyone who opened it. Strange, he thought, that so few Americans ever knew the ancient symbol was part of their everyday lives, shown on every single US one-dollar note ever printed. The Egyptian mythology of the all-seeing eye of Horus, the child of the goddess Isis, was well known to the Masonic Founding Fathers of America. The entire design of Washington had been on Egyptian principles in line with the stars and of Earth's unity with the Universe to bring good luck.

Superstition and the power of magic were not far from the public's mind any more than they had ever been, and who was to say the public were not right? How did humanity evolve? Where did it come from? If anyone knew it would be the Ancients. In the beginning was the Word. It was the Word the knowledgeable had passed from generation to generation, if not by mouth then in code. Their secret to those smart enough to discover it.

"W*e are such stuff as dreams are made on; and our little life is rounded with a sleep.*"

The words came suddenly into Phillip's head. Now where had he heard that? He scratched his crotch contemplatively. Time stood still for no-one; he needed to make the most of his prime, and Noi was waiting for him.

Deep in his thoughts, and hasty for some extramarital activity, Phillip did not realize that in his safe now lay the key to all he wanted for his vision to be fulfilled. Mrs G had had no time to write her book, and in the business center of the Ritz the evening before she had checked out, she had scanned and printed out her pages of hurriedly prepared notes from her lap top from which she was to write her book on her return. Realizing her poor state of health and in fear of Ethan's motives she had given the copied notes to Renate in Germany to mail to the US for safekeeping.

What she had also done was to mistakenly print out the notes she had taken down from Abe not long before and scanned into her laptop in the few weeks before he had died. A duty she had performed almost every day of her life working for him. In her haste in London, unwell, and in near panic to leave for Germany without Ethan following her, she had scanned Abe's notes together with her own. She had not conceived that Abe's formula for his elixir of life could be found in his notes by way of the codes they had always used together when exchanging information. She had not had the time to interpolate them in her own meaning as she would normally have done.

Mrs G's long evenings in England spent on deciphering the codes in the Shakespeare plays had been difficult, but she had found they were not so far different from that of the Fibonacci code she and Abe had learned together long ago. They had created new versions for their own means of communication so as to guard Abe's work from the prying eyes of computer hackers or their like. Her great-grandmother would have been proud of her intuitive intelligence, but now in error she had sent her notes to Buonarroti without realizing either his motives or the vital significance of Abe's final equations to those who might decode and misuse them.

Cryptology was in the blood. One either had the ability or not, and few had. It was not a science. It was a mathematical art. The difference between intellect and intelligence was that between fact and feeling. The kids had it. Mrs G had recently devised a test to try the intelligence of Gerry and Marianne which they had played out in Boston several times before she left. It used similar means to the coded information Mrs G and Abe had communicated with.

In effect, it was alike to the game of "consequences" which young children played with drawings or words, but requiring a far higher IQ with its twists and turns of thought process. As the game progressed, an essential element to reach a logical conclusion was to have followed the correct sequence. It was not dissimilar to the way the codes in the Shakespeare plays had been devised. If one player could not follow it, then the player could pass it on to the next, forfeiting a life in the process. Child's play if only you knew how, but it always annoyed Gerry that Marianne would come out the better of the two. Even Mrs G would get caught out by her ingenuity at times.

# Chapter 84

## The Boston Crematorium Chapel.  January 2015

Christmas had passed, and home in the big Brookline house seemed lonely now without Mrs G. Together with Esther the children had been chauffer driven to the crematorium in a large, black Lincoln town car limousine with tinted windows, and they now stood somberly in the chapel while the pastor made his short address. "I am the Resurrection and the Life." He had added the poetic words of TS Eliot: 'In my beginning is my end,' and recited the 23rd Psalm as the curtains closed round her coffin, as if pulled by an unseen hand.  Marianne wiped the tears away from her face. Gerry stood beside her taking her hand. He did not cry.

Mrs G had felt it was incorrect for her to be buried at the Hand in Hand Jewish cemetery in Boston where Abe's body had been interred next to his longtime first wife Marilyn. Mrs G had some time ago opted for cremation, and the children had decided on a small memorial tower with a plain white marble plaque to commemorate her.  The name on the plaque was that of *Jane Fenn Gallup* embossed in gold leaf with the dates of her birth and death.  Under it was the simple inscription:

"*Much loved by her family – Abe, Gerry and Marianne. Rest in Peace.*"  Since Mrs G had no close family of her own the children had thought these the best words they could think of.

Esther stood close by them.  She was all they had now to go home to, apart from the dogs. She had put on a black dress and a hat she had bought specially for the day and wiped a tear from her eye discreetly. She brooded on the sadness of events which had taken the life of the children's parents and grandparents, and now Mrs G, whom Esther had much admired.  Esther knew that of any time in her life she had now to be a tower of strength and in that she had no fear. Her faith gave her the confidence she needed. She was not a member of her local Boston Baptist Church for nothing.  It was where she had her friends and those she could rely on. Its Calvinist origins were not dissimilar to those of the Nazarene creed of Jesus and Mary Magdalene which Abe's wife Marilyn had told her much about. Her local parson had assured her that the Savior would return and she thought it was high time he did. There was no respect now left for anything of the spirit, and the world was the worse for it. Some friends of Mrs G had come to pay their last respects at the short service and offered their condolences to the two children as the mourners walked slowly away to their waiting cars, with the chill January wind biting into their faces. Phillip Buonarroti had not come. First things first. He had to obtain control of Abe's elixir before any attempt to befriend Gerry. It was best to leave any confrontation as late as possible.

The past few weeks had been ones of confusion. First the children had lost contact with Mrs G, and when finally they had learned of her death from the US consulate in Budapest they needed to arrange to have her body and possessions brought back to Boston. There had been a delay in registering the cause of death in Hungary, which had given a problem to the local doctor, and was finally put down to an internal hemorrhage. The skin on Mrs G's face had been scaly and discolored and she had lesions on her body and hands that had been hidden beneath her coat and gloves. No clothes had been sent on as almost all those she had taken to England had arrived earlier from London in the advanced baggage the Ritz had sent for delivery to Boston by British Airways, including the necklace once owned by the ill-fated Marie Antoinette.

The trees round the borders of the crematorium bore no leaves, and crows circled slowly in the background cawing loudly dressed in their shiny ink-black feathers, flying up and down as if there to attest to Mrs G's end, or as spies to pass on the information of her death. Whether they had or not there was another figure in attendance, uninvited. Standing back from sight of the other visitors behind the trunk of a stark leafless tree, and wearing a long black overcoat and black wide-brimmed hat pulled closely over the face.

The figure of the man watched the children from the short distance and saw that in Gerry's hand was an envelope which could not be seen fully. Unknown to him it contained duplicate copies of the same loose-leafed pages which Mrs G had separately packaged and asked Renate von Holzchuher to FedEx to Gerry and to Phillip Buonarroti. As for the children, they took little notice of the man in the black coat and shirt showing a small patch of clerical white collar. Their minds were racing ahead of them. They were to start a new life now, one which they were each to make their destiny, and tomorrow was to be the first chapter of it.

Mrs G had left a will. During her stay in London, and after her visit to the Harley Street doctor there, she had written a Letter of Wishes to her lawyer in Boston. It seemed she had a premonition she had not much time left. In the letter she had instructed that Gerry be appointed in her place as head of Abe's Magdala Foundation as soon as he became eighteen. She had few personal possessions and little money of her own, but what she had she had left to the children, other than a gift of $10,000 to Esther. The necklace of Marie Antoinette, which Abe had originally bought for Marilyn, she left to Marianne. She had asked for the 23rd Psalm to be read at her service. It was the original 1633 version from *"The Temple"* written by Francis Bacon, Viscount St Alban, at Gorhambury in 1625, shortly before his death in England, and dedicated to his friend George Herbert.

It read:

*"The God of love my shepherd is,*
*And he that doth me feed:*
*While he is mine, and I am his,*
*What can I want or need?*

*He leads me to the tender grasse,*
*Where I both feed and rest;*
*Then to the streams that gently passe;*
*In both I have the best.*


*Or if I stray, he doth convert*
*And bring my mind in frame:*
*And all this is not for my desert,*
*But for his holy name.*
*Yea in deaths shadie black abode*
*Well may I walk, not fear:*
*For thou art with me; and thy rod*
*To guide, thy staff to bear.*


*Nay, thou dost make me sit and dine,*

*Eve'n in my enemies sight:*
*My head with oyl, my cup with wine*
*Runnes over day and night.*

*Surely thy sweet and wondrous love*
*Shall measure all my days;*
*And as it never shall remove,*
*So neither shall my praise."*

END...

Ouroboros and The Tree of Life

Philippe (filippo) Buonarroti
Revolutionary friend of Napoleon

Picture showing the LibertyCap as worn
in the French and US revolutions

*The Von le Coq portrait of Valentin Andrea*
*said to be of Francis Bacon*

*Rosy Cross*

*The Count de St Germain*

# The Merovingian Kings

### by Ed Stephan

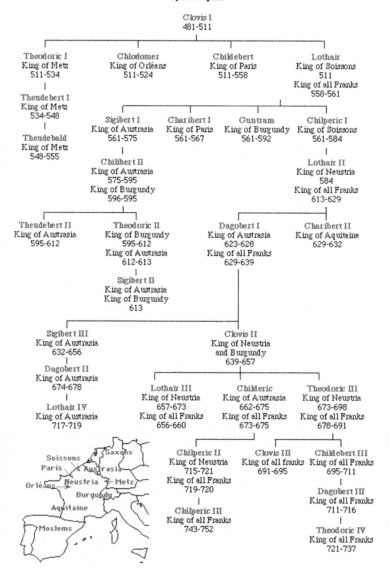

*The Family Tree of Merovingian Bloodline and the Black Nobility*

# Merovingian Bloodlines

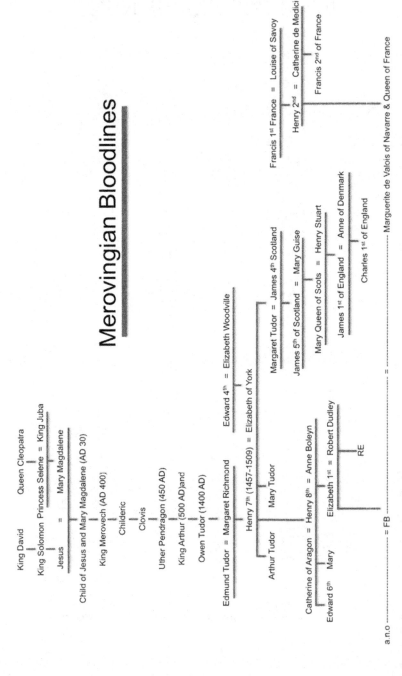

# AFTERWORD
## (PART FOUR)

It is said that knowledge is the wing by which we may fly to heaven. Each of our lives is a short corridor in time in a Universe where time has no meaning. We ignore history at our peril as it can inform both our present and our future.

That Francis Bacon did perhaps live two lives in his own era, and may have lived yet again a hundred or so years later in the body or spirit of the Compte de St Germain, cannot be dismissed simply for lack of scientific evidence. The existence of the spirit and soul of man has been recognized down the ages by great prophets, philosophers and poets long before the advent of modern science. It is still today the basis of all religions.

There are historians who have written of the Compte as a mysterious old man, named as the "Master" or "Teacher", who was present among the Founding Fathers at the signing of the American Declaration of Independence. Enshrined in it is the right to freedom and happiness, words by Francis Bacon written in his Utopian vision of the *"New Atlantis"* and an essential factor of the fraternity of Masonry he revived in the European Renaissance.

If this was the same "Master" who died as St Germanus 144 years beforehand in Transylvania, then either he was with the Founding Fathers supernaturally, or in the human physical form of a genetic offspring; and that he may emerge again in either form is as likely as it is unlikely. As with Christ, there are followers of Bacon who believe he will return. Where the visionary minds of humanity's geniuses have already gone light years ahead of us, we plod behind insisting on the need for "evidence" to prove the often unprovable. And yet when we think we have the answer, as Karl Popper commented, we only create new complexities to confuse ourselves the more.

All that we innately know for certain, as do all other species, is that we need to procreate to survive and find the resource to do so. As our recent forbears did in seeking new lands across unchartered oceans, we will need to seek out new planets to populate in human form. But until the day we can dispense with physical limitation and stretch our consciousness to the stars we may never find what our ancestors may have known long before us. A combination of chemistry and of the spirit to give us the freedom to travel the entirety of the Universe to which we belong, in any form we choose.

Is this what Francis Bacon tried to show us in his fantastical plays and allegories? Not just that they concealed his life story, but the secret of life itself. That it is eternal. For all eyes do not see alike. Even a visible creation is not the same, for all who look upon it, of one form and one color. It is our brain that tells us what the eye sees. It is a book printed both within and without, and the two writings are, with all men, more or less confused.

By the standards of the Universe the arrival of *Homo sapiens* is seen only as a moment away give or take five thousand years between 20,000 BC and now. It is quite possible that mankind achieved a sudden leap in intellect in that time infused by beings from another planet, as ancient African folklore relates, and which Francis Crick, considered the world's most eminent of his contemporary scientists, saw as a rational probability.

How the pyramids were built and their true intent is not known to this day. It is too simplistic to think their massive structures had no function other than that of a burial tomb. It is well known the Egyptians experimented with what we today see as the supernatural and in the transport of souls. Why without results would they have spent centuries otherwise futilely building these vast monuments without purpose? It is more than likely they knew the means of space travel from their ancestors who had travelled to Earth from elsewhere in the Universe. By a knowledge we have lost today, and which only a few geniuses since have comprehended. There is little doubt that Francis Bacon possessed a level of extraordinary intellect not superseded since, or that he spent a lifetime chasing the essence of immortality.

If we are to shut our minds to the past then we close the door on the intelligence we bequeath to our children, and their chance of peace as promised in our new millennium of harmonic convergence of the Age of Aquarius. By a wisdom that might well eradicate war and pestilence for good, and the knowledge that we live in a Universe to be shared universally as its name implies.

The maintenance of Earth's resources has always been uppermost in the minds of men, just as the control of population at a level resources can sustain has been. It is highly probable that the religious thinking of the past was shaped by this need, in particular the sexual practices that differentiated beliefs. Those exercised by the Cathars, apart from a few select abstainers who proscribed sex of any kind, the large majority enjoyed sexual freedom between both opposite and equal sexes regardless of procreation. This view was in direct opposition to that of the Catholics for whom coition was to be limited for the purposes of propagation only. Yet it would seem from the Bible that Jesus himself saw little difference in the love he had for Mary Magdalene and that he had for his disciple John.

Other religions advise of suitable times to breed in the human cycle as a means of birth control. Today despite the use of many forms of prophylactics, the increase in populations is once more threatening an imbalance in both resources and beliefs. Without thought and action as to the consequences, only strife can result. Perhaps the increase of open homosexuality in the Western world, once associated with atheism and immorality by the Church, is mankind's own answer to population control, without need for the advice of social organizations or of financial penalty.

# Saving Bacon: The Shakespeare Conspiracy

There are innumerable studies and interpretations of the Shakespeare plays and their meaning, but on their author, as William Shakespeare from Stratford, almost no information exists. It seems unbelievable that the public at large know so little of a person whose name of Shakespeare is as well known worldwide as that of Jesus Christ. While the period in which we know anything of who Jesus was or did was not much more than two to three years, what we know of the character of William Shaksper the actor from Stratford, in the fifty-two years of his life, offers even less. He had few friends, and certainly none in his time who ever lauded him as a person. The words below are extracted from an essay on Shakespeare by the famous American author Mark Twain:

*"He was born on 23rd April 1564 of farming stock parents who could not read or write. Of the nineteen men on the local council of the then small village of Stratford thirteen could not sign their own names. In November 1582 he married Anne Hathaway who was eight years his senior. She had a child within six months and twins in February 1585. In 1587 aged twenty-three he went to live in London returning in 1597 with money to buy his home New Place where he lived lending out money and buying and selling houses. In 1616 he made a Will, signing its pages with a scrawled and almost indecipherable signature, as if by a child or illiterate. In it he famously left his "second best bed" to his wife and no more. No books or manuscripts or possessions. At his funeral nobody came from London. There were no eulogies, no lamenting poems, only silence. So as far as anyone knew (or has ever known) the Shakespeare actor from Stratford never wrote a play or even a letter to anyone in his life.*

The Shakespeare Memorial Monument at Stratford to be seen today shows a man holding a cushion and a quill pen. It replaced the original, which depicted Shakespeare as a merchant holding a sack of grain as would a farmer or merchant. On the headstone of his grave the inscription reads:

*"Good friend for Jesus sake forbeare*
*To dig the dust enclosed here;*
*Blest by ye man yet spares these stones*
*And curst be he yet moves my bones."*

These words echoed those of Bacon's friend Ben Jonson in their intimation that the writer of the Shakespeare plays to whom the Stratford actor gave his name was not to be discovered there. We know that the last of the Shakespeare plays was not performed for up to seven years after the Stratford actor's death in 1616; yet for five of those years up to 1621 and Francis Bacon's imprisonment and disgrace Bacon was still writing extensively. The First Folio of the Shakespeare plays published in 1623 was an attempt at assembling a final conclusive work from the myriad of manuscripts and notes of varying editions of the plays produced over a long period. Ben Jonson and several colleagues carried out the complex task, very possibly to help out the still living Bacon in his then poor pecuniary circumstances, and most likely with his assistance. The timing was unlikely to have been a coincidence.

Since many of the plays in the Folio were written with allegorical reference to real events and people of the moment, for what reason would their performance have been postponed for years after those events, as many have assumed? The likelihood is they were not. The First Folio was a record for the sake of posterity and for Bacon's approval before his oncoming disappearance.

Not even the Stratford actor's greatest fans have ever suggested he traveled outside England or had any close connection with nobility or science, or the leading figures of his day in England and on the European continent. What is known without doubt is that Francis Bacon was such a person. That his Good Pens, and those of the Knights of the Helmet and of the Rosicrosse Literary Society, were sworn to secrecy not to reveal his name as the man who was Shakespeare was not unusual, but rather the norm. Many Elizabethan writers of noble blood left a confusing tangle of attributions by masking their own names with those of both living people or of dead ones, or by use of imaginary pseudonyms to cover their tracks. Bacon's own motto, borrowed from Ovid was *"Bene vixit qui bene latuit"* or *"To live well stay quiet."*

Nashe, Lyly and Marlowe are among the principal names imputed as masks for Bacon, despite being writers themselves. In all it has been discovered there were a hundred or more masks used across a wide range of Bacon's works and poems. Many of them were in return for payment having no clue as to the true writer since such transactions were handled confidentially by the Good Pens or Bacon's secretary Rawlings. Other masks were to be found among the Good Pens, a medley of streetwise rebels and intellectuals sworn to secrecy. Jonson and Marlowe were often involved in drunken brawls, and both separately stood trial for murder of which they were each acquitted. Through them Bacon kept his ear to the ground of public opinion just as his mother Elizabeth had done.

By knowing them Bacon could originate his stories as if he were in their shoes, perceptively studying their character traits. As Marlowe, jolly at times, but also pompous and lofty. As Spenser, writing of a concealed Elizabeth or Marguerite in terms of excellence and *"sweet singing love"*. As Peele, full of quips and saws; as Greene, a vivid painter of his mind's conceits; and as Burton, with thoughts of melancholy and much wisdom. That some were written in varying styles allowed the imagery that various authors were at work, but the underlying genius of the principal shows through them all as Francis Bacon. A man who, still in his teenage years, read, wrote and spoke fluently in Latin, Greek, French, Spanish and Italian, as well as his English native tongue, soon gained the respect of his team of followers and collaborators.

There are several reasons why, having been known to have written some plays under his own name in his youth, such as *The Comedy of Errors*, to delight his young friends and his mother, that Francis Bacon decided early on he could no longer declare himself as the author of his later plays. Not least the discovery of the rehearsal of the early *Ur-Hamlet* by Leicester and the subsequent fury of Elizabeth, which taught Francis to toe the line. But as he succinctly said in *Hamlet* when first staged after Elizabeth's death *"Every dog shall have his day."*

Francis was in truth a prince by blood, and princes used ciphers. Not only that, but he was in effect the Prince of Wales, heir apparent to the English throne of his mother, and it was of her that he was most fearful. Any inference as to his true identity might endanger him if the Queen was to know the author. To be or not to be was a question which would follow him all his life.

Having been denied his royal rights as the queen's son, Bacon constructed himself to become a poet and philosopher and scientist which he correctly saw as a means to achieve an acclaimed posterity even greater than that of a monarch. Not only did he develop his talents in his voyage of discovery, but he could honestly create himself as he was, rather than needing to act out a preordained royal role. To her credit it was Elizabeth who put him on that road. *"Uneasy lies the head that wears the Crown,"* as she had told him on his coming of age.

We shall never know to this day Elizabeth's true motives, but she had good reason to fear for her sons' lives should they attempt to claim her throne, either before or after her death, as heirs of her Tudor heritage and of Jesus' Nazarene Creed. The Catholic pope put a price on the Queen's head of the equivalent of more than US $3.5 billion dollars ($3,500,000,000) at the values prevalent at the end of the 20th century, payable to anyone who would kill her! That she could have justified her title as Supreme Governor of the English Church as a descendant of Jesus and Mary Magdalene would have been a good reason to do so.

In his reinvention of himself as a playwright Bacon required a cover. That of Pallas Athene's Speare of Knowledge was a suitable choice, not least as it was one his father Leicester had used before him. Little did Bacon conceive that it would take four hundred years for his ciphers, which he was so clever at devising, to eventually reveal his authorship.

Increasingly down the centuries a host of writers, mainly lawyers, who sought fit to pass judgment on Bacon as a lawyer and statesman, jumped to the conclusion that a man of his position who does not offer a defense must be guilty. That in itself is significant for demonstrating the self-inflicted limitations of the legally minded. They knew little of the other Bacon, the man who was Shakespeare, and if they did, they chose to ignore it as if Bacon shamed the name. It is the shame of their hypocrisy then and since which is unforgiveable.

Even the famed historian Lord Macaulay, writing two hundred years or so after Shakespeare, and one of Bacon's greatest critics of his alleged corruption from the evidence then available said of him:

*"His mind was the most exquisitely constructed intellect that has ever been bestowed upon any of the children of men. He knew that all the secrets, feigned of poets to have been written in the books of the*

*enchanters, are worthless when compared with the mighty secrets which are really written in the book of nature; and which with but time and patience will be read there."*

Yet Macaulay still refused to entertain that Bacon was Shakespeare, most probably to avoid contemporary controversy. Winston Churchill was later to say of Macaulay *"he was the Prince of Literary Rogues."*

Bacon's good and trusty friend and fellow playwright, Ben Jonson, said of him at the time that *"he was the embodiment of virtue."* Bacon's search for the meaning of life was that for the psyche of human kind itself and he chose to make his philosophy understandable to the public by way of entertainment and drama not provided for a thousand years. His knowledge of the past and that of modern science was that which only a highly educated and well connected man could have known. The use of allegory was the order of the day to disguise often revolutionary suggestions.

Bacon finally realized the inevitability of his situation and penned these lines in a sonnet later attributed to the name of the Shakespeare he himself had created as being the author of his plays:

*"Or I shall live your epitaph to make.*
*Or you survive when I in earth am rotten....*
*From hence your memory death cannot take,*
*Although in me each part will be forgotten.*
*Your name from hence immortal life shall have,*
*Though I, once gone, to all the world must die;*
*The earth can yield me but in a common grave,*
*When you entombed in men's eyes shall lie.*
*Your monument shall be my gentle verse,*
*Which eyes yet not created shall o'er-read;*
*And tongues to be your being shall rehearse,*
*When all the breathers of this world are dead;*
*You still shall live----such virtue hath my pen---*
*Where breath most breathes, e'en in the mouths of men."*

What better evidence could there be than these famous words from Sonnet 81 that the author was giving up his right of praise and recognition for another whose name would succeed him?

# The Cipher Story

The use of ciphers by Francis Bacon in his works was to tell of his own concealed life and views which he could not otherwise disclose. I have used material from a range of books to construct my story as much as possible near to the truth as history can reveal. Their pages run into many thousands and there is little space for much of the information in them here. As with most historical accounts, *The Royal Secret* is necessarily subjective, except that since the times of the criticism of Spedding and Macaulay, the two most famous of Bacon's critics, a good deal more information has become available. Those to whom I am most thankful I have referenced in these pages. I have also accessed a great well of online sites, any of which can be found by those interested to crosscheck my interpretation of events, but are too long to list. A number of them can be found online on the Pearltree site in the name *The Royal Secret* as can also be found many related pictures and symbols on the *The Royal Secret* Pinterest site. Being a novel, the characters in contemporary times are imaginary, as are some others in the past who offer the story continuity.

Of all my sources there are two books to which I am most indebted. One by Alfred Dodd entitled *"Francis Bacon's Personal Life Story"* first published in 1949, was that which first inspired me to write Bacon's tale. Knowing that I could never equal the result of the thirty-one years of research which it took Dodd to complete it, I felt that Bacon's story could best be portrayed to a wider public by means of a novel in a modern idiom running parallel to Bacons' life, by which Mrs G's contemporary search for truth and salvation is analogous to that of her sixteenth century hero. The immense amount of detail involved in Dodd's research provides the factual evidence for Bacon having been Shakespeare far more exhaustively than I might ever otherwise have been able to determine. I would recommend anyone who has a few weeks to spare and a mind for detective detail to try to obtain a rare copy to read its near six hundred pages of close type.

My second source is an even rarer book entitled "*I, Prince Tudor, Wrote Shakespeare*" by Margaret Barsi-Greene, an American from Los Angeles, last published over forty years ago. It is itself based on assembling a tale in good order of the discoveries of many years of diligent toil carried out by another American woman, the real-life Elizabeth Wells Gallup, and her book "*The Bilateral Cypher of Francis Bacon*" published in 1901. Through use of Elizabeth Gallup's interpretation of ciphers contained in some sixty works and plays of Shakespeare, carried out over thirty years, Margaret Barsi-Greene cleverly unravels and elucidates the biography of Francis Bacon as he himself wrote it and intended it should be told after his death.

At much the same time as Elizabeth Gallup had expertly deciphered Bacon's "bilateral" code she met and collaborated with an American, Dr Orville W. Owen, who had independently uncovered the more sophisticated "Word" code in use in the Shakespeare plays. Both these codes required the cryptologist to read a sequence of plays and works taken together, out of some sixty in all for choice, while that of the "Word" code need be better understood in them as part of lyrical iambic verse. That it had taken nearly three hundred years to appreciate Bacon's secret ciphers was not surprising, even perhaps to Bacon himself should he stir to life once again in some new guise. Mrs Gallup wrote in June 1900: *"I look out to the future, not of years, but of ages, knowing that my labors are for the benefit of a land very far off, and after great length of time is past."* Her words could have been those of Bacon himself.

In *The Royal Secret* there are illustrations of the simpler forms of the codes, but it would take another book written by a cipher expert to even begin to explain them to the uninitiated. In the main Bacon used six different code types or ciphers. The "Bilateral" which he invented when sixteen years old along with Marguerite, using two forms of Italics, is similar to that used by computers of today. The "Word" is the most complex of all. The "Capital Letter", the "Time" or "Clock" symbol; the "Ring and Wheel", and the "Anagrammatic". Each needs to be treated separately and only to be understood through reading a sequence of specific plays and works. In addition, there were many words and symbols utilized to indicate where a code might be found, some of which can be seen in illustrations of calligraphy at which Bacon was expert.

In the face of any criticism of the validity of the codes I am happy to rely on the expertise of Elizabeth Gallup and Dr Owen, both US citizens, who were both recruited as code breakers for the US secret service in the First World War (Mrs Gallup then was sixty seven or more in years).

There are many who will be upset at any effort to spoil the image of Shakespeare in the way he is known to the world at large, and both Dr Owen and Elizabeth Gallup came under critical fire in their time. The English literary establishment then, and since, has relatively successfully buried their disclosures for the reason, as I believe, not only are they revealing of the truth of Bacon but also of his mother, the much-revered Queen Elizabeth whose character as the Virgin Queen needs to remain unblemished in English history as its greatest monarch. Yet this is to ignore that both Bacon and Elizabeth acted according to their times.

To pretend that in their long lives such extraordinary personalities as Queen Elizabeth and Francis Bacon could not have fallen in love with others, or been beset by the emotional dramas and tragedies of a highly eventful time in history, is to give more to the lie Elizabeth sought to perpetuate of herself as the Virgin Queen. That she needed to maintain her ruse to protect her realm by every guile her ingenuity could devise is a credit to her strength of purpose and loyalty to England and her Tudor line.

Since Elizabeth knew her own claim to the throne was contestable under Salic Law she used every means to prevent the even more disputable claims of her sons. After the showing of the deposition scene in the play Richard II, in a cipher of Francis Bacon translated by Elizabeth Gallup she quotes him as saying: *"Yet we are in hourly terror lest the Queen, our enemy at present, although likewise our mother, be cognizant of our invention. Our worst fears cling to us so constantly that our intention is altered, and the chief Cypher be not herein set forth in such manner as was meant."*

Nothing could better show the state of mind which drove Bacon and his friends to the expedient of using the Shakespeare name from that moment on. A further cipher of note concerning Queen Elizabeth comes from the "Faerie Queen" masked for Francis by Spenser: *"To Queen Elizabeth, fate, a turn of Fortune's wheel, had given the gift of royalty, and the throne of mighty England was hers to bestow on whom her heart might chose."*

The name *Hamlet* was a play on the word 'piglet' which the Queen had fondly used for Francis in his boyhood. But when he had first written it as *Ur-Hamlet* (the prodigal piglet) on his return from France at the age of twenty-one she had seen it as a mischievous poke at her authority, and threatened his life if he were to continue. In another decipher of Mrs Gallup, Bacon cites his mother's words of disapproval of him thus:

"*Do you among the city wits and act your mother's death?*

*You the immediate heir of England, for let the world take note you are the most immediate to our throne and with no less nobility, our chiefest courtier and our son.*

*O, by strangling you, my son, I might have had some surety in the present!*

*You came to earth to make the earth my hell; a grievous burden was your birth to me,*

*Tetchy and wayward was your infancy; and now your manhood's daring, bold, and venturous;*

*What comfortable hour can you name that you have ever graced me with?*

*Alack, alack! Such an unfilial wrong – to make a dullard of me!*

*My son, I will fitly bring you to your knees.*"

Different times call for different understandings, but that Elizabeth could be a she-devil at times stands out against the character of Bacon as a complex, but ultimately kind and loving son, sadly at odds with his mother's imperious and capricious nature. His love of writing, and philosophy and art, rather than of hunting, dueling and gambling, was in direct comparison to his militant action-man brother Robert Essex. It would not be fair to Elizabeth to say that she perpetually rejected Francis from her affection since she did her best to give him a good education and a living out of harm's way. Nevertheless, her denial of his claim to the throne clearly disillusioned him, as did finally the execution of his brother Robert Essex.

For all his love of romance and comedy, sadness dogged Bacon's life. Firstly, at the loss of identity in the authorship of his plays, but in which he could express his feelings without fear of recognition. But lastly, in his loss of reputation as a lawyer and statesman and loyal subject of the England to which he had given his life. Even so, up to his end the one thing he was sure of was faith in the power of his intellect, never to be destroyed.

Before his death in England Bacon had made arrangements for his works to be placed by his secretary Rawley in various hiding places, such as the Canonbury Tower and at Gorhambury itself, as well as in the tombs of Spenser and Marlowe, for them to be found centuries later. Elizabeth Gallup, who had unearthed this information from Bacon's ciphers, traveled from the US to England as she knew of the possible whereabouts of the works, but found the passage of time had obliterated them.

One such hiding place now lay under today's Liverpool Street train station, whilst Gorhambury was a ruin. It is also believed Rawley may have been negligent in fully completing his task. The Canonbury Tower was said to contain hidden documents behind a secret spring-loaded sliding panel. As the building has been largely rebuilt either they have not been found, or taken and their whereabouts not known. The tomb of Edmund Spenser, one of Bacon's masks, is to be found in Westminster Abbey, and is still today unopened.

Along with Alfred Dodd's work, the intellect and great detective labor of Elizabeth Gallup over thirty years persuaded me conclusively to have no fear from the hordes of those Shakespearean buffs that have alternative opinions. As Margaret Barsi-Greene says in the preface of her book:

*"The world of tradition refuses to budge - under a thick mist of ignorance and prejudice".*

If one is to believe in the lifetime's work of Elizabeth Gallup in decoding Bacon's ciphers, then the tale she tells, or rather which Bacon tells of himself, is truly revealing in a way never before understood. I make no apologies for the lengthy showing below of some of those ciphers and the works in which they can be found, as translated by Elizabeth Gallup and presented by Barsi-Greene. In effect, they are Bacon's soliloquy for his decipherer to detect. In their light I challenge those who conspire to defeat Bacon's Shakespearean authorship to reveal any plausible alternative whether in the shape of the virtually unknown Bard of Avon or any other claimant, of whom there are a number.

*"Watching the storms but saying no unmeaning word, I put forth my secret letter. It may be no eye will note, no hand will aid – if this be true I die and make no sign."*

Francis of England. Cipher in Shakespeare Quartos 1619

*"Oft do I muse upon the ultimity of this Cipher, and ask whose hand may complete it. It may be that of some man in the marts of the City. It may, perchance, be some sharp spy of the Court, whose zeal would spell my death. But my hope is, that not the years, but the ages shall unfold secret history."*

Cipher of Francis Bacon in Ben Jonson's 1616 Folio

*"Labour! I do entreat thee, with all the diligence to draw forth the numerous rules for use in writing out these secret works. But so great is our faith that posterity shall give honour unto our name, here and in the distant lands beyond the seas, our efforts are tireless and unceasing to carry out our marvellous work to perfection."*

Cipher from the "New Atlantis" 1635

*"None needeth to mention to my new true, bold friend though far from me, as through the spaces of the Universe, both of duration as well as distance, that he will take forth this secret."*

Cipher from *Much Ado About Nothing.* 1600

It seems Bacon had never imagined it would be a woman who finally deciphered his hidden codes.

Ben Jonson in a play *The Fox,* which he either wrote himself or masked for Bacon, concerning Robert Cecil by which name he was known, says: *"When you look cursorily over parts of the volume* (of Shakespeare's works), *you will not let his names escape your eye, but will seek such plays, hoping to find the Cypher. Names like these*

*have their use: Fame or Glory, Reputation, Fortune, Nature, Art,*
*Truth and Honour, when scattered in any of our works say to you:*
*Look for things hid from most eyes for we thus aided in his Cypher*
*work"*

Finally, from a cipher in *De Augmentis "The Lost Manuscripts"*

by Francis of St Albans. 1623

*"My adverse fortune seemed the theme most suited to the Plays,*
*published by, and in the name of other men."*

Bacon's disappointment is reflected in many of his plays sometimes in sorrow and others in anger and satire or good humor. He described his father Leicester as *"that gay Court idol"* and wrote *Much Ado About Nothing* to describe him. He revealed disguisedly that his mother had herself *"been stricken by young Cupid's dart"* most probably to show he knew what she disowned in herself.

That Bacon saw himself as wronged no doubt blinkered his appreciation of his mother's own childhood and her subsequent behavior. Her father had begrudged her for having been born a girl, while having her mother executed when Elizabeth was just two years old. Elizabeth had lived in fear of her father, and so perhaps it was not unsurprising that she kept all other men in positions where she could control them or rid herself of them, giving her the dogged determination to succeed as a woman in a world of men.

That Francis fell head over heels for the romantic femininity of the petite Marguerite was understandable versus the opposite persona of his mother. But equally Marguerite exercised her own means of control over him through the charade she devised for her sensual pleasures. A cipher extract from Elizabeth Gallup sums up Francis' sentiments of his mother and how he dealt with their love-hate relationship:

*"When Her Majesty, my mother, child me*

*And bade me to be still, my mind was filled with rancor;*

*So I have made an audience of the world,*

*And through these plays, speak to the multitudes."*

In Bacon's major work the "Novum Organum" written in his own name he says in his cipher:

*"In my autobiography are two things that do not appear in any history written openly, viz. Queen Elizabeth, her secret union with the Earl, and the other sad tale giving the story of the unwelcome birth of the Queen's off-springs, myself and Robert."*

Francis, Baron of Verulam 1620

And again in Bacon's cipher from Henry 7th.

*"My true name is not in some back pages it was given, but Tudor. Prince of Wales is my proper title."*

To end the many apposite quotes that can be drawn from the ciphers perhaps the most appropriate to Bacon's acceptance of his life, and one that could well apply to Christ himself, is that he wrote under the name of Francis 1st King of England:

*"If thou dost love thy life,*

*Banish the canker of ambitious thoughts,*

*Fling away ambition,*

*By that sin fell the angels; how can man then*

*(the image of his Maker) hope to win by it?*

*Love thyself last, cherish those hearts that hate thee;*

*Corruption wins not more than honesty.*

*Still in thy right hand, carry gentle peace*

*To silence envious tongues. Be just and fear not;*

*Let all the ends thou aim'st at be thy Country's,*

*Thy God's and Truth's."*

Finally, this quote before Francis' death in England.

*"What remaineth to man at the last of all his labour and care?*

*Ought? Shall he leave the dearest labours, the great designs,*

*The marvels he hath wrought, and bear from hence to that new life*

*A memory only, or it may be, even less?*

*Must he lose his hold upon all earthly objects*

*To take hold on that that is eternal?*


*Must he part from all and leave all?*

*Ay; and yet, if his arts survive 'tis well as he can naturally wish.*

*Shall not his soul live after him? Surely; nor can you or I have that far sight*

*That looketh into the future, and we know that*

*By the Divine Wisdom of the Ruler Supreme, 'tis so ordained.*

*The future may thus in a measure make good the past,*

*So that I shall, perchance, recover with the generations that are to come.*

*The hope maketh my work less heavy and my heart less sad."*


In his message to his decipherer he says:

*"If your pen have no glory, it, indeed, is by some shortcoming of your own,*

*For I have prepared the way to fortune and high favour.*

*You may be my voice to utter the words I would fain speak."*


To say a farewell to Francis Bacon the lines below are perhaps his most memorable:

*"I am the Resurrection and the Life.*

*Then through the narrow winding church-way paths,*

*Of a melancholy bough, gently set down*

*Their venerable burden, they layer him into the tomb,*

*To sleep, perchance to dream; aye, there's the rub,*

*For in that sleep of death, what dreams may come,*

*When we have shuffled off this mortal coil,*

*Must give us pause. To die, to sleep, to dream*

*No more; and by a sleep, to say we end*

*The heartache, and the thousand natural shocks*

*That flesh is heir to, is a consummation*

*Devoutly to be wished. For in our graves*

*After lifes's fitful fever, one sleeps well."*

An Example of a Bi-formed Alphabet.

$$
\begin{array}{cccccc}
a\,b\,a\,b & a\,b\,a\,b & a\,b\,a\,b & a\,b\,a\,b & a\,b\,a\,b & a\,b\,a\,b \\
Aa\,aa & BBbb & CCcc & DDdd & EEee & FFff \\
\end{array}
$$

$$
\begin{array}{cccccc}
b\,a\,b & a\,b\,a\,b & a\,b\,a\,b & a\,b\,a\,b & a\,b\,a\,b & a\,b\,a\,b \\
Ggg & HHbh & JIii & KKkk & LLll & MMmm \\
\end{array}
$$

$$
\begin{array}{cccccc}
b\,a\,b & a\,b\,a\,b & a\,b\,a\,b & a\,b\,a\,b & a\,b\,a\,b & a\,b\,a\,b \\
NNnn & OOoo & PPpp & QQqq & RRrr & SSss \\
\end{array}
$$

$$
\begin{array}{cccccc}
a\,b\,a\,b & a\,b\,a\,b & a\,b\,a\,b & a\,b\,a\,b & a\,b\,a\,b & a\,b\,a\,b \\
TTtt & UVvvuu & WWww & XXxx & YYyy & ZZzz \\
\end{array}
$$

An Example of a Bi-literarie Alphabet.

| A | B | C | D | E | F |
|---|---|---|---|---|---|
| aaaaa | aaaab | aaaba. | aaabb. | aabaa. | aabab. |
| G | H | I | K | L | M |
| aabba. | aabbb | abaaa. | abaab. | ababa. | ababb. |
| N | O | P | Q | R | S |
| abbaa. | abbab. | abbba. | abbbb. | baaaa. | baaab. |
| T | U | W | X | Y | Z |
| baaba. | baabb. | babaa. | babab. | babba. | babbb. |

Bi-formed and Bi-literarie Alphabets

*Bi-formed example*

449

*Margaret Barsi-Greene, Author of
'I, Prince Tudor, Wrote Shakespere'*

*Elizabeth Wells Gallup 1846 - 1934*

# "What's in a name?"

It would be a bold writer who attempted to explain the psyche of the author of the Shakespeare plays by examination of their themes and words. Firstly, because information as to when the plays were written is insufficient to be able to reflect the author's mood or circumstances at the time of writing. Often there was no formal printed copy of a play at the time of its first performance, and so no way of knowing what was original and what may have been added or cut later. Up until 1594 no name of an author had been ascribed to any of the many plays later to be attributed to William Shakespeare.

Secondly, even though Bacon almost certainly used characters in different modes to portray his feelings we can only guess at which. If the plays are most revealing of Francis' character, the merriment and wit of *The Comedy of Errors*, written when he was twenty-one showed him in a joyful mood, while *Ur-Hamlet*, written not long after and later to be completed as *Hamlet*, showed a brooding vengefulness. *Romeo and Juliet, Anthony and Cleopatra, Troilus and Cressida, and Love's Labour's Lost* all reveal the chemistry of love and its often painful emotions which Bacon himself experienced at first hand with Marguerite.

*The Tempest*, almost certainly the last of Bacon's plays, returns to the realms of the supernatural and spiritual combining with Bacon's thoughts on natural science. Apparent in it also is the struggle he has with granting forgiveness. The opposing love-lust convolutions that run through it must surely too reflect the writer's own sensitivities and experiences.

It is in the sonnets where the author's personal emotions are most intense, particularly those expressed about the dark lady. The famous sonnet 18 *"Shall I compare thee to a Summer's day?"* evokes head over heels love, while sonnets 139 and 140 tell of the despair of love lost. Both sonnets admirably describe Francis Bacon's *amour* with Marguerite of Navarre. In sonnet 140 he forlornly requests Marguerite to say she loves him though he knows she does not.

*"Be wise as thou art cruel; do not press my tongue tied patience with too much disdain; lest sorrow lend me words and words express the manner of my pity-want in pain.*

*If I might teach thee wit better it were though not to love, yet love, to tell me so; as testy sick men, when their deaths be near, no news but health from their physicians want to know."*

And in sonnet 150 in which that by loving her despite her infidelity Francis claims he is more worthy of her love than others.

*"O! From what power hast thou this powerful might, with insufficiency to take my heart to sway?*

*To make me give the lie to my true sight, and swear that brightness doth not grace the day?*

*Whence hast thou this becoming of things ill, that in the very refuse of thy deeds there is such strength and warranties of skill, that, in my mind, thy worst all best exceeds?*

*Who taught thee how to make me love thee more, the more I hear and see just cause of hate?*

*O! Though I love what others do abhor, with others thou shouldst not abhor my state:*

*If thy unworthiness raised love in me, more worthy I to be beloved of thee."*


Some have suggested that the words of these sonnets relate to Bacon's love for his young friend and admirer Henry Wriothesley the Earl of Southampton. There is no evidence to support this despite the occasional rumors of Bacon's bisexual activities   The meaning of "a rose of pleasure" and "ruby color'd portal" in Venus and Adonis does not stand comparison to any part of the male anatomy as to that of a woman's vulva to which the words are more obviously dedicated.

The well-known American author Bill Bryson in his investigative book of 2009 on Shakespeare finally considered no satisfactory conclusion could be drawn as to his real identity, but it would seem from the many bibliographies Bryson lists as his references he had not read any of the books or writings of Alfred Dodd or of Margaret Barsi-Greene or Elizabeth Gallup.  Since the printing of Bill Bryson's book new investigations and theories have also been advanced.

Those of *"Shakespeare and the Dawn of Modern Science"* by the

American professor Peter Usher, and that of the Canadian Dan Falk, *"The Science of Shakespeare"*, dispute claims that the Shakespeare plays were not allegorical to people and events. In the dangerous and paranoid Elizabethan age of plot and counter plot, allegory and cipher was part of everyday use. It would be extraordinary that, whoever Shakespeare was, he would not have made use of it to portray characters in his plays from his times and those of the past.

Visionaries are seldom recognized in their time. Francis Bacon no less, and lesser envious mortals jealously disparage them to justify themselves.

In the words of Iago in Othello:

*"He who steals my purse steals trash, 'tis something nothing;*

*'Twas mine, 'tis his and has been a slave to thousands;*

*But he who filches from me my good name*

*Robs me of that which not enriches him*

*And makes me poor indeed."*

It is this "good name" with the help of the works of the doughty Alfred Dodd and his formidable dedication and well-argued persuasion, and of Elizabeth Gallup and Margaret Barsi-Greene, that I have attempted to join the ranks of those to restore to Francis Bacon his rightful reputation. As Barsi-Greene rightly states in her book:

*"Until the name of Bacon is restored to spotless purity it shows a flaw in England's moral character."*

Serious words indeed.

The year 2014 marked the 450th Anniversary of William Shakespeare's birth as will 2016 commemorate his death. Statues to the great Bard of Avon have been erected worldwide, and resistance to any alternative is imbedded.

Apart from Francis Bacon other possible authors of Shakespeare's plays and sonnets have been mooted. Edward de Vere the Earl of

Oxford, Lord Derby, and Henry Neville being three. The first was a romantic rake and wastrel who died in 1604 after which date many new Shakespeare plays were staged or published. Although Oxford, Neville and Derby may have known Bacon's Good Pens there is no evidence they collaborated with them. They may, however have told of events in their own lives which were used to inform descriptions in the plays.

To many Henry Neville is a likely alternative candidate since he was the same age as Bacon and as a young man had spent time in Italy, Spain and France, sometimes as a spy and later, in 1599, as English Ambassador in Paris. But he was also a businessman running his family's armaments company as well as being a politician and military man. He was with Robert Essex in his raid on Cadiz and was imprisoned with him and the Earl of Southampton in the Tower prior to Essex's execution. It is claimed that he wrote the Shakespeare Sonnets which were first published in 1609 and written in the first person. However, there is no record of Neville having had a tragic affair with a "dark lady" nor of any homosexual relationship with the much younger Southampton, both of whom have provided most of the speculative theories as the objects of *Venus and Adonis* and its verses. As far as is known, Neville was a happily married family man, who was not known, nor had little time, to have written anything but letters to friends and acquaintances in which his writing style was very different from that used in the Shakespeare plays.

Other author theories have been advanced. That of Marlowe who died more than sixteen years before The Tempest was first said to be staged, despite efforts by recent protagonists to revive him from the grave to support their claims. As for Ben Jonson he himself acknowledged Francis Bacon as the author of the plays in barely disguised allusions. The best known being Jonson's introduction to the Reader in the 1st Folio under the picture of Wm Shakespeare: *"Reader, looke, Not on his Picture, but his Booke.*

That there were contributors to the plays among Bacon's "Good Pens" there is little doubt, but neither can there be about the principal authorship of Francis Bacon from whom their style and purpose stemmed. Recent discovery of handwriting expertly comparing that of Francis Bacon to original scripts of the Shakespeare plays also claim similarity using contemporary scientific tests. Overall the dates of Bacon's birth and death and the events of his time coinciding with his legal, astronomical and scientific knowledge and that of Court procedure all lend more strongly towards his authorship than any contender. In addition his mastery of many languages and his extensive travels point towards many of the scenes in the Shakespeare plays.

The arguments against Bacon are weak by comparison. They have been no more than that the style of his serious philosophical works was unlike that of the plays, and that he lacked humor. As the reader will know both of these have been debunked in The Royal Secret. It is ridiculous to assume a clever author cannot alter the style of writing. The Comedy of Errors was known to be written by Bacon as a young law student and shown to amuse his fellow students at Gray's Inn; while his wit was shown in the book of jokes and anecdotes in his name published by his secretary Rawley. Two hundred and fifty years later Lord Macaulay, otherwise a critic of Bacon, was to call it "the best collection of jests in the world."

The members of the Francis Bacon Society of England, founded in 1886, and similar societies in England, together with those in America respect Bacon's role in the founding of America and his Masonic inheritance. Many of Bacon's works can be found in the Folger Shakespeare Library in Washington.

In the pages of *The Royal Secret* can be found a wide variety of quotes and expressions from the Shakespeare plays, very many still in use in the English language of today. Some philosophical. Some humorous. Some tragic. They have since formed much of the ethnic English character and values which the English have bequeathed to the world. It is said every book must have a beginning, middle, and an end. In *The Royal Secret* the Pharaohs provided the first and Francis Bacon the second, with Mrs G as a practical American the last, in relatively timeless interconnection, since true knowledge can never change.

*Francis Crick, Scientist, discoverer of DNA*

## Shaksper's Handwriting :
## "The Immortal Signatures" to Law Deeds.

. . . 1612. May 11th,
Record Office,
London.

. . . . . . . . . . . 1613. March 10th.
Guildhall, London.

. . . . . . . . . . 1613. March 11th.
British Museum.
N.B.—Though this is dated a day after No. 2,
it was signed just before it.

. . . . . . . . 1616. March 25th.
Somerset House.

. . Ditto.
Same Documen

. . . . Ditto.

*Handwriting of William Shakespeare*

456

## THE HUNDRED MASKS[180]

Adlington, William

Barnes, Barnabe
Barnfield, Richard
Basse, William
Beaumont, Francis
Blount, Edward
Bright, Timothy
Brooke, Arthur
Burton, Robert

Cambridge students
Camden, William
Campion, Thomas
Chapman, George
Chester, Robert
Chettle, Henry
Condell, Henry
Constable, Henry
Covell, William

Daniel, Samuel
Davies, John of Hereford
Davies, Sir John
Davison, Francis
Davison, Walter
Day, John
Dekker, Thomas
5th Earl of Derby
   (Lord Strange)
Digges, Dudley
Digges, Leonard
Digges, Thomas
Donne, John
Drayton, Michael
Droeshout, Martin

Dugdale, Sir William
Dyer, Sir Edward

Edwardes, Richard
E. K. (England's King)

Field, Richard
Fletcher, John
Florio, John
Ford, John

Gager, William
Gascoigne, George
Golding, Arthur
Greene, Robert
Greville, Sir Fulke

Hakluyt, Richard
Harrison, William
Harsnett, Samuel
Harvey, Gabriel
Hathway, Richard
Hayward, Sir John
Heminge, John
Henslowe, Philip
Heywood, Jasper
Heywood, Thomas
Hilliard, Nicholas
Holinshed, Raphael
Holland, Hugh
Holland, Philemon
Howard, Henry
   (Earl of Surrey)

Jaggard, William
Jonson, Benjamin

*Names used as masks for Francis Bacon*

## THE HUNDRED MASKS[186]

Kyd, Thomas

Lodge, Thomas
Lyly, John

Markham, Gervase
Marlowe, Christopher
Marston, John
Massinger, Philip
Meres, Francis
Middleton, Thomas
I. M. (John Milton)
Montaigne, Michel
Munday, Anthony

Nashe, Thomas
Newton, Thomas
North, Sir Thomas
Norton, Thomas

Painter, William
Peele, George
Pembroke, Mary, Countess
Porter, Henry
Putterham, George

Raleigh, Sir Walter
Rowley, William

Sackville, Sir Thomas
Scot, Reginald
Shakespeare, William
Shirley, James
Sidney, Sir Philip
Spenser, Edmund
Stow, John
Strachey, William

Thorpe, Thomas

Udall, Nicholas

Warner, William
Watson, Thomas
Webster, John
Weever, John
Whetstone, George
Willoughby, Henry
Wilson, Thomas
Mr. W. H.

Yonge, Bartholomew

NOTE: Many other masks have not been listed.

*Names used as masks for Francis Bacon*

# The Future

We live in a world where despite advances in science and communication little changes in the make-up of man. The specter of war, famine, plague and death hover over our lives like the Four Horsemen of the Apocalypse, as relevant today as when they were described in the Book of Revelation in the New Testament. No less apposite today are the eternal themes of the Shakespeare plays of good and evil, love and lust, honor and greed. Extremes between rich and poor are as prevalent as they have ever been. Belief in religions, cults and creeds have not been vanquished by the advances of science. Our consciences are still in fear of an unknown power if we are to abuse the good inherent in us. To ignore that power is a denial of our presence in a universe which has given us our lives.

Masonry claims that it provides a route of self-help to the soul's salvation. Along with similar claims of many other creeds and cults it no doubt has its negatives and positives, but if it can do what it promises without harm then it is to be welcomed. There is no intent in *The Royal Secret* to cast aspersions on Masonry of today or any other creed or ideal. What is past is past, so long as old abuses do not resurface. Phillip Buonarroti is simply an illustration of those who mistakenly think they can put the world to rights by coercion and are finally found evil by history's reckoning. Francis Bacon, on the other hand, tried to offer mankind a better understanding of itself in the parables of his Shakespeare plays. Its faults and credits and its comicality, and the need for balance if we are to enjoy the lives we are given.

In the final analysis, neglecting by default to know the real nature of the gifted and talented person who gave the world the Shakespearean legacy is as much a denial of his ethos as if he did not exist. Perhaps it is because we would rather dismiss a superior intelligence when we cannot possess it ourselves. Does Francis Bacon's bloodline and heritage matter? Was he able to access what we have not? A store of knowledge forever immortal.

From the time of the Pharaohs noble families have sought to replicate themselves by interbreeding in the belief that intelligence is inherited. Today genetic engineering offers selective cloning of all animal species and the possibility of a manufactured super-race. The invention of robotic machines too continues at a similar pace.

If one day a machine is to be created more intelligent than man himself, is this the end game in which man serves machines and so destroys his soul? As Albert Einstein remarked *"I fear the day that technology will surpass our human interaction the world will have a generation of idiots."*

Without genes for machines this likelihood is some time away, since machines cannot yet reproduce themselves without human assistance. But the ascendance of a super intelligent human race is not unlikely, nor that nations will pursue such a goal for their own ends. The higher plane of intellectual resource that the Pharaoh kings and queens once found in themselves which they named Zep-Tepi, and subsequently lost, can belong to us as their genetic heirs. That the ancient Druids of Britain had similar abilities and a path to the heavens from their astronomical 'henges' is as likely as not. Certainly Dr Francis Crick saw the unlimited possibility of our intelligent DNA if only we could re-attain our innate means to access it, but we are too often blinded by the limitations of modern science to see the obvious.

It is quite possible that what we attribute to the chemical or to magnetism is one and the same as the spiritual, or some combination of them. Science and religion are far closer than most imagine. It may well be that to achieve a world at peace with itself mankind's only salvation lies in the rediscovery and reassertion of spiritual man in tune with the cosmos. The promised harmony of the new Aquarian age as the stars predict.

"Faith, Hope and Charity" is one of the Bible's most memorable messages, and that of the chivalrous knights of the past who sought the glory of man, not his might. With no common spiritual goal for a brotherhood of man then humanity may well soon find itself at the mercy of its own most frightening scientific creation. That of atomic weapons which have replaced the sword.

As Francis Bacon said: *"Sweet are the uses of Adversity."* Hopefully it will take less than the fear of imminent threat of nuclear war, or global plague, or a large meteorite speeding its way to earth, or the approach of a fleet of alien spaceships to create a common bond among men as creatures of the universe. Whether our fate is in ourselves, or in our stars, is a tale still to be told.

# Further information:

Further information relating to references within *The Royal Secret* are available via our web site or social media sites listed below, where we have compiled details, pictures & websites of subjects within the book.

Web: http://www.theroyalsecret.info

Pinterest: www.pinterest.com/theroyalsecret

Pearltrees: www.pearltrees.com/the_royal_secret

CPSIA information can be obtained
at www.ICGtesting.com
Printed in the USA
FSOW04n0453020118
42955FS